The Sociology of Work

The Sociology of Work

Continuity and Change in Paid and Unpaid Work

Stephen Edgell

Los Angeles | London | New Delhi
Singapore | Washington DC

First published 2006
Reprinted 2010

SAGE Publications Ltd
1 Oliver's Yard
55 City Road
London EC1Y 1SP

SAGE Publications Inc.
2455 Teller Road
Thousand Oaks, California 91320

SAGE Publications India Pvt Ltd
B 1/I 1, Mohan Cooperative Industrial Area
Mathura Road
New Delhi 110 044

SAGE Publications Asia-Pacific Pte Ltd
33 Pekin Street #02-01
Far East Square
Singapore 048763

British Library Cataloguing in Publication data

A catalogue record for this book is available
from the British Library

ISBN 978 07619 4852 0
ISBN 978 07619 4853 7 (pbk)

Library of Congress Control Number available

Typeset by C&M Digitals (P) Ltd., Chennai, India
Printed in Great Britain by the MPG Books Group
Printed on paper from sustainable resources

Mixed Sources
Product group from well-managed
forests and other controlled sources
www.fsc.org Cert no. SA-COC-1565
© 1996 Forest Stewardship Council

Dedicated to the memory of my parents,
Grace (1914–95) and Don (1917–43)

Contents

● ● ● ● ● ● ● ●

List of Figures		x
List of Tables		xi
Preface and Acknowledgements		xii

1	**The Transformation of Work: From Work as an Economic Activity to Work as Employment**	**1**
	Work in pre-industrial societies	1
	Work in industrial capitalist societies	7
	Main features of work in industrial capitalist societies	8
	Women and work in the development of industrial capitalism	20
	Industrial capitalism, patriarchy, and the dominant conception of work	23
	Summary and conclusions	25
	Further reading	26
	Questions for discussion and assessment	27

2	**Paid Work and Alienation**	**28**
	Marx's theory of alienation	28
	Blauner's technology and alienation thesis	30
	Critique of Blauner's technology and alienation thesis	36
	Empirical research on the Blauner thesis	41
	Summary and conclusions	45
	Further reading	47
	Questions for discussion and assessment	47

3	**Paid Work in Industrial Society and Deskilling?**	**48**
	Braverman's deskilling thesis	48
	Critique of Braverman's deskilling thesis	53
	Braverman's supporters	58
	Summary and conclusions	59
	Further reading	60
	Questions for discussion and assessment	60

4 Paid Work in Post-Industrial Society and Upskilling?   **61**

Bell's upskilling thesis   61

Critique of Bell's upskilling thesis   64

The polarization of skills: support for Bell?   68

Summary and conclusions   71

Further reading   72

Questions for discussion and assessment   72

5 Fordism: Its Rise, Development and Demise   **73**

The rise of Fordism   73

The development of Fordism   77

The demise of Fordism as a system of mass production and consumption   80

Summary and conclusions   82

Further reading   82

Questions for discussion and assessment   83

6 Solutions to the Crisis of Fordism: Neo-Fordism (McDonaldism) and Post-Fordism   **84**

Solutions to the crisis of Fordism: (1) Neo-Fordist industrial work   85

Solutions to the crisis of Fordism: (2) Neo-Fordist service work (McDonaldism)   92

Solutions to the crisis of Fordism: (3) Post-Fordist work   95

Summary and conclusions   98

Further reading   100

Questions for discussion and assessment   101

7 Unemployment (Out of Paid Work) and Underemployment (Short of Paid Work)   **102**

Unemployment: meaning and measurement   104

Social consequences of unemployment   106

Class, age and gender, and the social consequences of unemployment   108

Underemployment: meaning and measurement   115

Social consequences of underemployment   118

Beck's underemployment thesis   119

Summary and conclusions   121

Further reading   124

Questions for discussion and assessment   125

8 Non-Standard Paid Work: Contractural, Spatial, Temporal and Total Destandardization   **126**

Contractural destandardization: self-employment   129

Spatial destandardization: homeworking   136

Temporal destandardization: temporary work   140

Total destandardization: paid informal work   142

Summary and conclusions		148
Further reading		151
Questions for discussion and assessment		152

9 Unpaid Work: Domestic Work and Voluntary Work **153**

Unpaid domestic work		156
Domestic work: conditions and technology		160
Gender and the division of domestic work: the symmetrical family thesis		162
Outsourcing domestic work		171
Unpaid voluntary work		172
Summary and conclusions		177
Further reading		180
Questions for discussion and assessment		181

10 Globalization and the Transformation of Paid and Unpaid Work **182**

Globalization		183
Causes of globalization		185
The parallel transformation of women's condition		187
The transformation of paid work?		189
The transformation of unpaid work?		192
Summary and conclusions		197
Concluding remarks on continuity and change and 'work'		200
Further reading		203
Questions for discussion and assessment		203

Glossary **204**

References **209**

Name Index **229**

Subject Index **235**

List of Figures

●●●●●●●●●

1.1 Types of society and main types of work in
     different historical periods   2

2.1 Blauner's model of causality   33
2.2 Blauner's historical trend of alienation   35

3.1 Why advances in automation can have contrary
     effects on skill requirements   52

4.1 Changes in skill and the occupational class structure   70

7.1 Employment situation and working hours   122

9.1 Spheres and types of work   156

10.1 Options beyond the male breadwinner/female carer model   195

List of Tables

●●●●●●●●

1.1 Work in pre-industrial society compared with work in
industrial capitalist society 9

1.2 Dominant conception of work in industrial capitalism
and threats to its hegemony 24

2.1 Blauner's four types of technology and characteristic industry 31

2.2 Blauner's four dimensions of alienation and polar opposites 32

2.3 Blauner's type of technology and degree of alienation thesis 34

4.1 Industrial and post-industrial societies: contrasting features 62

4.2 Change in skill and responsibility by class and sex 69

5.1 Key features of pre-Fordism and Fordism 75

6.1 Workers responding that it was difficult to find a relief worker
so they could leave their workstation to attend to personal
matters such as going to the toilet (%) 91

6.2 Key features of neo-Fordism (McDonaldism) and post-Fordism 100

8.1 Key dimensions of standard and non-standard
work/employment models 128

8.2 Percentage distribution of bad job characteristics
by employment status 141

9.1 Average weekly hours spent in paid work and
unpaid domestic work 165

10.1 Hours spent on housework by managers 193

Preface and
Acknowledgements

•••••••

I have been teaching the sociology of 'work' at the undergraduate level for over twenty years. In this field of sociological analysis, I was struck from the outset by the focus on regular paid work to the relative exclusion of all other kinds of paid and unpaid work. Such a narrow conceptualization of work is not only profoundly unsociological in the sense that it defers to the dominant idea that work equals a full-time job, it is also increasingly anachronistic given the growth of other types of work, notably what is referred to as non-standard employment. Therefore, the main purpose of writing this book is to redress the sociological balance.

The process of writing a book invariably involves the support, encouragement and assistance of others. In my case 'Jones' has provided invaluable help in many and various ways and Paul Kennedy took the time to express some critical thoughts on a draft of the material on globalization. Huw Beynon read the draft manuscript and his constructive criticisms and helpful suggestions are appreciated greatly. I am thankful to all of them, and to those cohorts of undergraduates who inadvertently contributed to the development of my ideas about 'work' by their telling comments and questions. Needless to say, the usual disclaimers apply. Finally, I am pleased to acknowledge the permission granted by the following for the use of the material listed below:

Lesley Hustinx and Frans Lammertyn for permission to quote from their paper 'Solidarity and volunteering under a reflexive-modern sign: towards a conceptual framework', presented at the *International Society for Third Sector Research*, Dublin. Ireland, July 2000.

John Eldridge for permission to draw upon his figures on Blauner's American Inter-Industry Comparison in *Sociology and Industrial Life* (M. Joseph, 1971: 186–7).

Monthly Review Press for permission to reproduce an amended version of an illustration from Braverman's *Labour and Monopoly Capitalism* (1974: 221).

Sage Publications Ltd. for permission to reproduce an amended version of Figure 1: 'The separation of spheres of work in traditional theory' in 'Extending conceptual boundaries: work, voluntary work and employment' by Rebecca Taylor in *Work, Employment and Society*, Vol. 18 (1), pp. 29–49 (© British Sociological Society, 2004).

Sage Publications Ltd for permission to reproduce an extract from 'Skill, craft and class' by Lee in *Sociology*, Vol. (1), p. 57 (© British Sociological Association, 1981).

Sage Publications Inc. for permission to reproduce an abridged version of Table 1: 'Percentage of bad job characteristics and mean number of bad characteristics by employment status' in 'Bad jobs in Britain: non-standard employment and job quality' by Patrick McGovern, Deborah Smeaton, and Stephen Hill in *Work and Occupations*, Vol. 31 (2), p. 236.

Oxford University Press for permission to reproduce an abridged version of Table 2.4 (p. 44) from *Restructuring the Employment Relationship* (1998) by Gallie, D. et al. and an adapted version of Figure 10.1 (p. 205) from chapter 'Discussion and Conclusions' by R. Crompton in *Restructuring Gender Relations and Employment: The Decline of the Breadwinner Model* (1999) edited by Crompton, R.

Wayne Lewchuk and David Robertson for permission to reproduce Table 4: 'Workers responding it was difficult to find a relief worker so they could leave their workstation to attend to personal matters such as going to the toilet (%)' from *Capital and Class* No. 63 p. 53, Autumn 1997.

Routledge for permission to reproduce an amended version of Table 14: 'Average weekly hours spent in different ways (diary sample: married men and women aged 30 to 49) by Young and Willmott in *The Symmetrical Family: A Study of Work and Leisure in the London Region* (Routledge & Kegan Paul Ltd, 1973: 113).

Blackwell Publishing Ltd. for permission to reprint Table 1: 'Hours spent on housework by managers' from 'The domestic basis of the managerial career' by Judy Wajcman in the *Sociological Review*, Vol. 14 (1), p. 619.

Whilst every effort has been made to trace/contact all the copyright holders, in the event that any have been inadvertently overlooked, I am confident that the publishers will be pleased to make the necessary arrangements at the earliest opportunity.

CHAPTER ONE

The Transformation of Work

From work as an economic activity to work as employment

Before the advent of industrial capitalism approximately 200 years ago in England, work referred in a generalized way to activities directed at satisfying the human need for survival, for the vast majority, at a subsistence level. In terms of the 40,000 years plus history of human societies, it is only in the recent past that work has become synonymous with regular paid employment, a separate sphere of specialized economic activity for which one receives payment. Thus, the current conception of work is a modern social construction, the product of specific historical conditions that are typically denoted by the term 'industrial capitalism'. The first part of this term indicates that work is a productive activity involving machines powered by inanimate energy sources that is undertaken outside the home in a dedicated building that one has to travel to each work day. The second part indicates that work involves monetary payment, typically agreed in advance in relation to time and/or output, and is part of a market system in which productive property is privately owned with a view to making a profit and that everything has a price, including labour. The term 'modern society' refers to industrial society and although the process of modernization may start with industrialization, it is one that covers all aspects of social change, not just economic change. At the beginning of the twenty-first century, there is some controversy about the extent to which the most advanced industrial capitalist societies have changed and how best to conceptualize it.

Work in pre-industrial societies

In order to appreciate the revolutionary character of the modern conception of work, it is useful to consider briefly the main features of work in pre-modern societies before comparing them with work in modern societies. However, such an exercise is not without its difficulties, notably that it implies, wrongly, that change is unilinear, and it understates the heterogeneity of work activities and beliefs in pre-modern societies,

Type of society	Approximate dates	Main kinds of work	Historical period
Hunting and Gathering (i.e., 'Stone Age')	40,000 BP+ to 10,000 BP (or 8,000 BP)	Hunting and gathering	
Horticultural	10,000 BP to 5,000 BP (or 3,000 BP)	Gardening	PRE-MODERN PERIOD
Agrarian	5,000 BP to late 18th century	Farming	
Industrial capitalist	19th and 20th centuries	Manufacturing	EARLY MODERN PERIOD
Post-industrial/ Informational/ Global capitalism	Late 20th century and early 21st century	Services (and information processing)	LATE MODERN PERIOD

BP: Before the present

Figure 1.1   Types of society and main types of work in different historical periods

Source: Pre-modern and early modern based on Nolan and Lenski (1999)

particularly with reference to the meaning of work and the division of labour. Since the objective here is to contextualize historically in a succinct way the contrast between work in pre-modern and modern societies, I have over-simplified the great variety of pre-modern societies by excluding hybrid societies and by collapsing the Nolan and Lenski (1999) classification based on the predominant method of subsistence into four types of society: (a) *hunting and gathering*, (b) *horticultural*, (c) *agrarian*, and (d) *industrial*.

Unless otherwise indicated, in the following discussion of pre-industrial societies, I have drawn heavily upon the vast amount of comparative material collated by Nolan and Lenski (1999). In the case of the most recent type of society, the indus-trial, two caveats are in order. First, the label 'industrial capitalism' is preferred since an essential element of the earliest and subsequently the most economically suc-cessful industrial societies which dominate the world economy is that they are capi-talist as well as industrial. Second, the development of human societies is ongoing, hence the debate about whether, and in what ways, advanced industrial capitalist societies have become post-industrial is indicated by the use of a broken line after the industrial type in Figure 1.1, which summarizes the main types of human society.

Hunting and gathering societies

The earliest known human societies were based on hunting and gathering and lasted longer than any other type of society, namely from the beginnings of human society, estimated to be at least 40,000 years ago, to around 10,000 years ago. Somewhat surprisingly given the globalization of industrial capitalism, a small number of these 'stone-age' cultures have survived into the modern era, for example, Aborigines in Australia and Pygmies in Africa. In these essentially nomadic and small-scale societies, their exceedingly limited technology, involving the widespread use of stone for tools and weapons, typically did not to produce a regular economic surplus or lead to marked inequalities. Consequently, everyone in such societies participated, to a greater or lesser extent, in productive work; the young and old, men and women, even political and religious leaders undertook their roles on a part-time basis. Biological differences between the sexes and age groups led to adult males specializing in hunting and fishing and adult females in gathering and food preparation, with everyone often contributing to the building of shelters. Preparation for the sex-based adult work roles in such a limited division of labour was informal, although formal ceremonies (initiation rites) typically marked the transition to manhood and womanhood. Sharing work and the products of work typified this stage of development since the survival of the group at this subsistence level put a premium on co-operative rather than competitive behaviour. In Veblen's terminology they were more peaceable than predatory societies (1964 [1914]).

Horticultural societies

The emergence of semi-nomadic and later settled horticultural societies based on the cultivation of plants and the domestication of animals about 10,000 years ago, combined with the use of metals instead of stone for tools and weapons, led to the creation of a more reliable economic surplus, an increase in the size of the population, and the differentiation of economic activities. Essentially, such societies are dominated by gardening work using a digging stick and hoe, and are characterized by an increase in socio-economic specialization, for example workers and warriors, and a corresponding growth of inequality associated with the beginnings of a stratification system dominated by male warriors. The increase in trade and the conquest of people were not only made possible with technological innovations such as metal working, but were found to be a viable economic alternative to the 'conquest of nature' (Nolan and Lenski 1999: 138). The production of a 'margin worth fighting for, above the subsistence of those engaged in getting a living', led Veblen to label this stage the first predatory era (1970 [1899]: 32). Thus in addition to the by now established pattern of women doing most of the productive work, in the more advanced horticultural societies, such as the one which prevailed in ancient China and the Mayan civilization in central America, the creation of a stable economic surplus by the majority, which often included slaves, allowed a minority to form an hereditary aristocracy of males who specialized in politics, religion and warfare.

Agrarian societies

The next major stimulus to production occurred sometime around 5,000 years ago, it involved the widespread use of the plough and the harnessing of animal power for agriculture and transport, and heralded the development of agrarian societies. The farming of fields using animals to pull a plough rather than gardening based on human energy to operate the hoe became the predominant method of cultivation. Following these technological innovations, production expanded markedly, the population grew, and social differentiation increased significantly, especially along class lines, with dominant groups specializing in the ownership of land and people, and subordinate groups specializing in a range of economic activities, including the production, transporation and distribution of everything from food and spices, to tools and weapons. Economic growth led to a greater diversity of occupations and the emergence of urban centres in which the use of money became the preferred medium of exchange, which in turn further stimulated trade and therefore production and community specialization. For the vast majority, home and work were still not separated, with the household being the unit of production as well as consumption for its members, not all of whom would have been related, for example, apprentices and servants. The expansion of those engaged in the increasing variety of occupations encouraged the establishment of craft and other specialist work associations, the pre-modern equivalent of trade unions, membership of which was open to both men and women (Applebaum 1992; Oakley 1976).

It was at this historical juncture that the important distinction between a productive class of people who worked for a living and a non-productive, parasitical leisure class reached its fullest development. In Europe this class prevailed during the feudal era when its members were 'not only exempt, but by prescriptive custom' they were 'debarred, from all industrial occupations' (Veblen 1970 [1899]: 22). This degree of social differentiation involved the emergence of work and leisure as separate spheres of activity for the dominant class, whereas formerly such activities were embedded in a range of other institutions, notably kinship, religion and politics. In Veblen's terms, there are upper-class and male-dominated leisure class occupations, such as government, warfare and religious observances, that are concerned with predatory, non-industrial activities and are accorded the highest social honour, and there are lower-class and female-dominated productive activities, such as farming and craft work, which are considered ignoble according to the standards of the leisure class. In order to further enhance their status, the leisure class demonstrated their superior wealth and power by engaging in a variety of other non-work activities, the defining features of which were that, in addition to the conspicuous abstention from useful work, they involved conspicuous expense and the conspicuous waste of materials; in short, the conspicuous consumption of time, money and resources, for example, sports, especially predatory ones such as hunting, plus the cultivation of elaborate manners, esoteric knowledge, collecting art and antiques, and more generally the consumption of the most expensive food, drink, clothes, and amusements.

Discussion: pre-industrial societies

Thus, prior to the growth of industrial capitalism, the main kinds of work were all non-industrial, such as hunting/gathering, gardening and farming, and varied from everyone working co-operatively on a minimally differentiated basis, to a degree of gender and class specialization culminating in some social groups being exempt from productive work whilst others spent virtually their whole lives working. The variation in terms of gender is particularly marked, ranging from women taken as trophies and enslaved following conflict between horticultural societies (Veblen 1970 [1899]), to women owning land and managing the production of linen and beer in agrarian England (Applebaum 1992). Notwithstanding such variations, the development of industrial society tends to enhance rather than impede the liberation of women (Boserup 1970), although this generalization is not without its complexities and critics (Walby 1990), as will become apparent later in this chapter.

Occupational specialization was minimal in the earliest known societies whereas in horticultural and agrarian societies 'occupational specialties numbered in the hundreds, and there was a complex division of labour that often involved specialization by communities and even regions' (Nolan and Lenski 1999: 206). Yet, as will become apparent in due course, compared with industrial capitalism, rural pre-modern societies were characterized by a relatively rudimentary and essentially ascriptive division of labour, such is the unparalleled degree of economic specialization intrinsic to modern industrial capitalist society. The increase in the division of labour was accompanied by a move from learning work roles informally via watching adults work and practical experience, to acquiring specialist knowledge and skills formally in dedicated organizations such as schools and universities. However, even in the most advanced agrarian societies, education was not universally available but restricted to the dominant classes in order to prepare its members for political, religious and military roles, rather than for economically productive ones.

Variations between the different types of pre-modern society also relate to beliefs about the meaning of work, although, as in the case of the division of labour, the multiplicity of meanings attached to work in such societies are revealed to be of minor social significance by the radically new and elevated meaning of work occasioned by the onset of industrial capitalism. In pre-industrial societies labour was typically unfree to a greater or lesser extent in the form of slavery, serfdom and bonded service, and persisted with the growth of industrial capitalism in both Britain and America (Corrigan 1977). It is unsurprising therefore that useful work tended not to be highly valued as an economic activity, despite its indispensability for the survival of everyone. Hence, it has been shown that in pre-modern societies as different as ancient Greece and medieval Europe, work was regarded negatively, as a necessary evil or as an expiation of sins committed by others in the past (Applebaum 1992; Tilgher 1977 [1930]). Moreover, even such vital activities such as farming and craft work received only limited approval from dominant political and religious leaders because, although they were conducive to an independent livelihood and produced goods and services for the parasitic ruling class, they detracted from the ability to engage in politics or spiritual contemplation. Consequently, physical labour, however essential or skilled, did not enjoy the wealth, power and therefore status of non-manual work, such as owning (land and people), governing or praying. Moreover, for the dominant classes of pre-modern society, productive work was ceremonially unclean, to be avoided at all costs. I know of no better illustration of this than the case of a king of France

> ... who is said to have lost his life through an excess of moral stamina in the observance of good form. In the absence of the functionary whose office it was to shift the master's seat, the king sat uncomplaining before the fire and suffered his royal person to be toasted beyond recovery. But in doing so he saved his Most Christian Majesty from menial contamination. (Veblen 1970 [1899]: 45–6)

The shame associated with certain kinds of work for particular social groups is not of course unique to pre-modern societies. In contemporary industrial capitalist societies the reluctance of unemployed men to undertake what they perceive as 'women's work' and a resistance among their wives to relinquish this type of work is not uncommon (Morris 1990). Similarly, neither is the tendency for certain high-status groups to avoid 'dirty work', defined in moral as well as physical terms, by delegating it to those of a lower status, notably for example refuse collection (Hughes 1958). The stigma that attaches to the performance of various kinds of manual work in industrial societies, particularly when it is conventionally undertaken by marginal groups, is due to a range of factors. Arguably, among the most important are the historical persistence of the indignity of manual work, namely cultural lag (Veblen 1970 [1899]), and the operation of a labour market in which the supply of unskilled manual workers exceeds the demand (Fevre 1992). Above all perhaps, the operation of an extensive and widely accepted social hierarchy, characteristic of modern occupational structures and the vast majority of work organizations, assigns zero prestige at best to jobs at the bottom of the pyramid (Rothman 1998). Whatever the source of the variation in status associated with different kinds of work in pre-modern agricultural societies, whether they are reflections of morality, economic value, prevailing social norms or political inequalities, work in pre-modern societies was not thought of as a separate entity, but an aspect, albeit a vital one, of the 'general social and spiritual framework' (Anthony 1977: 37).

In the transition to industrial capitalism in Britain and elsewhere, before wage labour became the norm for the vast majority, wage work in agriculture was common but it was typically irregular for the majority, and was merely one of a number of economic activities upon which people depended for their survival. For example, in addition to seasonal wage labour, they could obtain a supply of food via the cultivation of a small parcel of land, make and sell clothes, plus hunting and gathering (Malcomson 1988). Whatever the combination of different forms of work, the family remained the basic productive unit in the sense that all members contributed to its economic survival. This was a pattern which, like wage labour, persisted during the rise of industrial capitalism (Anderson 1971). Thus, it was not until the full development of industrial capitalism that a marked contrast between work in this new type of society and work in all pre-modern societies became apparent.

Work in industrial capitalist societies

Consideration of the many models of evolutionary change shows that there is near universal consensus regarding the social significance of the rise of industrial capitalism, namely that it involved a societal transformation which affected the life and work of everyone. Hence the tendency to focus on the contrast between this new type of society and all types of traditional rural societies and the plethora of dichotomies to summarize the differences, for example, mechanical and organic solidarity (Durkheim) and community and association (Tonnies). In the heyday of evolutionary theory around 100 years ago, an exception was Veblen, whose model emphasized the handicraft era by virtue of its importance in the establishment of a competitive market. However, even Veblen acknowledged that the advent of the machine age involved a radical departure from the past and consequently impressed him, albeit not entirely favourably, and in this respect he has more in common with Marx than Weber (Edgell 2001).

The term 'Industrial Revolution' is invariably used to convey the significance of this transformation, one that centres on the nature of work above all else. Such was the scale and intensity of this social change that it is widely thought to have prompted the rise of sociology as a distinct discipline (Giddens 1971; Kivisto 1998; Lee and Newby 1983; Nisbet 1970). Notwithstanding the ongoing and possibly never to be resolved debate about whether it was economic factors which changed ideas about work (Marx's view) or ideas about work which changed economic life (Weber's view), or a mixture of both (Veblen's view), what is certain is that work was transformed by the rise of industrial capitalism. What is also agreed is that the process of capitalist industrialization started in England towards the end of the eighteenth century, developed soon after in America, France and Germany, and subsequently the rest of the world to the point where it is now a global phenomenon in the sense that goods and services are not only made from materials sourced from many parts of the world, but are sold around the world.

The first part of the term 'industrial capitalism' refers to the use of inanimate energy sources such as electric, gas or nuclear power, and the consequent reorganization of production involving machine technology, which results in the establishment of large-scale specialized workplaces such as factories and the increased time synchronization of labour and technology in an economy based primarily on manufacturing rather than agriculture. 'Capitalism' refers to a profit-oriented system based on the private ownership of production, on an individual/family or corporate basis, that operates in a competitive market system in which the owners of capital employ free wage labour on a monetary basis. The apparent clarity of these definitions does not imply, in the case of the word 'industrial', any suggestion of technological determinism and, in the case of the word 'capitalist', any suggestion of admiration or antagonism. However, the use of the two words in combination does imply that industrialism and capitalism are inextricably linked without giving priority to either and, by implication, support for a theory of industrial society derived from the writings of Saint-Simon or for a theory of capitalism derived from the writings of Marx or Weber (Giddens 1973; Scott 1985).

An illustration of the interconnectedness of the industrial and capitalist dimensions of modern societies is afforded by consideration of the experience of workers. The spatial separation of home from work, initiated by the creation of specialist work sites following the introduction of inanimate energy sources to power machine technology, represents the first major change from what had been the norm in all pre-industrial societies, the unity of home and work. In a capitalist system in which making a profit is the priority, workers are recruited on the basis of potential productiveness rather than parentage. Hence the move from working and living at home in a rural community to working away from home in an urban area meant being treated as a cost of production and interacting with people to whom one was not related or even knew personally prior to working in the same workplace. In other words, the industrial (factory work) and capitalist (labour treated as a commodity) aspects of work reinforce each other, thereby accentuating the impersonality of the new work situation and the contrast between this and family relationships.

Finally, the characterization of work in industrial capitalism presented below applies to a greater or lesser extent to both the early organizational structure in which individuals, often members of the same family, owned and managed one or a relatively small number of local productive units, and the more recent form in which a large number of shareholders, individually or institutionally, own but tend to employ others to manage a relatively large number of productive units in many countries. This historical move from local family businesses to global corporate capitalism involves, among other things, the introduction of professional managers which has been interpreted as both a dilution and a strengthening of profit maximization (Edgell 1993).

Table 1.1 presents in summary form the ten main contrasts between work in pre-industrial society and in industrial capitalist society. It is not intended to be exhaustive

Table 1.1   Work in pre-industrial society compared with work in industrial capitalist society

Key features	Work in pre-industrial society	Work in industrial capitalist society
1 Production system	Hand tools/Water/Human/ Animal energy	Machine tools/Inanimate energy (coal, gas, oil, etc.)
2 Unit of production	Family/Household	Individual adults/Organizations
3 Division of labour	Rudimentary/Low degree of differentiation	Complex/High degree of differentiation
4 Time	Irregular/Seasonal	Regular/Permanent
5 Education and recruitment	Minimal/Generalized Particularistic/Family	Extensive/Specialized Universalistic/Individual adults
6 Economic System	Traditional/Non-market	Rational/Market
7 Meaning of work	Necessary evil	Work as a virtue
8 Purpose of work	Livelihood/Subsistence/ Short-term Profit	Maximum reward/Income/ Long-term profit
9 Payment	In kind/Cash	Wages/Salaries/Profits
10 Embeddedness of work	Embedded in non-economic institutions	Separate from other institutions

or to imply that some features are more significant than others. It is, however, intended to clarify the issues, albeit at the risk of exaggerating the discontinuities which are often less marked in practice than in theory. For instance, it is questionable how 'free' labour is under industrial capitalism, which is why Marx considered higher wages to 'be nothing but better payment for the slave' (1970 [1959]: 118), and others have noted that economic coercion prevails to this day, it is just a matter of degree (Corrigan 1977).

Main features of work in industrial capitalist society

(1) Production system

The re-organization of work could be said to have started with the introduction of new sources of inanimate energy to drive machinery, replacing water or wind power and human or animal muscle power. The key innovation was arguably the invention of the condensing steam engine to power cotton machinery in 1785 (Smelser 1972 [1959]). The steam engine not only revolutionized industry, but also transportation and mining, and led to a massive increase in production. An indication of this is afforded by the British textile industry in which output increased by over 300 per cent when power looms replaced handlooms during the early nineteenth century (Berg 1994).

The increased scale of the power sources and the complexity of the machines meant that a large amount of capital was required to finance production and work was moved out of the home and into factories, which in turn had profound implications for work. In contrast to pre-industrial production, in which 'the workman makes use of a tool', in the new factory-based system of production under the control of the capitalist, 'the machine makes use of him ... we have a lifeless mechanism independent of the workman, who becomes its mere living appendage' (Marx 1970 [1887]: 422). Also, the unrelenting uniformity of machinery that requires limited skills 'deprives the work of all interest' (Marx 1970 [1887]: 423). Marx used the term 'alienation' to describe the increasing estrangement and powerlessness of wage labour when confronted by the power of capital (1970 [1959]: 108); an issue that will be considered in the next chapter.

The deleterious impact of the introduction of the factory system on workers led them to contest the introduction of machinery, which threatened their livelihood and relatively independent way of life. Opposition often took the form of attacking in vain the machines (Luddism), which from the standpoint of displaced workers 'symbolized the encroachment of the factory system' (Thompson 1970: 599). The Luddites were depicted as being irrational whereas the new technology was considered the epitome of rationality (Grint and Woolgar 1997). Wherever industrial capitalism developed, workers organized themselves into trade unions and political parties in an attempt to temper the most harmful effects of the new system of production or even to overthrow it.

(2) Unit of production

The change from the household as the productive unit in which family and non-family members lived and worked together, pooling resources, and producing food and goods for their own consumption, to the factory and other specialist units of production, such as offices, in which individuals worked for wages, was gradual. Initially whole families were recruited to work in the factories, with parents effectively subcontracting work to their children. This system had many advantages; it maintained parental authority, facilitated occupational training, and enhanced the family income. Also, in the absence of state welfare, the family was the only resource available to individuals when faced with a crisis, such as sickness or lack of work (Anderson 1971). So long as these circumstances pertained, families 'continued to work and live as a unit' (Kumar 1988b: 157). Most importantly from the standpoint of capital, the move from household to factory production removed control over the product and the work process from the worker and enabled capitalists and their managers to supervise and discipline workers more easily, thereby reducing the costs of production (Marglin 1980).

In due course, the increased social control of employees by employers, facilitated by the introduction of the factory, was reinforced as alternative sources of income disappeared and non-family sources of labour and non-family relationships in general, eventually became more significant. Consequently, individuals became more independent of their family of origin and more dependent on the labour market and hence an employer. In other words, over time, '[f]amily members, male and female, increasingly come to think of their wages as their own, to be disposed of as they individually see fit' (Kumar 1988a: 190). By this stage, the process of individualization was virtually complete in the sense that a person's identity is no longer tied to family and place, as it was in the pre-industrial situation, but to 'one's occupation in the formal economy' of the industrial capitalist society (Kumar 1988a: 190). In effect, the loss of its productive function reduced the role of the family to that of consumption and reproduction; meanwhile, work, in the form of employment in the market economy outside the home, increased in importance as it became the sole or major source of income.

(3) Division of labour

The advent of capitalist industrialization reduced a range of pre-modern types of work, especially those connected to agriculture, such as blacksmiths and basket-makers, a large proportion of whom were self-employed, and created a vast number of new types of industrial work for employees in factories. Machines were designed, built, installed, supplied with energy and raw material, operated, maintained, and supervised by different types of worker who, following the separation of conception and execution, were divided by education (e.g., professional and elementary) and skill categories (e.g., skilled, semi-skilled, and unskilled). New professional specializations were created, notably those based on the application of scientific and technical knowledge such as mechanical engineering, and a mass of factory workers, consisting of 'individuals of both sexes and of all ages', were organized with 'barrack discipline' and divided hierarchically 'into operatives and overlookers, into private soldiers and sergeants of an industrial army' (Marx 1970 [1887]: 423–4). Weber concurred with Marx that 'military discipline is the ideal model for the modern capitalist factory', but unlike Marx, he seemed to admire its rationality and approved of 'the American system of "scientific management"', or Taylorism as it is also known (1961 [1948]: 261; see also 1964 [1947]: 261). This aspect of work in industrial capitalism will be considered more fully in Chapter 3.

The expansion of the factory system and the related increase in production led to an improvement in the means of transportation and communication, and an increase in the number of people employed to construct and work in new industries such as canals, railways, gas, electricity, post and telegraphy. The consequent change in the occupational structure can be illustrated with reference to the shift in employment from primary sector work which dominated pre-industrial societies (e.g., farming, fishing forestry, etc.) to secondary sector work (e.g., mills and factories) and tertiary sector work (e.g., services such as education and communication) which together dominate industrial capitalist societies. For example, in 1840 nearly 70 per cent of the American labour force worked in the primary sector and just over 30 per cent in the secondary and tertiary sectors; by 1900 employment in the primary sector had declined to 40 per cent and employment in the other two sectors had risen to 60 per cent (Nolan and Lenski 1999).

Another indicator of the impact of the Industrial Revolution on the pre-industrial occupational structure is the expansion of new job titles with its implicit differentiation of occupations. In the occupational classification of the census of Britain in 1841, the most advanced industrial capitalist society at that time, a mere 400 or so jobs were listed; by 1997 in America, the most advanced industrial capitalist society, there were over 20,000 different kinds of job listed (Nolan and Lenski 1999).

(4) Time

Prior to the rise of industrial capitalism, irregularity, especially in terms of work time, characterized the pattern of work. This was because work activities were influenced by the seasons, involved in obtaining sustenance from working on one's own plot of land, collecting food and fuel, and being hired out to work for others, and perhaps above all, because work tended to be task-oriented, work time tended to vary according to the job at hand (Thompson 1967). Consequently, the irregularity of work time applied to the working day, week, month, season and year, with the longest hours worked during the summer and the shortest in the winter (Kumar 1988b). At the risk of romanticizing the past, before industrial capitalism work involved a semblance of time freedom in that a person could decide when to start and stop work, and how hard to work. Work discipline, such as it was, tended to be minimal other than that imposed by the workers' definition of their needs and the weather (Thompson 1970).

In contrast to this pre-modern pattern of highly irregular work time, the introduction of the factory with its ubiquitous clock was a truly revolutionary event that came to dominate the lives of wage workers. Industrial factory work involved timed labour with the factory bell demarcating the relatively unstructured non-work time from the highly structured and supervised work time in which the tempo was set by the technology owned by the employers on whom employees were dependent for work: 'Industry brings the tyranny of the clock' (Hobsbawm 1969: 85).

Thus, work and life ceased to be task-oriented and characterized by independence, irregularity and variation, but became the epitome of dependence, regularity and routine, measured with increasing precision in hours, minutes and eventually even seconds. The stricter division between life and work and the increased synchronization of labour within the factory raised time-consciousness and created a need for time discipline, to which the growing school system and Methodism played their part by prioritizing punctuality and regularity (Thompson 1967).

Unsurprisingly, a key issue during industrialization, and since, was the length of the working day, especially those worked by children and women. In Britain the owners of capital initially extended the working day and resisted strenuously attempts to interfere with their freedom to exploit labour and maximize profits. It took nearly half a century of class struggle before the 'creation of a normal working day' of 12 hours was achieved by the middle of the nineteenth century (Marx 1970 [1887]: 299).

The centrality of time to work in industrial capitalism has led some to argue that the time piece rather than the steam engine symbolizes this era. For example, Mumford (1934) has argued that the increased scale of industrial production put a premium on the synchronization of people and technical processes and that this was achieved via the clock. Similarly, Thompson (1967) has claimed that what was different about work in industrial capitalism was its focus on time rather than tasks and a clearer distinction between work and non-work. Although Thompson has been criticized for underestimating the contested and variegated nature of time and work during the transition (Whipp 1987), the advantage of time is that it provides management with a standardized unit with which to co-ordinate the human and non-human elements of production and to measure the contribution of labour, with or without reference to output. Hence the tendency for pay to be based on the amount of time spent at work and the requirement to 'clock on and off' accompanied by a schedule of fines or dismissal for repeated lateness. Moreover, if a worker walked out, s/he could be prosecuted for breach of contract and imprisoned, whereas if the employer was in breach of contract the penalty was a fine at most (Marx 1970 [1887]). The importance of time discipline in the new factory system is also indicated by the rule that 'staying in the toilets "longer than necessary" was punishable by a fine' (Doray 1988: 30). Thus, in industrial capitalism time took on a new and exacting meaning; it was money.

(5) Education and recruitment

The rise of industrial capitalism increased both the technical or detailed division of labour by task specialization within occupations and the social or general division of labour between occupations in society. This necessitated a marked expansion of compulsory education in general, and specialized training in vocational subjects in particular, which in turn led to the growth of examinations and the award of credentials to certify competence for impersonal recruitment to different types of work (Collins 1979). Weber referred to this as the '"rationalization" of education and training' and noted that the process of bureaucratization 'enhances the importance of the specialist examination' (1961 [1948]: 240, 241).

The increasingly close link between education and work is reflected in Britain by the merger between the Departments of Education and Employment in 1995 (McKenzie 2001), subsequently renamed the Department for Education and Skills in June 2001 by the newly re-elected Labour government. The tendency for educational institutions to parallel the expected workplace experiences of their pupils has been called correspondence theory. This argues that

> major aspects of the structure of schooling can be understood in terms of the systematic need for producing reserve armies of skilled labour, legitimating the technocratic-meritocratic perspective, reinforcing the fragmentation of groups of workers into stratified status groups and accustoming youth to the social relationships of dominance and subordinancy in the economic system. (Bowles and Gintis 1976: 56)

During the transition to industrialization whole families, including young children, were recruited to work in the new urban factories, but over time the introduction of legal restrictions on the employment of children (and women) in factories, combined with state provision of education for all, undermined the kinship basis of factory labour. In Britain the first Act of Parliament to limit the employment of young children to a 12-hour working day was in 1802 but was restricted to cotton and woollen mills. Later Acts covered other workplaces and raised the age at which children could work, thereby reducing the number of child workers. Public funding of education was provided for the first time in 1833, but a national system of free elementary education up to the age of 10 was not established in England until 1891, and 1902 in the case of secondary education, well after similar reforms in other industrializing countries such as Germany and France (Hill 1971). Thus, gradually the recruitment of workers as individuals on the basis of their formal education and qualifications, replaced informal family recruitment and training, although in the textile industry in Britain the influence of the family lasted for most of the nineteenth century (Anderson 1971).

(6) Economic system

The rise of industrial capitalism involved the development of a market economy in which virtually all economic resources, including capital, labour, and the goods and services produced by business enterprises, are exchanged for money free of traditional social obligations and constraints such as restrictions on who could engage in certain economic activities. In other words, the idea and practice of free trade or *laissez-faire*. Most importantly, in industrial capitalism economic relations become separated, formally at least, from non-economic relations, and distinguished by the primacy accorded to the freedom to maximize economic gains by employing free wage labour. In contrast to pre-modern paternalism, employers had no obligations beyond paying the lowest wages possible in the new competitive market system, since to do other-wise risked economic failure, although industrial paternalism limited the more extreme operation of the free (labour) market culture (Joyce 1982).

From Marx's perspective, the fundamental capitalist feature is production for sale, and therefore profit, not use, involving the buying and selling of labour power in a market in which money wages are paid on the basis of the time worked and/or the output achieved. Hence, according to Marx, industrial capitalism is distinguished by its class dynamic which is rooted in the inevitable conflict of economic interests between the owners of capital and those they employ, namely exploited and oppressed propertyless free wage labourers. Separated from direct access to the means of subsistence, free wage labour is compelled in a competitive market system to sell their labour power in exchange for wages, which in turn are exchanged for the goods and services essential to maintain life. Thus, social relations under capitalism are reduced to market values expressed in monetary terms and, as a consequence of this commodity status, labourers are 'exposed to all the vicissitudes of competition, to all fluctuations of the market' (Marx and Engels (n.d. [1848]: 60). In contrast to the buying and selling of labour power in a profit-oriented market economy, social relationships in the private sphere of the family, which is now separated spatially and structurally from the public sphere of work, are not based on impersonal monetized exchange, but intimate reciprocity.

Although Weber agreed with Marx that industrial capitalism involves the develop-ment of a class system in which both capital and labour are freed from all restric-tions, arguably the key point for Weber was the rationality of a profit-seeking capitalist enterprise: 'capitalism is identical with the pursuit of profit, and forever *renewed* profit, by means of continuous, rational, capitalistic enterprise' (Weber 1976 [1930]: 17). In practical terms this meant making a calculation about the most effi-cient means to achieve certain goals, rather than selecting means with reference to historical tradition, namely on the basis of how things were undertaken in the past. This wholly new approach to work was exemplified by the rational principles of bureaucratic organization and book-keeping adopted by capitalist enterprises, and was in marked contrast to non-economic relations.

Thus, although Marx emphasized exploitation and Weber rationality, both agreed that in industrial capitalism the world of waged work (i.e., employment) is both separate and different from non-work, especially family life. Where previously the two spheres had been united in the form of the household economy, under industrial capitalism, the commodified and rational character of work is the opposite of the non-commodified and non-rational character of relationships beyond employment.

(7) Meaning of work

Weber argued that the rationality of economic action in industrial capitalist society required dispensing with the traditional attitude that work was at best something to be avoided and at worst a necessary evil, and replacing it with a positive evaluation as an activity that was considered virtuous. One of the main sources of this new rational attitude to work, which revolutionized economic and social life, was to be found in Protestantism, or more precisely in the symmetry between certain Calvinist beliefs, notably the calling of working hard to make money and the economic spirit of modern capitalism. Suitably imbued with the ethics of Protestantism, individuals work to please God and to demonstrate their worthiness to themselves and members of their group. Meanwhile, the asceticism of their religious beliefs discouraged people from spending their earnings wastefully. The unintended consequence of these religious prescriptions was accumulation rather than dissipation. In Weber's own words: 'When the limitation of consumption is combined with this release of acquisitive activity, the inevitable practical result is obvious: accumulation of capital through ascetic compulsion to save' (1976 [1930]: 172).

Work as a religious duty was exported to America with the Puritan settlers and a whole range of homilies emerged to sum up the modern spirit of capitalism and to inspire entrepreneurs and workers alike, for instance, 'time is money', and many others that praised 'industry', 'frugality' and 'punctuality', and deprecated 'idleness' (Weber 1976 [1930]: 48–9). In sum, ascetic Protestantism involved a major change in the meaning of work. In effect it meant a reversal of the traditional attitude of doing no more than is necessary, to one in which the creation of wealth via unrelenting hard work became the main object in life.

What had started as a peculiarly Protestant attitude to work became secularized in due course largely because this new conception of work was so 'well suited' to the emergent capitalist system in terms of encouraging workers to be diligent and employers to be profit-oriented, and over time 'it no longer needs the support of any religious forces' (Weber 1976 [1930]: 72). In other words, the Protestant work ethic became simply the work ethic, promulgated by non-religious institutions such as governments, business corporations and schools, although in the process the ascetic dimension has arguably declined as consumption has increased (Beder 2000).

An alternative perspective on the dramatic change in the meaning (and purpose) of work in industrial capitalism is provided by Marx, who argued that when workers are separated from the means of production and constrained to enter into a subordinate relationship to capital, they forfeit the ability to act creatively through work and instead become alienated since under industrial capitalism the competitive necessity to maximize profit requires that 'the labourer exists for the process of production, and not the process of production for the labourer' (Marx 1970 [1887]: 490). According to Marx: 'It follows therefore that in proportion as capital accumulates, the lot of the labourer, be his payment high or low, must grow worse' (1970 [1887]: 645). Thus, the meaning of work for Marx cannot be understood without reference to the antagonistic class relationships that lie at the centre of the labour process of industrial capitalism.

(8) Purpose of work

In pre-industrial capitalist societies the main purpose of economic activities that we call work was to provide the essential goods and services necessary for the survival of the group or household. For the vast majority, therefore, work was a matter of making a living. This changed markedly with the rise of the capitalistic organization of work, the main purpose of which became 'the pursuit of profit and forever renewed profit, by means of continuous, rational, capitalistic enterprise', for to do otherwise was to risk economic failure (Weber 1976 [1930]: 17). In other words, making things became subordinated to making a profit. If there was no profit to be obtained, things would not be made, however much people needed them. In Veblen's terms, the purpose of work changed from that of maximum production (workmanship) to maximum profits (predation), to the economic detriment of those who do not own capital (Edgell 2001).

On an individual level, the new idea of the relentless pursuit of profit by all work organizations, although sanctified by religion in the early years, was not embraced by everyone caught up in the rise of industrial capitalism. The privileged few who owned and controlled the business enterprises clearly had an interest in the accumulation of profit and therefore supported and promulgated the idea that hard work was not only a necessity that resulted in economic success, but morally worthwhile. However, for those recruited to work in the more routine and boring jobs for far smaller economic rewards, work remained more of a necessary evil than a virtuous activity in its own right. This kind of instrumental orientation to work, one that puts a premium on pay and security rather than on intrinsic interest and satisfaction, can still be found among manual workers (Goldthorpe et al. 1969). Finally, there is the case of professional workers who are considered to be motivated primarily by a commitment to provide a public service on the basis of their specialist knowledge, such as vocationally inspired health or education professionals. However, it has also been argued that the relatively high prestige and autonomy of certain professions, for example law, enables their members to act as much for their own benefit as they do for others. In other words, professional work can involve both a selfish orientation as well as a selfless one (MacDonald 1995).

(9) Payment

In pre-capitalistic societies, economic activities such as farming and handicraft work were organized on a small scale and were concerned primarily with 'earning a livelihood rather than with a view to profits on investment' (Veblen 1975 [1904]: 24). For the vast majority this meant subsistence, involving a mixture of payments in kind and in cash. However, once workers had been separated from the means of production, their only option was to seek work for wages as an employee in a business enterprise.

In the early phase of industrialization in England the payment of wages in kind rather than cash, known as the truck system, persisted until an efficient monetary system had been established. It was outlawed effectively following a series of Truck Acts, the most important of which were passed in 1831, 1854 and 1871 (Hilton 1960). It had been virtually universal in pre-modern England and took many forms; sometimes the workers were paid in the goods they had produced and at other times in coupons that were exchangeable only in shops owned by the employer, and at other times in a mixture of the two. Whatever form it took, the truck system was highly exploitative since it tended to lower wages via either the falsification of weights and measures, and/or high charges for materials and goods. Consequently, it was resented by workers, and even some employers, who regarded it as inflexible since it tied some workers to their employers through debt (Hilton 1960).

The truck system was a kind of transitional payment system between a predominantly payment in kind subsistence system, characteristic of pre-industrial capitalism, and a money payment system in which wages are the sole or main source of income and therefore sustenance. As the diversity of life-maintaining forms of work shrank, viable alternatives to wage labour declined markedly, although they did not disappear totally (Pahl 1984). By the late nineteenth century the transformation from a complex mixture of different forms of task work, common rights and self-provisioning, typical of pre-industrial England (Malcomson 1988), to a system characterized by regular, full-time employment in one job was well advanced (Kumar 1988b), although the change from the predominance of irregular to regular employment was a protracted one in that pre-modern forms of work persisted throughout the nineteenth century in Britain, especially in London where the seasonality of production, for example in high-value consumption goods, dock work and the building trade, favoured irregular casual employment (Stedman Jones 1984).

The gradual erosion of a culture characterized by multiple sources of income and sustenance to one way of making a living meant that to be without employment meant to be out of work, and by the 1880s in Britain the now familiar terms 'unemployed' and 'unemployment' had entered public discourse (Burnett 1994). The equation work equals employment is therefore only meaningful in a society, namely an industrial capitalist one, in which a wage via formal paid employment is effectively the only way of securing the means to obtain the goods and services necessary to sustain life.

(10) Embeddedness of work

The cumulative effect of all these radical changes to the nature and organization of work associated with the development of industrial capitalism was that work ceased to be embedded in non-economic social institutions, such as the family and religion, and became a separate, distinct institution in terms of space, time and culture. For example, it has been noted that the spatial separation of work from family also involved the differentiation of work time from non-work time, and a set of impersonal work relations which contrasted with the affective bonds of family life, although the extent to which economic relations were embedded in social relations in pre-modern society and the extent to which this pattern was reversed under industrial capitalism is a matter of some debate (Granovetter 1985).

To use more technical language, behaviour within the two realms of home and work in industrial capitalist society are guided by particularism and universalism respectively. In other words, participation in the modern world of work was no longer linked directly to family life in the sense that workers are typically trained, recruited, employed and dismissed by rational organizations in which they are not given preferential treatment. Thus, neither gaining qualifications, nor obtaining, retaining or progressing at work on the basis of a family connection or close friendship is regarded as fair or appropriate since it would compromise the rationality of the work system and risk the charge of cronyism. In theory at least, the equal treatment of all is the rule in the industrial capitalist economy and is typically backed up by the force of law. However, universalistic norms are so well established (i.e., institutionalized) and accepted (i.e., internalized) that, as economic actors, individuals in modern societies do not expect to be treated in a preferential way in any non-family structure, for instance not to be charged the train fare on the grounds that the ticket seller is related. Thus, the use of the law to enforce the rule of universalism tends to be infrequent in modern work organizations.

This model of the contrast between the particularism of family life and the universalism of work organizations associated with the rise of industrial capitalism is often referred to as structural differentiation and in many respects it is an idealized version of the two spheres (Smelser 1972 [1959]). In practice, notwithstanding the structural segregation of work from family in terms of space, time and culture, the autonomy of the two institutions is relative rather than absolute. This is largely because although the direct influence of family membership on the attainment of an occupational position has been disconnected, except where the inheritance of capital is concerned as in family businesses, family background continues to have an indirect influence via the purchasing of educational privilege, the acquisition of cultural capital, and the operation of social networks (Scott 1991). Consequently, even in multinational corporations it is not unusual to find a kinship link among top executives; for example, the current chief executive of Ford Motor Company is Bill Ford, the great grandson of the company's founder Henry Ford (*The Guardian* 30 October 2001). Similarly, lower down the corporate hierarchy, knowledge about the availability of work and from whom to buy or sell goods and services at work may be influenced by ongoing personal work networks (Granovetter 1985). In short, getting a job and getting on at work may depend as much on personal ties at the club or pub than impersonal factors such as formal qualifications and experience. Moreover, empirical research on the multiplicity of ways in which home and work intersect in modern societies, particularly for those who work at and/or from home, suggests that work has not been separated totally from home (e.g., Allen and Wolkowitz 1987; Edgell 1980; Finch 1983). Thus although it is difficult to deny the dislocation caused by industrial capitalism to family and work life, the thesis that the rise of industrial capitalism occasioned the separation of home from work tends to exaggerate the degree to which social life became segmented. This is especially the case for the early stages of the separation of the two spheres where recruitment to the new urban factories persisted on a kinship basis, either directly as in the case of the recruitment of family members or indirectly as in the case of recommending relatives to prospective employers (Anderson 1971). In due course, however, the increasing reliance on the wages from regular work as an employee contributed to the enhanced economic and social significance of paid work outside the home and the marginalization of all other kinds of work, including both paid and unpaid work inside the home. Thus, under industrial capitalism work became synonymous with paid employment, a distinctive and less embedded institution.

The unstable character of industrial capitalism

Although the terminology varies from 'contradictions' to 'irrationalities' and 'conflicts', the analyses of industrial capitalism by classical social theorists such as Marx, Weber and Veblen, all identified sources of instability that led invariably to tension and therefore change. However, their accounts of the nature and development of industrial capitalism diverged when it came to assessing the significance and implications of the instabilities they specified.

According to Marx, industrial capitalism is inherently unstable due to the conflict between the economic interests of the owners of capital and those of labour. The employers are constrained to exploit the labour power of workers by paying them less than the value of what they produce, to do otherwise would risk their survival in a competitive market system. Conversely, for their part, the employees typically respond by combining together to maintain or improve not just their wages, but also their working conditions. In other words, by creating specialist places of work dedicated to making profits, employers also created the opportunity for large numbers of workers to generate solidarity and challenge their power: 'What the bourgeoisie, therefore, produces, above all, is its own gravediggers' (Marx and Engels n.d. [1848]: 71).

Whereas Marx thought that the central contradiction of industrial capitalism would, hopefully, lead to its downfall and eventual replacement by socialism, Weber, as we have noted already, was also aware of the contradictory nature of industrial capitalism and took the view that it would result in adaptation rather than transformation. He argued that the 'capitalist market economy demands' the very features that define bureaucracy, notably precision and reliability, but the more bureaucratic an organization becomes the more it dehumanizes work relationships (Weber 1961 [1948]: 215). Weber considered this to be regrettable and likely to be exacerbated by socialism, yet also claimed that although bureaucracy was not unique to industrial capitalism, its growth was inevitable in modern societies because it was more efficient than any other known type of organization, such as those based on traditional or charismatic authority, both of which were pervasive in pre-modern societies.

Despite their contrasting conclusions regarding the 'inevitability' of the long-term failure and success of industrial capitalism, both Marx and Weber considered capitalism and industrialism to be so inextricably related that they did not differentiate clearly between the two concepts, whilst Durkheim did not use the terms 'industrial society' or 'capitalism', preferring instead 'modern' or 'contemporary society' (Giddens 1973: 203). For Veblen, on the other hand, the distinction between modern industry and modern capitalism was crucial since the former was concerned with mechanization and material gain whilst the latter was concerned with ownership and pecuniary gain (Veblen 1975 [1904]). Veblen argued that in advanced industrial capitalist societies, the capitalistic aspect of work organizations, namely maximum profit, increasingly dominated the industrial dimension, namely maximum output, and that this was to the detriment of the 'economic welfare of the community at large' (1975 [1904]: 27). For example, it is standard business practice to restrict output, make workers redundant, close factories, and withhold technical knowledge from competitors, all with a view to increasing profits. Moreover, Veblen claimed that the larger the scale and the more complex industrial capitalism became, the more unfit the 'businessman' to direct production, hence the tendency to employ specialist engineers to do the work for them. Thus, in Veblen's view, the fundamental contradiction of industrial capitalism involved the conflict between capitalist predation and industrial workmanship. Although Veblen considered conflict between business and industry to be unavoidable, he was unsure about the outcome, though he clearly sided with the interests of industry (Edgell 2001).

The issues raised in this summary of the main features of work in industrial capitalist societies will be discussed again at various points throughout this book, primarily but not exclusively with reference to Britain and America. In the meantime, in addition to the changes in the nature of work noted thus far, the gender dimension of the rise of industrial capitalism is central to any rounded sociological account of work.

Women and work in the development of industrial capitalism

The impact of capitalist industrialization on women, particularly the transfer of paid work out of the home and into the factory, has been the subject of considerable debate. The majority view, also referred to as the pessimistic perspective (e.g., Thomas 1988), is that the rise of industrial capitalism had a negative impact on the work prospects of women (e.g., Lewenhak 1980; Oakley 1976; Scott and Tilly 1975; Walby 1986). The minority view, correspondingly known as the optimistic perspective, argues the reverse (e.g., Goode 1970; Shorter 1976). The important study by Pinchbeck (1969 [1930]) has been credited with being the precursor of this optimistic viewpoint by virtue of her judgement that over the long term the industrial revolution benefited women because it increased their employment opportunities, which in turn contributed to their economic independence (Richards 1974). However, it has also been noted that Pinchbeck's account was not wholly unambiguous (Bradley 1989), and in this sense it is a forerunner of the most recent suggestion that the impact of industrial capitalism was mixed rather than simply beneficial or detrimental to women (Hudson and Lee 1990).

The ongoing debate about industrial capitalism and its impact on women and work affords numerous opportunities for disagreement, for example, the question of the gender division of labour before industrial capitalism and the time frame under consideration. Given the problematic character of this debate, the analysis will focus on agrarian Britain with reference to the initial impact of industrial capitalism, which in the case of textiles was the early nineteenth century, but later in other industries, and the impact over the longer term, namely the second half of the nineteenth century. Although these phases overlap, this distinction offers one possible way out of the debate between the 'pessimists' and the 'optimists'.

Initial Phase circa 1800–1840s

Official statistics on the gender pattern of work between 1801 and 1831 are relatively unhelpful because the unit of analysis was the household not the individual (Davies 1980; Hakim 1980). Consequently, historical research on the factors associated with female employment will be considered. This material suggests that there are several grounds for arguing that work opportunities for women expanded during the rise of industrial capitalism:

- the continuity of female labour in the transition to factory work (Scott and Tilly 1975);
- the decline of male-dominated guilds (Oakley 1976);
- the female input in trade unions and the co-operative movement (Lewenhak 1980);
- demographic forces which created a supply of female labour (Richards 1974);
- economic expansion and the demand for women workers (Hobsbawm 1969);
- physical strength ceased to be crucial to operate machinery (Hudson and Lee 1990);
- the relative cheapness of female labour compared to male (Rendall 1990);
- male reluctance to enter factories due to loss of independence (Thompson 1970);
- the perception that female workers were compliant (Pinchbeck 1969 [1930]);
- machines were designed with female workers in mind, namely their alleged greater manual dexterity (Berg 1994; Bradley 1989; Lown 1990).

Many of the factors that encouraged the employment of women during the initial phase of capitalist industrialization were mutually reinforcing, such as the tendency to employ female labour on the basis of their presumed docility, dexterity and, above all perhaps, cheapness. Similarly, the forces of supply and demand were complementary in that the greater availability of female labour coincided with increased opportunities for work in the expanding textile factories.

Studies of specific industries such as textiles and metals, confirm that the impact of this combination of factors was conducive to an increase in the employment of women during the early years of capitalist industrialization (Berg 1988). In the silk industry, which was slower to mechanize than cotton and wool, this gender pattern was repeated and by the middle of the nineteenth century there were at least two women workers for every man, and in areas such as Essex they outnumbered men in the workforce by over four to one (Lown 1990).

Although mechanization of the so-called 'sweated trades', namely work characterized by low pay, long hours and poor conditions, occurred much later than in textiles, it also led to an increase in the employment of women to the point where they became the 'majority of the workforce' (Morris 1988: 103). This came about as a result of the rise in demand for mass-produced, and hence relatively inexpensive, goods, which could not be satisfied by male craft workers. The work was subdivided and undertaken by cheap female labour at home, a workshop, or a factory. Significantly, the early legislation which sought to protect women by restricting their employment, notably the Mines Act of 1842 and Factory Act of 1844 did not cover the sweated trades (Rendall 1990).

Finally, in addition to being in the vanguard of those occupations affected by the initial impact of capitalist industrialization, women continued to work on an irregular, pre-modern basis, at and from home, and such work, especially by married women, was recorded inconsistently in the early censuses (Davies 1980), or not recorded even in 1851 (Anderson 1971). There is therefore a strong case for the view that during the initial phase of industrial capitalism women not only worked as they had done before when work was organized in the household, but became a prominent part of the waged workforce recruited by the first factory owners. Thus, whatever the actual timing of the capitalist industrialization of production, the absence of any legal or other constraints on the employment of women encouraged the employment of the cheapest labour available, which in the short run meant women (and children) rather than men, albeit in the less skilled and lower status work that had been mechanized.

Mature Phase circa 1850s–1890s

The separation of work from home and the initial increase in the employment opportunities for women created a problem for men in the short term and employers in the long term. It threatened male authority in the home and the supply of labour in the future, and raised the issue of who should care for vulnerable family members such as children. The solution was to exclude women from paid work outside the home and assign them primary responsibility for all things domestic. As a consequence, by the late nineteenth century the economic activity rate for women had declined to 32 per cent and the decline was even more marked for wives; in 1851 one in four married women was employed and by 1901 the proportion had shrunk to one in ten (Hakim 1980). Although the under-reporting of women workers was still an issue during this period, the decline in the employment rate of women occurred in the context of continued economic expansion and an increasingly greater number of women than men in the total population (John 1988). The exclusion of women from work outside the home was achieved by a combination of factors, including:

- male trade union restrictions on women workers (Hartmann 1979; Walby 1986);
- the campaign for a family wage by male workers (Creighton 1996; Land 1980);
- legislative restrictions by male parliamentarians (Bradley 1989; Walby 1986);
- the introduction of a marriage bar by male employers (Lewenhak 1980);
- limits on child labour and the introduction of compulsory education (Rendall 1990);
- the twin ideals of male breadwinner and female domesticity (Hudson and Lee 1990);
- the large size of the Victorian family (Richards 1974);
- the decline of the family production unit (Scott and Tilly 1975);
- lower pay rates for women discouraged them from working outside the home (Hudson and Lee 1990);
- changes in business structure which limited the possibility of women inheriting businesses (Hudson and Lee 1990; Walby 1986).

The patriarchal dimension of these factors is unmistakable, less obvious is the class dimension. Out of economic necessity, working-class women were far more likely to work outside the home than their middle-class counterparts, and as a result were criticized heavily for neglecting their domestic responsibilities (Roberts 1995). In marked contrast, there was no economic urgency for middle-class wives to go out to work. In fact they could afford to employ staff to undertake their domestic work, thereby creating employment for a large number of unmarried women (Oakley 1976). This left the middle-class wife free to engage in voluntary work, which, being unpaid yet time-consuming, demonstrated the economic status of the male head of the household (Veblen 1970 [1899]). Consequently, the Victorian ideals of full-time female domesticity and full-time male breadwinner were more likely to be achieved by the middle class than the working class. Conversely, the vast majority of women who worked outside the home during the mature phase of capitalist industrialization were working class (Scott and Tilly 1975) and unmarried (Hudson and Lee 1990).

Thus, the 'exclusion of women should be seen as a result of the intersection of patriarchal relations and capitalist relations' although the 'articulation of these factors varied between industries' (Walby 1986: 97). Considered together, the two phases of capitalist industrialization suggest that in terms of the paid work of women, 'the pattern was one of increase followed by decline' (Scott and Tilly 1975: 37). Finally, the decline in the proportion of women, especially married women, who worked outside the home during the second half of the nineteenth century paralleled the rise of women's work inside the home, as unpaid housewives or managers of domestic servants. In other words, the attempt to exclude women from paid work outside the home does not mean that women ceased to work; rather, it indicates a major change in the meaning of work.

—— Industrial capitalism, patriarchy, and the dominant conception of work ——

By the end of the nineteenth century in Britain, later in some countries, for example Germany, and somewhat more controversially elsewhere (Janssens 1997; Pfau-Effinger

Table 1.2   Dominant conception of work in industrial capitalism and threats to its hegemony

Dominant conception of work	Threats to its hegemony
Capitalist	**Non-capitalist**
Profit-oriented organizations	Non-profit-oriented organizations
Monetized market system	Barter system and gift exchange
Labour power exchanged for pay	Unpaid voluntary work
Industrial	**Global post-industrialism**
Outside the home	Working at/from home
Contractual regulation	Contractual deregulation
Fixed hours	Flexible hours
Modern	**Traditionalism**
Universalism	Particularism
Achievement	Ascription
Specialization	Non-specialization
Patriarchal	**Feminism**
Adult male worker	Adult female worker
Full-time	Full-time
Permanent	Permanent

2004), a model of work characterized by the male breadwinner and female home-maker had emerged. The term 'dominant concept of work' has been used to refer to this model (Callender 1985: 50; see also Hakim 1980; Ransome 1996). A systematic articulation of this model suggests that once industrial capitalism has become established, the defining features of the dominant conception of work are that it is work that is undertaken outside the home (i.e., industrial), for pay (i.e., capitalist), by adult males on a full-time and uninterrupted basis (i.e., patriarchal), and is allocated individually with reference to impersonal universalistic criteria (i.e., modern). This model is summarized in Table 1.2 along with the possible threats to its dominance.

With the maturation of industrial capitalism, this conception of work, or variations of it, such as the married woman who worked part-time, was dominant culturally and empirically. It became the only kind of work that was considered 'real' work, and this was reflected in the official data collected on work (Hakim 1980). Consequently, any work that did not conform to this dominant conception, such as housework, informal work and voluntary work, was not only excluded from the official statistics of work, but tended to be regarded differently, namely that it was a less important type of work. Since women were the largest social category who deviated from the dominant conception of work yet were over-represented in other kinds of work, notably housework, their economic role was correspondingly under-reported and under-valued (Hakim 1996). In effect, work became synonymous with employment which with the rise of Fordism became standardized in terms of contract, location and working time.

For those who worked as an employer or employee, the majority of whom were men, a regulatory framework developed covering eventually all aspects of work, namely pay and conditions. If a member of the permanent labour force was out of work, from the late nineteenth century onwards, they were considered to be unemployed and deserving of support, initially by charitable organizations and later the state (Burnett 1994). However, for those who worked unpaid in the home, the majority of whom were women, there was a complete lack of regulations covering their work; it was, and still is to a large extent, considered a private matter (Oakley 1976). Moreover, since eligibility for state benefits for the unemployed was related to one's degree of involvement in work as a form of employment, women typically found it more difficult than men to claim benefits when unemployed (Dex 1985). Thus, the development of industrial capitalism created a marked gender division of labour: a predominantly male group of adults who worked outside the home for pay on a regular basis, and a predominantly female group of adults who worked inside the home for no pay on a regular basis. The social category the unemployed and the role of full-time housewife are therefore both recent social constructions that emerged in the late nineteenth century in Britain and elsewhere.

The continuing relevance of this dominant conception of work is part of the rationale of this book and hence the implications of this model will be discussed in later chapters where relevant. In the meantime it is important to note that this conception of work is not a static phenomenon, but is subject to change. Over the past two decades or so, each of the dimensions of this dominant conception of work has come under threat from a variety of trends. First, as far as the capitalist dimension is concerned, the continued importance of certain forms of unpaid work, notably housework and voluntary work, the persistence of worker co-operatives (Mellor et al. 1988), and the growth of not-for-profit organizations suggest that not all work has been commodified and that non-monetized exchange remains significant (Williams 2002). Second, it has been argued that towards the end of the twentieth century, the industrial dimension was being undermined by globalization associated with the increasing emphasis on all forms of flexibility and the destandardization of work (Beck 1992). Third, the patriarchal dimension has been challenged widely and relatively successfully by feminism and the feminization of work over the past half-century (Castells 1997). Fourth, the modern dimension of the dominant conception of work is threatened by the revival of family-based enterprises and the persistent influence of family background on class destination (Edgell 1993). Moreover, who you know rather than what you have achieved can still influence whether or not the unemployed obtain paid work (Marsden 1982). However, it remains to be seen to what extent these threats to the dominant conception of work have been effective, an issue that will be discussed at the end of the book.

Summary and conclusions

At the risk of over-simplifying the complex and varied history of societies, it has been argued that in pre-industrial capitalist societies – stone age, horticultural and agrarian – work was viewed negatively and was embedded in wider social relations, notably those of kinship. The emergence of industrial capitalism, initially over a long period in Britain, and later over a shorter time span to the rest of the world, involved a clear break with all previous types of society. In ideal-typical terms, the main features of this new type of society include the use of machinery powered by inanimate sources of energy, the separation of home and work, specialist work roles and places, a profit-oriented market system, free wage labour, and a positive value associated with work. It is important to remember that these characteristics are neither uncontested, as the term 'wage slavery' indicates, nor universal, as the persistence of homeworking testifies.

During the early development of industrial capitalism in Britain, work opportunities for women increased, but thereafter declined, especially for married women, who were excluded from some kinds of work and restricted to certain other kinds of work, such as low-paid, unskilled work and unpaid housework. The distinct gender division of labour that emerged has been designated the male breadwinner and female homemaker model, although it was not universal. When this patriarchal dimension of work was combined with other key features of the new type of society – industrial, capitalist and modern – it created a dominant conception of work in which real work was equated with full-time employment for pay outside the home by adult males recruited on the basis of impersonal norms, and led to the devaluation of other kinds of work. This conception of work became standardized and dominated the twentieth century but is now under threat.

Two main conclusions may be drawn from the historical overview of the patterning of work. First, that the rise of industrial capitalism occasioned a major transformation in the nature of work which dislocated work to a greater or lesser extent from all other social institutions. Second, during the establishment of this revolutionary type of society, a dominant conception of work emerged that prioritized work that was capitalist, industrial, partiarchal and modern over other types work, such as unpaid housework, which did not conform to this model.

The purpose of this book is to cover paid and unpaid work, not just those in paid work, since a truly sociological account of work in advanced industrial capitalist society should not take its cue from the dominant conception of work, especially at a time when this model is arguably in decline.

Further reading

The history of work from a socio-cultural evolutionary perspective is provided by Nolan and Lenski (1999) *Human Societies: An Introduction to Macrosociology*, and more information on the key contrast between work in pre-modern and modern societies is provided by Applebaum (1992) *The Concept of Work: Ancient, Medieval and Modern*. For an in-depth account of Veblen's relatively neglected contribution to our understanding of changes in the nature of work in different eras, see Edgell (2001) *Veblen in Perspective: His Life and Thought*. As a corrective to the inevitable compression of the arguments and evidence concerning the gender dimension of work during the development of industrial capitalism, consult Walby (1986) *Patriarchy at Work* and John (1988) *Unequal Opportunities: Women's Employment in England 1800–1918*. A succinct account of the emergence of the specialist role of housewife as a consequence of industrialization can be found in Oakley (1976) *Housewife*.

Questions for discussion and assessment

1. Examine the view that economic development is associated with the increased differentiation of work roles with reference of pre-industrial societies.
2. What do you consider to be the defining features of work in industrial capitalist societies?
3. What are the major differences between work in pre-industrial and industrial societies?
4. What part did religion play in conceptions of work in pre-modern and modern societies?
5. Assess the claim that new technology played the crucial role in the development of industrial capitalism.
6. Evaluate the thesis that the initial development of industrial capitalism improved the work opportunities for women.
7. Account for the decline in the labour force participation of women in Britain during the late nineteenth century.
8. What is meant by the term 'the dominant conception of work' and explain which dimension you consider to be under most threat and why?

••••••••

CHAPTER TWO

Paid Work and Alienation

One of the most pivotal, if not the central, idea in Marx's sociological critique of work in industrial capitalist societies is his thesis that alienation is built into the nature of work under a capitalist mode of production. For Marx, alienation was both inevitable and universal in capitalist societies, but it could be overcome. In fact, de-alienation could be considered as Marx's life project.

Marx introduced the concept of alienation in his early philosophical writings in the 1840s, but they were published only in the 1930s and were not translated into English until the 1950s. Over the following half-century the idea of alienation was operationalized and used extensively in empirical research in the sociology of work (Blauner 1964) and political sociology (Finifter 1972), and entered popular discourse typically with reference to alienated youth. Yet an account of the economic elements of alienation can be found in Volume One of *Capital*, which was first published in the 1860s and translated into English in the 1880s. Marx's lifelong use of the concept alienation suggests that it 'is a vitally important pillar of the Marxian system as a whole, and not just one brick of it' (Meszaros 1970: 227).

This chapter will be concerned to evaluate the transformation of the concept of alienation from its nineteenth-century Marxian philosophical and political economic origins to its mid-to-late-twentieth-century use in empirical sociological research on waged work, the most renowned example of which is the study by Blauner (1964).

Marx's theory of alienation

For Marx, alienation is rooted in the structure of industrial capitalism, under which

> all means for the development of production transform themselves into means of domination over, and exploitation of, the producers; they mutilate the labourer into a fragment of man, degrade him to the level of an appendage of

a machine, destroy every remnant of charm in his work and turn it into hated toil. (1970 [1887]: 645)

In other words, work in industrial capitalist society is the dehumanized opposite of a satisfying experience which develops the human capacity for creativity. In Marx's most systematic account of alienation, he argues that there are four distinct yet related manifestations of alienation under industrial capitalism:

1 *Product alienation.* A worker is alienated from the product of his/her labour, which is owned by the employer: 'the worker is related to the product of his labour as to an alien object' (Marx 1970 [1959]: 108).
2 *Activity alienation.* The activity of work itself is alienating because it is involuntary and fails to develop a worker's creative potential: 'it is forced labour … that as soon as no physical or other compulsion exists, labour is shunned like the plague' (Marx 1970 [1959]: 111).
3 *Species alienation.* As a result of product and activity alienation, workers become alienated from their essential nature, what makes them human: 'In tearing away from man the object of his production, therefore, estranged labour tears from him his species life, his real objectivity as a member of the species and transforms his advantage over animals into the disadvantage that his inorganic body, nature, is taken from him' (Marx 1970 [1959]: 114).
4 *Social alienation.* Following from the above, workers are also alienated from each other: 'An immediate consequence of the fact that man is estranged from the product of his labour, from his life activity, from his species being is the estrangement of man from man' (Marx 1970 [1959]: 114).

Marx often used the word estrangement as well as alienation to describe the effect of being a wage worker under industrial capitalism. The literal meaning of this word, to become a disaffected stranger, implies that ideally work should be an enjoyable experience. Moreover, Marx wrote quite passionately about alienation, where he analysed the impact of capitalist manufacturing on workers: 'It converts the labourer into a crippled monstrosity, by forcing his detail dexterity at the expense of a world of productive capabilities and instincts' (1970 [1887]: 360).

It is not just the workers who suffer alienation. The employer is implicated in the treatment of workers as commodities and as a consequence they are also dehumanized by their role in the capitalist labour process, albeit less severely than workers. Hence, according to Marx, 'the whole of human servitude is involved in the relation of the worker to production, and every relation of servitude is but a modification and consequence of this relation' (1970 [1959]: 118). Thus, industrial capitalism is characterized by: 'Immorality, deformity, and dulling of the workers and the capitalists' (Marx 1970 [1959]: 121). The dehumanization of capitalists is emphasized by Marx but is often overlooked in contemporary discussions of alienation, although there are some notable exceptions (e.g., Ollman 1971; Swingewood 1975).

For Marx, the problem of alienation under industrial capitalism cannot be solved by tinkering with the capitalist system, for example paying higher wages or varying the range of tasks to be executed, since such reforms would merely alter the conditions under which exploitation takes place and alienation occurs. The only solution acceptable to Marx was the abolition of the structure which creates alienation, thereby achieving the 'emancipation' of both the sellers and buyers of labour power (Marx 1970 [1959]: 118). Following the abolition of private property and the end of the exploitation of workers by employers constrained by competition and the threat of economic failure to be concerned solely with production of goods and services for profit, a communist society, in which the 'complete return of man to himself as a social (i.e., human) being', namely de-alienation, can be established (Marx 1970 [1959]: 135).

Alienation and work are inextricably associated with Marx, but he was not alone among the founders of sociology in discussing the idea of alienation. Indeed, it has been argued that alienation was a major theme in nineteenth-century literature, for example, the novels of Dostoevski, as well as sociology (Nisbet 1970).

Blauner's technology and alienation thesis

The catalyst for the conversion of Marx's idea of alienation to a measurable concept was Seeman's article, entitled 'On the meaning of alienation' (1959). Whereas Marx's perspective was societal and in particular how the capitalist labour process gave rise to alienation on a universal scale, Seeman considered alienation from the standpoint of the individual. There is a second very important difference between the two approaches: for Marx, alienation was a political issue, a problem endemic to industrial capitalism that could only be overcome by revolutionary change and the creation of a communist society, but for Seeman the purpose of his analysis of alienation was not to change the world but to make the idea empirically usable. In other words, operationalize it. Also, in addition to Marx, Seeman drew upon the contributions of Weber, Durkheim and Veblen, plus various contemporary sociologists, including Mills, to examine the different meanings of alienation in classical and contemporary sociology.

Seeman distinguished five different meanings of alienation: (1) powerlessness, (2) meaninglessness, (3) normlessness, (4) isolation, and (5) self-estrangement. In the process of operationalizing the dimensions of alienation, Seeman recast them in terms of a socio-psychological framework of individual expectations and rewards, which he considered not too far removed from the Marxian legacy, aside from purging the concept of its political thrust.

The challenge to research alienation empirically with reference to work in industrial capitalism was taken up by Blauner (1964). Although Blauner accepted the 'Marxian premise that there are powerful alienating tendencies in modern factory technology and industrial organization', he rejected the assumption that alienation was inevitable under industrial capitalism on the grounds that the alienating tendencies emphasized by Marx are unevenly distributed among the labour force (1964: 4). His aim, therefore, was to investigate empirically the diversity of work environments in 'an

Table 2.1   Blauner's four types of technology and characteristic industry

1   Craft technology – Printing Industry
    Simple machines operated by hand.
2   Machine-tending technology – Textile industry
    Relatively complex machines minded by operatives.
3   Assembly-line technology – Car industry
    Conveyor-belt technology with limited tasks performed using small power tools.
4   Continuous-process technology – Chemical industry
    Automated technology monitored and maintained by operatives.

Source: Summarized from Blauner (1964: 6–8)

attempt to demonstrate and to explain the uneven distribution of alienation among factory workers in American industry' (1964: 6).

More specifically, he set out to research the conditions under which the different dimensions of alienation are heightened or lessened by comparing systematically four factory-based industries: printing, textiles, automobiles and chemicals. According to Blauner, the 'most important single factor which gives an industry a distinctive character is its *technology*', which he defined as 'the complex of physical objects and technical operations (both manual and machine) regularly employed in turning out the goods and services produced by an industry' (1964: 6, italics in the original). Blauner adopted a sociological conception of technology in that he refers to the mechanical hardware (tools and machines) and to the human activities associated with using the mechanical hardware (knowledge and techniques). The reasons Blauner advances for prioritizing technology above all other potential causal variables are that it is the most influential factor that 'determines the nature of the job tasks performed by blue-collar employees and has an important effect on a number of aspects of alienation' (1964: 8). For example, technology influences the kinds of work activity required of an employee and the amount of physical movement a worker experiences, both of which are thought to affect the degree of worker powerlessness.

In order to be able to achieve his stated aim of investigating variations in the patterning of alienation, Blauner distinguished between four types of technology (the independent or causal variable) and four dimensions of alienation (the dependent variable or phenomenon to be explained). The four types of technology and the industries selected to represent different historical phases of its development were: (1) craft – printing, (2) machine-tending – textiles, (3) assembly-line – cars, and (4) continuous-process – chemicals. These are summarized in Table 2.1. Blauner denies that his four types of technology conform to a unilinear model of industrial evolution, but admits that exceptions, such as instances of regression, 'are very rare' (1964: 8).

Blauner considered alienation to be a complex idea and therefore divided it into four dimensions: (1) powerlessness or lack of freedom and control at work, (2) meaninglessness or lack of understanding and sense of purpose, (3) social isolation or lack of a sense of belonging and an inability to identify with the organization, and (4) self-estrangement or lack of involvement and hence fulfilment at work. As can be seen in Table 2.2, these aspects of alienation are contrasted with their non-alienated

Table 2.2 Blauner's four dimensions of alienation and their polar opposites

Alienation	Definition/Key measures	Non-alienation
1 Powerlessness	Lack of freedom and control/ freedom to move physically and socially; control over quality and quantity of work	Freedom and control
2 Meaninglessness	Lack of understanding and purpose/ subdivided and limited work tasks	Understanding and purpose
3 Social isolation	Lack of belonging and identification/ formal and informal social interaction	Belonging and identity
4 Self-estrangement	Lack of involvement and fulfilment/ instrumental attitude and boredom	Involvement and self-expression

Source: Summarized from Blauner (1964: 15–34)

opposites, namely (1) freedom and control, (2) understanding and purpose, (3) belonging and identity or social integration, and (4) involvement and self-expression or self-actualization. Blauner claims that like Marx he too is adopting a multidimensional approach to alienation and makes the further claim that 'the connection between some of Marx's dimensions and those employed in the present chapter is clear' (1964: 16).

In between the independent variable technology and the dependent variable alienation, Blauner lists what may be called three intervening variables, which mediate between the cause (type of technology) and effect (form of alienation). First, variations in the division of labour or the extent of the subdivision of work tasks within a factory is thought to 'affect the meaning and purpose' experienced by workers (Blauner 1964: 9). Second, social organization or whether an industry is organized on the basis of tradition (personal ties) or bureaucratic principles (impersonal ties) is considered by Blauner to be an important factor that influences normative integration. Third, the economic structure of an industry and in particular its economic success is also thought to influence social integration. Figure 2.1 shows the direction of causality theorized by Blauner in his attempt to explain variations in worker alienation.

Blauner drew upon several data sources and used a variety of research methods to investigate empirically the technological (and economic and social conditions) which induce and intensify the different dimensions of alienation. First, he undertook a secondary analysis of a job attitude survey by Roper dating from 1947 which covered the four industries associated with his typology of technologies, namely printing – craft technology (n = 118), textiles – machine tending technology (n = 419), cars – assembly-line technology (n = 180), and chemicals – continuous process technology (n = 78). Second, he supplemented his relatively meagre number of chemical workers with his own re-analysis of a survey by Davis of another 230 blue-collar chemical workers conducted in 1959. Third, he utilized some case studies reported by others on automated plants and assembly-line workers that were published between

Independent variable	>	Intervening variables	>	Dependent variable
Technology	>	Division of labour Social organization Economic structure	>	Alienation

Figure 2.1   Blauner's model of causality

Source: Summarized from Blauner (1964: 6–11)

1950 and 1960. Fourth, he undertook some small-scale fieldwork of his own in 1961–62 amounting to 21 manual chemical workers selected randomly and involving formal interviews, informal discussions and observations. Fifth, he visited a number of cotton mills in southern USA in 1962 'in an attempt to supplement the observations of students of the industry' (Blauner 1964: 13). Finally, due to the limitations of his data, notably the problematic comparability of such a diverse range of studies, he referred extensively to various tables of comparative industrial statistics, the majority of which were official US statistics covering the years 1949 to 1960, on such topics as the proportion of female employees and the skill distribution of manual workers in different industries.

Blauner was well aware that his concern to gather empirical evidence from a variety of sources could not mask the limitations of his study: 'There was no over-all research design applied to the four industries which would have assured precisely equivalent materials for each', and noted modestly that his research findings were 'suggestive rather than conclusive' (1964: 13, 14).

As shown in Table 2.3, for Blauner the extent of alienation among workers varies – some work environments maximize alienation whilst others minimize it. For *printers*, *craft technology*, combined with favourable economic circumstances and a history of strong work organizations, 'result in the highest level of freedom and control in the work process among all industrial workers today' (Blauner 1964: 56). In addition, the long apprenticeship, relatively highly skilled, and small size of plants characteristic of the work of printers using craft technology leads to it being meaningful and involving, and engendering considerable identification with the occupation. Blauner concluded that the printer 'is almost the prototype of the non-alienated worker in modern industry', but wondered how long this situation would last given that the beginnings of automation were already apparent in the production of newspapers (1964: 57).

In the case of *textile workers*, the use of *machine-tending technology* requires little training and is associated with the subdivision of work into unskilled, uninteresting and unfulfilling jobs, all of which tend to enhance the powerlessness, meaninglessness and self-estrangement dimensions of the work. Conversely, Blauner suggests that despite the limited opportunities for social interaction and promotion in textile mills, social isolation is minimized and the impact of the other alienating tendencies are reduced for textile workers based in southern USA thanks to the socially integrating

Table 2.3 Blauner's type of technology and degree of alienation thesis

Type of technology (independent variable)	Degree of alienation (dependent variable)			
	Powerlessness	Meaninglessness	Social isolation	Self-estrangement
Craft technology (e.g., printing)	low	low	low	low
Machine-tending (e.g., textiles)	high	high	low	high
Assembly-line (e.g., automobiles)	high	high	high	high
Process technology (e.g., chemicals)	low	low	low	low

Source: Summarized from Blauner (1964) and Eldridge (1971: 186–7).

and involving nature of their non-work environment, namely their family, religious and community ties. Thus, for these workers, 'objective tendencies toward subjective alienation are overcome, not by fulfilling or creative work, but through the traditional integration of work and non-work concerns' (Blauner 1964: 88). This was especially so for women workers, who, notwithstanding their concentration in the less skilled and less rewarding jobs, were found to be less alienated than their male counterparts because '[w]ork does not have the central importance and meaning in their lives that it does for men, since their most important roles are those of wives and mothers' (Blauner 1964: 81).

The *automobile assembly-line worker* has long been regarded by sociologists as the archetypal, profoundly alienated modern worker, and Blauner reinforces this narrative. On every dimension of alienation, the car assembly-line worker scores extremely high: 'In fact, the result of assembly-line technology and work organization may be the highest level of dissatisfaction in all industry' (1964: 121). It is not difficult to see why this is since such work typically involves a series of highly synchronized simple tasks repeated at a pace determined by others. In short, assembly-line work tends to be physically demanding but intellectually unchallenging. Unsurprisingly, therefore, assembly-line work tends to maximize powerlessness, since workers have no control over the speed of the moving assembly line, maximize meaninglessness, since the work tasks have been fractionalized to an extreme degree, maximize isolation due to a lethal combination of bureaucratization, large-scale factory environment, homogenization of the workforce, limited opportunities for advancement, and the individualization of the work tasks, and maximize self-estrangement since the work is excessively monotonous, tiring, simple yet requiring attention to detail, resulting in a markedly instrumental attitude to work. In sum, alienation is maximized for the assembly-line workers because '[h]is work is unfree and unfulfilling and exemplifies the bureaucratic combination of the highly rational organization and the restricted specialist ... he is relatively powerless, atomized, depersonalized, and anonymous' (Blauner 1964: 122).

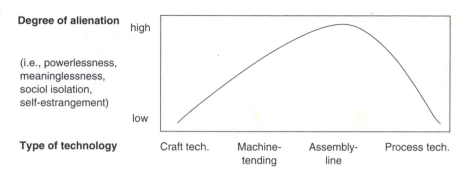

Degree of alienation high

(i.e., powerlessness,
meaninglessness,
sociol isolation,
self-estrangement)

low

Type of technology   Craft tech.   Machine-   Assembly-   Process tech.
                                           tending   line

Figure 2.2   Blauner's historial trend of alienation

Source: Based on Blauner (1964)

Finally, *chemical workers* operating *continuous-process technology* regain a sense of control, meaning, social integration, and self-fulfilment due not only to the auto-mated technology which places a premium on individual responsibility as part of a production team, but also to the favourable economic situation of the chemical industry which improves job security and welfare benefits, and to the small-scale and decentralized plants which enhance communication and social interaction, even between management and workers. According to Blauner, therefore, the historical trend of increasing alienation is reversed by 'the unique combination of technologi-cal, economic, and social forces which counteract alienation in the chemical indus-try' (1964: 164). However, Blauner did note that even among the chemical workers he interviewed in a plant characterized by a 'remarkably high degree of morale and social cohesion', a minority were 'clearly alienated' (1964: 164).

Blauner concluded that, looked at historically: 'Alienation has travelled a course that could be charted on a graph by means of an inverted U-curve' (1964: 182). This trend (shown in Figure 2.2) reveals that alienation is at its lowest in the early indus-trial period when craft technology was dominant, increases steeply with the intro-duction of machine-tending technology, and reaches its peak in the assembly-line technology industries during the mid-twentieth century. However, with the advent of continuous-process technology, a countertrend occurs and alienation declines from its previous high point 'as employees in automated industries gain a new dig-nity from responsibility and a sense of individual freedom' (Blauner 1964: 182). In an important footnote, Blauner qualifies his optimistic conclusion by suggesting that in the future, automation will not necessarily lead to 'a continuation of the major trend toward less alienation' because of the diversity of automated technology and economic conditions (1964: 182). This theme is continued by Blauner where he also notes that his study covers extreme situations, highly alienated textile and car work-ers, and non-alienated printing and chemical workers. Consequently, for most fac-tory workers the situation is 'probably' less clear-cut (1964: 182). Hence in the final analysis he concludes that 'alienation remains a widespread phenomenon in the factory today' (Blauner 1964: 183).

Blauner's proposed solutions to the problem of worker alienation included an increase in the quantity and quality of leisure time, job enlargement and job rotation, research on industrial design and job analysis 'oriented to the goals of worker freedom and dignity as well as the traditional criteria of profit and efficiency', and, in the case of anti-union companies, government intervention to enable trade unions to contribute to the lessening of alienating working conditions (1964: 185). These policies and his reference to the legitimacy of private profit are indicative of reformism rather than radicalism.

Critique of Blauner's technology and alienation thesis

The criticisms of Blauner's technology and alienation thesis can be summarized under three headings: (1) methodological, (2) theoretical/conceptual, and (3) interpretative.

(1) Methodological limitations

Blauner's attempt to measure the extent of alienation among workers using different kinds of work technology is an example of verificational research. That is to say that he sought to test, using relevant empirical data, the Marxian hypothesis that alienation is universally high among workers in industrial capitalism. The bulk of Blauner's data was derived from a re-analysis of two attitude questionnaire surveys: one on job satisfaction conducted in 1947 which contributed 795 responses and the other on attitudes to job redesign conducted in 1959 which contributed 230 respondents. An additional 21 chemical workers were interviewed by Blauner to compensate for the paucity of research on this relatively new industry. It has been noted that: 'Given his specific interests this data base was inherently unsuitable' (Gallie 1978: 26). For example, 98 per cent of Blauner's empirical data was dated and collected not with alienation in mind but job satisfaction and attitudes to a programme of job redesign. In other words, Blauner's research was primarily a study of job satisfaction masquerading as one of alienation. Furthermore, levels of job satisfaction are known to be very context-sensitive (Gruneberg 1979), hence attitudes to job satisfaction in the immediate post-war period in 1947 are likely to be different from those expressed after more than a decade of economic growth in 1959. Thus, the appropriateness of the data used to analyse alienation by Blauner is highly questionable.

Moreover, Blauner's survey data was collected and analysed in terms of four particular industries that he considered to have 'distinctive technological arrangements', yet he also admitted that 'no industry has a completely homogeneous technology' (1964: 7). Consequently, there is no way that Blauner could know how many of the workers in the studies he drew upon worked with the technologies characteristic of the industries selected. For example, as Blauner himself noted, in the American automobile industry in 1959, less than 20 per cent of manual workers in this industry 'actually worked on the line' (1964: 91). This led Eldridge to comment that since the

180 respondents from the automobile industry were not 'differentiated', 'it is difficult to get at the significance of assembly line work *per se* in assessing attitudes' (Eldridge 1971: 188). Similarly, in the case of the respondents selected from the chemical industry: 'Neither we, nor Blauner ... can know precisely what proportion of workers in his sample were in fact working in a highly automated setting' (Gallie 1978: 26). Even in the case of the chemical industry workers chosen at random and interviewed by Blauner, it is impossible to know how many were involved directly with the highly automated continuous-process technology because they were drawn from three different departments of the company – operations, maintenance and distribution. In his discussion of this point, Gallie noted that: 'If the departments had equal numbers he [Blauner] may have interviewed seven operators, hardly enough to provide a solid grounding for the argument [that technology determines alienation]' (Gallie 1978: 329).

(2) Theoretical/conceptual limitations

Blauner's study was inspired by the Marxian theory of worker alienation and he claimed that 'the connection between some of Marx's dimensions of alienation and those employed in the present chapter are clear' (1964: 16). However, in his discussion of his four dimensions of alienation he draws upon Marx only with reference to powerlessness and self-estrangement, and even here the congruence between his conception of these two dimensions differs markedly from Marx's. In the case of powerlessness, Blauner differentiated 'four modes of industrial powerlessness': '(1) the separation from ownership of the means of production and the finished products, (2) the inability to influence general managerial policies, (3) the lack of control over the conditions of employment, and (4) the lack of control over the immediate work process' (1964: 16). He contended that the first two forms of powerlessness are not important to workers since they are accepted widely as a 'constant in modern industry' and a '"given" of industry' respectively (Blauner 1964: 17, 18). Conversely, Blauner argued that employment conditions powerlessness 'is considerably more meaningful to American workers' and that immediate work process powerlessness is 'greatly' resented (1964: 18, 20). Consequently, Blauner focused on the last two modes of powerlessness, especially control over the immediate work process, rather than the first two modes. It has been argued that dismissing the sociological significance of ownership powerlessness and decision-making powerlessness, on the basis of minimal evidence, 'is implicitly to acknowledge the universality of alienation in that society' (Eldridge 1971: 190).

Although the nature of alienation is not without ambiguity in Marx's original works, it is clear that as far as the fate of workers was concerned, capitalism was the main villain, albeit aided and abetted by industrialization (see Chapter 1). However, in Blauner's transformation of the concept of alienation into a measurable feature of work, the major source of alienation in general, and powerlessness in particular, is industrialization, specifically technology, whereas capitalism plays an occasional minor role. An example of this can be found in his discussion of the cost structure of textile companies where Blauner suggests that it 'furthers the tendency to use the workers as "means", as commodities in the classic Marxist sense' (1964: 180). The same can be said in the case of car workers, who, due to the insecurity of their employment, are 'likely to feel' that management view them 'only as a number, an instrument of production, and not as a human being' (Blauner 1964: 110). To the extent that Blauner prioritized industrial factors, such as technology, over capitalist ones, such as ownership, he reversed completely Marx's theoretical explanation of worker alienation, and in the process distorted the Marxian meaning of the concept of alienation.

It has also been argued that by focusing on the subjective experience of alienation Blauner trivialized Marx's conception of alienation in the sense that he reduced it to a study of job satisfaction (Eldridge 1971). Notwithstanding Mills' argument that 'whatever satisfaction alienated men gain from work occurs within the framework of alienation' (1968 [1951]: 235), to the extent that Blauner attempted to link job satisfaction to structural conditions, his analysis aspired to a more complete account by including both the objective and subjective features of work.

(3) Interpretative limitations

The interpretation of data is invariably problematic, especially so in a study that relies on several data sources. Blauner's interpretation of his data is open to criticism with reference to the causal significance of trade unions, the role of gender in his account of textile workers, his optimistic interpretation of working in the chemical industry, and the deterministic thrust of his analysis.

In his first chapter Blauner outlined the factors that may influence alienation with top causal billing being given to technology and supporting roles to the division of labour, social organization and economic structure. In the case of the intervening variable social organization, the importance of trade unions is hinted at where Blauner refers to the move from traditional to bureaucratic principles of organization and its impact on the 'situation of workers in economic organizations (including their relations with their employers)' (1964: 9). By subsuming the potential causal significance of organized labour in this way, Blauner effectively minimizes the importance of this non-technological factor whilst simultaneously introducing a highly contradictory element into his account (Gallie 1978; Hill 1981).

This can be seen most clearly when, in marked contrast to the minor role allocated to organized labour in the opening chapters, his analysis of three of the four selected technologies/industries – craft/printing, machine-tending/textiles, and assembly-line/ autos – Blauner provided evidence to show that trade unions, or labour unions as they are known in America, are a vital force whose presence/absence can lessen/ heighten alienation. More specifically, the 'unusual power of the [printing] union' to influence the printers' control over the pace of their work and their freedom from supervision, which reduces the powerlessness dimension of alienation, is fully acknowledged (Blauner 1964: 44). In the case of textile workers, only a minority are protected by union agreements because the majority of textile companies are anti-union, which suggests to Blauner that, among other things, a 'strong labour union' would 'reduce the powerlessness and improve the working conditions of textile employees (1964: 186). In the car workers union (United Automobile Workers), Blauner noted that 'it has reduced through the years the worker's individual and collective power-lessness against the forces of technology and management' (1964: 114–15). It is only in the chemical industry that trade unions are viewed by Blauner as virtually irrelevant since he considered that integration in this industry 'is an outcome of continuous-process technology, favourable economic conditions, and worker satisfaction with superior wages and employee benefits' (1964: 154).

Thus, on the basis of Blauner's own data, there would seem to be good grounds for arguing that the power of trade unions is a major, not a minor, factor that influences alienation, particularly powerlessness via their impact on the conditions of employment. That Blauner was aware of the importance of organized labour is unsurprising given his background as a unionized ex-factory worker who had received financial support from a trade union; that he underplayed the causal importance of trade unions and left himself open to the criticism of faulty interpretation on this point is somewhat more surprising.

Interpretative problems have also been identified in Blauner's analysis of textile workers. It has been argued that 'the sexual division of labour characteristic of the middle period of industrial capitalism' (see Chapter 1) led to the emergence of 'two sociologies of work' which corresponded to the separate spheres involving the male breadwinner role and the female domestic role, namely a job model for men and a gender model for women (Feldberg and Glenn 1979). The different assumptions behind each of these models are that studies of male workers tend to assume that paid work outside the home is the key factor in the analysis of their relationship to work, whereas in the case of female workers, it is invariably assumed that family life is the main influence on their relationship to work.

Feldberg and Glenn examined Blauner's study to illustrate the way in which the use of these models can distort the interpretation of data. They found that Blauner oper-ated with the job model in his analysis of male-dominated industries, namely printing, automobiles and chemicals, but in his interpretation of the textile industry, in which there are a large number of women workers, he 'switches to the gender model to analyse the women's response to employment' (Feldberg and Glenn 1979: 528). Feldberg and Glenn note that Blauner's data confirms that women are concentrated in the least skilled jobs in the textile industry and therefore tend to experience the most alienating work conditions. Understandably, more women than men complained that their work was too fast and tiring, yet Blauner 'shifts, without warning or justification, to a gender model to interpret women's responses' (Feldberg and Glenn 1979: 528). In other words, he attributes the women's higher degree of pressure and fatigue to their biology ('less physical stamina than men') and to their family responsibilities ('working women often double as housewives and mothers') (Blauner 1964: 71).

Feldberg and Glenn suggest that there are two interpretative problems with Blauner's analysis of textile workers: it 'obscures the previously argued link between working conditions and workers' responses', and it 'ignores data which show that women's work conditions are more demanding' (1979: 528–9). Thus, in addition to contradicting his main thesis that technology determines alienation, Blauner compounds his problematic interpretation by relying on assumptions about the primary roles of men and women rather than evidence in his analysis of male and female textile workers. In other words, instead of considering variations in working conditions and family responsibilities for male and female textile workers and relating them to his dependent variable, alienation, Blauner's interpretation of textile workers is flawed because alienation is explained inconsistently in terms of both his overall thesis and his account of male and female textile workers. With regard to the latter, the alienation of male textile workers is analysed with reference to the assumption that work is a central life interest for employed men, which discounts the possibility that their family role may influence their work attitudes and behaviour, whereas the alienation of female textile workers is explicated in terms of the assumption that the family is a central life interest for employed women, which discounts the possibility that their work conditions may influence their work attitudes and behaviour. Thus, Blauner's interpretation of textile workers is distorted by his selective incorporation of different assumptions about men and women, which may be plausible but are introduced into the analysis without the support of any empirical evidence.

Blauner's interpretation of chemical workers has been criticized on the grounds that he provides 'an exaggerated picture of the positive aspects of work life in a continuous-process factory' (Gallie 1978: 85). Blauner argues that: 'Since work in continuous-process industries involves control, meaning and social integration, it tends to be self-actualizing instead of self-estranging', hence it is essentially non-alienating (1964: 154). At the same time Blauner provides evidence which seems to contradict this rosy picture of work in a chemical plant. For example, he notes that the complexity of continuous-process technology threatens the meaningfulness of the work and that working with highly automated technology on an 'invisible product' is conducive to sensory deprivation (Blauner 1964: 145). In addition, he notes that 'considerable dissatisfaction' arises where expectations of rapid promotion are thwarted and that the work can be quite monotonous, especially for shift workers 'when there are no bosses around and no maintenance workers to make repairs and pass the time with' (Blauner 1964: 152, 156). It has also been pointed out that Blauner 'cites one oil refinery personnel executive who has placed a limit on the IQs of workers hired for operating jobs, and another who calls them "only watchmen"' (Braverman 1974: 224). Thus, far from being non-alienating, work in a chemical factory could, on the basis of Blauner's own data, be considered acutely alienating, especially for workers of above average ability.

Blauner was fully aware therefore that work in a chemical plant using continuous-process technology was alienating in certain respects for some workers, yet he chose to emphasize the non-alienating features and to generalize on the basis that they were applicable to the majority of workers. Hence the suspicion remains that his interpretation of this highly automated work is an accurate one for those chemical workers at or near the top of the team hierarchy, but an inaccurate one for all those at the bottom of the hierarchy. Given that there are invariably more people at the bottom of a hierarchy than at the top, Blauner's conclusion that there are 'proportionally fewer' alienated workers in the chemical industry is questionable (1964: 164).

Finally, arguably the most common criticism of Blauner is that he advanced a technological determinist account to the extent that he explained variations in alienation largely in terms of variations in technology to the relative exclusion of other factors, most importantly the meanings workers create and attach to work (Goldthorpe 1966; Silverman 1970). A strong example of this line of criticism is provided by Hill, who has asserted that Blauner's support for technological determinism 'surpasses anything in previous industrial sociology' (Hill 1981: 95). Thompson affords a much weaker example where he noted that studies such as Blauner's 'merely tended to add a touch of determinism' to research on the technological influences on work (Thompson 1983: 21).

Blauner certainly supplied his critics with plenty of material with which to construct a case in that he placed disproportionate causal weight on technology. At the beginning of his study Blauner made two statements that appear contradictory. Initially he asserted that 'modern factories vary considerably in technology, in division of labour, in economic structure, and in organizational character. These differences produce sociotechnical systems in which the objective conditions and inner life of employees are strikingly variant' (1964: 5). On the next page Blauner argued that of the four variables, technology was the 'most important single factor that gives an industry a distinctive character' (1964: 6). Throughout his subsequent analysis, Blauner focused on the role of technology more than any other influence, although he continued to proffer evidence to the contrary, notably in the case of his analysis of women workers in the textile industry and his references to the role of trade unions, as noted above. In his final chapter, although Blauner reiterated his technology plus other factors argument in the context of advancing his inverted U-curve thesis, he qualified his technological determinism in two ways in the space of one footnote: 'Automated technology will take many forms besides continuous-process production, and the diversified economic conditions of future automated industries will further complicate the situation' (1964: 182). As Eldridge has indicated, this point 'ought perhaps to be emphasised' (1971: 189). I would concur since had Blauner done so, his vulnerability to the charge of technological determinism would have been reduced.

Blauner was clearly uncertain throughout his analysis about the significance of the causal status of technology and intervening variables. Arguably, this nagging uncertainty was reflected in interpretative inconsistencies, particularly with respect to the ability of trade unions and community ties to alleviate alienation. The root of Blauner's hesitant technological determinism can be traced to his empirical evidence and his interpretation of it, which from the standpoint of his explanation of alienation, could also be considered a theoretical/conceptual limitation.

Empirical research on the Blauner thesis

At the extremes of alienation, non-alienated print workers and alienated car workers, there is an unusual degree of unanimity among sociologists that Blauner's description, though not necessarily his theoretical understanding, of craft work and assembly-line work was accurate. Thus studies of craft workers (e.g., Harrison and Zeitlin 1985) and assembly-line workers (e.g., Beynon 1975) have shown that the former tend to enjoy a considerable degree of power, control, and so on at work, whereas the latter tend not to. However, it does not necessarily follow that assembly-line workers are invariably alienated or that technology is the major determinant of work attitudes and behaviour since non-work factors, such as consumption and family-centredness, may lead such workers to adopt an instrumental orientation to work (Goldthorpe et al. 1969).

As far as textile workers are concerned, one reassessment of alienation using 1980s data produced only mixed support for Blauner (Leiter 1985), whilst others have suggested that they were an inappropriate choice since in certain respects machine-tending technology is hardly any more advanced than that used by printers (Hull et al. 1982). Interestingly, at the end of his study Blauner conflated machine and assembly-line technologies on the grounds that they were both involved in 'routine low-skilled operations' (1964: 169). These points tend to reinforce the problematic nature machine-tending technology and Blauner's questionable interpretation of this case study data.

More generally, in a re-examination of Blauner's data, an analysis of their own empirical research on over 100 industrial organizations and 245 printers whose work had been automated following the introduction of computer technology, plus a review of the research on Blauner's increasing technology and decreasing alienation thesis, Hull et al. concluded that, when the problematic textile workers are excluded, 'the inverted U-curve hypothesis is supported' (1982: 33). Although the Hull et al. empirical research has been criticized strongly on conceptual, theoretical and methodological grounds (Vallas and Yarrow 1987), their review of the research literature involving continuous-process technology is also problematic because it is highly selective in two ways. First, their review excludes consideration of one case study which contradicts the Blauner thesis, namely the research on chemical workers by Nichols and Beynon (1977). Second, their summary of the apparently supportive literature tends to overlook the limited nature of that evidence. For example, the research by Cotgrove (1972), cited by Hull et al. (1982), focused on only one of Blauner's dimensions of alienation, self-estrangement, and although the findings confirmed that process work is relatively non-alienating, Cotgrove's data on job interest and monotony revealed marked variations and is generally less convincing than the comparable data in Blauner.

Continuous-process technology is arguably the pivotal issue for Blauner's technology and alienation thesis since his predicted long-term trend that increasing automation leads to decreasing alienation is predicated on the adoption of this technology. Therefore, a more detailed review of the post-Blauner empirical research on continuous-process technology workers in chemical plants is crucial before one can conclude unambiguously that Blauner's historical thesis is correct or incorrect.

In Britain during the 1970s there were three major studies of chemical workers which provided empirical evidence of direct relevance to Blauner's thesis that the introduction of continuous-process technology leads to decline in all the dimensions of alienation. Wedderburn and Crompton (1972) used similar indicators to Blauner and came to similar conclusions with respect to the powerlessness, meaningfulness and social isolation dimensions of alienation, namely that continuous-process workers were comparatively less alienated than workers using other types of technology. However, in terms of the self-estrangement dimension, Wedderburn and Crompton 'found little evidence of positive identification with the firm' and an instrumental orientation to work (1972: 149). This study conformed to Blauner's approach in that it accepted his theoretical point of departure that technology is an important variable for understanding work attitudes and behaviour. Thus, they not only confirmed his findings but also his main theoretical premise, albeit with the caveat that technology is a sound starting place but not the whole picture since it fails to look beyond the factory gate.

The research by Nichols and Beynon was based largely on conversations with chemical workers at one plant over a three-year period and contains no statistical tables but a description of what work is like in a chemical plant for the majority of employees (over 75 per cent) who do the unskilled 'donkey work' (1977: 10). Nichols and Beynon provide plenty of qualitative evidence to show that Blauner's thesis does not apply to the majority of chemical workers since they perform very similar work to that 'found on traditional assembly lines in technically less "progressive" sectors' (1977: 68). As far as the minority were concerned, namely the operators who monitored the process technology, the work was certainly less physically demanding but most of them worked alone rather than in a team, disliked the shift work, especially the double shift, and felt more trapped than secure. In marked contrast to Blauner, this study emphasized that complex technology was 'not designed to make chemicals, but to make chemicals for profit' (1977: 69). Thus, Nichols and Beynon not only repudiated Blauner's thesis, but rejected his assumption that the effect of technology can be understood without reference to the capitalist mode of production.

Finally, the empirical research undertaken by Gallie (1978) involved a comparative study of chemical workers at two British and two French oil refineries. Gallie found that the French continuous-process workers were 'deeply alienated from the system of authority' and that consequently the 'predominant feeling was one of powerlessness', whereas the British workers 'felt that they had a fairly high level of control over decisions' that affected their immediate experience of work and regarded strategic financial decisions as a matter for management (1978: 145). As far as meaninglessness was concerned, Gallie reported that due to the complexity of the technology and the limited inter-unit flexibility, knowledge of the overall process was confined to a small number of multi-skilled workers. For the majority of French and British oil refinery operators, 'the job was probably less meaningful than many jobs in traditional industry' (1978: 80–1). Blauner's argument that a sense of belonging was enhanced by teamwork within a decentralized factory was also found wanting. Gallie reported that although the 'growth of a semi-team system among operators seems to have facilitated better relations in both countries', control had not been decentralized to the work team to the same extent in France as it had in Britain, and as a consequence French managers retained more power and French workers perceived a greater social distance between themselves and management (1978: 236). Gallie also noted that although work in a chemical plant is less boring and physically demanding, 'automation does not make work a deep source of satisfaction' sufficient to achieve self-actualization, and that '[t]he commonest attitude towards work in all our refineries was one of indifference' (1978: 87, 104). In sum, Gallie's findings show that French chemical workers were more alienated than their British counterparts in that they were highly alienated on every dimension of alienation whereas the British workers were highly alienated on only two dimensions, meaninglessness and self-estrangement. He concluded: 'It is extremely doubtful whether automation leads to the overcoming of alienation in work in any profound sense of the term' (Gallie 1978: 296).

Since the technology was similar in all the plants in both countries in the Gallie study, the explanation of the variations in alienation between the French and British workers must be attributed to non-technological factors such as managerial and union policies. In contrast to Blauner, Gallie did not ignore completely the capitalist context of his analysis. For example, he considered the issue of capitalist ownership versus forms of non-capitalist ownership and found a small majority in favour of the status quo in both France and Britain (54 per cent and 63 per cent respectively). Yet other capitalist features, such as exploitation and profitability, were neglected by Gallie, which is surprising since his conclusions are more in line with those of Nichols and Beynon (1977), who are not cited, than with those of Wedderburn and Crompton (1972), who are cited.

Empirical research on the Blauner thesis was taken one step further by Shepard (1971), whose large-scale study included both factory workers and white-collar workers. He replicated Blauner's dimensions of alienation almost exactly with respect to powerlessness and meaninglessness, but defined and operationalized social isolation and self-estrangement differently and referred to them as normlessness and instrumentalism respectively, and added a fifth dimension of alienation that he called self-evaluative involvement. He adopted a quota sampling method to ensure that 'only workers performing tasks corresponding to the different stages of technological development were selected', and distinguished between three types of worker–technology relationship: non-mechanized (i.e., industrial craft workers and traditional clerical workers), mechanized (i.e., industrial assembly-line workers and office machine operators) and automated (i.e., industrial continuous-process workers and computer operators and other types of computer worker) (Shepard 1971: 17). In the case of the factory workers he found that, with the exception of powerlessness, 'alienation was lower among craftsmen, reached a peak among assemblers, and declined again among monitors to a level below that of either assemblers or craftsmen' (Shepard 1971: 40). With regard to white-collar workers Shepard revealed some inconsistent patterns, such as the tendency for female computer workers to be more alienated in certain respects than female clerks and machine operators, although in certain other respects his office worker data broadly supported Blauner's thesis. Shepard concluded that whilst Blauner's thesis that 'automation reverses the historical trend toward increased alienation from work among factory workers appears to be supported', the impact of automation on alienation among white-collar workers is more variable

(1971: 117). In the light of these findings, Shepard did not place as much weight on technology as an independent variable as Blauner: 'Factors affecting attitudes towards work are too many, and their interrelationships too complex, to assume that the technologically determined attributes of the job alone constitute an explanatory variable' (1971: 126). Thus, despite designing his research within Blauner's non-capitalist, industrial society framework, and operationalizing the independent and dependent variables in a broadly similar way, Shepard's evidence on blue- and white-collar workers using different types of technology provides mixed support for his thesis and he fails to endorse unequivocally Blauner's (alleged) technologically determinist theoretical position.

Summary and conclusions

The key points of Blauner's study are that: (1) it was a test of Marx's theory that all workers are alienated under industrial capitalism; (2) the data sources included a secondary analysis of attitudinal survey data, some purposefully collected interview data, and comparative industrial statistics; (3) four types of technology/industries were examined – craft technology/printing industry, machine-tending technology/textiles, assembly-line technology/cars, and continuous-process technology/chemicals; (4) four dimensions of alienation were distinguished – powerlessness, meaningfulness, social isolation, and self-estrangement; (5) it hypothesized that not all workers were equally alienated and that differences in technology were primarily responsible for the variation; (6) alienation was found to be relatively low for the least automated print workers, that it was higher for textile workers, highest for the mass-production assembly-line workers, but lower again for the most technologically advanced chemical workers; (7) when this pattern of variations in alienation was placed in historical context, it was described as an inverted U-curve; and (8) it concluded that increasing alienation was not inevitable due to the liberating influence of advancing technology.

The main criticisms of Blauner's technology and alienation thesis were reviewed under three headings and these suggested that, methodologically, his data sources were not ideal, his conceptualization of alienation vulgarized Marx's original idea, and that his interpretation was sufficiently problematic, especially with regard to the textile workers and his tendency to idealize continuous-process work, to cast doubts on the consistency of his theory, analysis and his conclusions.

Subsequent research on the impact of different types of technology on worker alienation provided mixed support for Blauner's thesis. In the case of the non-alienated craft workers and highly alienated car workers, Blauner's assessment has received broad support, but his analysis of textile workers has not been confirmed unambiguously. More generally, the closer a study replicated Blauner's industrial society model and key variables, the more likely that the findings would support his thesis (e.g., Wedderburn and Crompton 1972) and vice versa (e.g., Nichols and Beynon 1977). However, a replication study by Shepard (1971) that sought to extend

Blauner's thesis by including a sample of office workers as well as factory workers, failed to confirm unequivocally his historical thesis in the case of the former but did so in the case of the latter.

Virtually all Blauner's critics and those who have attempted to replicate his research, have tended to distance themselves from what some have considered to be the main weakness of his account of technology and worker alienation, namely its alleged technological determinist thrust.

Although Blauner's study has been criticized extensively and replicated several times with mixed success as far as his thesis is concerned, many of his detractors have also lauded his research as a 'classic study' (Feldberg and Glenn 1979: 528), in part on the grounds that it has been 'highly influential' in the field of technology and work (Vallas and Yarrow 1987: 127). Similarly, specialists in the sociology of work have noted that his project was an 'ambitious' one that 'has never been surpassed as a study of automation that is empirical and speculative in equal measure' (Rose 1988: 223).

In the seeming welter of negative comments, one should not lose sight of the many strengths of his contribution to our understanding of some of the influences on the attitudes and behaviour of workers in industrial capitalism. Blauner was one of the first sociologists to undertake a theoretically informed empirical test of Marx's important theory of worker alienation. Given that the meaning of this concept is contested by Marxists and non-Marxists, it is unsurprising that his attempt to operationalize this complex idea would generate considerable criticism. Second, rather than simply assume that the structure of industrial capitalism would result in increased alienation for all workers, Blauner tried valiantly to analyse the main causal variables that could explain variations in alienation among the industrial labour force, and the links between the objective and subjective aspects of alienation. As a consequence, he was successful in demonstrating that the diversity of work situations and associated degrees of alienation are to some extent due to variations in the type of technology that prevails in different industries. Third, Blauner's account of alienation may be viewed as flawed, especially from a Marxian perspective, but it was historically sensitive and cautiously presented. For example, he contextualized his types of technology historically and qualified his thesis by noting, albeit in a easily overlooked footnote, that, in the future, despite advances in technology and other relevant factors, such as economic conditions, further declines in alienation are not guaranteed. Finally, although Blauner's study was primarily concerned with how different types of technology, in combination with other variables, influence alienation, it was also concerned with what has since become known as the skill debate. Behind his inverted U-curve thesis was the evidence-based argument that whereas machine-tending and assembly-line technology deskills workers, continuous-process technology both increases the demand for traditional craft skills, for example on the part of maintenance workers, and changes the nature of skills required from manual dexterity to non-manual responsibility, although both types of work 'require considerable discretion and initiative' (Blauner 1964: 168). Looked at from this perspective, therefore, Blauner's thesis was a pioneering study of the historical fate of skill levels or, more precisely, an early example of the upskilling thesis, with a hint of polarization where he noted that 'a considerable amount of routine work that negates the dignity of the worker will very likely persist in the foreseeable future' (Blauner 1964: 169).

The overlap between the debates about declining alienation and upskilling is illustrated clearly by the inclusion of Blauner's study on the upskilling side of the debate (e.g., Vallas 1988). The issue over whether or not workers have been deskilled or upskilled continues to divide sociologists, and will be considered in the next two chapters.

Further reading

Before embarking on a journey into the Blauner-related literature, it is of course imperative to read the original: Blauner (1964) *Alienation and Freedom: The Factory Worker and His Industry*. Consideration of the material critical of Blauner should start with the important review by Eldridge (1971) *Sociology and Industrial Life*, which covers both Marx's and Blauner's conceptualizations of alienation. A critique of the gender dimension of Blauner's analysis can be found in the article by Feldberg and Glenn (1979) published originally in the journal *Social Problems*. The study by Gallie (1978) *In Search of the New Working Class: Automation and Social Integration within the Capitalist Enterprise* combines a critique of Blauner's study with an analysis of cross-national data of workers who operate continuous-process technology. For an alternative understanding of chemical workers, consult Nichols and Beynon (1977) *Living with Capitalism: Class Relations and the Modern Factory*. The overlap between the alienation and the skill debates is readily apparent in the article by Vallas (1988) published in the journal *Work and Occupations*, which is also a good introduction to the next two chapters.

Questions for discussion and assessment

1. How Marxian is Blauner's operationalization of alienation?
2. Do you agree with the criticism that Blauner's account of the relationship between technology and alienation was technologically deterministic?
3. Aside from Blauner's alleged technological determinism, what do you consider to be the major weaknesses of his study?
4. To what extent does the post-Blauner research support his technology and alienation thesis?
5. Discuss the view that the gender dimension is the main weakness of Blauner's study.

●●●●●●●●

CHAPTER THREE

Paid Work in Industrial Society and Deskilling?

It is widely thought that one of the major consequences of the rise of industrial capitalism was the destruction of skill following the introduction of machinery. From the start of capitalist industrialization therefore the concept of skill has been in the forefront of debates about changes in the nature of work. Subsequent technological advances, particularly the use of computers to design, direct and control production, has ensured that the concept of skill has remained a focal point in the sociology of work.

Despite the centrality of the concept of skill in the sociological analysis of work and its widespread use in everyday discussions of occupations, there is little agreement about how best to define and measure this familiar idea. This lack of agreement is reflected in the ongoing debate concerning the historical direction of skill change. Basically, there are the 'pessimists', who have tended to use a definition of skill which emphasizes the skill content of a job and the amount of task-specific training required to do it and who argue that work has been deskilled. On the other hand, there are the 'optimists', who have tended to use a definition of skill which focuses on the change from manual dexterity to the exercise of responsibility and the increased educational qualifications required to exercise this new skill and who argue that work has been upskilled. There is also a third perspective, which typically combines definitional elements of both the above and whose advocates argue that skill polarization is occurring. The purpose of this chapter is to evaluate the first of these views. (The other views will be considered in the next chapter.)

Braverman's deskilling thesis

Braverman's historical account of deskilling is the leading and most powerful version of the pessimistic position. His thesis draws upon Marx's theory of work in industrial capitalism in that he starts from the proposition that in such a society workers are constrained economically, by the absence of alternatives, to sell their labour power to employers who are similarly constrained to seek a profit or go out of business. This is the capitalist mode of production, at its core is the unequal relationship between employer and employee, and Braverman's aim is to examine 'the manner in which the labour force is dominated and shaped by the accumulation of capital' (1974: 53). Whilst Marx's empirical reference point was Britain in the nineteenth century, Braverman's was America in the twentieth century – respectively the first industrial capitalist society and the most advanced.

Braverman's ambitious analysis of the development of the capitalist mode of production over the past hundred years or so was predicated on the Marxian assumption that human labour power is unique in that it is 'intelligent and purposive' (1974: 56). These distinctive characteristics make human labour exceedingly adaptable, with unlimited potential for production. From the standpoint of the capitalist this is good news, but the downside is that, in the context of the inherently 'antagonistic relations of production', there is 'the problem of realizing the "full usefulness" of the labour power' that has been purchased (Braverman 1974: 57). Thus, if all the capitalist really buys is potential, it is imperative to exert control over the labour process in order to maximize the productive potential of labour and therefore profits.

By the end of the nineteenth and beginning of the twentieth century, capitalist production in America had developed on a large scale, was increasingly based on scientific knowledge and was concentrated among a declining number of big corporations. Consequently, the control of labour issue had become more complex. In an attempt to solve this problem capitalists turned to developments in management and machinery, which not only enhanced the control of labour but also progressively deskilled the worker.

In the quest for managerial control, scientific management, or Taylorism, after the world's first management consultant who coined the term and pioneered it, is of first importance to Braverman for its practical implications and, above all perhaps, because it is 'a theory which is nothing less than the explicit verbalization of the capitalist mode of production' (1974: 86). For Braverman, it is a capitalist approach to the question of control, notwithstanding its claims to the contrary via the language of scientific objectivity. In other words, scientific management, and all those management experts who followed in Taylor's footsteps (notably Mayo, who is associated with the human relations approach to work) were more interested in developing and prescribing ways to ameliorate the alienating conditions of work in industrial capitalism than in abolishing the forces that gave rise to them in the first place. It is as a capitalist ideology therefore that Taylorism came to dominate managerial ideas about 'how best to control alienated labour' (Braverman 1974: 90).

Taylor exemplifies this point well in that he regarded workers as inherently lazy, and 'soldiering', namely the tendency to work consistently at less than maximum output, as universal. He was also less than impressed by managers since they allowed workers to shirk and restrict output. In order to overcome what Taylor therefore regarded as the natural recalcitrance of workers he recommended that managers should approach the organization of work more scientifically and take total control of the labour process, including every aspect of production, however small. Braverman summed up Taylor's systematic or scientific approach to management with reference to three related principles: 'the first principle is the gathering and development of knowledge of the labour processes', 'the second is the concentration of this knowledge as the exclusive province of management – together with its essential converse, the absence of such knowledge among the workers', and 'the third is the use of this monopoly over knowledge to control each step of the labour process and its mode of execution' (1974: 119). Implicit in these principles is the separation of conception from execution, namely the transfer of all mental labour from the worker to the manager whilst simultaneously simplifying the manual tasks that the worker is instructed to perform. In short: 'The production units operate like a hand, watched, corrected, and controlled by a distant brain' (1974: 125).

Braverman considered this separation to be of prime importance and that it was only feasible when the scale of production plus associated resources had advanced to the point where a class of managers could assume total responsibility for designing, planning and supervising the subdivided tasks of manual workers. The main effects of the insitutionalization of the separation of conception from execution, mental from manual work, are that, for the capitalist, 'the cost of production is lowered', and that it has a 'degrading effect upon the technical capacity of the worker' (Braverman 1974: 127). Although Braverman acknowledged that in expanding industries there are increased opportunities for a few workers to move into planning and supervisory positions, thereby hinting at polarization, he also noted that such a short-term tendency obscured the overall trend of progressive deskilling. Importantly, over time, 'the very standards by which this trend is judged become imperceptibly altered, and the meaning of "skill" itself becomes degraded' (Braverman 1974: 130).

Braverman's historical benchmark was the craft worker, who epitomized the unity of hand and brain work, and he noted that the initial opposition to Taylorism was not directed at the time study feature of his system, but at its attempt to denude the craft workers of their knowledge and autonomy. However, the effects of scientific management were felt far beyond the nineteenth-century (predominantly) male craftsman when, in due course, it was introduced into office work during the first decades of the twentieth century. As in the case of Taylorized factory work, office work was reorganized on the basis of the same principles with the same results, namely increased output to the benefit of capital and reduced skill to the detriment of labour. The class implications of Braverman's deskilling thesis are therefore inextricably linked to the work dimension; in a word, proletarianization.

According to Braverman, the control of blue-collar and white-collar work, and as a consequence deskilling, was aided considerably by mechanization. For capitalists, the great advantage of machinery is that it not only increases the productivity of labour, but that it also enables the managers of capital to control workers impersonally and unobtrusively by mechanical means in addition to organizational means. More specifically, so long as it is maintained in good working order, machinery, or dead labour, has three major advantages over workers, or living labour: it is invariably more predictable, consistent and acquiescent. In other words, the use of machinery instead of people ensures that the same precise actions are performed repeatedly and without question. By comparison, a worker, however assiduous and conscientious, will tire, become distracted, perform variably, and protest about the conditions and rewards of work if necessary. In addition to these productivity advantages, capital also benefits from savings by reducing the number of workers required, plus the training time and pay of those retained. In short, mechanization cheapens labour whilst simultaneously deskilling it, both in the interests of capital. Little wonder that capitalists are keen to design machines that incorporate the knowledge and skill of the worker, ideally to the point where the few remaining workers who are employed are reduced to monitoring the automatic production process.

Interestingly, in support of this part of his analysis, Braverman cites the research on automation and skill by Bright (1958), as did Blauner before him, but interprets his research findings quite differently. Blauner picked out one of only two dimensions of Bright's research which showed a mixture of an increase/decrease in skill with the most advanced mechanization, namely responsibility, and relegated to a footnote Bright's point that 'automation does not necessarily raise skill requirements. In some cases it actually reduces skill levels' (Blauner 1964: 134). However, Braverman noted that all the other skill indicators used by Bright, such as dexterity, general skill, experience, decision-making and so on, showed that the skill requirements of advanced automation were either decreased or nil, and quoted his conclusion that 'there was more evidence that automation had reduced the skill requirements of the operating work force, and occasionally of the entire factory force, including the maintenance organization' (Braverman 1974: 220). As an alternative to Blauner's inverted, U-shaped declining alienation curve (see Chapter 2, Figure 2.2), Braverman cited Bright's inverted, U-shaped curve of declining skill (presented here as Figure 3.1) and, in marked contrast to Blauner, argues that even in the most technologically advanced industries using continuous-process technology, such as the chemical industry, the automation of production places it 'under the control of management engineers and destroys the need for knowledge or training' (Braverman 1974: 225).

Consideration of Bright's analysis of automation and skill shows that Braverman's interpretation is more in tune with his conclusions than was Blauner's. For example, in an article summarizing his research, Bright claims that the conventional wisdom that automation results in higher workforce skills is a myth since it 'often tends to reduce the skill and training required of the work force' (1958: 97). In the pivotal case of the potentially counteracting trend in which automation leads to increased responsibility, Bright concluded that 'those who appreciate the evolutionary nature of mechanization will anticipate that, at some future time, automatic controls will be introduced to provide for this "responsibility" function, too. Eventually even this operator contribution will be reduced or eliminated' (1958: 98).

Whilst Bright (1958) and Blauner (1964) focused on the skill implications of the mechanization of factory work, Braverman analysed factory work, office work, and somewhat more briefly service work, in relation to both scientific management and mechanization and skill. In particular, Braverman noted that in the nineteenth century

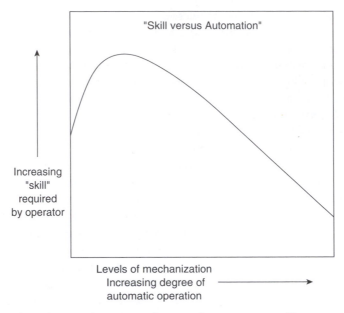

Figure 3.1 Why advances in automation can have contrary effects on skill requirements (as charted by James R. Bright)

Source: Adapted from Braverman (1974: 221)

the work of the clerk was similar to that of the manual craftsman in the sense that it involved various craft tools (pen, ink, paper, envelopes and ledgers), control over the various office processes, such as record keeping and scheduling, and was a multi-skilled type of work that enjoyed considerable responsibility and status. During the twentieth century Braverman argued that the twin forces of scientific management and mechanization have reduced office work to a stream of paper 'which is processed in a continuous flow like that of the cannery, the meatpacking line, the car assembly conveyor, by workers organized in much the same way' (1974: 301). Moreover, the feminization of the clerical labour force during the twentieth century in Britain and America 'has made it possible to lower wage rates' (Braverman 1974: 353). Thus, the deskilling of skilled factory work is paralleled by the deskilling of skilled office work. In terms of the class structure, according to Braverman both types of employment have been proletarianized.

   In his final chapter Braverman turned his attention to the 'impressionistic' and 'self-evident' theory that the increased mechanization of work requires an increasingly better educated and trained workforce, namely the upgrading of work thesis (1974: 424). Braverman noted that the terms used in this debate, such as skill, training and education, are problematic in their vagueness and that those who advocate the upgrading thesis tend to rely on two alleged trends: first, that there has been a shift of workers from lower to higher occupational categories and, second, that the average amount of time spent in education has increased.

Braverman argued that the retrospective introduction of the category operatives who are deemed to be semi-skilled achieved, 'with a mere stroke of the pen, a massive "upgrading" of the skills of the working population' (1974: 429). In other words, the upgrading of large numbers of manual workers is a statistical illusion that is compounded by the growth of non-manual work and the 'prejudice' which assumes all such work to be more skilled than manual work (Braverman 1974: 435). Regarding the second reason commonly advanced in support of the upgrading thesis, Braverman agreed that the length of time spent in education prior to entering the workforce has lengthened, but argued that the 'connection between education and job content is, for the mass of jobs, a false one', since, for the majority, their educational achievements exceed those required by most jobs (1974: 440). Thus the raising of the school-leaving age and the growth of educational certification has more to do with reducing unemployment and screening, 'even when job content is not necessarily becoming more complex or requiring higher levels of skills', than it does with the alleged need for a better educated workforce (Braverman 1974: 338).

Braverman was not the first deskilling theorist (arguably Marx was), but he is the best-known contemporary one by virtue of the commitment and comprehensiveness of his account. Notwithstanding the important non-Marxist contributions by Mills (1968 [1951]), Friedmann (1955), and Bright (1958), all of whom were cited by Braverman, the case for deskilling remains dominated by Braverman's thesis.

Critique of Braverman's deskilling thesis

Braverman's deskilling thesis has been the subject of a veritable plethora of critical comment as befits a study that sparked a prolonged bout of 'Bravermania' (Salaman 1986: 17). After more than two decades of extensive criticism and research on the capitalist labour process, Braverman's account of deskilling has been accorded the status of a classic book on the grounds that it transformed both the sociology of work and the sociology of class (Burawoy 1996). The numerous criticisms that have been levelled at Braverman's deskilling thesis can be summarized with reference to four main interrelated ones concerning his limited craft definition of skill, powerful managers and powerless workers, gender-blindness, and that he understated the possibility of upskilling.

(1) Braverman conceptualized skill from a craft perspective since he claimed that '[f]rom the earliest times to the Industrial Revolution the craft or skilled trade was the basic unit, the elementary cell of the labour process', and proceeded to depict factory work and clerical work in the nineteenth century as crafts (1974: 109). His craft perspective is also clear from his concluding chapter on skill, where he noted that, '[f]or the worker, the concept of skill is traditionally bound up with craft mastery – that is to say, the combination of knowledge of materials and processes with the practiced manual dexterities required to carry on a specific branch of production' (Braverman

1974: 443). Thus for Braverman the decline of skill is the equivalent of the decline of craft work.

The main problem with this key aspect of Braverman's deskilling thesis is that of romanticizing the pre-modern skilled manual worker (Cutler 1978; Littler 1982; Rose 1988). This line of criticism is more than a matter of idealizing the past; it concerns the empirical question of the representativeness of the craft worker prior to the rise of scientific management and mechanization in America from about 1900 onwards. On this crucial issue Braverman implied that craft workers were central to all production processes in the nineteenth century, which 'distorts their numerical importance since skilled workers did not constitute even a majority of the labour force' (Stark 1980: 94). It has been noted that the majority of the pre-industrial capitalist labour force were not craft workers, but 'farm-labourers and domestic servants' (Rose 1988: 317). Consequently, assuming Braverman was correct in his claim that manual and non-manual craft-based workers were deskilled by the twin forces of Taylorism and mechanization, this process was not the experience of the majority of workers. Even among craft workers, there were clear variations in the extent to which they yielded to managerial power and were therefore able to resist deskilling, as point (2) below shows.

Braverman's tendency to idealize atypical craft work applies not just to manual workers but to non-manual workers. Braverman likened clerical work to a craft and contrasted the 'small and privileged clerical stratum of the past' with the enlarged Taylorized and mechanized and hence deskilled clerical class of today (1974: 304). Research covering clerical workers in Britain and America has shown that Braverman's highly skilled clerical workers 'were a small minority (5 to 10 per cent) of [Victorian] clerks' (Attewell 1989: 369). In other words, there was an office hierarchy in the late nineteenth century and the majority of clerical workers undertook work of a routine and repetitive kind. It is difficult to avoid the conclusion that such 'false nostalgia' is an inadequate basis upon which to advance a theory of universal deskilling (Attewell 1989: 384).

In the case of the development of data-processing work during the middle of the twentieth century, Braverman also argued that for a short time it 'displayed the characteristics of a craft' (1974: 329). However, 'along with the computer a new division of labour was introduced and the destruction of the craft greatly hastened' (Braverman 1974: 329). At the upper echelons of the computer hierarchy a small number of technical specialists are retained but below this minority a mass of operators undertake work that has been 'simplified, routinized, and measured', ensuring the increasing similarity between work in an electronic office and a factory (Braverman 1974: 335). Evidence on the degradation of computer work in support of Braverman is at best mixed. First, it has been argued that whilst Braverman's thesis with respect to the computerization of office work applies well to the USA, where Taylorism was implemented more extensively than elsewhere, it applies less well to Europe, notably Germany where secretarial work and skills 'are regarded as professional' (Webster 1996: 121). Second, it has been shown that the computerization of office work involves a 'shift in personnel requirements', with an increased emphasis on social skills such as communication and the ability to learn new technical skills as the pace of technological change increases (Woodfield 2000: 35). Either way, and notwithstanding the problem of getting social skills acknowledged and valued as highly as technical sklls, the gender aspect of which is discussed below under point (3), at the very least this suggests that the degradation of computer work is far from assured. In fact, the use of advanced technology such as computers has been found to be 'strongly associated with having experienced an increase in skill requirements' (Gallie et al. 1998: 48).

(2) *Braverman's picture of powerful managers* and *powerless workers* has lead to the claim that this aspect his account of deskilling is 'seriously deficient' (Brown 1992: 206). The claim is that 'Braverman portrays the capitalist class as veritably omniscient and the working class as infinitely malleable', hence he overestimates the extent to which capitalists were able and willing to implement Taylorism and underestimates the degree to which workers, especially craft workers, resisted individually and collectively the deskilling impact of Taylorization and mechanization (Stark 1980: 92).

Three main reasons have been advanced for the reluctance of managers to embrace Taylorism. First, Thompson has suggested that they were unconvinced about the 'value' of Taylorism (1983: 14), in part because it has been shown that implementing scientific management in a thorough manner could take between two and four years (Layton 1971), and in part because Taylorized piece-rate schemes did not eradicate the problem of workers deceiving managers and continuing to restrict output (Edwards 1979). Second, managers were concerned that the introduction of scientific management might provoke conflict in the form of strikes in the short run and jeopardize worker co-operation in the longer term (Friedman 1977). Third, managers considered that their authority and hence their position was threatened by the new efficiency engineers who might be more interested in productivity than profits (Stabile 1984). Taylor himself was certainly aware of the reluctance of managers to adopt his methods since at the first conference on scientific management held in 1911 he noted in his address that '[t]hose in management are infinitely more stubborn, infinitely harder to make change their ways than are the workers' (quoted by Stabile 1984: 47). This has been confirmed by several historians of American business, who have concluded that during his lifetime Taylorism encountered far more opposition from managers than from workers (Stark 1980).

Worker opposition to scientific management was particularly widespread during the early attempts to implement it in America such that in 1914 the government commissioned an investigation into the relationship between scientific management and labour, known as the Hoxie Report (Stark 1980). In terms of Braverman's pivotal craft workers, historical research in America and Britain has shown that they were often successful in defending their control of the labour process, and hence their status as skilled workers, via a combination of local and national collective action (Montgomery 1979; Zeitlin 1985). Thus, whilst some craft workers conformed to Braverman's theory in the sense that they were unsuccessful in their efforts to resist the deskilling impact of Taylorism, notably engineers in Britain between 1890 and

1914, other craft workers, such as compositors, were able to defend and even enhance their position in the division of labour during the same period. According to Zeitlin: 'A crucial determinant of the balance of forces between skilled workers and employers in each case lay in the relative cohesion and capacity for collective action on each side' (1985: 238).

The combination of managerial and worker resistance to Taylorism meant that the ideas of scientific management, advocated by, among others, Henry Ford and Lenin, met with more approval than its practices (Friedman 1977). It has been calculated that at the time of Taylor's death in 1915, approximately 1 per cent of American industrial workers were operating under a fully Taylorized production system (Edwards 1979). After Taylor's death some of his more liberal followers became more sympathetic towards labour and some of the less radical trade unionists responded by adopting a less hostile view of scientific management (Rose 1988). As a consequence, Taylorism was implemented widely in America, although not necessarily in a pure form and not without continued opposition, whereas in Europe, it was adopted more slowly and unevenly, again often in a modified form and in the face of managerial and worker resistance (Littler 1982).

Braverman was not unaware that in America Taylorism 'antagonized workers and sometimes management as well' but his 'self-imposed limitation' to consider only 'the shape given to the working population by the capital accumulation process', ruled out an analysis of the practical (class) consequences of the attempt to introduce scientific management (1974: 27, 87). This restriction not only left Braverman vulnerable to the criticism that he exaggerated the power of managers to implement Taylorism and underestimated the power of workers to resist it, but it also exposed him to further criticisms; that his account of deskilling was 'one-sided' and hence deterministic since he considered deskilling to be the inevitable outcome of the spread of Taylorism and increased mechanization without analysing the relationship between the managers and the managed (Mackenzie 1977: 249). Such an analysis would have shown that, among other things, in the process of using their union based bargaining strength to defend successfully their status and pay as skilled workers, some groups of male workers sought to exclude women from the same relatively privileged position (Rubery 1980; Walby 1986). The pattern of resistance to Taylorism indicates that the working class is not as homogeneous as Braverman claimed, it is divided by gender, an issue which is addressed in the next section.

(3) Braverman's gender-blindness is apparent from his failure to examine how patriarchy contaminates definitions of skill. Braverman defined skill in a gender-neutral way by reference craft mastery, namely 'the combination of knowledge of materials and processes with the practiced manual dexterities required to carry on a specific branch of production' (1974: 443). This approach to skill has been called 'technicist' because it defines 'skill as technique, a combination of manual and mental capacities for manipulating objects and tools' (Blackburn and Mann 1979: 292). The alternative to Braverman's essentially technicist approach to skill is one that acknowledges that skill contains a social dimension in addition to a technical one, sometimes called the

'political' aspect of skill since it involves the element of power (Blackburn and Mann 1979: 292; see also Cockburn 1983: 116).

Patriarchal assumptions can influence the definition of skill in two main ways. First, irrespective of the content of a job, the 'work of women is often deemed to be inferior simply because it is women who do it' (Phillips and Taylor 1980: 79). A good example of this is provided by Phillips and Taylor, who cite some empirical research in which the male workers who were undertaking less skilled work than women in a technical sense were classified as semi-skilled whereas the women were classified as unskilled. In another example of the same tendency, Phillips and Taylor quote the researcher's conclusion that for some women workers 'the only way to become skilled was to change sex' (1980: 83). Thus, upon entering work outside the home, women carry with them their subordinate status, namely that they are seen and treated by male managers and workers, and sometimes by women also, as being primarily responsible for the domestic sphere, the concomitant of which is that paid work is considered to be of lesser importance to women. Needless to say, the tendency to devalue women workers is to the advantage of employers in the form of lower wages and to male workers in the form of higher wages.

A second form of patriarchal bias is the tendency to undervalue female skills, notably emotional, social and caring skills, on the specious grounds that these kinds of skill are part of being a woman and as such are gained without formal training or via workplace experience (Davies and Rosser 1986). Although there are clear parallels between these skills and those associated with being a wife and mother, they tend to be devalued by virtue of this association (Thornley 1996). For example, historically, nursing has been a female-dominated type of work, and although it requires extensive knowledge and training, it has not been regarded as a 'technical job because it is women's work and therefore undervalued' (Wajcman 1991: 36). Similarly, a study of life assurance sales work showed that a range of skills are required, some of which are associated with masculinity (e.g., ambition and competitiveness), whilst others are associated with femininity (e.g., caring and communication). It was found that masculine attributes were overvalued by management during recruitment and promotion, whereas feminine ones were not even included in job descriptions, to the advantage of men and to the detriment of women (Collinson and Knights 1986). In non-traditional areas of female employment, such as insurance sales, the sexual harassment of women by their male colleagues was also used to exclude women from this type of work (Collinson and Collinson 1996).

Braverman indicated his awareness of patriarchy and its implications for work when he noted: 'The sex barrier that assigns most office jobs to women, and that is enforced both by custom and hiring practice, has made it possible to lower wage rates in the clerical category' (1974: 353). To this extent his approach was not entirely technicist, but he failed to examine the extent to which the meaning of skill is influenced by ideas about gender as well as technical considerations. Ironically, social skills, which have been associated historically with femininity and hence undervalued, have become more important as a result of the growth of service work, especially in terms of the upskilling of women (Gallie et al. 1998). The possibility that upskilling exceeds deskilling is the subject of the fourth major criticism of Braverman's thesis.

(4) *Braverman underestimated the extent of upskilling* in a valiant attempt to counter the prevailing conventional wisdom that there has been a general upgrading of work, especially with regard to clerical workers. Braverman considered this to be a major myth promulgated by the 'practice of academic sociology and popular journalism' (1974: 293). Although he was aware of the unevenness of the deskilling process as a result of social changes in the organization and mechanization of production which created 'new crafts and skills and technical specialties', he considered such eventualities as temporary (1974: 170). According to Braverman, the best workers could hope for is to delay the 'historical process of devaluation of the worker's skill' when managers opt for 'patience' rather than 'a bitter battle with the union' (1974: 203).

In the case of the increased demand for maintenance workers and technical specialists, such as engineers, who are responsible for the conceptualization and planning of production, it is the same story. Braverman argued that there was a tendency for their work to be 'standardized in much the same fashion as that of the production worker', due in large part to the introduction of 'computers and numerical control instrumentation' (1974: 223, 244), although Braverman did concede that the computerization of clerical work creates the 'exception of a specialized minority whose technical and "systems" skills are expanded' (1974: 339). However, this exception to the deskilling imperative inherent in industrial capitalism is not thought by Braverman to be a threat to his thesis since the majority of new technical specialists are rationalized in due course, degraded via the familiar twin forces of Taylorism and mechanization.

Research on industrial workers, which focused mainly on the period between 1940 and 1980, concluded that 'skilled workers remain a central grouping within the division of labour in both America and Britain', and that whilst some skilled jobs have declined, such as compositing skills in printing, 'this has been compensated for by the rise of welding, sheetmetal working, car repairing and machine maintenance skills' (Penn 1990: 166). A similar conclusion was reached in a study of skill and organizational and technical change, namely the introduction of teamwork and robots, and car workers in America during the mid-1980s. It was found that already deskilled production workers remained deskilled or experienced further deskilling following these changes, whereas skilled workers experienced considerable upgrading, and that this was particularly marked for the 'high-tech maintenance workers' (Milkman and Pullman 1991: 143). A case study of clerical workers also came to the conclusion that new technologies, such as computers, create new skills as well as destroy old ones, with women carrying out the majority of the deskilled office work (Crompton and Jones 1984; Crompton and Reid 1982).

Braverman's supporters

The combined force of these criticisms of Braverman's deskilling thesis can be interpreted as suggesting that little merit attaches to his analysis. This would be a mistake since there are several studies that are supportive of Braverman, notably Burawoy's American research of a piecework machine-shop (1979) and Cooley's British study of the impact of computer-aided design (1987 [1980]), as well as accounts of the debate about deskilling that are broadly favourable of Braverman's approach and conclusions (e.g., Thompson 1983).

Burawoy endorses Braverman's deskilling thesis but adds two important qualifications. First, he suggests that the destruction of craft skills was a more 'uneven' process than Braverman allows, and, second, he argues that capitalist control over workers is achieved not just by the coercive influence of Taylorism and mechanization, but by the active complicity of the workers themselves (Burawoy 1979: 198). He focuses on the ways in which consent is generated as the workers participate in work games, such as meeting output targets: 'Workers are sucked into the game as a way of reducing the level of deprivation' (Burawoy 1979: 199). Consent is therefore 'manufactured' via the managerial organization of work within the factory, which 'allows the degradation of work to pursue its course without continuing crisis' (Burawoy 1979: 94). This more subtle analysis of how capitalism accomplishes the co-operation of exploited and oppressed workers has been criticized for overestimating the degree of consent achieved by game playing, thereby underestimating the radical potential of workplace culture (Rose 1988; Thompson 1983).

Cooley's analysis of the impact of computer-aided design (CAD) unambiguously supports Braverman: 'There is already evidence to show that CAD, when introduced on the basis of so-called efficiency, gives rise to deskilling of the design function and a loss of job security' (1987[1980]: 72). This study lends powerful support to Braverman, especially the myth of the politically neutral technology dimension of his thesis, although it also opens him up to the same line of criticism, namely that the technological bias of capitalist domination tends to overstate the powerlessness of workers.

Summary and conclusions

The idea that in industrial society work is inevitably deskilled as part of the capitalist process of profit seeking derives from Marx's writings. Braverman exemplifies this approach clearly and thoroughly and has been credited with transforming both the sociology of class in general and the sociology of work in particular. Braverman starts with a craft model of skill, which emphasizes task-specific training, and goes on to argue that the combination the Taylorism and technology have a deleterious impact on work skills. For Braverman, deskilling was therefore inherent in the structure of work in industrial capitalist society.

Although Braverman's contribution to the debate about deskilling is widely considered to be seminal, it has not escaped extensive criticism. He has been accused of idealizing craft work, portraying managers as all-powerful and workers as impotent, patriarchal bias, and underestimating the possibility of upskilling. However, his thesis is not without support, especially from those who share his Marxist approach, such as Burawoy. Consequently, it is impossible to ignore Braverman's deskilling thesis and his focus on the labour process renewed interest is this neglected concept.

The issues raised by Braverman's deskilling thesis remain the subject of research and debate in the sociology of work (e.g., Aronowitz and DiFazio 1994), especially with reference to part-time work (e.g., O'Reilly and Fagan 1998) and gender (e.g., Webster 1996). Arguably, the key question prompted by Braverman's contested thesis is whether or not deskilling is a major or minor trend. In order to address this point, the issue of upskilling needs to be considered. This is the subject of the next chapter.

Further reading

In addition to reading Braverman's famous study, the collection of articles in Wood (ed.) (1982) *The Degradation of Work? Skill, Deskilling and the Labour Process* cover the range of criticisms directed at Braverman's thesis. The specialist textbook by Thompson (1983) *The Nature of Work: An Introduction to Debates on the Labour Process* provides an in-depth analysis Braverman's thesis.

Questions for discussion and assessment

1. On what grounds did Braverman advance his deskilling thesis?
2. Assess critically Braverman's deskilling thesis.
3. Evaluate the strengths of Braverman's deskilling thesis.
4. Consider the view that the gender dimension is the main weakness of Braverman's study.
5. What is the lasting significance of Braverman's contribution?

CHAPTER FOUR

Paid Work in Post-Industrial Society and Upskilling?

In order to assess fully the issue of deskilling, upskilling also needs to be considered. In the same way that deskilling theories can be traced back to Marx, upskilling theories have their origins in the writings of Weber on the increased demand for educational qualifications by the expanding number of bureaucratic organizations (Edgell 1993). This is readily apparent in Bell's version of upskilling, with its emphasis on the centrality of knowledge and the growth of technical specialists (1976 [1973]). Bell's version of post-industrial upskilling is not especially original but it is arguably the 'most frequently quoted' and 'most systematic' (Kumar 1978: 196, 197).

Bell's upskilling thesis

Like Braverman, Bell's empirical reference point is America, but in marked contrast to Braverman, Bell argues that in the post-industrial society, the possession of private property as a source of power will be relatively less important compared to the possession of knowledge: 'while property remains an important base [of power], technical skill becomes another, sometimes rival, base with education the means of access to the attainment of technical skill' (1976 [1973]: 115). He also claims that in the post-industrial society the 'non-profit sector' would expand, particularly health, education and research (Bell 1976 [1973]: 147). Thus at the core of Bell's post-industrial society upkilling thesis is the idea that theoretical knowledge is the key factor of production in the sense that it becomes the 'source of innovation and policy formulation for the society' (1976 [1973]: 14). Although Bell notes that 'the concept post-industrial society is an analytical construct, not a picture of a specific or concrete society', he considers that the 'United States is no longer an industrial society', but the first post-industrial society, and in the 1970s the only one (1976 [1973]: 133).

Table 4.1   Industrial and post-industrial societies: contrasting features

	Industrial	Post-industrial
Regions	Western Europe	USA
	Soviet Union	
	Japan	
Economic sector	Goods	Services
Occupational slope	Semi-skilled worker	Professional and technical
	Engineer	Scientists
Technology	Energy	Information
Primary institution	Business enterprise	University
Design	Game against fabricated nature	Game between persons
Stratification: Base-	Property	Skill
Access-	Inheritance	Education
Axial principle	Economic growth:	Centrality of and codification
	state or private control	of theoretical knowledge
	of investment decisions	

Source: Summarized from Bell (1976 [1973]: 117, 118)

Bell's idea of a post-industrial society focuses on changes in the social structure with reference to the economy, the occupational system, and science and technology. From a sociology of work perspective, the main contrasts between an industrial society (IS) and a post-industrial society (PIS) are outlined in Table 4.1. This shows that:

- IS produce goods whereas a PIS produce services and that the majority will no longer be employed in industry but in the service sector;
- created energy is the transforming resource of an IS whereas in a PIS it is information in the form of computer and data-transmission systems;
- the strategic resource of an IS is financial capital but in a PIS it is knowledge;
- access to capital is via inheritance in an IS and via education in a PIS;
- the key technology of an IS is machine technology but in a PIS it is intellectual technology epitomized by the computer;
- the skill base changes from one dominated by the engineer and semi-skilled worker in IS to one in which the scientist and technical and professional occupations predominate in PIS;
- work involves a 'game against fabricated nature' in IS and a 'game between persons' in PIS (Bell 1976 [1973]: 116); and finally,
- the axial principle of economic growth characteristic of an IS is superseded by the codification of theoretical knowledge in a PIS.

In short, a post-industrial society is a white-collar society dominated by service work and the 'centrality of theoretical knowledge' in which the system of social stratification is transformed by the creation of a new 'division between the scientific and technical classes and those who will stand outside' (Bell 1976 [1973]: 112). In this new type of society the 'central person is the professional, for he is equipped by his education and training to provide the kinds of skill which are increasingly demanded in a post-industrial society' (Bell 1976 [1973]: 127).

Somewhat surprisingly, given the thrust of his thesis, neither skill nor work appear in the index of Bell's book, although these inextricably related issues are discussed widely in the text, usually with reference to education. For example, Bell emphasizes that technical knowledge as a factor of production puts a premium of the acquisition of technical and professional skills, and this in turn 'makes education, and access to higher education, the condition of entry to the post-industrial society itself' (1976 [1973]: 128, see also 426). In a post-industrial society the demand for more services combined with the 'inadequacy of the market in meeting people's needs for a decent environment as well as better health and education lead to a growth of government' (Bell 1976 [1973]: 128). Thus, according to Bell, a post-industrial society is also a more communal society in that economic decisions are 'subordinated to, or will derive from, other forces in society' and that other major decisions 'are made by the government, rather than through the market' (1976 [1973]: 344, 364).

In addition to the quantitative changes associated with the emergence of a post-industrial society, notably the decline of blue-collar workers and the increase in white-collar workers, especially the scientific and technical occupational category, Bell also outlines some of the concomitant qualitative changes in relation to work. For example, first and most importantly, he argues that in a white-collar society dominated by service work 'the fact that individuals now talk to other individuals, rather than interact with a machine, is the fundamental fact about work in the post-industrial society' (Bell 1976 [1973]: 163). In other words, instead of working to the 'rhythms of mechanization' which put a premium on physical strength, information is all important since work relationships are characterized by 'encounter and communication' whether one is selling an airline ticket or teaching a student (Bell 1976 [1973]: 162, 163). Second, hierarchical work structures will be modified 'by encouraging committees and participation' which, when combined with 'the inevitable end of the "fee-for-service" relationship in medicine and other non-profit sectors, will lead to the 'emergence of new structural forms of non-bureaucratic organization' (Bell 1976 [1973]: 153, 154, 324). Third, compared to the large corporation typical of industrial society, 'the distinctive character of the services sector is the small size of the unit enterprise. ... Even where unit size is larger, in hospitals and schools, what is different about these enterprises is the larger degree of autonomy of smaller units ... and the greater degree of professional control' (Bell 1976 [1973]: 161). The contrast to work in an industrial society is marked; brains have replaced brawn, democracy has replaced despotism, and small organizations have replaced large-scale ones.

In sum, Bell's upskilling post-industrial society thesis is a mixture of quantitative changes, such as the dramatic increase in education and white-collar work, and qualitative changes, such as the tendency for service work to involve interacting with people rather than machines. For Bell, this all adds up to a new type of society, a post-industrial society that is totally different from its predecessor, the industrial society, especially in terms of the predominant kind of work and workers, namely post-industrial services.

In support of his upskilling thesis Bell presents a large number of statistical tables and other quantitative data that purport to show that America is already well on the way to being a post-industrial society and that on the basis of trends at the time Bell was writing, by the end of the twentieth century it will be one of about a dozen post-industrial nation states, and arguably the most advanced, with New York as the economic capital of the world.

In a later exposition of his thesis, Bell preferred the label 'information society' to his earlier one, post-industrial society, although this concept had already been used (1976 [1973]: 467). Unsurprisingly, the basic thrust of his thesis remained unchanged, namely the inexorable rise of 'information workers' who displace industrial workers as the 'largest single group in the workforce' (Bell 1980: 523). Hence Bell still refers to the growth of post-industrial services, both 'human' ones, such as teaching and health, and 'professional' ones, such as the programming and processing of information (1980: 501). Thus the change from a goods-producing to a service or information society involves the proposition that the organization and processing of information influences the 'character of the occupations and work in which men engage' (Bell 1980: 500).

Critique of Bell's upskilling thesis

Bell is widely credited with advancing an upskilling thesis in the context of his theory of post-industrial society (e.g., Gallie 1991; Penn 1990). The basic claim that modern societies are dominated by service workers, not agricultural or industrial workers, is not disputed. What has been disputed is Bell's interpretation of this trend. He has been extensively criticized on four major interconnected grounds: that he idealized service work, understated the growth of routine white-collar work, misjudged the sociological significance of the expansion of professional work, and neglected the gender dimension of work in post-industrial society.

(1) Bell idealized service work in the post-industrial society in the sense that he tended to 'take as the general pattern of work the conditions in the most attractive and prestigious parts of the service sector' (Kumar 1978: 206). Aside from the problem that the distinction between an industrial sector and a service sector does not 'illuminate effectively the type of work performed' since service workers can be found in both sectors (Webster 2002: 47), most work in the expanded service sector is of a routine nature, typically undertaken by women, minorities, and those without a university education, often on a part-time basis (duRivage 1992; O'Reilly and Fagan 1998).

For example, work in telephone-based customer services or call centres, 'has become the fastest growing job market in the UK' and is expected to account for over 3 per cent of all employees by 2008 (Kilpern 2001). In marked contrast to Bell's optimism regarding the upskilled character of service sector work, in this type of service work the 'typical call centre operator is young, female' and 'is increasingly likely to be a part-time permanent employee' (Taylor and Bain 1999: 115). Moreover, 'irrespective of the quality of service workflow', the majority of call-centre workers experience work routinization and intensification in the form of highly scripted and therefore repetitive conversations that are monitored, involving minimal discretion or creative responsibility (Taylor et al. 2002: 148). This evidence is far more supportive of Braverman's deskilling thesis than Bell's alternative upskilling thesis.

Thus, the growth of the service sector is far from synonymous with upskilling, and although service work often involves the demand for new communication skills and specialist knowledge highlighted by Bell, recent research suggests that this does not apply to the majority of call-centre or other types of service workers, such as fast-food restaurant staff (MacDonald and Sirianni 1996). In short, Bell can be criticized for generalizing from the work experience of a relatively small and unrepresentative group of scientific and professional workers. Most service sector work, as the following overlapping criticism makes clear, does not conform to Bell's model of the upskilled knowledge worker, working autonomously and interacting with others in a small, non-hierarchical organization.

(2) *Bell understated the growth of routine white-collar work* when he argued that '[t]he expansion of the service economy, with its emphasis on office work, education, and government, has naturally brought about a shift to white-collar occupations' (1976 [1973]: 17). Within the emerging white-collar majority, Bell emphasized the 'startling' growth rate, 'twice that of the average labour force', of professional and technical employment, and in particular noted that the 'growth rate of the scientists and engineers has been triple that of the working population' (1976 [1973]: 17). He concluded that this massive growth would lead to the 'dominance of the professional and technical class in the labour force' (Bell 1976 [1973]: 125).

As with the first criticism, the claim that the post-industrial society is a white-collar society is incontestable on the basis of the available employment statistics. However, the suggestion that white-collar work is qualitatively different in that it requires a college education and involves working with people rather than machines, particularly in non-profit organizations, and helps to promote a sense of community, and that such work is more skilled and satisfying, is less than convincing given the 'tendency to glamorize white-collar work by drawing selectively on some of its more attractive but quite unrepresentative areas' (Kumar 1978: 209).

Although many of the newer white-collar jobs do indeed involve interacting with people rather than machines, Bell underestimated the extent to which such work has been rationalized, mechanized and, as a consequence, routinized by the imperative to make a profit in a competitive market system, in the manner described by Braverman and discussed in the previous chapter (Kumar 1978). Post-Braverman research on white-collar work has shown that computerization aided the Taylorization of work, and hence extended deskilling to clerical work and even managerial and professional work (Kumar 1995). For example, one British study of the impact of computerization on clerical work concluded: 'The clerk now typically performs more exclusively the functions of (deskilled) labour, being increasingly peripheral to the performance of the computer and having little or no responsibility for the co-ordination and completion of the many separate work tasks in the process as a whole' (Crompton and Reid 1982: 176). Similarly, as noted in the previous chapter, professionals such as industrial designers have found their work standardized and hence deskilled by the introduction of computer-aided design (Cooley 1987 [1980]). Given the higher pay of managers and professionals, there is a major economic incentive to Taylorize their work, and at least one researcher has suggested that it is professional workers who are most at risk of being deskilled (Baran 1988).

Thus, Bell's focus on the expansion of white-collar work, and especially the upper echelons of the hierarchy, combined with his neglect to consider the potential and extent of Taylorization among non-manual occupations following the widespread adoption of computers in the workplace, contributed to his underestimation of the persistence of routine white-collar work.

(3) Bell misjudged the sociological significance of the expansion of professional work in the sense that he overlooked a range of influences on such work which undermine his upskilling thesis. Apart from the tendency to re-label work that is essentially relatively unskilled manual work in a way that implies a degree of technical expertise, for instance referring to a garbage collector as a 'sanitary engineer' (Bell 1976 [1973]: 153), as noted above, professional workers are far from immune to the logic of the capitalist market system. Hence the growth of public sector professional workers, emphasized by Bell, has been accompanied by changes in the political and economic context in which they operate (Crompton 1990). For example, government policy during the 1980s and 1990s in Britain and America exposed public sector professional workers to market forces via different forms of privatization of state services and the introduction of quasi-markets in the provision of state services, notably health (Edgell and Duke 1991; Gabe et al. 1990; Schiller 1996), which suggests that Bell's optimism regarding the 'inevitable end of the "fee-for-service" [doctor–patient] relationship' is misplaced (1976 [1973]: 154). Thus professional work in the public sector in Britain has become more like work in the private sector due to what has been termed 'entrepreneurial government' (Osborne and Gaebler 1992: 19) and associated tendencies such as the commodification of knowledge (Smart 1992). These changes have led to an emphasis on accountability, targets, league tables, competition, and value for money, all of which have undermined rather than enhanced the status and autonomy of the professional. Bell is not unaware of what he calls the 'constraints' on the changes he envisages, such as the productivity and cost of professional services, but it does not seem to have tempered his optimism regarding the future of work in a post-industrial society (1976 [1973]: 154).

Moreover, Bell's emphasis on the growth of research spending as an indicator of the increasing centrality of theoretical knowledge overlooks the extent to which such budgets, and the researchers employed to work on them, are subordinate to the interests of capital (Robins and Webster 1989). Part of this process is the tendency for university research to be placed on a commercial footing (Schiller 1996). As a consequence, the expansion of scientific work, like that of routine white-collar work, is subject increasingly to the influence of the capitalist market system, including Taylorization (Kumar 1995). This is in contrast to the claim that in a post-industrial society non-market forces would become stronger and that therefore it would be a more 'communal society' (Bell 1976 [1973]: 159).

In advancing his case for the increased importance of professional and technical workers in post-industrial society, Bell placed great weight on the expansion of higher education and presented many tables to support his argument (Bell 1976 [1973]: especially Tables 3.1 to 3.21). Yet again the bare statistical 'facts' are impressive and are interpreted to show a direct and simple relationship between more education and an upskilled workforce, which encouraged Bell to proclaim that a post-industrial society is a 'knowledge society' (1976 [1973]: 212). In an early critique of this line of reasoning Braverman argued that the lengthening of the period spent in education prior to entry to the labour force has 'many causes, most of them bearing no direct relationship to the educational requirements of the job structure' (1974: 437). He suggests that the expansion of education limits the rise of unemployment and expands the employment opportunities of 'teachers, administrators, construction and service workers' (Braverman 1974: 439). He concluded that the 'commonly made connection between education and job content is, for the mass of jobs, a false one' (Braverman 1974: 440; see also Kumar 1978). In support of his alternative interpretation of the expansion of education, Braverman cited Berg, who had concluded that 'educational "achievements" have already "exceeded requirements in most job categories"', thereby undermining the argument that technical change requires a better educated workforce (1974: 441). Thus, far from improving productivity, this suggests that a better educated workforce may be disadvantageous to employers since it is associated with job dissatisfaction.

More recent research that shows that the expansion of higher education has led to 'significant levels of over qualification in employment' is not good news for Bell's thesis that there has been an upskilling of the workforce in response to technological change (Brynin 2002: 650). Consequently, using the historical expansion of educational qualifications as an indicator of the increased importance of knowledge and as evidence of upskilling is problematic.

(4) *Bell's neglect of the gender dimension of work in post-industrial society* is indicated by the small number of pages (less than ten) he devoted to the issue of women and work. Yet Bell noted that 'a service economy is very largely a female-centred economy' and that 'the proportion of women in the labour force is bound to rise – the efforts of women's lib apart – simply because of the expansion of service industries' (1976 [1973]: 146). Thus, the main problem raised by this trend is the difficulty faced by trade unions in recruiting women workers: 'Fewer women have thought of their jobs as "permanent" and have been less interested in unions; many female jobs are part-time or "second jobs" for the family, and the turnover of the number of women at work has been much higher than that of men' (1976 [1973]: 146).

Surprisingly, in view of his awareness of limitations of female service sector work (see also Bell 1976 [1973]: 134), he neglected to examine the significance of the low skill content of such jobs for his upskilling theory. If he had, he may have modified his theory to take account of the tendency for the majority of the new jobs created in those societies that fit best his model of a post-industrial society to be lower-level ones involving the delivery of basic services and routine information (Kumar 1978, 1995).

Importantly, the whole thrust of Bell's account of women and work betrays a traditional view in that he stereotypes all women as workers for whom paid work outside the home is not as central as their family roles. This approach to women and work has been addressed by Feldberg and Glenn (discussed in Chapter 2 in relation to the work of Blauner), who argue that to adopt a gender model for female workers and a job model for male workers distorts the analysis of work behaviour and influences what is researched, for example by defining 'job conditions as problematic for men and family responsibilities as problematic for women' (1979: 532). This is exactly what Bell does when he discusses the issue of corporations employing more women: 'A child-care centre is a necessary component of job satisfaction for young women, even though it may add costs to a company far beyond the "gains" in productivity from such women' (1976 [1973]: 290). For Bell, low skill and low pay are less of a problem for women workers than the lack of child-care facilities! Moreover, in the process of viewing all women as uncommitted workers, Bell neglects the tendency for women who work full-time to 'differ very little in their work commitment' from men who work full-time (Hakim 1995: 433). Thus, Bell's upskilling theory fails to take women workers into account in any serious way and when this issue is considered, albeit briefly, the heterogeneity of the female labour force is overlooked in favour of an outdated stereotype that labels all women workers as primarily concerned with family life rather than paid work.

These interrelated criticisms of Bell's upskilling thesis have led one critic to conclude that Bell's 'whole project is deeply flawed empirically, theoretically and methodologically' (Webster 2002: 33). Rather than posit a single skill trend, it is possible that changes in the process of controlling and exploiting workers and/or in the technology used at work result in both deskilling and upskilling. This implies that social change is more complex than either Braverman or Bell suggest, hence the pursuit of overall trends, such as progressive deskilling or upskilling, 'are likely to be both theoretically and practically in vain' (Wood 1982: 18). The key question, therefore, is that if the pattern of skill change is uneven, is deskilling or upskilling the dominant trend?

The polarization of skills: support for Bell?

In the research literature on the sociology of work skills there are hints of polarization as far back as Bright (1958: 93) and Blauner (1964: 169), both of whom noted counter-trends in their studies of automation and skill, notwithstanding their contrasting conclusions, namely deskilling and upskilling respectively. The latest research on the sociology of work skills in several advanced industrial capitalist countries has been broadly supportive of the polarization of skills thesis.

An American study examined the impact of increased automation on workers at a single car assembly plant and found that the effect was to polarize the workforce within the factory: 'Skilled trades workers experienced skill upgrading and gained enhanced responsibilities, while production workers underwent deskilling and became

Table 4.2   Change in skill and responsibility by class and sex

	Increase in skill (cell %)		Increase in responsibility (cell %)	
	Men	Women	Men	Women
Professional/managerial	72	77	80	77
Lower non-manual	75	68	77	62
Technician/supervisory	78	56	81	66
Skilled manual	65	55	62	57
Semi- and non-skilled	50	41	55	46
All employees	66	60	70	61

Source. Adapted from Gallie et al. (1998: 44).

increasingly subordinated to the new technology' (Milkman and Pullman 1991: 123). More generally, in terms of occupational trends, further evidence from the USA has confirmed that polarization is occurring in the form of a highly educated and highly paid minority of information workers whose work is intrinsically satisfying (e.g., designers) and a poorly educated and poorly paid majority of production service workers whose work is not satisfying (Reich 1991). Reich estimates that the highly skilled minority constitute around one-fifth of the workforce whereas the unfortunate 80 per cent undertake all the routine and mundane jobs.

A representative British survey (Gallie 1991: 325) used five indicators of skill: educational qualifications, length of training after completing full-time education, time taken to acquire job proficiency, responsibility for supervising the work of others, and subjective assessment of whether or not their work was skilled. The main findings of this comprehensive national survey on the pattern of skill change in the 1980s were that the 'experience of deskilling was very rare and this was true for all occupational classes' and that the 'argument that is best supported [by the data] is that of a polarization of skill experiences between classes' (Gallie 1991: 349; Gallie et al. 1998). The dominant upskilling trend was related to technological change, especially the use of computers at work, and the increased importance of social skills in work, particularly for women's work. However, there were several caveats, notably that there was a 'deep gender divide in skill experiences', with men gaining most from upskilling and women the least, and that this was mainly related to the tendency for women to be employed part-time (Gallie 1991: 350). As Table 4.2 shows, further research by Gallie et al. confirmed the 'growing polarization in skill experiences between lower manual workers and other employees', but also showed that 'the trend over time has been for gender differences in skill to diminish' (1998: 56).

A similarly representative survey of Dutch workers showed that automation produced a net upskilling for white-collar and professional workers, but a 'pocket' of deskilling among blue-collar workers due to a process of internal differentiation among this group (de Witte and Steijn 2000: 260). These findings confirm the aforementioned British data since they show that polarization is occurring and that the white-collar majority are more likely to experience upskilling than manual workers.

Finally, in the context of advancing what amounts to an updated version of Bell's post-industrial society thesis, Castells concluded, on the basis of a mass of cross-national statistical data, that '[t]he hardening of capitalist logic since the 1980s has fostered social polarization in spite of occupational upgrading' (Castells 2001: 280). However, for Castells, the pivotal point about the transformation of work is not deskilling or upskilling, but the pressure on all workers to be flexible – an issue that will be considered more fully in the later chapters.

On balance, the empirical evidence regarding the polarization of skill tends to be more supportive of Bell's thesis in two respects. First, his focus on new technologies and social skills has been shown to be closely related to upskilling. Second, upskilling has been found to be far more prevalent than deskilling, although intensification often characterized upskilled work and deskilling was still apparent, particularly at the bottom of the occupational hierarchy, and especially for part-time female work.

The transformation of work can be considered from the standpoint of changes in the class structure in the manner advocated by Lee (1981). From this perspective, Lee has suggested that the debate about skill and the class structure may be summarized by noting that Braverman's thesis posits that exploitation leads inevitably to falling skill levels and eventually to proletarianization, and that, conversely, Bell's thesis posits that technical change leads inevitably to rising skill levels and eventually to professionalization or embourgeoisement. This model is summarized in Figure 4.1.

The capitalist view:
Exploitation → Falling skill levels → Proletarianization

The technicist view:
Automation → Rising skill levels → Professionalization

Figure 4.1   Changes in skill and the occupational class structure

Source: Adapted from Lee (1981: 57)

The usefulness of approaching the debate about skill trends in terms of the contrast between Marxist (e.g., Braverman) and post-industrial (e.g., Bell) conceptions of social change has been acknowledged implicitly by Wright (1997). His study of changes in the class structure of America, the most advanced industrial capitalist society, shows that the post-industrial expectation of upskilling was confirmed, whereas the Marxist expectation of deskilling was not. This was especially marked during the 1980s and came as a major surprise and disappointment to the Marxist Wright. In mitigation, as it were, Wright pointed out that the Marxist theory of class proletarianization applies to capitalism in general and not 'national units of capitalism' (1997: 110). In other words, upskilling may be occurring in the first world, but the deskilled jobs have been transferred to the third world. Hence, Marx was correct for global capitalism but wrong in the case of the most developed capitalist nation states.

Summary and conclusions

Upskilling theories tend to draw upon Weber and focus on technological imperatives such as the need for a better educated and skilled workforce. The best-known version of this tendency is Bell's post-industrial theory of upskilling. However, in contrast to the deskilling theories which draw upon Marx, focus on capitalist imperatives such as the need to make a profit, and tend to operate with a craft model of skill which emphasizes task-specific training (discussed in Chapter 3), Bell tends to operate with an educational model of skill which emphasizes knowledge and responsibility. Corresponding to their different conceptions of skill, upskilling theories have been criticized for idealizing white-collar work, whereas deskilling theories have been criticized for idealizing highly skilled manual work. Both theories have also been accused of neglecting the gender dimension of work, and exaggerating certain trends among the labour force. Furthermore, in their desire to advance a general skill trend, Bell and Braverman both tend to be deterministic, play down counter-trends and over-simplify the issue of skill.

The search for a general tendency towards either deskilling or upskilling is thought by some to be a false trail since post-Braverman and Bell research has found evidence of both. This has led to the emergence of a polarization of skill thesis which has been largely confirmed empirically in that in advanced industrial capitalist societies the dominant tendency is upskilling rather than deskilling. Most tellingly, research by the avowed Marxist Wright (1997) found that changes in the American class structure between 1960 and 1990 supported Bell's post-industrial upskilling theory, not Braverman's Marx-inspired deskilling theory.

However, many workers, notably women and relatively less skilled manual workers, are more likely to experience deskilling than upskilling, even in highly developed societies. Moreover, the growth of low-skilled part-time work in such societies during the past couple of decades and the emergence of the deskillers being deskilled following the introduction of computer-aided design, suggest that the debate about deskilling is not yet over, especially if the global picture rather than any one nation state is considered (Aronowitz and DiFazio 1994; Cooley 1987 [1980]; O'Reilly and Fagan 1998; Wright 1997).

One way of looking at skill trends is to consider them in relation to how work is organized. Thus, deskilling is associated typically with Fordist mass production, which declined from the 1960s onwards in the most advanced industrial capitalist societies, and upskilling with post-Fordist alternatives to mass production (Wood 1992). Hence among other things, the incidence of either deskilling or upskilling will depend on how work has been organized historically in different types of societies. The alleged transformation of Fordism into neo-Fordist and post-Fordist production systems is the subject of the next two chapters.

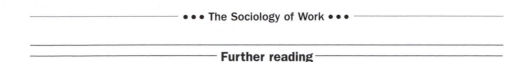

Further reading

In addition to reading the original works of Bell, the critiques of his upskilling thesis by Kumar (1978) *Prophecy and Progress: The Sociology of Industrial and Post-Industrial Society*, and Webster (2002) *Theories of the Information Society* (2nd edn) should also be read, although neither cover the gender dimension in depth. Recent research on the sociology of skill should be consulted, notably Crompton et al. (eds) (1996) *Changing Forms of Employment: Organizations, Skills and Gender*, and Gallie et al. (1998) *Restructuring the Employment Relationship*.

Questions for discussion and assessment

1. Examine critically the grounds upon which Bell advanced his upskilling thesis.
2. Assess the strengths of Bell's upskilling thesis.
3. Consider the view that the gender dimension is the main weakness of Bell's study.
4. How convincing is the evidence for the polarization of skills thesis?
5. To what extent has the post-industrial society theoretical expectation of progressive upskilling been confirmed?

CHAPTER FIVE

Fordism Its Rise, Development and Demise

Implicit in much of the discussion of alienation (in Chapter 2) and skill (in Chapters 3 and 4) was the idea that the organization of the production of goods and services during the twentieth century has changed and that this has influenced the extent to which workers are alienated or deskilled. This can be seen clearly in Blauner's model of the evolution of manual work from highly skilled and non-alienating craft work, to relatively unskilled and alienating assembly-line work, and the change to '"non-manual" responsibility called forth by continuous-process technology' (Blauner 1964: 169). Blauner's prescience was also apparent where he speculated that 'a more affluent and educated public, reacting against the standardization of values and products in a mass society, may increase its future demand for unique and individuated articles' (1964: 168).

In the sociological history of production systems a range of concepts have been developed in an attempt to comprehend the complexity of these kinds of changes. Among the most widely used are Fordism, and the systems that replaced it, namely neo-Fordism (McDonaldism) and post-Fordism, although the precise meaning of these terms often varies (Jessop 1994). Here the focus will be on the production or labour process dimension of Fordism and its successors. However, even within this limited objective there are variations regarding the use of these terms. For example, such is the overlap between Taylorism and Fordism that in the index of a sociology of work book, under Fordism there is an instruction to 'see scientific management' (Brown 1992: 270), whilst another sociologist prefers the terms neo- and post-Taylorism to the more usual Fordisms (Lomba 2005). The purpose of this chapter is to consider the rise, development and fall of Fordism with special reference to car making and the implications for the experience of work.

The rise of Fordism

During the course of the nineteenth century the factory became the dominant image of work in industrial capitalism in Britain, yet manufacturing often still involved a mixture of machine- and hand-made products by machine operators and craft workers producing a range of small batch and individual products (Samuel 1977). The great variety and complexity of factory production systems in the nineteenth century makes it difficult to generalize about pre-Fordism. However, those who have attempted such an exercise typically emphasize the role of highly skilled craft workers operating general purpose machines, the assembly of a whole product or large part of a product by one worker, and the use of non-standardized parts to produce a small number of high-quality products (Womack et al. 1990). As a result of this way of organizing production, complex products, such as cars, were extremely expensive to build and buy.

At the beginning of the twentieth century Henry Ford combined the organizational innovations of Taylorism, namely the separation of conception from execution and associated task fragmentation and simplification, with the introduction of special or single-purpose machine tools which made standardized and therefore interchangeable parts, and arranged production in a continuous flow in the form of a moving assembly line derived from meatpacking (Edwards 1979). The effect of these innovations transformed production from small to large scale and reduced markedly the costs of production.

The final pieces in the Ford production system were the reduction in the working day to eight hours and the more than doubling of wages to $5 a day in 1914. However, these benefits were only available to those who had worked for Ford for six months, were aged 21, and who conformed to Ford's idea of an appropriate lifestyle, involving cleanliness and no drinking, smoking or gambling. This was not an act of altruism but a policy calculated to reduce exceptionally high labour turnover, absenteeism, growing worker dissatisfaction, and the threat of unionism (Beynon 1975). Increasing pay dramatically had the extra advantages of generating extensive free publicity and creating many additional potential customers (Hounshell 1984).

These changes did not occur overnight but evolved following experimentation and modification over a number of years. For example, the moving assembly line was the culmination of many mechanical transfer devices introduced between 1910 and 1914, including an overhead monorail more than a mile long (Williams et al. 1992). The first moving assembly line was introduced in the sub-assembly section concerned with the production of flywheel magnetos in 1913 and extended to other areas of production until an endless and highly synchronized chain conveyer for final assembly was achieved in 1914 (Hounshell 1984). The flow production principle was basically an organizational innovation which saved time by restricting workers to their position on the line.

The three main elements of the production system implemented by Ford after years of continuous refinement, and which inspired the term 'Fordism', are summarized in Table 5.1 where they are contrasted to pre-Fordism. They include:

- the fragmentation and simplification of work via Taylorized tasks,
- managerial control over the pace of work via the moving assembly line, and
- the standardization of parts and products via single-purpose machines.

Finally, the consent of workers was achieved via higher wages for those who complied with Ford's model of good behaviour, and in due course this was underpinned

---

Table 5.1   Key features of pre-Fordism and Fordism

Pre-Fordism: type of production system characterized by:

1   Craft skills
2   Stationary assembly
3   Non-standardized parts and a low volume of high-quality products

Fordism: type of production system characterized by:

1   Fragmented and simplified (Taylorized) work tasks
2   Moving assembly line
3   Standardized parts and a high volume of low-quality products

---

by state welfare policies which sought to provide an economic safety net for unemployed workers. This created a virtuous circle in which the gains in productivity meant that there were only winners. The employer achieved larger profits, the employee received higher wages, and the consumer was able to purchase cheaper products. In sum, the Fordist system of mass production democratized consumption by making what were previously luxury goods for the few available in a standardized form to potentially everyone.

The success of Ford's new system of mass production can be gauged by the impressive increase in production, profits and worker loyalty which were achieved in just a few years. Between 1909 and 1916, production of the Model T increased from under 14,000 to nearly 600,000, profits rose from just over $3 million to nearly $60 million, with Ford's share of the cheap car market rising to over 90 per cent (Williams et al. 1992), and whereas 'the Ford employment office had to replace up to 60,000 men in 1913, in 1914 only 2,000 men left their jobs on the line' (Beynon 1975: 24). Ford's success is also apparent from the extent to which the new methods of mass production were adopted not only by other car manufacturers in America and eventually Europe, but also by makers of other products, such as houses, furniture, and consumer goods generally (Allen et al. 1992). From the standpoint of the potential consumer of Ford cars, the price fell impressively from $950 in 1909 to $360 in 1917, and reached its lowest price ever of $240 in 1924 (d'A.Jones 1965). The steep decline in the price of Ford cars led to a corresponding growth in car consumption that was stimulated by advertising and financed increasingly by instalment buying, with 75 per cent of cars purchased via loans in 1924 (Rhode 2002/03). Such was the success of Ford, a prominent Boston businessman of that time, Edward Filene, declared that competition 'will compel us to Fordize American business and industry' (cited by Ewen 1977: 24).

This rosy picture of the rise of Fordism is not without its complexities. First, the earliest American car maker to mass produce cars on an assembly line was Ransom Eli Olds in 1901, nearly a decade before Henry Ford (d'A.Jones 1965). In the following years the popularity of Oldsmobile cars, which became part of the General Motors Corporation in 1908, enabled this new form of transport to overtake the horse, with which it was contrasted in the advertisements in the early 1900s, as the favoured form of transport in America, and outsell Fords (www.oldsmobile.com).

Oldsmobile's lead over Ford was short-lived and this may have been due to 'obsolescence through technological innovation, such as alters the differential advantage enjoyed by one business concern as against its competing neighbours in the same line of industry' (Veblen 1966 [1915]: 128). Veblen referred to this tendency as the 'penalty for having been thrown into the lead and so having shown the way' (1966 [1915]: 132). Possibly the Oldsmobile assembly line predated the full appreciation of Taylorism that accompanied the rise of Ford. In the mid-1920s General Motors introduced a wider choice of inexpensive cars and displaced Ford as the model of manufacturing success (Williams et al. 1992). This suggests that in due course Ford also paid the penalty for taking the lead.

Second, there is some debate about the exact relationship between Taylorism and Fordism. Hounshell (1984) has pointed out that Ford had a time study department and that there was a clear division in Ford factories between the management who organized the work and workers who undertook the fragmented tasks assigned to them. On the other hand, Taylor was concerned to improve the efficiency of work using the existing technology, whereas Ford sought to improve efficiency via the displacement of workers by mechanization and the concomitant re-organization of work. Perhaps the safest conclusion is that Taylorist principles were clearly apparent in the Ford system of mass production and that they both involved the deskilling of work (Allen et al. 1992).

Third, the extent of the diffusion of Fordism has been questioned, most notably by Williams et al. who have argued that 'even in America there was only limited imitation' of Ford's production methods (1992: 537). This was partly because when Ford first produced relatively cheap cars on a large scale, there was a massive demand, but when the market became more complex and consumers demanded a greater range of models in the 1920s, Ford's focus on one model and their declining market share meant that the company 'was no longer a shining example, but a cautionary tale' (Williams et al. 1992: 539). In Europe, the introduction of Fordism was limited by weaker markets and stronger trade unions, especially craft workers, who resisted the displacement and deskilling aspects of Fordism (Beynon 1975).

Conversely, it has long been argued that Henry Ford's pride in his achievements and his unusual openness about his production methods encouraged technical journalists to tour his factories and write about them. As a consequence of this positive publicity, Ford's methods of production were spread throughout manufacturing industry: 'The Ford Motor Company educated the technical community in the ways of mass production' (Hounshell 1984: 261). American engineers also travelled abroad disseminating their knowledge of the new production techniques, most notably to the Soviet Union where factory walls were adorned with pictures of 'the two men who had "revolutionized" the twentieth century', namely Lenin and Henry Ford (Sussman 1974: 450).

Fordism was exported to Europe when Ford purchased a derelict factory in Trafford Park, Manchester, in 1911, although the assembly-line method of production was not introduced until 1914. Ford also exported Taylorism, anti-unionism, and an ultra strict approach to discipline, prompting one former employee to describe working for

Ford in its first European manufacturing plant as 'worse than Alcatraz', tolerated due to the relatively high wages and lack of alternative job options (McIntosh 1995: 75). Later Ford established foreign subsidiary companies elsewhere, for example, Japan, and General Motors followed suit when it took over the British car maker Vauxhall in 1925 (Littler and Salaman 1984). Foreign car makers such as Louis Renault from France, Giovanni Agnelli from Italy, Herbert Austin and William Morris from England, and Kiichiro Toyoda from Japan, visited the Ford plants in Detroit and applied the knowledge they gained of Ford's assembly line-based mass-production methods, albeit with modifications 'to accommodate simultaneous production of different models with a variety of specifications' (Shiomi 1995: 4). Fordism became a global system when mass production was relocated to developing countries such as Brazil, to take advantage of lower wages and weaker trade unions (Peck and Tickell 1994).

Thus, the dissemination of technical knowledge nationally and internationally, plus the rise of the multinational corporation, facilitated the diffusion of Fordism. Ford's success inspired the term 'Fordism', which became a shorthand for standardization; a standardized product produced by standardized machinery using standardized methods and standardized human labour employed for a standard working day (Doray 1988). Ford's achievement in creating a new way organizing production was acknowledged at the time and since as epoch-making.

The development of Fordism

So far the discussion of Fordism has focused primarily on what this concept means in terms of production, but as has been indicated with reference to the conditions attached to qualifying for extra pay, and the growth of credit and mass consumption, from the outset Fordism was more than a matter of how work was organized. Ford was interested in the behaviour of his workers outside as well as inside the factory, hence the creation of the Ford Sociological Department to administer the momentous 8-hour $5 a day deal in 1914 (Beynon 1975). Thirty investigators were recruited to ensure that Ford employees were not only punctual and performed their detailed work well, but also conformed to the non-work behaviour deemed appropriate by the company, including certain standards of cleanliness at home and avoidance of alcohol and gambling. In return for satisfying these work and non-work prescriptions, Ford offered the prospect of regular work for higher pay, initially only to men but extended to women in late 1916. In these and other ways, such as by encouraging adult male workers to buy houses, cars and life insurance, Ford can be seen as promoting the idea of full-time male workers as 'responsible heads of households' (Lewchuk 1995: 228). For the many immigrant workers among the Ford workforce, English language tuition was provided. Social provision also included a Ford hospital, Ford school, Ford shops selling cut-price goods, and a Ford newspaper (Doray 1988).

This kind of self-interested paternalism, or fraternalism according to Lewchuk (1995), was characteristic of nineteenth-century industrial capitalism, especially family-owned businesses, before the advent of state welfare (McIvor 2001), but Ford took it further in a less than benign direction. The Sociological Department was renamed the Service Department and expanded for an enhanced disciplinary role. Three and a half thousand private policemen were employed to discourage union activity, spy on employees at work and at home, and punish and reward them accordingly. Ford was vehemently anti-union as well as anti-drinking and gambling, and his zeal for control over his workers inside and outside work led to him being referred to as an 'industrial fascist' (Beynon 1975: 28). A more subtle version of his paternalist tradition was still in evidence at the beginning of the twenty-first century when Ford, in a deal arranged with the union, offered to give every employee a personal computer with internet access for $5 a month (Hammersley 2000). In a comment on the same article, Copps (2000) pointed out that this act of apparent generosity by Ford has several potential benefits for the employer: it opens up a new form of direct communication with employees when they are at home; it may increase loyalty to the company; and it could increase the computer skills of the workforce which in turn may enhance both production and sales.

As far as Ford's fundamental objection to trade unions is concerned, in 1941, after three decades of often bitter and sometimes extremely violent opposition, Ford was the last of the 'Big Three' American car makers, who between them supplied 90 per cent of the market during the 1930s, to concede the right of workers to join a trade union (Beynon 1975). This is somewhat ironic since one of the features of the fuller development of Fordism is the idea that it involved standardized settlements between labour and capital, organized centrally as part of a negotiated accommodation. This has been called the 'Fordist compromise' and this strand refers to the acceptance by unions and employers of the legitimacy of each other, including the understanding that productivity gains that accrue from the extreme rationalization of work will be shared (Lipietz 1992: 6).

The other main party to the Fordist compromise was the state, which provided a legal framework within which employers and employees negotiated, notably the right to join a union and therefore enjoy representation, and the provision of minimal income and welfare services. The term 'Fordist welfare state' has been used to describe the development of state welfare policies that are compatible with mass production and mass consumption (Lipietz 1994: 351). For example, in addition to ensuring the supply of healthy workers, the state adopted Keynesian monetary policies in an attempt to smooth out the booms and slumps of the business cycle, and introduced welfare benefits to enable those who are not in full-time employment to avail themselves, albeit at a reduced level, of the products of mass production (Jessop 1994).

As a result of these compromises, workers became integrated to the extent that they accepted the legitimacy of the hierarchical structures that play such a large part of their lives – the private company, the trade union, and the capitalist state. The sum total of this arrangement as it developed during the middle of the twentieth century in various industrial capitalist societies has been well expressed by Beck in the process of contrasting the Fordist model involving the standardization of work and life with the risk model involving the individualization of work and life:

... the Fordist growth regime ... did not only mean fixed times for holidays and other activities that underpinned and standardized life together in family, neighbourhood and community. It was also shaped and reinforced by a 'mode of regulation', which supported the growth machine culturally, politically and legally. This involved a wide range of strategies, actors and conditions which tied company management, banks, trade unions and political parties, as well as governments, to a relatively uniform philosophy of growth and a corresponding set of measures that held out a promise of success. The cultural-political targets of these measures were citizens in full-time employment, who had expectations of rising living standards and job security, while the main recipes were workforce participation, free collective bargaining, strong trade unions, government intervention and Keynesian macro-politics. ... The basic rule of Keynesianism was that rising demand would result in corporate investment and new jobs. Thus, under the conditions of Fordism ... rising consumption, public affluence and social security constituted the 'social cement' of the regime. (Beck 2000: 69)

In short, Fordism culminated not only in standardized production, standardized work and standardized employment, but also in standardized consumption, and standardized lifestyles, even standardized politics, often referred to as the post-war consensus.

According to this view, first advanced by Gramsci whilst in prison during the inter-war years (1971), ultimately Fordism involved much more than a new way of working. It involved a new way of life, or to be more precise, an American way of life characterized by increasing prosperity for all via mass production and mass consumption. Industrial capitalist societies in the rest of the world implemented Fordism slightly differently, hence the use of the term 'national Fordisms' to indicate the global reach of Fordism and the variations in its development beyond the USA, including 'blocked' (GB), 'hybrid' (Japan) and 'peripheral' (Brazil) Fordism (Peck and Tickell 1994: 285–7).

Thus the development of the Fordist compromise was the culmination of work trends discussed towards the end of the first chapter, namely the emergence of a dominant conception of work epitomized by the employment of full-time male workers. Fordism, in its broadest sense, therefore not only contributed to the creation of standardized production work, but, after much conflict, also promoted the creation of a standardized worker with a standard employment contract (Beck 1992). This relationship focused primarily on full-time, permanent male employment and the ensuing regulatory framework stabilized the bargain struck between capital and labour at work and outside work. This was especially the case in the car industry which was more male-dominated during the rise of Fordism than other assembly-line industries, such as food, clothing and electrical goods, in which the predominantly female workforce was not married (Glucksmann 1990).

As noted above with reference to the fraternalism of the 8-hour, $5 a day deal in 1914, prominent among the employment policies associated with Fordism from the beginning was that in addition to the class dimension of the compromise, an implicit gender compromise operated in which the continuously employed male worker was excused responsibility for domestic work whereas women were correspondingly restricted in the labour market due to their assumption of family obligations (Pfau-Effinger 1993). Although a large minority of women have worked full-time since the beginning of industrial capitalism, the rate remained relatively stable at approximately one-third between the 1950s and 1980s in Britain, suggesting that the prevailing Fordist norm was that permanent full-time work was a male prerogative (Crompton and Harris 1998; Hakim 1996). In the same way that there were national variations in the adoption of Fordist production methods, there were differences in the gender contracts, which varied from a strong, male breadwinner and female carer pattern in Japan and Germany, to a weaker or modified version in Sweden and the USA (Gottfried 2000).

The Fordist model of standardized mass production and the standardized male factory worker and female homemaker reached its peak in western industrial capitalist societies in the 1950s and 1960s, since when it has undergone a process of destabilization and decline. It is argued that by the mid-1970s, the post-1945 era of prosperity and social stability that was Fordism was in crisis.

The demise of Fordism as a system of mass production and consumption

There are a number of theories regarding the issue of what happened to Fordism (Amin 1994b). The two discussed here, the regulation approach and the flexible specialization approach, have been selected because they are among the most influential and connect to the topics discussed in the previous chapters, namely the historical development of industrial capitalism (Chapter 1), alienation (Chapter 2), and skill (Chapters 3 and 4).

Regulation theory was developed in France and claimed that, as a capitalist production system, Fordism is inherently alienating and inevitably involves deskilling. It is argued that the experience of alienating and deskilled work is likely to provoke a negative response from workers, no matter how well paid they are, and that discontented workers are not good news for productivity and hence profits. The theory of flexible specialization was developed in America and claimed that as a production system, Fordism is intrinsically inflexible in that it is unable to respond to variable demand, especially once mass markets have been saturated and consumers' tastes have changed in the direction of more individualized and higher-quality products. It is argued that this break-up of mass markets provided the opportunity to introduce more flexible workers and technologies, which leads to less alienating, more skilled work. The thrust of these approaches is that Fordism was becoming less profitable, which in turn stimulated changes in production methods (Amin 1994b).

More specifically, the regulationists argue that during the Fordist phase of the development of industrial capitalism the problem of alienated and deskilled work 'multiplied during the course of the 1960s' and that this was reflected in an increase in accidents, absenteeism, defective products, and conflict at work (Aglietta 1987 [1976]: 120). The increased scale of labour dissatisfaction contributed to declining productivity and higher costs of production, and therefore reduced profits, for example by constraining employers to devote extra time and resources to quality control. Thus the demise of Fordism was due primarily to 'a crisis of the labour process, which, because it dehumanizes the worker, ends up by not being efficient, even from the employer's point of view' (Lipietz 1992: 17). This economic crisis for labour and capital impacted on the ability of the state to fund the ensuing recession out of declining taxable income, thereby prompting cuts in welfare benefits, which compounded the problem as well as threatening the political dimension of the Fordist compromise.

Alternatively, the flexible specializationists argue that the dominance of mass production at the expense of craft production, since the first industrial divide during the nineteenth century, was coming to an end by the 1960s with the decline in the mass market for Fordist products and that this cultural change encouraged manufactures to 'radically modify, if not completely abandon' their Fordist principles (Sabel 1984: 201). This was in part attributed to market saturation, especially in America, where by 1970 the overwhelming majority of households had a range of such goods, including a car, television, radio, fridge, washing machine and vacuum cleaner, and in part due to the break-up of mass markets as consumers demanded a greater range of higher-quality products (Piore and Sabel 1984). In practical terms this involves moving from the inflexible production of standard products for mass markets to that of a diversity of products using more flexible forms of organization involving computer technology and multi-skilled labour, for the increasingly individualized pattern of consumption, and constitutes the beginning of the 'second industrial divide' (Piore and Sabel 1984: 252).

Although these arguments have different points of departure, they end up in the same place, namely that Fordism had reached the limits of its shelf life as a profitable system of mass production and consumption. The first approach starts from the supply-side and argues that Fordism is incapable of overcoming workers dissatisfaction, whereas the second starts from the demand-side and argues that Fordism is incapable of overcoming consumer dissatisfaction. Both approaches conclude that by the 1970s Fordism was in 'crisis' (Aglietta 1987 [1976]: 383; Piore and Sabel 1984: 252).

Both approaches to the crisis of Fordism have been criticized extensively. As far as regulation theory is concerned, it has been pointed out that the rise in labour disputes in the 1960s may not have been due simply to the nature of the Fordist labour process, but to other factors, such as the wider political and economic conditions prevailing at that time, and that the alleged progressive degradation of labour may be overcome, partially at least, 'by further automation and labour displacement' (Sayer 1989: 669; see also Sayer and Walker 1992). The theory of flexible specialization has been criticized on the grounds that replacement demand and new products compensate for market saturation and that the argument about the break-up of mass markets 'does not rest on any sound empirical basis' (Williams et al. 1987: 427; see also Williams et al. 1992). Of the two competing explanations of the demise of Fordism, the former, supply-side perspective seems to have more evidence to support it than the latter, the demand-side approach, not least because Fordism had been capable of a degree of product differentiation since the mid-1920s.

Notwithstanding these critical comments on the reasons for the crisis of Fordism, there is broad agreement that in the advanced industrial capitalist societies there was an emerging crisis in the Fordist way of organizing production during the 1960s. How Fordism changed in response to the crisis is the subject of the next chapter.

Summary and conclusions

The rise and development of Fordism during the twentieth century was responsible for the achievement of mass production and consumption in the industrial capitalist societies in which it grew and predominated. It marked a clear departure from the craft-based, non-standardized, low-volume production and consumption characteristic of pre-Fordism. Yet, from the outset it was a system that entailed social and economic, and ultimately political, disadvantages as well as the well-known advantages of mass production and consumption, and political stability. By virtue of its defining features, namely fragmented and simplified work, assembly-line production, and standardized parts and products, it became inextricably associated with deskilled work, conflict between labour and capital, and low-quality goods. In the process of stabilizing this problematic production system, it became synonymous with the standardization of work and workers characterized by regular work and contractual benefits, underpinned by a state welfare system, all of which culminated in the full-time male worker and the full-time female homemaker model.

Various theories have been advanced as to why this successful yet flawed production system experienced a crisis in the 1970s. Among the most influential are regulation theory, which attributed the crisis in Fordism to worker dissatisfaction, and flexible specialization theory, which attributed it to consumer dissatisfaction. There would seem to be more empirical support for the former explanation of the demise of Fordism than the latter. Whatever the merits and demerits of these views, there is broad agreement that there was a crisis of profitability and that an alternative to Fordism was needed.

Further reading

A good overview of 'Fordism and modern industry' can be found in the chapter of this title by Allen in Allen et al. (eds) (1992) *Political and Economic Forms of Modernity*. There are some excellent articles on the sociological, economic, geographical and political aspects of the debate about Fordism (as well as neo-Fordism and post-Fordism) in Amin (ed.) (1994a) *Post-Fordism: A Reader*. The key studies on the Fordist crisis include the first few chapters of Lipietz (1992) *Towards a New Economic Order: Postfordism, Ecology and Democracy* and Piore and Sabel (1984) *The Second Industrial Divide*.

Questions for discussion and assessment

1. What are the defining characteristics of Fordism and how do they differ from pre-Fordist ways of organizing production?
2. Assess the advantages and disadvantages of Fordism with reference to (a) workers, (b) employers, and (c) consumers.
3. In what ways was Fordism much more than just a new method of production?
4. Account for the demise of Fordism.

CHAPTER SIX

Solutions to the Crisis of Fordism

Neo-Fordism (McDonaldism) and Post-Fordism

Fordism and variants of it predominated for most of the twentieth century in industrial capitalist societies. Since this system of organizing production entered a crisis in the mid-1970s, there have been various attempts to transcend the difficulties associated with it, including automating production, internationalizing production, and re-organizing production (Wood 1992). The first often involves the use of industrial robots, 50 per cent of which are in car factories (Williams et al. 1987), which has the effect of displacing labour and reducing the amount of heavy and repetitive work for those who are retained. A second option is to relocate Fordist production in less developed countries where non-unionized, low-skilled and much cheaper labour is widely available, as was noted in the previous chapter with reference to 'peripheral Fordism' (Peck and Tickell 1994: 287). These options are not mutually exclusive, though the focus here will be on the third strategy, the re-organization of production, including services as well as manufacturing.

Among the many solutions adopted to solve the crisis in the Fordist organization of industrial production there are essentially two alternatives. The first is referred to as neo-Fordist or new Fordism since it is an adaptation of Fordism in that it continues to be informed by the original principles of Fordism. Neo-Fordism has been relatively neglected in discussions of what happened after the demise of Fordism. This is in marked contrast to the second solution to the fall of Fordism, namely post-Fordism or after Fordism, indicating that it involves a complete break with Fordism.

Neo-Fordist industrial work solutions will be discussed first, followed by neo-Fordist service work in fast-food restaurants (McDonaldism). Finally, post-Fordist solutions will be considered, including what is generally regarded as the 'best known contribution', namely flexible specialization (Sayer and Walker 1992: 191), and the most recent addition to the debate, the idea of a 'new informational paradigm of work and labour' that accompanies the rise of the network enterprise (Castells 2001: 256). There is considerable debate about the exact meaning of these key terms (Amin

1994b; Clarke 1992; Sayer 1989; Wood 1992), hence part of the purpose of this chapter is to attempt to outline schematically the main differences between neo-Fordism, McDonaldism and post-Fordism from the standpoint of the experience of production work.

Solutions to the crisis of Fordism: (1) Neo-Fordist industrial work

A neo-Fordist solution implies modifications to, rather than the complete abandonment of, the key elements of the Fordist production system that were discussed in the previous chapter. In the light of these points, neo-Fordism involves modifications to one or more of the following: (a) the fragmentation and simplification of work via Taylorized tasks, (b) managerial control over the pace of work via the moving assembly line, and (c) the standardization of parts and products via single-purpose machines. In this section, two alternatives to Fordist car manufacturing will be considered: the Swedish and Japanese models of production work, arguably the most innovative and the most influential respectively.

Swedish vehicle manufactures

Swedish vehicle manufacturers conducted some of the earliest and most notable experiments to modify the Fordist organization of production, a process that was started by Volvo at their Kalmar car plant in 1974 and culminated in a highly automated 'holistic assembly' system at the Uddevalla car plant in 1989 (Berggren 1993a: 238).

In terms of the three defining features of the Fordist organization of production, at Kalmar task fragmentation was addressed by using a computer-controlled assembly carrier that 'functions both as a transport device and assembly platform' and 'makes it possible to choose between various organizational forms in the planning of the assembly work' (Aguren et al. 1976: 9). Importantly, this included the preferred expedient of workers co-operating as a team, among whom a greater variety of tasks (job rotation) and/or extended tasks, such as taking more responsibility for quality (job enlargement), are distributed. Second, control over the pace of work at Kalmar was increased by dividing an assembly line either into sections, separated by buffers, in which dock assembly takes place, or mini-lines, also separated by buffers, based on the aforementioned assembly carrier technology. In each case the assembly carrier allows teams of workers to work on stationary cars that can be tilted to make assembly work less awkward for the operative, and allows them to vary the speed at which they work, including the possibility of working ahead to gain time that can be used for additional work breaks. Third, at Kalmar the destandardization of parts and products was achieved by the same 'flexible carrier system' which 'makes it easier to rearrange production – for example, during a model change' (Aguren et al. 1976: 16).

As implied by the references to the new assembly carrier technology, introduced by Volvo as part of their ongoing experiments in alternatives to conventional assembly lines, these modifications to Fordist car production often occurred together (Berggren 1992). In other words, by redesigning a car factory to enable workers to operate as teams, tasks can be rotated and enlarged quantitatively to extend the work cycle and qualitatively to increase responsibility for quality and control over the pace of work. Moreover, these new ways of organizing work can be adjusted more easily when modified or new models are introduced.

An evaluation of the early Volvo experiments has shown that 'the work itself is still divided among different work stations, more or less in the traditional manner' and Taylorist time and motion studies were still used to establish the time allowed to complete a task (Aguren et al. 1976: 19). Although the workers expressed satisfaction about teamwork, job rotation, and the opportunity to influence the way they worked, the majority of assembly workers thought that their influence was either small (50 per cent) or non-existent (25 per cent). The researchers concluded that the type of production system implemented at the Volvo Kalmar plant contained a 'definite framework for how and where work can be done ... and how long the work is to take', planned by management with the assistance of time and motion experts and controlled by management with the help of a central computer (Aguren et al. 1976: 25). Thus, at best, the work teams experienced 'controlled autonomy' to make decisions and minimal freedom to control the pace of the work (Coriat 1980: 36). Another review of the Swedish experiments concluded that the re-organization of production that followed this technological innovation was so limited that it was called 'flexible Taylorism' (Berggren 1992: 201).

These attempts to re-organize production by Volvo overcame some of the problems of Fordism to the extent that they improved working conditions, increased job satisfaction, decentralized quality control, raised the quality of work, reduced absenteeism and labour turnover, and achieved assembly times that were the same as those for a conventional assembly line. In relation to the earlier analyses of alienation and skill, by modifying Fordism, work on the more flexible assembly lines at Volvo was possibly less alienating and involved a wider range of skills, including some responsibility. However, research assessments of these experiments have shown that they were still essentially neo-Fordist since task fragmentation had been ameliorated rather than reversed, and worker control was constrained by managerial responsibility for the order, how long, and with what tools, tasks were accomplished, although the production lines were less rigid (Aguren et al. 1976; Berggren 1992). Thus attempts at Volvo to re-organize production humanized it to a small degree but did not constitute a radical break with Fordism. The assembly-line innovations at Kalmar appeared more revolutionary than they actually were and once the economic conditions changed from expanding demand and labour shortages in the 1970s, to declining demand and labour surpluses in the early 1980s, 'intensive rationalization measures were carried out at Kalmar' and the plant reverted to a traditional assembly line (Berggren 1992: 183). Similarly, the Uddevalla plant, 'conceived as a "noble experiment in humanistic manufacturing"' was at a disadvantage during a recession (Berggren 1993a: 239).

Japanese vehicle manufacturers

Japanese vehicle manufacturers developed the other famous solution to the Fordist organization of production and they overtook American companies as the leading car makers in the world in terms of volume and, most importantly, productivity by the 1980s (Cusumano 1985). The success of the Japanese car companies was based on their ability to motivate a co-operative workforce to mass produce cars to a higher quality and at a lower cost than their American and European competitors, thereby overcoming two of the inherent problems of Fordist production, namely worker dissatisfaction and poor quality (Dohse et al. 1985). This provoked international interest in their methods of production and a reverse of the pattern earlier in the century when foreign car makers visited American car plants. In the 1980s US and European car companies sent executives to Japan in an effort to understand the reasons for their success (Elger and Smith 1994). Diffusion of Japanese production methods was furthered by the establishment of transplant factories in the west by Japanese car manufacturers during the 1980s and by joint ventures, for example, between General Motors and Toyota in America, and Rover and Honda in Britain (Cusumano 1985; Oliver and Wilkinson 1997). Ironically, many of the ideas about how to organize production exported by Japan originated in America, for example quality control, but were adopted so successfully by Japanese companies that they became known as the Japanese model and were re-imported back into America under the pressure of competition (Jürgens 1992). The multi-directional international diffusion of new ideas about how best to organize production has continued in the form of the 'westernization' of Honda transplants in North America and Europe (Mair 1994: 323).

Thus, the Japanese way of organizing production has many variants historically and geographically, hence there is no one Japanese model, yet within this diversity there are some sufficiently distinctive elements to justify the use of the term 'Japanization'. Accounts of Japanese production innovations suggest that the main interconnected features of Japanization are the Just-in-Time production system, total quality control, and teamworking (e.g., Cusumano 1985; Elger and Smith 1994; Oliver and Wilkinson 1997; Sayer and Walker 1992). The issue is whether or not the innovations associated with Japanese car manufacturers amount to a new way of organizing production, namely one that is post-Fordist, or is a modified version of Fordism (i.e., neo-Fordist)?

The development of Just-in-Time (hereafter JIT) method of production is credited to Toyota and refers to the supply of materials, parts and subassemblies for final assembly when they are 'needed, "just-in-time" for their operation', rather than in advance (Cusumano 1985: 265). Sometimes JIT is also known as the 'pull method' since it is demand-driven, as opposed to a Fordist 'push method' which is a supply-driven production system (Ohno 1988: xvii). This way of organizing production reduces the size of buffer stocks and requires the use of a *kanban* (or tag) to ensure that each part is available when and where needed, thereby ensuring the continuous flow of production which saves on materials, space, conveyors, stock inventories and labour – in other words, lean production (Womack et al. 1990). For this system to work smoothly it is essential that components are produced and delivered defect-free 'in lots as small as possible' (Cusumano 1985: 265). Imperfect parts would disrupt production which is wasteful and therefore costly, hence the need for workers to check for mistakes when they receive the part they need. Small batches of components require reduced set-up times to be economical, which is achieved 'simply by standardizing all dies and using rollers or carts to move dies and other fixtures', plus '[m]echanizing part of the set-up process, such as adjustments of the height of the machinery' (Cusumano 1985: 287). The JIT system is flexible in terms of its ability to vary the range and quantity of models produced (product flexibility) and in terms of its ability to vary the number of workers (numerical flexibility) and the tasks they undertake (functional flexibility), all of which requires the co-operation of employees.

An effective, defect-free JIT system places a premium on quality control and is so integral to it that it is also referred to as Just-in-Time/Total Quality Control (e.g., Schonberger 1982). The need to ensure that all materials, parts and so on arrive when needed in perfect condition alters the training and role of the production worker. Quality control training programmes were introduced and lasted longer than comparable American or European sessions to enable workers to identify defects and correct them, and 'responsibility for maintaining quality' was shifted from specialist staff, such as inspectors, to shopfloor workers (Cusumano 1985: 321). In practical terms this means that workers have to be multi-skilled and adaptable or flexible – namely, they undertake a variety of tasks (job rotation) and use their discretion (job enlargement). To encourage a company-wide culture of quality control, Japanese car makers instituted quality control circles in which work groups meet to study quality issues and make suggestions. It has been claimed that between 1974 and 1984 quality circles saved Nissan $160 million or about $5,000 per circle (Cusumano 1985). Quality circles also benefited the company since they boosted 'morale by allowing employees to work in groups to solve problems' (Cusumano 1985: 334). Cusumano has further suggested that worker co-operation in implementing innovations in production, including transferring responsibility for quality control from staff to the production line, was made easier by the 'absence in Japan, after the mid-1950s, of powerful industrial unions' (1985: 33; see also Ohno 1988). Some commentators have suggested that the emphasis on zero defects is informed by the idea of continuous improvement of the production process or *kaizen* (e.g., Oliver and Wilkinson 1997; Williams et al. 1994). When *kaizen* is translated into work practices it involves workers as well as managers seeking to improve working methods and arguably empowers workers and reunites mental work with manual work.

Finally, the concept of teamwork is associated indelibly with the Japanese production model outside Japan, so much so that Oliver and Wilkinson have declared that it is 'a central characteristic of Japanese work organization' (1997: 39). Thus Ohno, the architect of the Toyota JIT system, has noted that 'Just-in-Time is the teamwork involved in reaching an agreed-upon objective' (1988: 7). Although this concept does not appear in the index of Cusumano's book on the development of Nissan and Toyota, as will become apparent below, it is implicit in his account, especially with reference to the 'weakened distinction between management and labour', and in his analysis of quality circles (1985: 171). Following from this and the discussion of the Swedish and Japanese conceptions of teamwork by Berggren (1992), there are two interrelated senses in which the term 'teamwork' is used in the Japanese organization of production. The first refers to a company culture that emphasizes co-operation between management and workers, namely a 'we' culture instead of a 'them and us' culture. For instance, at Nissan an attempt was made to 'publicize and strengthen their philosophy of cooperation rather than confrontation by establishing … the Association for Research on Modern Management–Labour Relations' (Cusumano 1985: 171). The second refers to the organization of work teams who are expected to co-operate when participating in quality circles. For example, the introduction of quality circles involving foremen and shopfloor workers at Nissan and Toyota continued the tradition of study groups that was 'common in Japanese schools' (Cusumano 1985: 334). Both forms of teamwork evoke egalitarianism and are part of the rhetoric of a managerial discourse that encourages all employees to identify with the company and its goals, thereby blurring social divisions within the workforce (Gottfried and Graham 1993).

In terms of the three key features of Fordism that have been the focus of this account of the Fordist organization of production and beyond (i.e., task fragmentation, control over the assembly line, and the standardization of parts and products), although the Taylorist fragmentation of tasks has been modified in the Japanese model to the extent that workers are trained to undertake a variety of tasks, are given responsibility for ensuring quality, and are expected to suggest ways of improving the production process, the essence of Taylorism was not only retained but applied more thoroughly. For example, at Toyota, time and motion studies were used to revise 'standard operation sheets to make it easier for unskilled workers', and to 'redistribute worker motions and cycle times to eliminate idle time … for machines or workers' (Cusumano 1985: 272). Also, standard job cycle times were varied according to the requirements of production so that during a period of slack demand line speeds and workers were reduced, whereas when demand was strong line speeds and workers were increased. Thus work intensification, or workers working fast to precise standards, was the norm whatever the circumstances.

Research on Japanese transplants has shown that the rhetoric of job enlargement, job rotation and multi-skilling tends to obscure the extent of 'rotating easily learned, repetitive jobs', hence the term 'multi-tasking' rather than multi-skilling (Rinehart et al. 1994: 171; Rinehart et al. 1997). This suggests that job rotation and enlargement 'are simply the ultimate extensions of the principles of Fordism and Taylorism' (Aglietta 1987 [1976]: 128; see also Palloix 1976). Reservations have also been expressed about the reunification of mental and manual labour since workers have always used their brains as well as physical capabilities, typically to make their work easier, and that under a Japanese production system the appropriation of a worker's knowledge via quality circles is more about cutting costs and raising productivity than work humanization (Graham 1995; Rinehart et al. 1994). This has led to the view that 'the Japanese out-Taylor us all – including putting Taylor to good use in QC circles or small group improvement activities' (Schonberger 1982: 193). This is acknowledged by Ohno, who has noted that Taylorism in the form of industrial engineering (or IE) 'is a system and the Toyota production system may be regarded as Toyota-style IE' (1988: 71). Thus, the Japanese model is 'neo-Taylorist' and therefore neo-Fordist in the sense that it is a more developed form of work rationalization (Garrahan and Stewart 1992: 90; see also Dohse et al. 1985).

The second key feature of Fordist production concerns control over the pace of the assembly line, and, as implied in the above paragraph, in Japanese plants management adjust the speed of the line as they see fit (Schonberger 1982). Unlike the Swedish experiments, the Japanese model does not deviate from the conventional Fordist assembly line. Consequently, the experience of work on the line remains the same, or worse, than before. This is because the continual search to eliminate waste in the form of idle machines and idle labour (for instance, by the flexible deployment of labour at the discretion of management, involving one worker operating many machines) ensures that the pace of assembly-line work is relentless. An autobiographical account of working on the Toyota assembly line revealed that it achieves worker flexibility but at the cost of greater work intensity due to faster line speeds, extra tasks, and compulsory overtime, all of which can lead to tiredness and accidents, even fatalities (Kamata 1984).

Studies of Japanese transplants in Britain and North America have confirmed the oppressive character of work on an assembly line. Research at the Nissan plant in England concluded that 'the new, integrated (JIT) production cycles do not present an unambiguously different experience of assembly line work' (Garrahan and Stewart 1992: 128). This study also showed that the Nissan production system did not lead to upskilling or an improvement in the quality of the work experience, although it did emphasize the importance of quality work. Similarly, at a Canadian transplant, quality was a priority yet typically combined increasing line speeds with shorter job cycles, with a 'high incidence of work-related injuries' (Rinehart et al. 1997: 80). This study also noted that though teamwork limits the isolation of workers, it generates peer pressure to keep up with the pace of the line, which remains 'the heart of production. The logic and pace of the line set the tone and tempo of work for the entire plant' (1997: 201–2). Instructively, at one North American car plant before Japanization, workers were kept busy 45 out of 60 seconds; after Japanization they were busy 57 seconds of every minute (Rinehart 2001). Finally, a Canadian study of Japanization found little evidence that workers were empowered, as Table 6.1 shows (Lewchuk and Robertson 1997). Unsurprisingly, the Japanization of transplants has been termed 'management by stress' (Parker and Slaughter 1990). Thus from a worker's perspective, the Japanese system seems to increase the intensity of the assembly line, and is therefore clearly neo-Fordist.

Third, the destandardization of parts and products was achieved in Japanese production systems by an attempt to 'avoid the use of dedicated facilities and equipment', and by making every effort 'to put together specialized, yet versatile production processes through the use of machines and jigs that can handle minimal quantities of materials' (Ohno 1988: 40). In order to be able to respond to the demand for a variety of products, and avoid 'undermining the benefits of mass production', some

Table 6.1 Workers responding that it was difficult to find a relief worker so they could leave their workstation to attend to personal matters such as going to the toilet (%)

Lean plants	All direct production*	Male direct production*	Female direct production*
General Motors	62.10	62.78	57.32
Chrysler	64.50	63.10	70.37
Ford	57.56	56.95	71.43
CAMI (GM/Suzuki)	63.53	62.12	66.67
Total	62.40	61.99	65.32

*Mostly assembly-line workers

Source: Adapted from Lewchuk and Robertson (1997: 53)

standardization of parts as well as worker operations was retained, and most importantly set-up times were reduced markedly, from two to three hours in the 1940s to three minutes in the late 1960s (Ohno 1988: 40). In effect, the Japanese system typically involves the flexible production of a large number of small lots rather than the inflexible production of a small number of large lots. In this respect the Japanese model of flexible production contrasts with the Ford system of 'planned mass production' (Ohno 1988: 37). Yet, the Japanese system is still a mass production one in that it is not averse to using 'simple inflexible machines' where appropriate. Hence the term 'flexible mass production' has been used to describe the Honda transplants in America that are 'close copies of their Japanese sister factories' (Mair 1994: 208, 214). However, of the three key features of Fordism under review, this dimension of Japanese manufacturing success is arguably the one that is most distinctive, especially in relation to its ability to respond quickly to diversified demand. Ironically, this aspect of the Japanese production system was pioneered by General Motors in the 1920s, who 'built a degree of variety into mass production', although this strategy arguably involved more superficial variations than those achieved by contemporary Japanese and western car makers with their great variety of models, engine sizes, options, and ability to supply a car to a customer's specification (Elam 1994: 56).

This assessment of the three key features of Fordism suggests that the Japanese production model is more of a development of, rather than a radical departure from, Fordism. Consequently, for the majority of production workers, it has not solved the twin problems of alienation and deskilled work inextricably linked to Fordism (Rinehart 2001). First, the Japanese model is characterized by restricted numerical and functional flexibility in relation to production tasks, notwithstanding the pervasiveness of a company ideology that stresses equality and harmony. Second, it is characterized by a more flexible use of the assembly line, whilst increasing the intensity of work. Third, it is characterized by the use of more flexible machinery, faster set-up times, and greater responsiveness to the diversification of consumer demand. Hence, in contrast to Fordism, Japanization involves 'flexibility of a limited kind' in terms of both numerical and functional flexibility, but greater flexibility in terms of products, yet, as noted above, even here there are echoes of Fordism since American car makers had been concerned about product variation since the 1920s. Thus, contrary to those who claim that the Japanese model is more post-Fordist than neo-Fordist, notably Kenney and Florida (1988), whose argument tends to overlook the impact of lean production on workers, Womack et al. (1990), who provide no relevant empirical evidence (Berggren 1993b), and Graham, who has also conceded that it 'incorporates Taylorism' (1995: 3), the limited flexibility and increased intensification of work under a Japanese production system disqualifies it as an unambiguous exemplar of post-Fordism (Tomaney 1994).

The successful implementation of the Japanese model depends in large part upon a compliant workforce which lacks independent trade union representation and hence tends to co-operate with management over a range of production rationalizations, including assigning one worker to more than one machine and assembly-line speed-ups. Japanese car makers prefer employees to belong to a company union or to a union that has been marginalized by the company, and favour transplant locations that lack a tradition of trade unionism. This is a consistent theme in the Japanization literature dating from accounts of Japanese production (e.g., Cusumano 1985), to studies of Japanese transplants (e.g., Garrahan and Stewart 1992), and even by those who claim that it is post-Fordist (e.g., Kenney and Florida 1988). This has lead to most analysts taking the view that Japanization 'is simply the practice of the organizational principles of Fordism under conditions in which management prerogatives are largely unlimited' (Dohse et al. 1985: 141). In this respect, Japanization is identical to early Fordism in its opposition to trade unions and, like the original, has found that attempts to neutralize union activity does not guarantee conflict-free industrial relations (Maguire 2003; Rinehart et al. 1997).

Thus the continuities between both the Swedish and Japanese attempts to re-organize production and Fordism are extensive, particularly in the case of the Japanese model with its emphasis on lean production and which also involves a system of industrial relations that is predicated upon a diminished role for independent trade unions. This suggests that they constitute neo-Fordist solutions to the crisis of Fordism rather than post-Fordist ones, notwithstanding the teamwork rhetoric and emphasis on quality and product variation.

Solutions to the crisis of Fordism: (2) Neo-Fordist service work (McDonaldism)

It was noted in Chapter 4 on upskilling, with reference to Bell's post-industrial society theory, that more people are employed in the service sector of advanced industrial capitalist societies than in any other. Yet, aside from some notable exceptions, sociologists of work, particularly those concerned with flexible specialization and/or post-Fordism, have continued to focus more on the increasingly shrinking number of factory workers than on the ever expanding number of service workers. Among the exceptions are studies of what have been called 'interactive service work', such as working in a fast-food restaurant (Leidner 1996: 29). The purpose of this section is to consider the nature of such work from the standpoint of Fordism and neo-Fordism.

The 'fast-food factory' is characterized by speedy service from a limited menu and was developed by McDonald's in the early 1950s (Love 1995: 20). The success of this form of highly rationalized food production was imitated by other restaurant chains in America and the same organizational model was adopted in virtually every part of the service sector, including education, health and leisure (Ritzer 1996, 1998).

The Fordist character of McDonald's and other fast-food restaurants is unmistakable since they are 'based on speed, lower prices, and volume' and therefore conform to the three key features of Fordism discussed throughout this chapter (Dick McDonald, quoted in Love 1995: 14). That is to say McDondalism involves (a) fragmented work tasks, (b) assembly-line production, and (c) standardized parts and products. Moreover, work routines, including worker–customer interaction, are standardized to an extreme degree and training for the low-skill tasks is minimal. For example, the heavily scripted interaction is conducive to 'pseudo interactions' involving fake sincerity (Ritzer 1996: 82). Second, production and consumption are based on the assembly-line system with each part of the product being assembled by workers in an automatically set time before being passed on to the next worker over the shortest distance possible. Furthermore, '[e]ven customers must face a kind of assembly line, the drive-through window being the most obvious example' (Ritzer 1996: 26). Third, 'rigid technologies' are used to produce a narrow range of identical products so that whenever and wherever a McDonald's burger is purchased it would be the same in every respect (Ritzer 1996: 152). Fast-food restaurants are therefore excessively Fordist in that the production of the standardized output is organized with a precision that is measured in seconds, degrees and ounces, all designed to fill orders as fast as technologically and humanly possible. The degree of detail specified by McDonald's is Taylorist in the extreme – 'workers are instructed in the precise arm motion to use when salting a batch of fries' (Leidner 2002: 17). Thus in the same way that Fordism dehumanized factory work and democratized car ownership, it has also dehumanized service work and democratized eating out.

However, there are some important differences between interactive service work and Fordist assembly-line work in a car factory. First, the presence of customers in the work process creates a 'three-way dynamic of control' which produces a less stable and less predictable situation than the simpler worker and management dynamic typical of industrial work (Leidner 1996: 38). Leidner's research showed that in response to this situation McDonald's attempted to control the behaviour of both employees and non-employees. For example, employees' appearance and interaction with customers was standardized by the compulsory wearing of uniforms and company rules covering everything from fingernail length to emotions, and scripted sentences, although some monitored variation was allowed 'to avoid sounding like robots' (Leidner 1996: 33). As far as the customers are concerned, McDonald's had 'trained' them via advertising and restaurant design so successfully that virtually all the customers studied by Leidner conformed to the behaviour expected of them (1996: 36). Consequently, they did not sit at a table and wait to be served, but queued, ordered their meals in the required sequence, and cleared away the waste. These attempts by management to control employees and non-employees are not always successful. For instance, McDonald's window workers are required to engage in suggestive selling, and when this caused irritation to customers they tend to resolve the situation by siding with the customer. Generally, though, McDonald's workers' ability to resist managerial control was reduced by the involvement of customers in the work process since customers shared many interests with management, notably for quick and polite service, and employees were in a subordinate position to both managers and customers (Leidner 1996). Although Leidner refers to the cultural dimension of interactive service work at McDonald's, overall his account suggests that they are essentially Fordist in terms of the organization of unskilled, repetitive manual work and the volume production of a limited range of standardized products.

Conversely it has been argued that interactive service work is different from industrial work because 'part of what is consumed is the quality of the social interaction' (Urry 1990: 273). Allen and du Gay develop this point by suggesting that service work cannot be understood 'within the discourse of manufacturing, even when many of its constituent elements have been subject to standardization and routinization' (1994: 267). They suggest that the inclusion of social skills, such as communication and presentation, renders interactive service work a 'hybrid' occupation (Allen and du Gay 1994: 266). This interpretation implies that, notwithstanding the excessive rationalization of interactive service work, it involves a semblance of multiskilling and upskilling and is therefore not entirely Fordist but has post-Fordist features. However, this argument is somewhat undermined by research which shows that the inauthenticity of interactive service work can lead to depression (Erickson and Wharton 1997).

A second difference between Fordism and McDonaldism concerns the recent policy to offer increased choice and quality at 'affordable' prices on a mass basis, termed 'mass customization' (Pine 1993: 44). The achievement of what would appear to be a contradictory combination was made possible by advances in both technology and management, namely the 'two Japanese systems: the adaptable marketing system (AMS) and the flexible manufacturing system (FMA)' (Taylor et al. 1998: 109). These innovations enabled fast-food restaurants to move beyond their Fordist origins and respond quickly to the demand for a greater variety of products. For example, the recent fragmentation of mass markets led McDonald's to expand their menu to include eggs, fish and chicken, albeit in a standardized form (Taylor et al. 1998). Thus the essentially Fordist fast-food business has been modified in a manner comparable to the neo-Fordist Japanization of car production in order to be able to meet the new market conditions.

The third difference between Fordism and McDonaldism is the attempt to organize work on a team basis, as implied by the use of the term 'crew' to refer to kitchen staff. Hence, in addition to an emphasis on social skills, training courses at McDonald's

Hamburger University include one on team-building (Love 1995). The production and consumption of fast food is organized with military precision using a well drilled team with no previous experience of working in a restaurant or knowledge of cooking, but are trained in the detailed operating procedures that define '*the* successful method' to produce a milk shake, hamburger and french fries (Love 1995: 141). Although crew members are trained to do a variety of tasks, job rotation is often limited because it is a potential threat to efficiency. Yet teamwork is crucial due to the tendency to minimize both staffing and idle time, much the same as in Japanese car plants. Once again, Fordist elements, notably the standardization of work and a high labour turnover (Royle and Towers 2002), are combined with neo-Fordist ones such as teamwork and multi-tasking.

Ritzer rejected the view that McDonaldism is post-Fordist and emphasized its continuities with Fordism. He concluded: 'Fordism is alive and well in the modern world, although it has been transformed into McDonaldism' (1996: 152). Yet there is evidence of the intrusion of neo-Fordist features into the organization of work of fast-food restaurants. This is clear in the case of multi-tasking associated with social as well as production skills, increased quality and variety of products, and teamwork. To this extent interactive service work is not just a hybrid occupation, fast-food restaurants are hybrid work organizations in that they are a mixture of both Fordism and neo-Fordism, though still predominantly Fordist given the limitations of the neo-Fordist elements.

Solutions to the crisis of Fordism: (3) Post-Fordist work

As indicated earlier in this chapter, two developments beyond Fordism will be considered here: post-Fordist flexible specialization and the network enterprise thesis.

Flexible specialization

Flexible specialization (FS), as advanced by Piore and Sabel, was mentioned above in the context of the crisis of Fordism. Here the focus is on what is alleged to have replaced it. This theory is based on the distinction between two models of industrial production or 'industrial divides' – mass production and FS (Piore and Sabel 1984: 5). The former emerged at the beginning of the twentieth century and involved the use of special-purpose machines and deskilled labour to mass produce standardized goods. Mass production and consumption dominated for most of the last century when, as discussed in the previous chapter, this Fordist system experienced a crisis and declined. Piore and Sabel's 'speculative' thesis is that one way out of this crisis was to implement a new system of production, namely FS, based on the use of flexible machinery and skilled labour to produce a range of high-quality customized products (1984: 258). This solution involves the resurgence of craft methods via the 'fusion of traditional skills and high technology', and promises a 'revitalized' worker, production system, and economy (Piore and Sabel 1984: 279). In other words, skilled workers using computer technology can adjust production relatively easily, quickly and cheaply in response to changes in demand for specialist goods, thereby reversing the Fordist pattern of deskilled workers producing standard products on a mass scale.

The *locus classicus* of FS is the 'Third Italy', found in the centre and north-east, to distinguish it from the First Italy, which was characterized by the mass-production industries in the north, and the Second Italy, characterized by peasant small-holders in the south (Piore and Sabel 1984: 266). In this 'high-technology cottage industry', skilled workers operate the 'most advanced numerically controlled equipment of its type' in workshops which design the products for niche markets all over the world (Sabel 1984: 220). This case of FS is unambiguously post-Fordist in terms of the three key features of Fordism discussed throughout this chapter. Thus instead of task fragmentation and simplification there is unity of conception and execution, instead of repetitive work on an assembly line there is collaboration among flexible, multi-skilled workers to create a whole product, and instead of standardized parts and products there are destandardized parts and customized products. FS involves the renaissance of craft work combined with advanced computer technology which results in a reversal of the Fordist tendency for the worker to be subordinated to machinery.

From the standpoint of the sociology of work, several difficulties with the theory of FS have been noted. First, it has been argued that the fundamental distinction between Fordist mass production and post-Fordist FS is 'unworkable because empirical instances cannot be identified' (Williams et al. 1987: 438). Thus, it may be conceptually neat, but it is not so easy to place a factory unambiguously in one of the two categories. For example, mass production typically involves a mixture of dedicated and general purpose equipment, and product differentiation occurs in both mass-production and FS systems. Moreover, the introduction of FS does not guarantee increased skills or job satisfaction (Wood 1992). These points raise doubts about the viability of the binary divide that it at the heart of the theory of FS.

Second, it has been suggested that Piore and Sabel exaggerate the extent of FS in the 'Third Italy' by playing down the persistence of companies organized along more Fordist lines (Murray 1987). Furthermore, even within the 'artisan sector', not all the workers are performing 'post-Fordist craft labour' but semi-skilled assembly work and heavy manual work (Murray 1987: 88). The contradictory nature of FS has also been noted by Harrison (1997), who has shown that low-skill, low-wage workers support high-skill, high-wage workers in the Italian industrial districts. A similar pattern of unevenness is apparent in the UK where one study found that there was 'little evidence of the growth of multiskilled teamworking or craft-based flexible specialization' (Elger 1991: 63). Post-Fordist FS would seem to be less of a trend and more of a restricted regional tendency than its supporters imply.

Third, and following from the above point, it has been contended that Piore and Sabel's account of FS is gender biased in the sense that 'if flexible specialization is accepted in a gender-blind way it will reinforce and even strengthen unequal gender relations' (Jenson 1992: 155). In view of the feminist critiques of Blauner's 1960s alienation thesis and Braverman's 1970s deskilling thesis, to overlook the gender dimension whilst advancing a new theory of production in the 1980s is a major omission by Piore and Sabel.

These criticisms of FS suggest that it is not as widespread as Piore and Sabel claim and that even where it has emerged, not all workers enjoy upskilled work or have more control (Vallas 1999). Thus this FS theory would seem to be an overly optimistic account of recent developments in the organization of production work.

The network enterprise thesis

The network enterprise thesis (NET) by Castells is the latest contribution to the debate about the transformation of work. Although the NET thesis is within the tradition of post-industrial society theory, contrary to Bell, Castells argues that it is not the theoretical character of knowledge that is crucial, since it is important in all societies, but the 'technology of knowledge generation, information processing, and symbolic communication' (2001: 17). For Castells, this heralds a new type of society, a network society based on 'improving the technology of information processing as a source of productivity' (2001: 17). The network society contrasts with an industrial society whose source of increased productivity was, as noted in Chapter 1, the use of new forms of energy. A network society has three key elements: it is informational, global and networked. That is to say, it is characterized by the production of knowledge and information on a global scale in which the business model is the network enterprise 'made up from firms or segments of firms, and/or from internal segmentation of firms' (Castells 2000: 10).

According to Castells: 'We have entered *a new technological paradigm*, centred around micro-electronics-based, information/communication technologies', the distinctive feature of which is maximum flexibility of production (2000: 9, italics in the original). In order to transcend the crisis of Fordism and succeed in the ever-changing competitive environment of the global economy, flexibility is essential, especially technological capability and the organization of work. For example,

> to be able to assemble parts produced from very distant sources, it is necessary to have ... a micro-electronics-based precision quality in the fabrication, so that the parts are compatible with the smallest detail of specification; and ... a computer-based flexibility enabling the factory to program production runs according to the volume and customized character required. (Castells 2001: 123)

Second, the vertical bureaucracy associated with Fordism is superseded by the horizontal corporation characterized by 'organization around process, not task; a flat hierarchy; team management; measuring performance by customer satisfaction; rewards based on team performance; maximization of contacts with suppliers and customers; information, training, and retraining of employees' (Castells 2001: 176).

Third, Castells subscribes to the upgrading and polarization thesis discussed in Chapter 4 on the grounds of actual and projected evidence from the USA between 1990 and 2005 which shows that 'there are simultaneous increases at the top and bottom of the social ladder, although the increase at the top is of greater magnitude' (2001: 241).

But the skill issue is of declining significance in the informational society since both highly skilled and unskilled workers are subject to the flexibilization of work.

Fourth, a 'new model of flexible work, and a new type of worker: the flex-timer' becomes the 'predominant form of working arrangements' in the network society (Castells 2001: 281, 2000: 11). The new flexible employment arrangements include part-timers, temporary workers, self-employment, contract workers, and informal and semi-formal workers. Castells claims that these types of non-standard employment are expanding at the expense of standard work in the most advanced sectors of the network society, such as Silicon Valley, and that the 'feminization of labour leads to the rise of the "flexible woman", gradually replacing the "organization man", as the harbinger of the new type of worker' (2000: 12).

To be able to benefit from all these flexibilities, Castells suggests that the corporation has to be transformed into a network enterprise, spelling the demise of individual (e.g., the entrepreneur) and collective (e.g., the corporation) units of capitalist economic activity. Castells notes that flexibility is not inevitable since the introduction of every kind of flexibility involves human decision, though he also suggests that 'current technological trends foster all forms of flexibility' which unhindered will 'evolve into multifaceted, generalized flexibility for workers and working conditions, both for highly skilled and unskilled workers' (2001: 295). Thus the network enterprise is totally flexible, with firms and their workers reaping the benefits of flexibility, 'epitomized' by the Californian company Cisco Systems (Castells 2001: 180). Even unemployment is viewed by Castells as a temporary problem since in this new type of society, more jobs of a superior kind are created than destroyed.

Aside from noting that Fordism is 'an historical relic' in developed societies but extensive in industrializing ones, Castells does not address in a detailed way the debate about what replaced Fordism (2001: 258). Yet there is little doubt that the network enterprise form of production is post-Fordist in all respects since it involves flexible multi-skilled workers, flexible production, and product flexibility.

A limitation of the NET is that generalizing from a model of work based largely on the possibly atypical experience of technologically advanced firms in California is problematic. Second, and following from the first point, Webster has questioned the claim that 'the Information Age represents an epochal break' with the past (2002: 121). Third, Castells discusses key issues such as teamwork without any detailed analysis. For instance, a lack of information about teamwork in network enterprises precludes any firm judgement about whether it approximates to the Japanese or Swedish models of teamwork, as outlined by Berggren (1993a). Research undertaken in what could be regarded as a nascent network society (Finland) addressed the issue of teamwork and produced mixed results in relation to Castells' NET (Blom and Melin 2003).

Summary and conclusions

Solutions to the crisis of Fordism include attempts to reform the organization of production, termed neo-Fordism, among the most prominent examples of which are the Swedish and Japanese strategies to ameliorate what were regarded as the most problematic features of Fordism, such as the monotony of repeating simplified tasks on an assembly line whose speed was controlled by management, and the limited range of relatively low-quality products, plus a focus on endless improvement to efficiency and product quality.

The Swedish experiments were arguably the more radical in that they involved assembling cars that were stationary by teams of workers assembling whole cars. However, the work teams only enjoyed limited autonomy and with the onset of a recession a more conventional moving assembly line was reinstated.

The Japanese method of organizing production, sometimes termed 'lean production' because it is based on the just-in-time rather than the just-in-case principle, has had a global impact. Studies of its development in Japan and diffusion to Europe and North America show that the rhetoric of multi-skilled flexible workers co-operating to continuously improve the quantity and quality of production is such a long way away from the actual experience of work in a lean production system that it is more accurately described as a mean system. In particular, researchers have documented heavy work loads, the rotation of relatively unskilled, repetitive tasks, and assembly-line speed-ups, all of which contribute to a highly stressful work environment, one that often lacks independent trade union representation.

Categorizing the Swedish and Japanese production systems as neo-Fordist does not mean that there are no important differences between them. For example, the Swedish version of teamwork focused on autonomy, whereas in the Japanese model it involved more managerial control (Berggren 1992). It is also important to bear in mind that some researchers consider the Swedish and Japanese production methods as examples of post-Fordism (e.g., Rubery and Grimshaw 2003).

In the case of service work, the emphasis on social skills and teamwork, the increased attention to quality and consumer choice, are considered by some to mitigate the Fordist features of McDonaldism, such as the fragmentation and simplification of assembly-line tasks. Conversely, and more convincingly, it has been argued that the centrality of the assembly line, the focus on the speed of production and consumption, and that not all service work involves interaction, and even jobs that require social skills, the repetition of standardized scripts engenders monotony. Thus, McDonaldism is unambiguously neo-Fordist.

More radical solutions to the crisis of Fordism which deviate markedly from the Fordist system of mass production and consumption, termed 'post-Fordism', include flexible specialization and network enterprises. Both of these solutions claim that a new type society based on flexible information technology is emerging. Moreover, they suggest that upskilling, not deskilling, will predominate in this new type of society. These optimistic accounts of work changes have been criticized for exaggerating the extent of flexible specialization and network enterprises, whilst underestimating the persistence of Fordist and neo-Fordist forms of production and consumption (Vallas 1999).

Table 6.2 attempts to summarize the main points raised in this chapter on neo-Fordism, McDonaldism, and post-Fordism. It shows that neo-Fordism and

Table 6.2   Key features of neo-Fordism (McDonaldism) and post-Fordism

Neo-Fordism (McDonaldism): type of production system characterized by:

1   Qualified Taylorized work tasks and organization (e.g., job rotation, teamworking)
2   Modified assembly-line production
3   Limited destandardization of parts and a wider range of higher-quality products/services

Post-Fordism: type of production system characterized by:

1   Flexible multi-skilled work and organization
2   Flexible micro-electronic computer technology
3   Flexible parts and high-quality, customized products/services

Note: These are ideal-typical categories, hence in practice it is likely that any one production system will be characterized by a mixture of features. For example, even under Fordism, product variation was not unknown.

McDonaldism may be considered expressions of reformed Fordism in that they are relatively more flexible but continue to exhibit continuities with Fordism, whereas post-Fordism is a totally flexible system that involves a clear break with Fordism. This pattern of development is associated with a wider range of better quality products with neo-Fordism and McDonaldism, and a diversity of high-quality products with post-Fordism. The fluidity and even development of different types of production system, not revealed in Table 6.2, suggests that diversity rather that uniformity is likely to characterize the globalized future.

Whilst there is widespread agreement that the dominance of Fordism, especially in the most advanced industrial capitalist societies, has come to an end, and with it the security of standard work, there is less agreement about what has replaced it. The relatively neglected concept of neo-Fordism constitutes an important theoretical possibility between Fordism and post-Fordism and the empirical evidence suggests that it is far more prevalent than advocates of post-Fordism admit. The development of both neo-Fordist and post-Fordist ways of organizing production, plus the growth of post-industrialism, involved a major restructuring of economic activity, all of which are associated with the expansion of unemployment and non-standard forms of work in advanced industrial capitalist societies following the demise of Fordism. The social consequences of unemployment and the nature and extent of the various kinds of non-standard work will be considered in the next two chapters, again mainly, but not exclusively, with reference to the UK and the USA.

Further reading

The literature on neo-Fordism is limited, even in the otherwise excellent collection of articles on various aspects of the complex debate about what came after Fordism, edited by Amin (1994a) *Post-Fordism: A Reader*. For material on the nature and impact of Japanization, see Elger and Smith (eds) (1994) *Global Japanization? The Transnational Transformation of the*

Labour Process. The equivalent book on the Swedish experiments is by Berggren (1993a) *The Volvo Experience: Alternatives to Lean Production in the Swedish Auto Industry.* Aside from Ritzer's many books on McDonaldization, notably the (1996) revised edition of *The McDonaldization of Society: An Investigation into the Changing Character of Contemporary Social Life,* there are fewer accounts of service work, as yet, though one of the more wide-ranging is MacDonald and Sirianni (eds) (1996) *Working in the Service Society.* Piore and Sabel's theory, *The Second Industrial Divide* (1984), is essential reading, as is the critique by Tomaney in the aforementioned book edited by Amin. A review and critique of Castells from an information society perspective is provided by Webster (2002) *Theories of the Information Society* (2nd edn).

Questions for discussion and assessment

1. Assess the view that the Swedish car production system is neo-Fordist.
2. Examine the claim that Japanization is more neo-Fordist than post-Fordist.
3. Do you agree that fast-food production and consumption is essentially neo-Fordist?
4. To what extent is flexible specialization post-Fordist?
5. Evaluate critically Castells' network enterprise thesis.

CHAPTER SEVEN

Unemployment (Out of Paid Work) and Underemployment (Short of Paid Work)

Prior to the advent of industrial capitalism, self-provisioning of an essentially subsistence kind was of primary importance and regular paid work was of secondary importance for the vast majority. Hence, 'there was no unemployment because there was no norm of work' (Beck 2000: 13). The revolutionary change inaugurated by industrial capitalism constituted a complete reversal of these priorities. In due course, as was noted in the first chapter, the dominance of wage labour resulted in work becoming synonymous with employment. In such a society, to be without regular full-time employment, namely unemployed, involved exclusion from the main form of work and therefore from an income necessary for economic survival since all other legal avenues to alternative sources of income had more or less vanished.

It is entirely logical and fitting that the first society to industrialize on a capitalistic basis, Britain, was the first in which the twin issues of unemployment and underemployment in a time-related sense were raised politically by radicals as early as the 1820s (Thompson 1970), and the first to introduce compulsory state insurance against unemployment in 1911 (Burnett 1994). In between, the issues of unemployment and underemployment were theorized by Marx and Engels in the 1840s – the reserve army of workers theory (Marx and Engels 1962 [1845]) – surveyed by Mayhew in the 1850s and Booth in the 1890s (Stedman Jones 1984), and were the subject of an academic conference organized by the Sociological Society and held at the London School of Economics in 1907 (Burnett 1994). The main lesson of these diverse contributions was that economic well-being in a market system was almost entirely dependent on avoiding unemployment and underemployment, that is to say total/partial unemployment.

However, the economic theory that informed government policy between 1910 and 1940 considered unemployment to be an unavoidable consequence of the business cycle (Ashton 1986). According to this view, there was little that a government could or should do except relieve the worst of its deleterious economic impact on the unemployed. Yet the political salience of mass unemployment often led governments to focus on the plight of the unemployed in a pragmatic way when faced with the threat of social unrest (McIvor 2001). In Britain, the government offered tax incentives to companies to locate factories in areas of high unemployment and adopted an assisted migration policy to encourage the unemployed to move from depressed to prosperous parts of the country (Burnett 1994). In the USA, in the aftermath of the stock market crash of 1929 and subsequent depression, in order to quieten political disorder, provide economic relief in the form of employment and inculcate the habit of work, an interventionist programme of public investment known as the New Deal was implemented (Piven and Cloward 1974). A generation after it was pioneered in Britain, unemployment insurance was introduced in the USA in 1935 (Ashton 1986).

In the light of these pragmatic policies, plus the experience of successful state regulation of labour during the Second World War, governments in Britain and the USA were eventually converted to the Keynesian idea that the state could do more than merely provide limited financial support, namely that it could create employment by attempting to influence the market via public investment (Ashton 1986). By the 1950s the ideal of full employment was adopted as a policy objective and realized to a large extent in industrial capitalist countries. This was the culmination of the state dimension of Fordism that was part of what was referred to in Chapter 5 as the Fordist compromise between the interests of employers and employees. Thus, under the Fordist model of mass production and consumption, state polices tried to ensure that demand for goods and services remained relatively stable, despite the vicissitudes of the market.

The crisis of Fordism in the 1970s provoked another change in policy as rapid increases in inflation and unemployment reduced support for state intervention and strengthened the argument that market forces should operate without interference from governments or trade unions (Ashton 1986). During the mass unemployment of the 1980s, the new orthodoxy was identical to that which had prevailed between 1910 and 1940, namely that unemployment was inevitable in a market society. The recrudescence of individualistic values and what were perceived as the twin virtues of free competition and minimal state intervention in the economy was complete when the Conservative governments of the 1980s abandoned the objective of full-employment and substituted the primary policy aim of controlling inflation (Edgell and Duke 1991). Governments in Britain and the USA have continued to follow essentially neo-liberal policies ever since, although opinions are divided on the inevitability of large-scale unemployment in the context of advancing technological change and increasing globalization; there are pessimists (e.g., Aronowitz and DiFazio 1994) and optimists (e.g., Castells 2001) regarding the scale of unemployment in the advanced economies this century.

From the standpoint of the unemployed, the two eras of mass unemployment in the twentieth century coincided with the dominance of the view that unemployment was a necessary consequence of a market economy and that the state should not intervene for fear of exacerbating the problem. Thus we find that during both depressions welfare benefits for the unemployed were cut (Edgell and Duke 1991). Two other factors informed public policy during these mass unemployment eras: that the state could not afford to fund such large numbers when its income was shrinking and that generous unemployment benefits might undermine the incentive to work (Ashton 1986). First, the cost argument is somewhat specious since fiscal prudence does not seem to apply to non-welfare state spending, such as defence (Edgell and Duke 1991). Second, there is little evidence to support the theory of benefit-induced unemployment (Eichengreen 1989). On a positive note, in terms of the sociology of unemployment, the two major unemployment eras of the twentieth century stimulated extensive research on this issue.

More recently, it has been argued that there has been an expansion of forms of work in between regular full-time employment (i.e., the Fordist model) and unemployment, namely different types of underemployment, sometimes referred to as destandardized work (Beck 1992) or non-standard work (Carré et al. 2000). Although underemployment was prevalent in nineteenth-century Britain and was the norm before the rise of industrial capitalism (Kumar 1988a, 1988b), its growth in the late twentieth century is now seen as part of the trend towards the increasing flexibility of labour (Beck 1992).

In the light of this contemporary social change in the patterning of work, this chapter will review the sociological significance of both unemployment and underemployment.

Unemployment: meaning and measurement

There are major difficulties in comparing changes in the scale of unemployment over time in any one country and between countries. The main reason for both is that nation states frequently alter the way unemployment is measured, often for essentially political motives. For example, between 1979 and 1989 Conservative governments in the UK changed the way unemployment was measured in official statistics 30 times and virtually every one had the effect of reducing the unemployment total (Edgell and Duke 1991). However, most governments increasingly measure unemployment using the International Labour Organization's (ILO), a specialist UN Agency, definition of unemployment, or one that is similar to it, which enhances the consistency of cross-national comparisons over time. The ILO classifies people as unemployed if they are (a) without a job, (b) actively seeking employment, and (c) available for work. This is a less restrictive definition than the one also used by the current UK government that involves only counting those who are (a) jobless, (b) registered as unemployed, and (c) in receipt of unemployment-related state benefits, such as a Jobseeker's Allowance. Not unsurprisingly, given that they measure different things, the ILO measure typically produces a higher level of unemployment than the so-called 'claimant count', although more often than not they move broadly in the same direction (www.statistics.gov.uk 2004).

However it is measured, in the era of the Fordist compromise unemployment was consistently low compared with the major pre-war and post-war recessions. For example, the unemployment rate (proportion of the labour force 'unemployed') in the 1950s and 1960s was typically below 2 per cent in the UK and under 5 per cent in the USA, whereas the unemployment rates in both countries were around 20 per cent in the early 1930s and 10 per cent in the mid-1980s (Ashton 1986). At the beginning of the twenty-first century, that is from 2000 to the third quarter of 2003, the unemployment rates in the UK and USA were averaging just over 5 per cent of the labour force on the basis of the ILO definition of unemployment. The annual unemployment rate in the rest of the industrialized world was higher, at over 6 per cent, during the same period and over 8 per cent in the Eurozone (www.oecd.org/dataoecd January 2004). This suggests that the post-1945 Fordist era was a golden age as far as full employment was concerned since the relatively low unemployment rates during the 1950s and 1960s have not been achieved since Fordism started to decline.

From the perspective of the unemployed, the sociological significance of the recent high rates of unemployment in advanced industrial capitalist societies, which reached a peak during the major global recession of the 1980s, is that 'the economic and social consequences of job loss are much more severe for the individual than in times of full employment when other jobs are readily available' (Ashton 1986: 37). Given that research into the impact of unemployment tends to be undertaken when unemployment rates are at their highest, the findings are likely to reflect the greater hardship experienced during such a period.

Further, the 1980s resurgence of large-scale unemployment in advanced industrial capitalist societies has led some to argue that aside from professional workers, the work ethic was in decline (e.g., Gorz 1999). There are also those who have expressed doubts about the pervasiveness of a work ethic during the development of industrial capitalism in the nineteenth century (Kelvin and Jarrett 1985; Rose 1989). Yet the continuing centrality of work is readily apparent from surveys, including those undertaken during a severe recession. For example, when the unemployment rate was at its highest in the UK in the mid-1980s, a representative survey found that the majority of respondents (92 per cent) expressed a strong commitment to work, reflecting the persistence of a secularized version of the Protestant work ethic (Mann 1986). This study concluded: 'Even if work is boring or low paid, it is central to most people's notion of their own moral, as well as material, worth' (Mann 1986: 24). Moreover, even among those made redundant, commitment to the work ethic has been shown to remain high (Westergaard et al. 1989). For instance, another survey during the same recession found that the unemployed are 'more committed to employment than those in work' (Gallie and Vogler 1994: 124). Similarly, surveys in the USA have shown that the decline of the work ethic is a myth. This is unsurprising given the emphasis placed on it by the capitalist state, corporations, the media and educational institutions (Beder 2000). Thus, large-scale unemployment does not seem to undermine the work ethic since the unemployed retain a moral commitment to work in addition to an instrumental one. In sum, work is typically perceived as crucial not only to one's economic well-being, but also to one's sense of moral and social worth. It is invariably in this context that the effects of unemployment have been understood since the pioneering research of the 1930s.

Social consequences of unemployment

The classic study of unemployment by Jahoda et al. (1974 [1933]) was a comprehensive, in-depth account of the social consequences of unemployment for the inhabitants of an industrial community in Austria decimated by the economic crash of 1929. The fieldwork was undertaken between 1931 and 1932 when three-quarters of the families in Marienthal were dependent on unemployment relief for their economic survival. Apart from cultivating vegetables on an allotment and breeding rabbits, opportunities to make a living legally were minimal, hence the first and most obvious effect of unemployment was financial. The economic impact was more than a matter of not going out for a drink. Such was the extent of economic desperation in this unemployed community that '[w]hen a cat or dog disappears, the owner no longer bothers to report the loss; he knows that someone must have eaten the animal, and he does not want to find out who' (Jahoda et al. 1974 [1933]: 22).

In addition to a markedly reduced standard of living, effectively a dramatic form of downward social mobility, the loss of employment also involved a decline in social activities due as much to a feeling of resignation as straightened circumstances. For example, despite the growth of free time, the unemployed typically attended the library and various social and political organizations less often than before. Thus the loss of confidence and sense of shame associated with unemployment seemed to contribute to the tendency to withdraw from social interaction outside the home.

For those among the study living on an income 'which averages just one quarter of normal wages', careful budgeting is vital, and it is significant that all the quotations used to illustrate this point are by women (Jahoda et al. 1974 [1933]: 31). This is indicative of the differential impact of unemployment on men and women, as the material on the use of time demonstrates clearly: 'For the men, the division of the day has long since lost all meaning' (Jahoda et al. 1974 [1933]: 67). They tended to idle away the time, doing virtually nothing, with the vast majority not wearing a watch. In marked contrast, the women, though strictly speaking they were not unemployed, were extremely busy running the household. In other words, their 'day is filled with [domestic] work' (Jahoda et al. 1974 [1933]: 75).

More generally, the data on time use revealed that for the men, the absence of paid employment meant that their daily lives, indeed weekly, monthly and annual routines, lost the time structure that was hitherto organized around work. Time no longer had any significance beyond the reference points of the physical needs to eat, sleep and get up, with punctuality of the unemployed men being a source of marital conflict since the mealtimes were set by their wives. The problem of marital discord was also mentioned in the context of the general deterioration of personal relationships as hope of employment faded. At best, minor quarrels increased in frequency and at worst 'difficulties became more acute' (Jahoda et al. 1974 [1933]: 86).

Not unrelated to the loss of a sense of time was the tendency for the majority (over 70 per cent) of the families, including the children and adolescents, to respond to unemployment with a feeling of resignation, characterized by the 'absence of long-term plans' and general 'aimlessness' (Jahoda et al. 1974 [1933]: 59). Although the initial reaction tended to be one of shock, even panic about the prospect of debt, it was followed by optimism, as reflected in the numerous job applications sent in the first few months of unemployment. However, failure to get a job and the inexorable deterioration in economic circumstances as any savings ran out, clothing and household items wore out, and unemployment benefits are 'superseded by emergency relief', optimism turns to pessimism (Jahoda et al. 1974 [1933]: 80). Eventually any lingering resilience tends to fade and apathy becomes the norm, the whole process 'intensified by the concomitant decline in health' (Jahoda et al. 1974 [1933]: 82).

This pioneering study of mass unemployment has had a major influence on the sociology of unemployment. First, it revealed that in addition to the manifest function of providing an income vital for economic survival, work as employment in modern societies performs a range of latent functions and that, as a consequence, unemployment involves a number of other unintended yet important losses. In sum:

- the loss of time structure for one's daily, weekly, monthly and annual routines;
- the loss of social contact outside one's immediate household;
- the loss of a sense of collective purpose and achievement;
- the loss of self-esteem, status and identity; and
- the loss of regular activity.

The thesis is that the loss of full-time employment involves not just economic hardship, but a range of social and psychological costs that have major implications for a person's well-being, ranging from an increasing sense of purposelessness to social isolation, including a marked deterioration in physical and mental health, and family conflict. Contemporary reviews of research on the economic, social and psychological consequences of unemployment (Hakim 1982) and the specific tests of the Jahoda et al. thesis (Gershuny 1994) have confirmed that, notwithstanding the growth of the welfare state, prolonged unemployment involves a wide range of interrelated negative consequences. In short, the multiplicity of 'losses' associated with unemployment suggest that work in the form of employment is still the main way that individuals connect to the wider society. Unemployment therefore has the potential to threaten not just one's economic survival but also one's identity, even one's life. Thus the tendency to understand the human consequences of unemployment through the prism of paid work as employment is the lasting legacy of the Marienthal study of unemployment.

Second, this study showed that there was a clear gender dimension to the social impact of prolonged unemployment with unemployed women being far less affected by the loss of the time structure provided by full-time employment than men. In large part this particular social consequence is predicated on the relatively traditional division of household tasks, which provided an alternative time structure to the day, that prevailed in Marienthal, namely that domestic chores were considered the wife's responsibility. Contemporary unemployment research has broadly confirmed this pattern in that traditional gender roles tend to prevail where the husband and wife are both unemployed, although some small changes are apparent when the wife is employed full-time and the husband is unemployed (Gallie et al. 1994).

Third, the Marienthal study suggested that reactions to long-term unemployment typically followed a pattern that started with shock, was followed by optimism and pessimism, and ended in total apathy. This phase model was confirmed by other research on long-term unemployment during the 1930s (Jahoda 1982). When mass unemployment re-emerged during the recession in the 1980s, this stage model was adopted widely, though not uncritically. A major criticism of this model is that it is based on the male experience of unemployment, and therefore applies well to men, especially those who subscribe to the work ethic, but that their experience of unemployment cannot easily be generalized to other social categories, such as young people and women (Burnett 1994). This suggests that these stages are neither universal nor inevitable and that it is necessary to consider the possibility that the social consequences of unemployment vary among different social categories.

Class, age and gender, and the social consequences of unemployment

Certain social categories in the working-age population are over-represented among the unemployed, especially during a recession, notably the working class, younger and older workers, women, and particular ethnic minorities, such as Pakistani and Bangladeshi groups in Britain. The social consequences of unemployment with respect to class, age and gender are discussed below since they are numerically the most important in industrial capitalist societies, with the exception of the USA where race or ethnicity is a major consideration.

Class

Ashton has argued that among the factors which influence the way in which unemployment is experienced are 'a person's status in the labour market, the extent to which their occupational identity is central to their self-image, their financial situation and their identity in the family' (1986: 122). More specifically, Ashton suggests that the '[t]ype of work experience is perhaps the most important factor influencing the experience of unemployment because it determines the level of income available and the opportunities for the development of an occupational identity' (1986: 124). On the basis of this systematic approach, Ashton claims that the most significant social consequence of unemployment for professional workers is the threat to their work identity whereas for semi-skilled and unskilled workers it is financial insecurity.

Ashton's class analysis of the social consequences of unemployment is supported by surveys of the unemployed, notably by the large-scale longitudinal survey of the unemployed undertaken by Daniel (1990). This showed that although the shortage of money was a problem for all unemployed people, it was a bigger problem for the manual working classes than for the non-manual middle classes. Conversely, a sense of shame was more significant for non-manual workers and skilled workers than for semi-skilled and unskilled workers. Research on white-collar unemployment by Fineman (1983) has also shown that the stigma of being unemployed was particularly acute among this social class. The main reason for this is that for the middle class employment represents a high social status and hence the loss of their occupational status is experienced as a major source of shame and therefore stress.

This was illustrated dramatically in the film, *The Full Monty* (1997), in which the most middle class of the redundant steelworkers featured in the firm continued to pretend to be employed. The class dimension of this reaction to unemployment is also apparent in Japan, where the shame of unemployment induces numerous 'salarymen' to 'haunt the business districts of downtown Tokyo, unable to stay home or in their neighbourhoods between the morning and evening rush hours' (French 2000: 10). Attempts to conceal the discreditable status of being unemployed is fraught with difficulties, not least that it can lead to what has been termed 'derivative stigmata', such as feeling 'duplicitous or untrustworthy', which in turn can compound the problem of managing the original stigma (Letkemann 2002: 511).

Not unrelated to the stigma experienced by the unemployed middle class is the finding that 'the parasuicide rate [attempted suicide] varies inversely with social class', suggesting that those most at risk are middle-class males (Platt 1986: 160). This is in line with Ashton's theory that unemployment is more of a shock to those who had previously enjoyed a high status and relatively secure position in the labour market.

However, less extreme forms of mental ill health, such as feeling depressed, seem to be experienced by all classes, although a slightly larger proportion of higher occupational classes than the lower ones, including those in the skilled manual category, reported feeling depressed (Daniel 1990). This class pattern can be interpreted as showing that all males are attached to paid employment, but those who are most attached for both intrinsic and extrinsic reasons, which tends to be the higher occupational classes, are likely to experience unemployment even more negatively in terms of psychological well-being.

Retaining the conventional middle-class and working-class occupational model, Ashton has also argued that professional and managerial careers maximize the tendency to 'develop an identity with an occupation' whereas relatively unskilled jobs minimize this possibility, and that, as a consequence, the threat to one's work identity is correspondingly greater for the former than the latter (1986: 124). The assumption here is that the middle classes are more likely to identify with their work, and thus are likely to experience a greater sense of loss if they become unemployed than the working class. However, research on occupational communities by Salaman (1974) has shown that identifying with an occupation is not an exclusively middle-class phenomenon. Hence the threat to one's work identity occasioned by unemployment is not necessarily restricted to professional workers.

On the basis of British data from the late 1980s, it was confirmed that the financial consequences of unemployment were understandably also far more dire for the working class than the middle class, especially for those in relatively low-paid and insecure jobs (Gallie and Vogler 1994). This occupational class pattern is entirely consistent with Ashton's emphasis on the relevance of the kind of work undertaken prior to job loss that is crucial to the economic impact of unemployment. More generally, it has been found that the experience of unemployment increases significantly 'the probability of downward occupational mobility' and lessens 'the chances of moving to less vulnerable positions' (Layte et al. 2000: 170).

Age

Ashton does not systematically examine how the length of time in work affects the social consequences of unemployment except to note that for young people about to enter the labour market: 'Their financial needs are not of the same order as those of prime-age males or females with families to support' (1986: 131). Yet evidence shows that the economic and social impact of unemployment is particularly severe for middle-age, full-time workers, but far less so for those approaching retirement (Daniel 1990). This is not to suggest unemployment for those aged over 55 is unproblematic since employers are typically reluctant to recruit older workers (Gallie and Vogler 1994). In other words, older people are likely to experience unfair discrimination on the basis of their age (ageism) in the labour market, not unlike several other segments of the working-age population, notably women and ethnic minorities, although in most advanced industrial capitalist societies legislation has been passed banning sexism and racism in employment, but not ageism, yet (Hakim 1998). In the case of older men who are unemployed, many are reluctant to see themselves as retired and there is a clear class pattern with early retirement being more of a non-manual option than it is for former manual workers (Casey and Laczko 1989).

According to Ashton's analysis of youth unemployment, the main social consequences for this age group are that their transition to adult status is delayed and becomes 'more problematic', whilst they remain dependent upon their family of origin for economic and social support (1986: 132). Aside from a study of male apprenticeship in the 1945–75 period, which argues that transitions in the past were also extended and not entirely unproblematic (Vickerstaff 2003), these points have been broadly confirmed by research which shows that not only has the 'period of the transition … been lengthened', but that it has also 'become much more fluid and uncertain' (Coffield et al. 1986: 199). Similarly, the study by Allatt and Yeandle confirmed the delay and increased fluidity of the transition into adulthood thesis, and went further in attributing a wider form of social exclusion to prolonged youth unemployment by suggesting that 'young people who might never hold a job were consigned to a second order of citizenship, unable to contribute to the community' (1992: 145). Revealingly, in light of the link between unemployment and ill health, this study reported that the language of illness was often used by the young to describe their experience of unemployment.

The alleged fragmentation of the transition to adulthood during the recent past has not only been attributed to the growth of youth unemployment, a distinctive feature of the 1980s compared with 1930s, but to the '"sexual revolution" of the 1960s and in the women's movement' (Hutson and Jenkins 1989: 154). A similar line of argument has been advanced by Irwin, who has suggested that the 'delay in household and family formation by young couples [is], in part, a consequence of the increased importance of the earnings of young women relative to young men in resourcing new households, and becoming parents at a standard of living commensurate with orientations towards general, societal levels of consumption' (1995: 312). These contributions to the debate about unemployment and the transition to adulthood do not seem to be denying the relevance of youth unemployment, they are simply noting that it is not the only factor causing a delay.

Empirical research on the increased fluidity aspect of the unemployment and the delayed transition to adult thesis has suggested that where there was once, at the height of Fordist full-employment, a relatively small range of 'smooth transitions' from education to employment, fractured particularly by class and to a lesser extent gender, this pattern became more complex during the decline of Fordism in the recession of the 1980s (Roberts 1984: 43). In effect, during the 1950s and 1960s the (male) working class left school and became manual workers, whereas their middle-class counterparts stayed on in full-time education before entering the labour market as non-manual workers. The gender dimension was apparent in that young women typically entered the labour market with the expectation that they would leave it when they became mothers (Martin and Roberts 1984). The decline of manual occupations following deindustrialization and the growth of non-manual occupations following the rise of the post-industrial service society, led to the creation of a greater variety of possible transitions into employment, including the distinct possibility that the young unemployed from disadvantaged class backgrounds were more likely to 'end up incarcerated (if male) or as a single parent (if female) as they mature' (Blanchflower and Freeman 2000: 8).

Thus, in addition to the traditional transitions, which in the meantime have become less distinct as more young people stay on in academic and non-academic full-time education, at least two other possibilities have become apparent. These can be summarized as government training schemes and underemployment (Roberts and Parsell 1988). With only a small minority of young people entering the labour market at the minimum school-leaving age, thereby reducing the scale of youth unemployment, the transition into adulthood has not only become more protracted, but also far more fragmented (Roberts et al. 1994). Despite the growth of options, the influence of class background has persisted into the new era in that it continues to have a cumulative effect on the selected route from education to employment broadly in the form of an academic trajectory for predominantly middle-class high achievers and vocational training for the rest, namely those from working-class social origins (Roberts and Parsell 1992). Similarly for gender, studies have shown that 'as transitions into employment have been prolonged, despite equal opportunity policies, new schemes and courses have quickly become segmented into masculine and feminine tracks, just like older opportunities' (Roberts et al. 1994: 50). This suggests that, notwithstanding what has been called the 'destandardization of the lifecourse' (Brannen and Nilsen 2002), the main routes from education into employment and their associated class and gender patterns, have changed little since the decline of Fordism and the expansion of options.

Ashton's analysis of the distinctiveness of youth unemployment is qualified with reference to both class and gender in that he suggests that the threat to the realization of an occupational identity is greater for middle-class youths than working-class ones, and that for young males the impact of unemployment on their transition to adulthood is 'mediated by their involvement in peer group activities which can provide an alternative source of status and prestige' (1986: 132).

As indicated already, the influence of class, gender and age can be seen to converge in the controversy regarding the link between unemployment and crime. In a review of the research literature, Hakim concluded that 'parental and youth unemployment increase juvenile delinquency' and that unemployment is particularly associated with property crimes, such as burglary and theft (1982: 450). One way of interpreting the relationship between unemployment and crime is via Merton's famous 'anomie theory', which argues that when legitimate opportunities to achieve success are blocked, namely employment, illegitimate means are adopted, namely crime (1957). It has been contended that young people, especially males, who are unemployed for a long duration, are most likely to respond in a deviant manner (Blanchflower and Freeman 2000; Box 1987). Youth unemployment is perceived as a potential threat to social order, hence it tends to be the main focus of government policies on unemployment (Jordan 1982).

Gender

Until recently the issue of female unemployment had been neglected, possibly a reflection of the pervasiveness of the idea that work outside the home is less important to women than to men (Marshall 1984; Sinfield 1981). This form of patriarchy was discussed in Chapter 1 with reference to the dominant conception of work. Yet, female unemployment is arguably more complex than male unemployment because, in contrast to adult men, the vast majority of whom conform to the continuous employment pattern of work, there are three options for women: a full-time work career, a discontinuous work career, or a full-time homemaker career (Hakim 1996). The first two patterns of work history are most relevant to women's experience of unemployment since the homemaker career woman is unlikely to seek work outside the home except under economic duress.

The first large-scale study of female unemployment in Britain examined continuous and discontinuous work history patterns and noted that the former involved three elements: that 'paid employment is central, mandatory, and constant' and typically applies to virtually all adult males and some women, whereas in the case of the latter, paid employment is 'marginal, optional, and discontinuous' and typically applies to most women but rarely to men (Cragg and Dawson 1984: 70). The contrast between the predominantly uniform male relationship to the labour market and the uneven female one, which varies from continuous to discontinuous, suggests that female unemployment is more of a 'continuum, rather than a discrete phenomenon with a comprehensive checklist of identifying characteristics' (Cragg and Dawson 1984: 70). Moreover, even among those women who were actively seeking paid employment, many did not consider themselves to be unemployed, partly because they were seeking part-time work which does not conform to the dominant male model of the unemployed breadwinner, and partly because 'most married women felt that their primary concern lay with their domestic responsibilities' (Cragg and Dawson 1984: 71). Consequently, many unemployed women reject the label 'unemployed' especially if they are married, under no financial pressure to find work, and are constrained by domestic responsibilities.

In Marienthal it was clear from the use-of-time data that when women were made unemployed, the majority reverted to what they regarded as their primary responsibility, that of homemaker. This aspect of the Marienthal study has been confirmed by recent research in the sense that it found 'some support for the view that the more substantial responsibilities that women undertake in the domestic sphere provide a sense of identity and a patterning of activity that helps to offset certain of the psychological consequences of unemployment that have been identified in studies focussing on the male unemployed' (Gershuny 1994: 216–18). This suggests that the social consequences of unemployment for men and women are different, especially in the case of married women, since their occupational identity is not threatened due to their lower commitment to full-time employment and their family role is not threatened because they can revert to their domestic role on a more full-time basis.

In Ashton's account of the various work and family factors that affect the experience of unemployment, he claims: 'It is in the household division of labour that the main source of women's distinctive experience of work and unemployment is to be found' (1986: 133). His argument seems to be that the more women identify with a family role, the more likely that this will constrain their labour market involvement and the less likely that their work identity will be threatened by unemployment. According to this analysis, women's experience of unemployment is different from that of men. However, Ashton also notes that even among women who work part-time to fit in with their family responsibilities, the loss of employment can have financial consequences for them and their families and reduce their sense of independence. This suggests that just because women's work history pattern is discontinuous and, for many, particularly those with young children, there is the option of enlarging their domestic role, it does not necessarily follow that their experience of unemployment is completely different from that of men.

Ashton's suggestion that women's experience of unemployment may not be too different from that of men is supported by surveys and case studies of female unemployment during the 1980s recession in Britain. For example, the survey of unemployed women by Cragg and Dawson (1984) showed that, like men, they worked for economic and non-economic motives and that the loss of employment had a not dissimilar financial and social impact that it had on men in terms of the threat to their economic and social well-being. Coyle's (1984) study of women made redundant from two factories also showed that women were strongly attached to paid work, not just for financial reasons but for the status and satisfaction it provided. Consequently: 'As for men, unemployment for women means financial hardship, isolation, and depression', and 'women's domestic role is no compensation' (Coyle 1984: 121). These studies suggest that women's and men's experience of unemployment are quite similar in that, for both, it has negative economic and social consequences. However, Coyle has also suggested that there was one major difference between male and female unemployment: for men unemployment can trigger a 'crisis of gender identity' whereas for women the option of an enlarged domestic role effectively precludes this possibility and instead unemployment for women often involves a 'crisis of autonomy' (1984: 121).

There are two features of women's unemployment that are distinctive. First, unemployed women are less willing to be geographically mobile in order to find work than unemployed men (Gallie and Vogler 1994), and second, unemployed women, especially if they are married and have children, are more likely to take a part-time job than unemployed men (Hakim 1996; see also Cragg and Dawson 1984). Hence, for women, the lack of a threat to their gender identity and their reluctance to be geographically flexible in their search for employment, yet be more flexible than men in terms of the number of hours worked, suggests that women's labour market behaviour is still influenced by their domestic responsibilities.

In conclusion to this part of the analysis, studies of unemployment in the 1930s, such as that undertaken by Jahoda et al. (1974 [1933]), found that the social consequences were essentially negative and that different social groups of the unemployed experience the range of losses to a greater or lesser extent both quantitatively and qualitatively. These findings were broadly confirmed by the next wave of unemployment research, occasioned by the major recession of the 1980s, showing that despite the growth of the welfare state, in Britain the connection between prolonged unemployment and poverty remained (Ashton 1986). The uneven development of what have been called 'welfare regimes' affects the risk of poverty and social exclusion due to unemployment and the nature and extent to which the experience of unemployment is gendered (Gallie and Paugam 2000). For example, the risk of poverty is high for the unemployed in countries with minimal welfare provision, such as Portugal and Greece, whereas in countries with a more universalistic welfare system, such as Denmark and Sweden, there is a much lower risk of poverty. Hence the degree of poverty and social exclusion experienced by the unemployed in contemporary societies varies depending on the welfare regime in a particular country.

However, it is argued that the experience of poverty in the 1980s is relative rather than absolute, as in the 1930s, since contemporary economic deprivation is no longer a matter of bare necessities, but the extent to which the poor fall below the standard of living considered acceptable, which may include not owning a car as opposed to not having sufficient food (Burnett 1994; Jahoda 1982). The same authors have also suggested that the higher standard of living of the 1980s, and associated rise in expectations, means that the sense of relative deprivation for the long-term unemployed is more intense nowadays compared to the more basic lifestyle of the 1930s. The contemporary deprivation of the unemployed is also exacerbated by greater financial commitments (Burnett 1994) and cuts in the welfare state benefits (Jahoda 1982). Thus, absolute poverty may not be as acute as in the past, but in relative terms the unemployed may well feel just as deprived in the more affluent present.

Conversely, it has been argued that the greater availability of financial compensation to the unemployed in the 1980s in all Fordist welfare states, on a comprehensive basis in the Europe and a fragmentary one in the USA, but especially in the UK thanks to the Redundancy Payments Act of 1965, cushioned those made unemployed involuntarily from severe and immediate hardship (Ashton 1986). The cuts in unemployment benefits in the UK and USA during the 1980s reduced rather than removed some of the social foundations of the Fordist welfare state.

Thus far, the social consequences of unemployment have been considered in relation to individuals, but it is important to note that collective responses to the loss of paid work are not uncommon. Unionized workers are particularly prone to resist redundancy and, during the demise of Fordism, sit-ins or occupations became a popular collective reaction to factory closures, albeit of limited success (Greenwood 1977). By the 1980s, the typical collective response to the steep rise in unemployment was the establishment of job creation co-operative enterprises in the UK, USA and other industrial capitalist societies (Mellor et al. 1988). However, most of the new co-operatives were small in scale and not always successful, despite state support, often on a local basis. A notable exception to these generalizations is the Tower Collery in South Wales, which was saved from pit closure in the mid-1990s by a worker co-operative financed out of the redundancy pay of over 200 miners and a bank loan (Cato 2004). The success of this relatively large-scale worker co-operative is regarded by Cato (2004) as indicative of a possible alternative to private capitalism, although there is little evidence as yet that this message is having any noticeable influence on the nature and direction of global capitalism.

Underemployment: meaning and measurement

A social consequence of unemployment not considered in the Marienthal project is that the recently unemployed are more likely than the employed to obtain non-standard forms of employment such as part-time and temporary work, typically at a low-skill level (Payne and Payne 1993). Involuntary, time-related underemployment is the most 'visible' type of underemployment. Other less visible forms include education or skill-related underemployment, in which someone is employed below their education or skill level, and low pay or income-related underemployment involving work which is considered to be at a poverty level (Simic 2002a: 414). All forms of underemployment involve inadequate employment situations and are not mutually exclusive. For example, the graduate who is a reluctant part-time worker in a fast-food restaurant on low wages is experiencing time-related, education-related and pay-related underemployment. Of these meanings of underemployment, only the first will be discussed here, on the grounds that this type of underemployment is easier to quantify, discussed most often, and there is now an ILO definition that has been adopted for the analysis of statistics in the UK (Simic 2002b). In contrast to time-related underemployment, there is no emergent standard definition of education-related or pay-related underemployment, which suggests that they are particularly difficult to measure.

The ILO defines time-related underemployment as people of working age who were 'willing to work additional hours, meaning that they wanted another job in addition to their current job(s), wanted another job with more hours instead of their current job(s) or want to increase the total number of hours worked in their current job(s)' (Simic 2000b: 512). Employment situations that differ from permanent full-time employment, which was considered to be standard during the height of Fordism, include part-time work, which will be considered in this chapter, plus self-employment, informal work and temporary employment, which are the subject of the next chapter. These types of paid work are referred to as contingent work (duRivage 1992), non-standard work (Carré et al. 2000) or flexible work (Castells 2001). They often overlap, hence it is difficult to obtain an accurate measure of the extent of non-standard work. Time-related underemployment is therefore just one form of non-standard work in that it refers to a partial lack of paid work, as opposed to a total lack of paid work, or unemployment, and is the opposite of overemployment, that is those who want to work fewer hours, which could also be considered a form of inadequate employment (Simic 2002b).

Part-time employment, along with other forms of non-standard work, expanded following the demise of Fordism to the point where, by 1998, it constituted between one-fifth and one-third of the employed labour force in many advanced capitalist countries (Castells 2001). In the UK it has been estimated that by the 1990s nearly 40 per cent of the labour force were engaged in non-standard work, 'most of it in the form of part-time work, of which 85 per cent was done by women' (Beck 2000: 56). Beck commented that '[t]he United Kingdom, which once pioneered the standardization of work, is now pioneering its individualization', or destandardization (2000: 65).

A notable exception was the USA, which suggests 'that when there is labour flexibility in the institutions of the country, non-standard forms of employment are not deemed necessary' (Castells 2001: 285). However, Castells went on to note that, 'in spite of the institutionally embedded labour flexibility, non-standard forms of employment are also significant in the United States', amounting to just under 30 per cent, with part-time work at around 17 per cent (2001: 286). Instructively, in Silicon Valley, 'at the centre of the new economy', the expansion of non-standard work, or flexible labour, including part-time employment, was even more marked (Castells 2001: 288).

The growth of non-standard work in Britain since the 1980s, especially part-time and other types of flexible employment, has been attributed to the change in labour use strategies associated with the rise of neo-Fordism and post-Fordism (Hakim 1988,

1996). As noted in the previous chapter, in contrast to Fordism, the concern to increase workforce flexibility and reduce labour costs is characteristic of these production systems. It has also been explained with reference to the expansion of the service sector (discussed in Chapter 4) and its need to match the availability of labour to peaks in demand irrespective of the type of production system (Smith et al. 1998).

The social profile of the underemployed is the opposite of that of the overemployed – that is to say, the young, low-skilled/educated and low-paid were most likely to be underemployed whereas the older workers, high-skilled/educated and high-paid, were most likely to be overemployed (Simic 2002a). In addition to these age and class characteristics of the underemployed and overemployed, there is also a clear gender dimension in the pattern of time-related underemployment. Underemployment includes a high proportion of part-time workers and in the UK between 1987 and 2002 the number of part-time workers increased by nearly one-third to 25 per cent of all employees, the vast majority of whom were women. Among female part-time workers, in most advanced industrial capitalist countries, 'the involuntary proportion of all part-timers ranges from between 20 and 30 per cent, and that in most cases, a higher proportion of women than men state that they work part-time because they cannot find a full-time job' (Dex and McCullock 1997: 159). In the UK in 1994 less than 10 per cent of married women worked part-time because they could not find a full-time job, whereas for non-married women the figure was 20 per cent (Hakim 1996; see also Hakim 2000). This suggests that most women prefer part-time work in order to be able to combine the roles of paid worker and unpaid houseworker.

Hakim's preference theory has been criticized for failing to take into account that a woman's choice of part-time work is 'shaped by their available options', notably the lack of affordable child-care provision. Hence national underemployment statistics, which show only a small proportion of women who work part-time do so involuntarily, may understate the extent of women's time-related underemployment (Crompton 1997: 35). An empirical assessment of Hakim's preference theory concluded that 'a complete explanation of women's labour market choices after childbirth and the outcomes of those choices, depends as much on understanding the constraints that differentially affect women as it does on understanding their preferences' (McRae 2003a: 334–5; see also Hakim 2003). Accordingly, it may well be that women have preferences, but it is also the case that women experience constraints in the form of welfare regimes and gender ideologies that influence individual preferences and the ability to act on them (Crompton and Harris 1998; McRae 2003b).

In the USA nearly all of the growth in part-time work has been involuntary rather than voluntary (Tilly 1992). This suggests that 'companies are deliberately creating both peripheral and internal low-wage labour markets for employees on contingent work schedules' (Harrison 1997: 205). In other words, increased flexibility in the form of time-related underemployment tends to be in the interests of capital not labour, hence Harrison's use of the phrase 'the dark side of flexible production' as a chapter title (Harrison 1997).

However it is measured, time-related underemployment, and other forms of non-standard work, seem to be expanding, and therefore affects a far larger number of people than unemployment. Women, the young, and the working class are over-represented among the underemployed although there are national variations, particularly in relation to women and part-time work.

Social consequences of underemployment

The main social consequence of part-time work, and other forms of underemployment, is that it 'results in economic hardship unless there is recourse to additional income transfers within the family or Welfare State entitlements' (Fagan and O'Reilly 1998: 6). This is because part-time work is notoriously low-skilled, low-paid, with limited fringe benefits, or opportunities for training and promotion (O'Reilly and Fagan 1998: Rubery 1998). It is also highly concentrated in the service sector where it is female-dominated and provides employers with flexibility (Smith et al. 1998).

The issue of the working poor, 'in which people work for a living but do not earn a living wage', is particularly noticeable in the USA, where 'the devolution of national welfare into workfare is expected to greatly worsen the relative income position of the poorest citizens in the country' (Harrison 1997: 272). Harrison cites data which shows that whilst the proportion of voluntary part-time workers without health insurance has declined between 1983 and 1988, during the same period an increasing number of involuntary part-time workers have no health insurance. For Harrison, the decline in the proportion of the American labour force who are not entitled to employee benefits 'is truly a dark side of flexible production', and seems to be particularly widespread among network firms (1997: 204). Thus, the combination of low wages, few or zero employee benefits, low skill, few training opportunities and limited promotion prospects shows the major social consequence of female-dominated, time-related underemployment, namely part-time work, is economic deprivation, notwithstanding the growth of multiple job holding among part-timers (Tilly 1992).

One of the most recent and systematic empirical studies of underemployment has suggested that time-related underemployment is a form of disguised unemployment since it involves employment situations which fall somewhere between full-time employment and zero employment, yet it found that underemployment had similar 'psychosocial and health costs' as unemployment (Dooley and Prause 2004: 201). This study also considered pay-related underemployment and concluded that 'falling into various types of underemployment is associated with a variety of undesirable outcomes', including lower self-esteem and increased depression (Dooley and Prause 2004: 201). In the same way that unemployment has been linked to negative social consequences such as mental ill health, time-related underemployment and other forms of underemployment have comparable social consequences both quantitatively and qualitatively, and, to the surprise of the researchers, minimal gender differences.

The similarities between the social consequences of unemployment and under-employment also extends to the stigmatization of part-time work irrespective of whether or not it is voluntary or involuntary, and the controversial issue of crime. For example, an American study of part-time lawyers, most of whom were women, concluded that such work was 'often stigmatized for its violation of the profession's norm' [of long hours] (Epstein et al. 1999: 134). This was in addition to part-time workers experiencing difficulties obtaining training and promotion. Another American study found that 'states in which a high proportion of young adult [male] employment is characterized by low hours and/or low pay have high rates of young adult property crime' (Allan and Steffensmeier 1989: 118). This finding is not only consistent with the theory that one of the social consequences of unemployment for those of a certain age and sex is crime, but suggests that other types of economic marginality are also linked to crime, namely time- and pay-related underemployment.

It would seem that the available empirical evidence suggests that the social consequences of time-related underemployment are comparable to those of unemployment in terms of low income, reduced status and poor health, and that consequently the part-time worker is more on a par with the zero employed than the fully employed.

Beck's underemployment thesis

The idea of underemployment is central to Beck's thesis concerning the demise of the standard employment system and the global development of flexible, destandardized labour that will be discussed in the next two chapters (1992, 2000). Meanwhile, it is pertinent to note that Beck contends that the Fordist system of mass production, mass consumption and standardized full-employment is in the process of being transformed, especially in the service sector, due largely to the growth of knowledge and information technology, by a 'risk-fraught system of flexible, pluralized, decentralized underemployment' (1992: 143). In this new pattern of employment 'unemployment disappears, but then reappears in new types of generalized risky underemployment', one of which is part-time work characterized by greater insecurity (Beck 1992: 144). There is the distinct possibility that automation will displace many unskilled and semi-skilled workers who will be replaced by a small number of upskilled, specialized workers. Moreover, spatial destandardization of labour and production will accompany temporal destandardization as information technology reduces the need for people to work next to each other in designated places such as offices and factories.

According to Beck, the growth of underemployment, and the economic insecurity associated with it, affects those at the top as well as at the bottom of the education and skills hierarchy – the low-skilled and fast-food restaurant worker and the highly educated university lecturer. Thus the demise of full-time employment provides the opportunity for all those who embark on flexible forms of underemployment to 'achieve greater time-autonomy and a new and better coordination of paid work and domestic labour, of work and life' (Beck 2000: 81). At the same time, underemployment tends to be accompanied by the 'privatization of the associated risks to health and psychological well-being' (Beck 2000: 81). For Beck, we are living in an era of increased job insecurity for all, but especially for the underemployed.

From an employer's perspective, the expansion of underemployment is beneficial in that '[i]t reduces wage costs, increases flexibility and shifts the burden of risk on to the workforce' (Beck 2000: 89). However, from the perspective of the employee, since it does little for their economic well-being, it encourages them to work longer hours and/or take on more than one part-time job and other forms of under-employment, both legal and illegal, such as informal employment. Beck concludes: 'Work and poverty, which used to be mutually exclusive, are now combined in the shape of the *working poor*' (2000: 90, italics in original). This has led the view that this does not represent a new type of society but an extreme form of industrial capital-ism, one that is characterized by increased exploitation (Crouch 1999). The less than celebratory discussion of flexible companies and their flexible employees by Sennett tends to confirm this interpretation in that it suggests that the experience of risk on a daily basis by all workers is disorienting and 'corrodes trust, loyalty and mutual commitment' (1998: 24).

Beck's thesis that flexible yet risky, insecure underemployment is spreading and signals the emergence of a new type of society to that which prevailed during the Fordist era is supported by the evidence noted above regarding the pay, prospects and benefits of part-time work, but the key growth and security dimensions are more problematic. First, the expansion of part-time work predates the demise of Fordism (Robinson 2000), and since the 1980s it has not grown everywhere – in some coun-tries it has actually fallen (Smith et al. 1998). Second, although part-time workers may still be legally at a disadvantage in terms of employment protection legislation in many countries, it does not follow that they have less job security in practice (Gallie et al. 1998). The majority of part-timers are permanent in the UK (Purcell 2000) and in the USA there is no evidence that part-time jobs are less secure than full-time ones (Houseman and Osawa 1998). However, job insecurity is also a matter of perception (Heery and Salmon 2000) and women feel less insecure than men, possi-bly because men still adhere to the breadwinner role (Charles and James 2003).

Beck's thesis shares many of the ideas that feature in the contributions of those who have written within the tradition of post-industrialism (e.g., Bell, discussed in Chapter 4, and Castells, discussed in Chapter 6). This includes an emphasis on the future, the role of knowledge and information technology, upskilling, the service sector, and the claim that work is being transformed. The commonalities are most marked in the case of Castells, who uses similar terms to Beck to advance essentially the same thesis: 'the individualization of labour and the labour process', charac-terized by 'multifaceted, generalized flexibility for workers and working conditions, both for highly skilled and unskilled workers' (2001: 282, 296). Beck does not express the same degree of optimism of Bell and Castells in that he suggests that the current transformation of work involves the rationalization of work-time and the growth of various forms of precarious underemployment largely in the interests of capital. However, his thesis has been criticized on similar grounds, namely that he exag-gerates the extent of the changes in the employment system and is insensitive to the persistence of class, gender and ethnic inequalities and geographical variations (Mythen 2004).

Summary and conclusions

Prior to industrial capitalism various types of precarious work and therefore income prevailed and unemployment as we know it today did not exist. However, once alternative sources of income other than wage labour had virtually disappeared and work had become synonymous with employment, the twin issues of unemployment, or zero employment, and underemployment, or partial-employment, became major social problems in the sense that they both became associated with hardship and insecurity.

The two major eras of mass unemployment during the twentieth century, the 1930s and the 1980s, when the levels of unemployment reached around 20 per cent and over 10 per cent respectively in industrial capitalist societies, stimulated empirical research on the social consequences of unemployment. The growth of non-standard types of work in general and involuntary part-time work in particular since the 1980s had a similar effect on time-related underemployment research.

The ILO definition of unemployment is now universally recognized, whereas the ILO definition of time-related underemployment is in the process of being adopted by various nation states, notably the UK, though other forms of underemployment, such as those relating to skill and pay, are more difficult to quantify and a standard measure has yet to be developed. Consequently, whilst the measurement of unemployment is relatively easy and facilitates cross-national and historical analyses, data on time-related and other forms of underemployment are less reliable, which makes analysis of the extent of underemployment problematic. However, this has not inhibited attempts to calculate the incidence of standard full-time employment and various forms of non-standard employment, a large proportion of which is time-related underemployment.

It has been estimated that non-standard employment during the 1990s was around 40 per cent in the UK and 30 per cent in the USA, well above the levels of unemployment during the same decade. In both countries the largest proportion of this diverse type of employment was female-dominated, time-related underemployment in the form of part-time work. Assuming this trend continues, during this century the proportion of non-standard workers is likely to equal or even exceed that of standard workers. This suggests that Beck and Castells are correct to note that the historical focus on the distinction between zero employment and regular full-time employment is obsolete since it no longer represents the diversity of employment situations of advanced industrial capitalist societies.

On the basis of these estimates, in the UK and the USA in the 1990s between 5 per cent and 10 per cent of the labour force were unemployed, about 30 per cent underemployed or involved in other forms of non-standard employment, and approximately 60 per cent were fully employed, of which up to 10 per cent were overemployed.

Type of employment situation			
Unemployment	Underemployment	Full-time employment	Overemployment
Zero	Under 40	Around 40	Over 40
Hours per week			

Figure 7.1 Employment situation and working hours

Thus employment is no longer a simple matter of being in or out of work, employed or unemployed, but more a matter of degree characterized by an employment continuum that ranges from zero employment to overemployment. This contemporary range of employment situations is summarized in Figure 7.1.

In industrial capitalist societies, work in the form of employment is effectively the only legal way to earn a living. It is unsurprising, therefore, that the main social consequence of unemployment is economic deprivation, which in terms of class amounts to downward social mobility. The pioneering research on unemployment in the 1930s by Jahoda et al. (1974 [1933]) showed that the importance of work goes far beyond the manifest function of the satisfaction of material needs. Permanent full-time work performs a range of latent functions such as a time structure, social contact, sense of purpose, achievement, self-worth and status, and regular activity. These latent functions of work are also threatened by unemployment and are experienced as losses, although '[d]ifferent groups of unemployed experience the absence of one category of experience or another with differing intensity' (Jahoda 1982: 85).

The class contrasts in the social consequences of unemployment suggest that economic deprivation was marked for the working class whereas status deprivation was more acute for the middle class. In terms of age and the social consequences of unemployment, both young and old were affected by loss of income, but in different ways. The middle-aged unemployed were more concerned about maintaining their standard of living, but for the young unemployed it meant a prolonged and more fluid transition to economic independence and therefore adulthood. The issue of gender and the experience of unemployment is complicated by the heterogeneity of women's involvement in the labour market. Thus, for women who conform to the male model of continuous employment, the impact of unemployment is likely to be similar to that for men, namely severe economic and social deprivation. Conversely, for women who participate discontinuously in the labour market, the economic and social consequences of unemployment may not be so acute, especially if they are married and can opt for a life of secondary earner and/or primary homemaker. The social consequences of unemployment are essentially negative for everyone but the precise impact depends on a variety of factors, including class, age and gender, and how they combine in any one case. The degree of the economic hardship experienced by the unemployed in contemporary societies will also be affected by the extent to which the social foundations of the Fordist welfare state have been eroded. Collective responses to unemployment include worker sit-ins and worker co-operatives.

Time-related underemployment is an increasingly important issue that relates to the demise of Fordism and the rise of the destandardization of employment. The social consequences of this form of underemployment are remarkably similar to those associated with unemployment. In other words, underemployment typically involves economic hardship, low social status, stigma even, and poor mental health. Although some people prefer part-time work, notably students and married women, many do not, since the poor pay often necessitates having two or more part-time jobs. Yet it also has the potential of improving one's work–life balance. The contradictory nature of time-related underemployment has been confirmed by empirical research which shows that whilst part-time work may help solve the problem of family commitments, it tends to be seen by employers and employees as a sign of reduced work commitment and, as such, is stigmatized. Thus time-related underemployment may be expanding numerically, but full-time work is still regarded as the norm, especially in professional work cultures.

Time-related underemployment is highly gendered in the Beechey and Perkins (1987) sense in that it is considered to be women's work and consequently tends to be poorly paid and low in status, with limited opportunities for training and promotion. However, some debate surrounds the extent to which women choose freely this flexible form of employment. Hakim has advanced a preference theory which claims that for the majority of women it is a work–lifestyle choice, whereas critics such as Crompton and McRae have pointed out that women's employment choices are constrained by structural and cultural forces and that women vary in their capacity to surmount constraints.

The (uneven) growth of part-time employment in Europe and other industrial capitalist societies is symptomatic of a wider trend towards labour market flexibility which has clear economic advantages for employers but economic disadvantages for employees. Since women, especially married women, make up the majority of the part-time labour force, it can be argued that it is women who tend to pay the price of this flexibility in terms of low pay and limited promotion. However, the recent increase in male part-time work in Europe suggests that this form of destandardized employment is in the process of being de-gendered (Delsen 1998). If so, it may lead to its de-marginalization too.

Beck's underemployment thesis is an integral element of his more general claim that Fordist standarized work is being superseded by a risk regime of destandardized work. The insecurity dimension of his thesis is not supported by the data on part-time work and may be criticized on the grounds that the growth of this type of non-standard work predates the decline of Fordism and that he tends to underestimate the persistence of class and gender inequalities. The parallels between Beck's thesis and theories of post-industrial society include a focus on the role of technical change and knowledge.

In the light of Beck's destandardization of work theory, and specifically the underemployment component, the key issue now, and increasingly in the future, is not unemployment but underemployment of various kinds. Thus, underemployment is the new form of unemployment, or in the words of Dooley and Prause, 'disguised unemployment' (2004: 1). Whilst this may be good news for politicians, it is bad news for those who no longer appear on the unemployment register, who work part-time or in another type of destandardized employment, and therefore do not qualify for unemployment benefits. Hence the growth of time-related underemployment is likely to increase rather than reduce the incidence of economic hardship.

The wider implications of the continued expansion of destandardized work in general, and time-related underemployment in particular, include the possibility that the labour force will become more polarized between the affluent and relatively economically secure and the poor and relatively economically insecure. The former are also likely to be overemployed and therefore experience a shortage of non-work time, whereas the latter are likely to suffer from an excess of non-work time. These are arguably yet further manifestations of the polarization of skill discussed in Chapter 4.

If the gendered nature of time-related underemployment does not alter significantly, the expansion of this form of non-standard work is unlikely to disrupt the traditional division of labour by gender that allocates primary responsibility for income generation to men and primary responsibility for domestic and child-care work to women. This is the logic of Hakim's analysis of the feminization of the labour force and suggests that Beck's claim regarding the advent of a new type of society is misplaced in this respect since the male breadwinner model associated with Fordism is likely to be reinforced rather than transcended (Crompton 2002). The impact of changes in the patterning of paid work on unpaid work will be explored in Chapter 9.

Thus, the Fordist welfare system and social norms that still reflect the traditional distinction between the male breadwinner and female homemaker to a greater or lesser extent in many advanced industrial capitalist societies, such as Britain, may not be undermined easily. This is because in addition to the persistence of women's over-representation in time-related underemployment, there is the possibility of institutional and cultural inertia, as well as political resistance, especially from those men and women who still support the idea of male breadwinning and female homemaking.

However, a fuller consideration of the many ramifications of Beck's underemployment thesis, especially the key insecurity dimension, requires an analysis of all types of destandardized work, including self-employment, temporary work, homeworking and informal work, not just part-time work. These other forms of non-standard paid work are the focus of the next chapter.

Further reading

Ashton's (1986) *Unemployment under Capitalism: The Sociology of British and American Labour Markets* contextualizes the sociology of unemployment both historically and comparatively, and covers the class, gender and age variations in the experience of unemployment. The influential study by Jahoda et al. (1974 [1933]) *Marienthal: The Sociography of an Unemployed Community* is still worth reading, alongside Jahoda's more recent analysis of the social consequences of unemployment, *Employment and Unemployment: A Social-Psychological Analysis* (1982). An evaluation of Jahoda's theory of the manifest and latent consequences of unemployment, plus analyses of the class, gender and age dimensions of the experience of unemployment are covered in the the collection of articles by Gallie et al. (eds) (1994) *Social Change and the Experience of Unemployment*. The most comprehensive book on the part-time form of underemployment is O'Reilly and Fagan (eds) (1998) *Part-time Prospects: An International Comparison of Part-time Work in Europe, North America and the Pacific Rim*. Beck's underemployment thesis is advanced in two books: *Risk Society: Towards a New Modernity* (1992) and *The Brave New World of Work* (2000). The best critique of this aspect of Beck's theory of risk is contained in Mythen (2004) *Ulrich Beck: A Critical Introduction to the Risk Society*.

Questions for discussion and assessment

1. What are the main social consequences of unemployment?
2. To what extent are the social consequences of unemployment the same for everyone?
3. Evaluate critically Hakim's preference theory.
4. Compare and contrast the consequences of unemployment and underemployment.
5. Outline and assess Beck's underemployment thesis.

CHAPTER EIGHT

Non-Standard Paid Work Contractural, Spatial, Temporal and Total Destandardization

In the previous chapter it was noted that Beck and Castells were of the view that non-standard work was expanding and that standard work was declining. Their conceptions of non-standard work were similar in that they covered the overlapping categories of part-time work, self-employment, temporary work in the case of Castells (2000), and 'part-time work, inconsequential and temporary employment, and spurious forms of self-employment' in the case of Beck (2000: 56). On the basis of these categories they calculated that by the 1990s over one-third of the labour force were engaged in non-standard work in most advanced industrial capitalist societies, and the proportion was increasing. In some regions, notably Silicon Valley, California, the non-standard workforce was growing at least twice as fast as the overall workforce (Benner 2002). Beck (2000) and Castells (2000) also noted that informal work was expanding and that there was a tendency for the distinction between formal and informal work to become blurred.

The clear implication of these analyses is that non-standard forms of paid work are increasing, albeit unevenly, and will soon be as prevalent as standard work in modern societies. For Beck and Castells, this is a revolutionary change that heralds a new type of society, the emergence of which is due mainly to the competitive pressure for flexibility and the global adoption of information technology: 'All around the world, flexible work and insecure terms of employment are growing faster than any other form of work' (Beck 2000: 84); 'Competition-induced, technology-driven trends toward flexibility underlie the current transformation of working arrangements' (Castells 2001: 282). This growth of what has been called 'just-in-time' employment (Carré et al. 2000: 3) complements just-in-time production methods (discussed in Chapter 6) and involves workers across all skill levels.

The one-third of the labour force figure for the scale of non-standard work is broadly comparable to Standing's (1997) calculations for most industrial capitalist societies for 1993, Robinson's (1999) calculation for the UK in 1997, and the estimate for the USA in 1997 by Polivka et al. (2000). Unlike Beck and Castells, with the exception of Standing, these researchers were far less sanguine about the transformation of work and society in that Robinson noted that the growth of non-standard work was marked in the early 1980s but has since 'slowed down' (1999: 90), and Polivka et al. showed that the proportion of non-standard workers in the USA actually fell slightly between 1995 and 1997, 'in contrast to the popular perception of burgeoning non-standard work arrangements' (2000: 44–5). These and other even more sceptical contributions to the debate about the changing character of paid work (e.g., Bradley et al. 2000; Pollert 1988), suggest that the growth of non-standard work may have stalled, which implies a resurgence of standard work and a return to the recent past.

This view is supported by the most recent survey of changes in working arrangements in Britain which found that '[t]he overwhelming majority of paid jobs remain full-time and permanent and physically located in a specific place of work' (Taylor 2003: 7). One cross-national study confirmed that the 'stable core still accounts for the dominant form of employment' (Auer and Cazes 2000: 405). This may be because employers are seeking to achieve greater flexibility from within their standard workforce by varying the number of hours they work and the tasks they perform (Burchell et al. 1999). Thus the distinction between standard and non-standard work is no longer as clear-cut as in the past, a point that is reinforced by the tendency for standard employment to become less secure and some forms of non-standard employment, such as part-time work, to become more secure (Benner 2002; Gallie et al. 1998). Thus, whilst non-standard work has certainly expanded at the expense of standard work, standard work is also changing.

The idea of non-standard paid work, or flexible work as it is also known, is predicated on the standard work pattern that emerged with the rise of industrial capitalism and, as noted in Chapter 5, reached its fullest development under Fordism. According to Beck, this standard form of paid work was 'based on high degrees of standardization in all its essential dimensions: the labour contract, the work site and working hours' (1992: 142). The contrast between standard and non-standard models of work are summarized in Table 8.1. These features of standard work were referred to in the first chapter under the heading 'Industrial' and were part of a wider conceptualization of work that included capitalist and patriarchal elements. From the perspective of the dominant conception of work, the standard worker was a male breadwinner who worked full-time in his employer's premises in exchange for a regular wage or salary. Such was, and to some extent still is, the dominance of this model of paid work that other forms of paid work have been marginalized and other forms of unpaid work under-valued. Part of the purpose of this chapter, and indeed this section of this book, is to redress the picture by giving greater prominence to non-standard forms of paid and unpaid work than is usual.

The decline of standard paid work and the growth of non-standard paid work has been attributed to the tendency for employees and employers to prefer the flexibility of non-standard work arrangements around which the former can organize their personal lives more independently and effectively and the latter can organize production more efficiently and economically. Evidence from the US labour market

Table 8.1   Key dimensions of standard and non-standard work/employment models

Dimensions	Standard work/employment	Non-standard work/employment
Contractural	Highly regulated* and collectively negotiated	Deregulated and individually negotiated
Spatial	Spatially concentrated, specialist site away from home	Spatially variable, multiple sites, including at/from home
Temporal	Full-time, permanent	Variable time, impermanent
Gender system	Male breadwinner/female houseworker	Dual earner/variable houseworker

*Regulations covering hours, wages, redundancy, health, safety and benefits such as pensions, holiday and sick pay, etc.

suggests that the expansion of non-standard work 'mainly reflects employer, not employee, preference' (Rosenberg and Lapidus 1999: 76). From the perspective of an employer, non-standard work offers the advantage of reduced costs, notably the expenses involved in providing employees with premises and benefits, and in adjusting the number of workers to changes in demand for goods and services. In other words, in the context of an increasingly competitive market, employers can simultaneously overcome the rigidities associated with Fordism and reduce costs. Furthermore, advances in information technology make it possible for employers to transfer work to an employee's home, thereby saving on overheads such as heating and lighting. Castells has summarized neatly this demand-side explanation of the growth of non-standard work: 'Competition-induced, technology-driven trends toward flexibility underlie the current transformation of working arrangements' (2001: 282). Beck (2000) also emphasizes the role of technology, especially in relation to the global growth of destandardized work. Both Beck and Castells envisage the continued expansion of non-standard work, albeit unevenly in terms of types, regions and industries, with economic benefits for firms and social benefits for workers, notably an improved life–work balance.

Whatever the reasons for the decline of standard employment, it is widely agreed that working arrangements are no longer uniform, but are increasingly diverse and overlap with each other. Casey has calculated that in the UK '54 per cent of temporary workers are also part-time workers ... while 9 per cent of both are part-time and self-employed' (1991: 182). Moreover, the growth of the various types of informal work is uneven in different countries. For example, during the 1980s and 1990s self-employment expanded markedly in Italy and the UK but not the USA, whereas temporary work expanded significantly in Spain and Australia but not Denmark and the Netherlands, and part-time work expanded in most industrial capitalist societies with the exception of the USA and Denmark (Castells 2001). The range and combinations of non-standard forms of paid work is a challenge to those seeking to establish trends and explain them, problems that are particularly acute in the case of informal work since it is unrecorded income generating economic activity and therefore does not appear in conventional statistics on work and employment.

In the light of the diversity of non-standard work, Beck's and Castells' seminal contributions are an appropriate point of departure. The remarkable parallels between them is readily apparent from Beck's three key aspects of standardized work, namely the contract, site and working hours noted above (1992), and the 'four elements in the transformation of work', the 'social contract between employer and employee', 'location', 'working time' and 'job stability', which can be subsumed under the heading 'contract', outlined by Castells (2001: 282). Here the contractural, spatial, and temporal destandardization of work will be discussed with reference to self-employment, homeworking and temporary work respectively, plus informal work which represents the total destandardization of work, but not part-time work since this was discussed in the previous chapter under the heading 'underemployment'. The main thrust of both theses is that the decline of standard work and the expansion of non-standard work involves the development of 'risk-fraught system of flexible, pluralized, decentralized underemployment' (Beck 1992: 144), or 'multi-faceted, generalized flexibility for workers and working conditions' (Castells 2001: 296). Both Beck and Castells contend that the flexibilization and individualization of work affect all skill levels, with Beck emphasizing the growth of insecurity for all, and Castells highlighting the trends of extreme polarization and fragmentation. These theories raise the possibility that the destandardization of work involves more low-quality jobs. The purpose of this chapter is to redress the balance of accounts of work which focus almost entirely on standard work, and to review the nature and extent of different types of paid non-standard work.

Contractural destandardization: self-employment

Self-employment represents the exact opposite of standard employment in that typically it does not involve a contract of employment and consequently the self-employed person is treated differently from an employee in relation to tax, national insurance and social security entitlements. For example, in the UK the self-employed are not eligible for unemployment benefit, earnings related additions to the state pension and invalidity benefit, and statutory sick pay (Eardley and Corden 1994). Also, the self-employed do not receive holiday pay or work fixed hours. Consequently, in contrast to the standard employee, the self-employed have to rely on private insurance to cover risks associated with working since they are excluded from the key areas of social protection achieved under the Fordist compromise between the employer, the employee and the state. In an American study of the quality of standard and non-standard forms of work it was found that the self-employed were in between standard employees and other non-standard workers, such as part-time and temporary workers, in terms of access to benefits, although some earned higher incomes than standard workers (Kalleberg et al. 2000).

However, even from the standpoint of this social security and tax perspective, the category of self-employment is not unproblematic. On the one hand, there are those who are technically self-employed according to the tax and social security authorities, such as labour-only subcontractors and homeworkers, but whose work is controlled by an employer. Conversely, there are those who are technically a dependent employee, for example, directors of limited companies, yet who are in control of their work. These anomalies are statistically important since it has been calculated that they can lead to very different estimates of the size of the self-employed workforce (Dale 1991).

In ideal-typical terms, the self-employed own the means of production and conse-quently have autonomy in their work, hence the above references to control (Dale 1986). This simple definition masks the diversity of this status, which ranges from part-time self-employment without employees, to full-time self-employment with (often unpaid) family workers and (typically paid) non-family labour, although the vast majority work alone. Arguably, what unites the various manifestations of self-employment is the element of independence (or autonomy). This is the most distinctive feature of self-employment and the one that separates this employment status most clearly from that of dependent employee (Bechhoffer and Elliot 1968).

However, there is a gap between the ideology of autonomous self-employment and the reality of being at the beck and call of customers, whether they are individuals or subcontracting employers, or at the mercy of bank managers. Moreover, typically, the self-employed work long, unsocial hours, for uncertain, sometimes relatively low financial rewards, and often rely on other family members to contribute as unpaid workers. In a recession small firms are particularly vulnerable since they lack the financial resources essential to survival (Wigley and Lipman 1992). Thus they may have escaped the alienation characteristic of being supervised closely as a dependent employee, but the self-employed are not only overworked and risk failure, but are 'indirectly controlled by others' (Scase and Goffee 1982: 76). Hakim has summed up this general finding by noting that the 'illusion of autonomy' is emphasized 'in order to give moral value to, and to rationalize a work situation that would otherwise be intolerable' (1988: 434).

Yet the idea of being in control, being one's own boss, is a 'deeply held belief' (Bechhofer et al. 1974: 114), a widely held 'aspiration' (Wright 1997: 115), and the main reason that people are attracted to self-employment (Nisbet 1997) in advanced industrial capitalist societies like Britain and America. Self-employment is a more highly valued status than that of employee. The idea of independence is a key element of a nexus of what may be regarded as basic capitalist values, including self-reliance and initiative. Accordingly, the self-employed are regarded as the guardians of vital capitalist virtues who help to keep alive the idea that prosperity can be achieved via individual initiative and hard work, although they do not necessarily see themselves in this way (Scase and Goffee 1982). Hence self-employment is important ideologically in that 'it buttresses the present system of inequality and offers it legitimation' (Bechhofer et al. 1974: 124). Given the historic tendency for multinational corporations to dominate economic activity, the political significance of the ideological function of self-employment cannot be underestimated.

Prior to the development of industrial capitalism, the independent farmer, craft worker, shopkeeper, trader, and so on, was the norm. However, as the scale of production expands there is a concomitant increase in the amount of capital needed to compete, which concentrates ownership among a few and limits the opportunities of the many to become business owners. According to this analysis, self-employment or small-scale capitalism was typical of pre-industrial capitalism but increasingly atypical in advanced industrial capitalism. This transformation in the organization of production and the structure of competition was articulated by Marx in the first volume of *Capital* (1970 [1887]). Weber too outlined a similar process when he noted that before the advent of industrial capitalism 'every worker could be said to have been primarily interested in becoming an independent small bourgeois, but the possibility of realizing this goal is becoming progressively smaller' (1964 [1947]: 427). However, for Weber, the driving force behind the 'expropriation of the individual worker from ownership of the means of production' was the greater rationality and hence efficiency of a bureaucratic organization of production in a market system (1964 [1947]: 246). The Marx–Weber thesis that self-employment in particular, and small-scale capitalism in general, was destined for terminal decline corresponded to the historical trend in industrial capitalist societies – until recently. For example, Wright has calculated that in the USA the percentage of the labour force who were self-employed declined from over 40 per cent in 1870 to under 10 per cent in 1970, with a comparable though less steep decline in other modern societies (Wright 1997). Unsurprisingly, the view that self-employment was in terminal decline became the dominant one, with education replacing entrepeneurialism as the conventional route to occupational success (Scase and Goffee 1980).

Since the 1970s, though, there has been an unexpected reversal of this historical trend in many industrial capitalist societies, including the USA, and most notably the UK where self-employment, mainly without employees (Hakim 1988), increased from 7.3 per cent of total employment in 1979 to 12.4 per cent in 1987, and was particularly marked among women (Casey 1991). Although the growth of self-employment fluctuated during the 1990s, it was still around 10 per cent of the working population in the spring of 2002 (Weir 2003). In the twelve months to September 2003 self-employment increased significantly again, with part-time self-employment exceeding the increase in full-time self-employment, whereas the number of employees remained more or less static (Macauley 2003). The growth of self-employment in the 1980s may have reached a plateau in the 1990s, but it is still higher than it was in the 1970s. The expansion of self-employment during the 1980s in the UK and elsewhere has been attributed to a range of interrelated economic, political and socio-cultural factors that will be considered next.

Economic factors

Economic factors include, first, deindustrialization, characterized by the decline of capital-intensive manufacturing, and the growth of labour-intensive services which require a smaller financial outlay, thereby encouraging self-employment (Scase and Goffee 1980). There is empirical support from the USA for the claim that 'the expansion of self-employment is significantly linked to post-industrialism' (discussed in Chapter 4 with reference to skill), in the sense that post-industrial occupations, such as business and professional services, tend to contribute hugely to the growth of self-employment (Wright 1997: 135). Although women are under-represented in self-employment, they tend to be concentrated in the service sector, the growth of which partly explains the doubling of female self-employment in the UK between 1979 and 1987 (Casey 1991). The service sector was prominent in the most recent upsurge in self-employment in the UK, especially in banking, finance and insurance (Macauley 2003).

Second, organizational restructuring, characterized by the conversion of employee jobs into self-employed jobs as part of the tendency for firms to seek numerical flexibility and reduce costs, was discussed in the context of post-Fordism in Chapter 6 (Hakim 1988). This can take various forms, two of the most prominent being self-employed subcontracting and self-employed freelance work. The former is associated with manual work whereas the latter is with knowledge work, and along with other types of non-standard work, such as part-time work and temporary work, they are seen as either highly risky forms of employment in Beck's destandardization of work thesis (discussed in the previous chapter), or highly rewarding flexible forms of employment in Castells' network enterprise thesis (discussed in Chapter 6). Historically labour-only subcontracting has been widespread in the UK construction industry (Bresnen et al. 1985), but during the 1980s this form of self-employment spread to manufacturing industry (Fevre 1987) and the service sector (Hakim 1988). Freelancing also increased, such as in the production of television programmes in the UK, largely in response to the competitive pressure to reduce costs, and has involved the transfer of risks from employers to employees (Dex et al. 2000). Recent research has shown that although the majority of subcontracted and freelance workers are pushed into self-employment by organizational restructuring, levels of work satisfaction were high and focused on the freedom to exercise initiative and use their abilities (Smeaton 2003).

Third, technological innovations have encouraged self-employment by reducing the cost of setting up a business and by offering the advantage of flexibility or, as Castells has put it, 'as new technologies make it possible for small business to find market niches, we witness a resurgence of self-employment and mixed employment status' (2001: 236). For Beck, the teleworker in the electronic cottage is an 'extreme' example of 'decentralized', non-standard work, thereby emphasizing the temporal and spatial dimensions of destandardization of work rather than the contractural (1992: 147). Empirical research on the contractural aspect of telework in Britain found that in six cases only two involved self-employment and in both instances they were contracted to a single company, one of which provided support 'until full independence was established' (Stanworth and Stanworth 1991: 41). Thus the majority of teleworkers are not self-employed in the sense of owning the means of production and working autonomously since teleworking tends to be initiated by companies with a concern for costs and flexibility rather than an individually inspired conversion to self-employment.

Fourth, according to the post-Fordist interpretation of industrial capitalist development, the change from mass consumption to more individualized consumption is thought to have encouraged small-scale production, hence self-employment, for example by craft workers for niche markets (Burrows 1991). The impact of the increased demand for specialist goods and services on the organization of production was discussed in Chapter 6 with reference to flexible specialization. Understandably, the fragmentation of consumption has been referred to as '"post-Fordist" consumption' (Lash and Urry 1994: 174). The problem with this explanation of the expansion of self-employment is that it lacks any empirical evidence (Fine 1995). This does not mean that this intuitive line of reasoning is totally without merit since Beck's individualization thesis implies not only the destandardization of work but also consumption, though research on the latter is less advanced than it is on the former.

Fifth, unemployment during the 1980s is thought to have stimulated entry into self-employment via a combination of limited opportunities for waged work, receipt of redundancy payments that can fund starting a business, and the availability of relatively inexpensive equipment during a recession (Curran and Blackburn 1991b). There is evidence from the USA which shows that as unemployment rises so does self-employment (Wright 1997), and from the UK which shows that unemployment does spur people on to enter self-employment (Bogenhold and Stabler 1991). Hence unemployment is both cyclical and a 'push' factor, especially for men (Granger et al. 1995: 499) and ethnic minorities, who often turn to self-employment when they are unable to obtain work as an employee (Phizacklea and Ram 1996). However, only a small proportion of entrants to self-employment were previously unemployed (Hakim 1988), and even with the state financial support to help the unemployed become self-employed, a policy that was not unique to the UK (Yeandle 1999), the move from unemployment to self-employment is a risky one that often ends in outright failure or a struggle to survive in an area of high unemployment (MacDonald 1996). This was just one UK government initiative during the 1980s concerned with encouraging self-employment and small businesses generally, and reflects the political salience of both high unemployment and self-employment.

Political factors

Political factors include direct influences such as government policies to encourage self-employment (discussed below) and indirect influences to alter the political culture in a pro-enterprise direction (discussed in the next section).

In the UK between 1979 and 1989 successive Conservative governments introduced 'over 200 legislative initiatives designed to make starting, running and expanding a small firm easier' (Burrows and Curran 1991: 20). These measures included advice and training, loans and tax incentives, and a general relaxing of the regulations affecting the self-employed and small businesses in order to reduce their bureaucratic burden. Prominent among the measures introduced during the early 1980s were the Loan Guarantee Scheme (1981), to provide guarantees for bank loans, and the

Enterprise Allowance Scheme (1982), to provide funds to facilitate the transition from unemployment to self-employment.

The policy to encourage self-employment via direct legislative action has been continued by Labour governments since 1997. The most recent manifestation of this twin-track approach was the launch of an 'Enterprise Insight Campaign' in June 2004 by the Chancellor of the Exchequer, at which he announced that new funds for enterprise capital would be made available and that a National Enterprise Week was planned for November (www.hm-treasury.gov.uk/newsroom_and_speeches/press/2004). There are clear parallels between the Enterprise Initiative inaugurated in 1988 by the then Conservative government and the Enterprise Insight Campaign introduced in 2004 by the Labour government in that both policies regard a culture of enterprise as a panacea for Britain's alleged economic ills.

Socio-cultural factors

Socio-cultural factors refers to changes in attitudes and behaviour in relation to work and employment that favour self-employment over dependent employment and are typically summed up by the problematic concept of 'enterprise culture' (Keat and Abercrombie 1991; Richie 1991). From a right-of-centre political perspective, enterprise culture denotes a distinct set of attitudes and values, notably risk-taking, self-reliance and individualism, which contrast with a dependency culture characterized by risk-aversion, reliance on others and collectivism (MacDonald 1996). In the UK in the 1980s, successive Conservative governments sought to encourage an enterprise culture and discourage a dependency culture as a solution to the perceived long-standing problem of the relative inefficiency and lack of dynamism of the economy. The policy to foster an enterprise economy involved not just financial incentives and the support of the local and central arms of the state, but also implicated the state educational system. Enterprise education was incorporated into the national curriculum of secondary schools and into undergraduate and postgraduate programmes in higher educational institutions (Wigley and Lipman 1992). This is entirely logical given that the aim was to inculcate a spirit of enterprise and that education is the main socialization agency under the control of the state. However, the idea of enterprise was also extended to other spheres of public provision, including policing (Hobbs 1991) and welfare (Kelly 1991). Once again, the policy to engender an enterprise society, initiated by Conservative governments in the 1980s and early 1990s, has been continued by Labour governments since the late 1990s, as can be seen by the scope of the 2004 Enterprise Insight Campaign (2004), which covers schools and universities as well as potential and actual entrepreneurs of course.

Discussion

The significance of the attempt by successive Conservative and Labour governments in the UK since the 1980s to encourage self-employment directly via self-employment and small business-friendly economic measures, and indirectly via the creation of an enterprise culture, is a matter of some dispute. On the one hand, politicians tend to claim credit for the apparent success of their policies and can point to the take-up of its various measures, such as the Loan Guarantee and Enterprise Allowance Schemes (Wigley and Lipman 1992). On the other hand, the empirical evidence is mixed in that research on the Loan Guarantee Scheme shows that it was effective in stimulating new small-scale capitalism (Ridyard et al. 1989), whereas research on the Enterprise Allowance Scheme shows that it was a minor source of entry to self-employment (Hakim 1988) and that the long-term survival rate of the 'new self-employed would seem to fall far below those estimated officially and, more importantly, the quality of their experiences do not support the idea that we are witnessing the (re)birth of a local enterprise culture' (MacDonald 1996: 434). MacDonald concluded that in a high unemployment area the experience of self-employment was more a matter of survival than an expression of either the enterprise culture or dependency culture. There is also a gender aspect to the Enterprise Allowance Scheme in that it effectively discriminated against women via the benefit eligibility rule (Richardson and Hartshorn 1993).

As far as the enterprise culture is concerned, the above discussion of economic factors suggests that there are four reasons to be sceptical about its value as an explanation for the rise in self-employment since the 1980s in the UK. First, the growth of services, with their lower start-up costs, local markets and labour-intensive character, imply that self-employment would have expanded irrespective of the alleged emergence of a more enterprising culture (Curran and Blackburn 1991b). Second, organizational restructuring tends to be employer-sponsored, hence the conversion of dependent employees into self-employed subcontractors or freelancers is often on an employer's terms and involuntary, not inspired by a spirit of entrepreneurialism (Hakim 1988). This point also applies to the strategy of franchising, which involves an ambiguous employment status (Felstead 1991) and the growth of reluctant entrepreneurs (Boyle 1994). The lack of genuine autonomy and continued subordination to one employer among those who have been converted from an employee to self-employed status at the instigation and in the interests of capital has led Rainbird to argue that 'self-employment constitutes a form of disguised wage labour' (1991: 214). Third, teleworkers are often only nominally self-employed and the motivating force for women homeworkers to become self-employed was not the aspiration to be enterprising, but the need to fit their work around their domestic commitments (Stanworth and Stanworth 1991). This is indicative of a general tendency for women to be more concerned than men with the schedule flexibility that self-employment offers (Carr 1996). Fourth, the tendency for unemployment to push people into self-employment, with or without government support, suggests that this tends to be more of an involuntary push than a spontaneous response to the attractiveness of being part of an enterprise culture (Wright 1997).

In view of the limited salience of enterprise culture in relation to these various routes to self-employment, it seems that many of the new recruits to self-employment during the 1980s in Britain were constrained by circumstances rather than inspired by the appeal of a culture of enterprise. Hence it has been argued that the idea of an enterprise culture is best understood as a rationalizing discourse that helps to make sense of the change from the more collectivist recent past to a more individualist present (Burrows 1991). Thus the unexpected growth of self-employment in Britain and elsewhere over the past quarter of a century was the product of a variety of factors, mostly economic.

There are three possibilities regarding the future of self-employment:

1　Demise theory: the trend of self-employment could revert to the pre-1980s historical pattern of long-term decline;
2　Marginalization theory: self-employment could stabilize at the current level of approximately 10 per cent of the labour force of industrial capitalist societies;
3　De-marginalization theory: self-employment could continue to grow at the expense of standard wage labour (Edgell 1993).

The first possibility (demise theory) is unlikely since the owners of small-scale businesses can 'pass on their capital assets to their children' (Scase and Goffee 1982: 187), and because '[a] history of self-employment in a family is repeatedly found to be a significant factor in people taking up self-employment, and in success' (Hakim 1988: 432). It is also a popular option with high levels of work satisfaction, notwithstanding the myth of autonomy and intrinsic insecurity due to the risk of failure. Moreover, with governments embracing the idea of an enterprise economy with practical and ideological support, the extension of self-employment to the public sector, employers converting employees into self-employed subcontractors of various kinds, further advances in technology which, among other things, reduces start-up costs, and the continued expansion of the service sector, the first possibility seems even more remote. Whether or not self-employment has peaked (marginalization theory) or will continue to grow (de-marginalization theory) depends in part upon one's definition of self-employment in that it could be argued that much of the recent growth of self-employment is spurious and that the rhetoric of enterprise seems to be flourishing better than self-employment itself. In the short term the current trend of self-employment suggests that it will continue to fluctuate. Meanwhile, it is too early to tell if the recent rise in self-employment was a relatively brief historical aberration or the beginning of a long-term trend.

Spatial destandardization: homeworking

Working at home was the norm prior to the rise of industrial capitalism. The introduction of the factory system, and its associated division of labour, necessitated the transfer of production to specialist sites (discussed in Chapter 1). Thereafter home-based work declined in industrial capitalist societies as the economies of large-scale factory production rendered it relatively inefficient and therefore costly. The consequent spatial separation of work from home became a central element in the social construction of the standard form of work that achieved dominance in the mid-to-late twentieth century. However, homeworking or work that is located in the home, predominantly of a manual kind and undertaken primarily by women, persisted in less developed societies and never disappeared completely in the more developed societies, where it survived hidden in the increasingly private sphere of the family (Boris and Prugl 1996). For example, in nineteenth-century Britain it was prevalent in the clothing industry and the production of many other goods, such as boots and shoes (Pennington and Westover 1989). Towards the end of last century home-working expanded and this trend was apparent in both developing societies and the most advanced societies (Boris and Prugl 1996).

Homeworking, like other forms of destandardized work, overlaps with self-employment and may be temporary, as well as part-time or full-time. Moreover, as with self-employment, discussed above, the employment status of homeworkers is certainly problematic. For example, in a study of homeworking in Britain it was found that approximately one-third of homeworkers considered themselves as self-employed and an equivalent proportion thought that their work provider considered them to be self-employed (Felstead and Jewson 1996). Thus well over half of all homeworkers in Britain were self-employed and consequently excluded from the range of employment protections applicable to employees, such as redundancy, lay-off, and maternity pay. The same survey also reported that the remainder either did not know how their provider viewed them or could not specify their employment relationship! Furthermore, incredibly, nearly 90 per cent of homeworkers interviewed by Felstead and Jewson did not have a written contract of employment, two-thirds do not receive an itemized pay slip, although they were typically paid on a piece-rate basis, and the vast majority were not entitled to various fringe benefits, including holiday and sick pay. The lack of employment rights, irrespective of the national regulatory framework, are compounded by relatively low pay, especially for women and ethnic minority homeworkers, and a higher risk to the health and safety of homeworkers compared to those who work in dedicated work spaces, namely factories and offices (Felstead and Jewson 2000). The contemporary vulnerability of homeworkers suggests that little has changed as far as their employment and work conditions are concerned since the late nineteenth century when homework was 'one of the burning issues of the women's trade union movement up to the Trade Boards Act of 1909' (Pennington and Westover 1989: 121).

Along with other types of non-standard work, such as self-employment, home-working is thought to have expanded in recent years in Britain, the USA, and other modern societies, although variations in the way it is defined and therefore measured suggest that statistics on the incidence of homeworking should be treated with caution. For example, 'estimates based on whether any work is done at home widens the focus, while those based on whether work is done mainly at home narrow it' and the distinction between working at or from home is a further source of variation (Felstead and Jewson 2000: 49). Notwithstanding this problem, Felstead and Jewson have noted that studies have estimated that homeworking increased by over 50 per cent in the USA between 1980 and 1990 to 3.4 per cent of the employed population, and by two-thirds in Britain between 1981 and 1991 to 5 per cent of the working population. More recently, in the UK at least, homeworking remained unchanged between 1996 and 2000 (Social Trends 2001), which suggests that, like self-employment, the 1980s expansion of homeworking may have stalled, despite it being preferred to working outside the home by two-thirds of homeworkers (Felstead and Jewson 1996).

The main reasons for the dramatic increase in homeworking in Britain and the USA during the 1980s are technological innovations, notably the computer, and managerial strategies to enhance numerical flexibility in an attempt to reduce costs via outsourcing work to home-based production in the face of global competition (Felstead and Jewson 2000). These two factors often operate together in the form of a cost-cutting restructuring of an organization, as in the case of Rank Xerox where managerial specialist staff were converted from conventional employees to self-employed new technology homeworkers during the early 1980s (Stanworth and Stanworth 1991). Stanworth and Stanworth (1991) have also suggested that the key factor is the development of new technology because it facilitates the spatial destandardization of work by allowing work to be undertaken in the home, thereby reversing the historical trend since the rise of industrial capitalism for work to be concentrated in specialist work spaces. However, evidence from the USA and the UK on homeworking shows that around half of the increase in this type of non-standard work is not dependent on new technology, but on old technology such as the telephone (Castells 2001; Felstead et al. 2001).

Irrespective of whether or not homeworkers are utilizing computing technology or not, Felstead and Jewson have argued that what is unique about homeworkers is that 'they are engaged in a distinctive type of struggle, on a routine basis, to define and to bring into being aspects of their working lives that workplace producers rarely if ever encounter', namely 'the processes of the management of the self that are the bedrock on which the meaning and experience of home-located production rests' (2000: 112). In contrast to those who view homeworking as either totally autonomous (e.g., Bailyn 1988) or minimally autonomous (e.g., Allen and Wolkowitz 1987), the former being associated with high trust, non-routine homeworkers, and the latter with the opposite (Dimitrova 2003), Felstead and Jewson emphasize that home-workers have to manage their work and how it fits in within the household. In practical terms this means that homeworkers have to organize the space they work in and their working time. They also have to supervise themselves to ensure that the quantity and quality of their work is maintained. Finally, they have to manage the juxtapostion of homework with home life, which challenges the idea that paid work is something that takes places outside the home and creates a number of dilemmas since the home is primarily an emotional space. Yet the prospect of earning an income whilst looking after children was by far the most often mentioned advantage of homeworking (Felstead and Jewson 1996). Homeworking therefore puts a premium on self-management skills, and in his respect there are clear parallels between self-employment and homeworking.

Time flexibility is considered to be one of the main advantages of homeworking for employees, although for male homeworkers it is mainly a matter of managing work and leisure time, whereas for women it is typically about managing work and domestic responsibilities (Felstead and Jewson 2000). Thus men were concerned to establish a work routine and a separate space that mirrored working in a non-home environment, whereas women often organized their paid work around their unpaid house and child-care work and undertook their paid work in shared rather than dedicated space. This makes it easier for male homeworkers to work in an uninterrupted way and more difficult for female homeworkers to resist the perception that they are housewives.

For both male and female homeworkers time flexibility may be undermined by a combination of an uneven supply of work, a piece-rate payment system, and the lack of a fixed working day/week, which can result in little control over their work pattern and a tendency to work intensively for long hours, plus the involvement of other family members as unpaid workers (Harvey 1999). Consequently, although homeworkers have the power to decide how, when and where to work, such decisions are often made with reference to their employer or supplier and/or other family members. Limited rather than total flexibility would seem to characterize homeworking.

From the perspective of an employer or supplier, homeworkers not only provide the advantage of numerical flexibility, but do so at a lower wage rate and without the costs associated with employment in a factory or office, such as heating, lighting and employee benefits (Felstead and Jewson 2000). However, homeworking is not without its difficulties for an employer since maintaining control over workers at a distance puts a premium on trust, and a manager's delegational and communication skills (Stanworth and Stanworth 1991). In practical terms, controlling and motivating workers at a distance is more difficult than doing so in a face-to-face situation (Pyoria 2003) and may jeopardize teamwork (Dimitrova 2003). For these reasons, both Stanworth and Stanworh, and Pyoria have suggested that a combination of home and office working would be an arrangement that suited both employers and employees. Potentially, the mixed location solution could also mitigate the problem of staff training and social isolation, which are considered to be two of the major disadvantages for homeworkers.

On balance, potentially, the advantages of homeworking for employees and employers seem to outweigh the disadvantages, yet homeworking in general, and teleworking in particular, remain very much a minority pattern. This suggests that homeworkers are fully aware that this type of non-standard work involves poor working conditions, poor career prospects, and relatively small economic rewards, and that prospective employers of homeworkers are reluctant to relinquish their conventional control of standard workers. Also, perhaps the idea that work is something that is undertaken outside the home is more entrenched in organizational cultures and has been more thoroughly internalized by workers than is realized by those who advocate and celebrate homeworking.

Temporal destandarization: temporary work

In addition to part-time work, discussed in the previous chapter, temporary work is another form of temporal destandardization and, as with other types of non-standard work with which it overlaps, temporary work is an elastic term. The usual definition of temporary work is short-term employment and, as such, it is intrinsically insecure. However, this definition is deceptively simple in that it embraces various overlapping types of temporary work, including casual, seasonal, contract and agency work, plus other types, such as freelance work and self-employment, and can range from a casual couple of hours to full-time temporaries who are effectively permanent (Atkinson et al. 1996; Purcell 2000). Also, as with other types of non-standard work, it was widely but wrongly assumed that the development of the Fordist model of work, characterized by permanent contracts of employment and a range of 'rights, benefits and forms of protection', signalled the historical demise of temporary work (Campbell and Burgess 2001: 171). Yet temporary work persisted, not least due to seasonal demand in agriculture and tourism.

Notwithstanding the usual definitional and measurement problems that afflict all forms of non-standard work, it has been shown that during the 1980s and early 1990s it increased in nearly all industrial capitalist countries (Castells 2001). Moreover, even where the proportion of temporary work grew but remained relatively low, some forms of temporary work increased dramatically, notably that for agencies in Silicon Valley, where they function as a 'substitute' for those with 'poor social networks' (Benner 2002: 228). In the USA as a whole, the temporary help agency workforce increased from just over 400,000 in 1982 to over 2,600,000 in 1997, although the sum total of temporary workers remained quite small (Castells 2001). Similarly, temporary work in the UK remained stable during the 1980s at the relatively low level (Casey 1991), increased slightly during the 1990s to around 7 per cent (Robinson 1999), but from 1984 to 1999 agency temporaries increased fivefold from 50,000 to 250,000 (Forde 2001). More recently, temporary employment increased in most advanced societies except in America and the UK (Burgess and Connell 2004; McOrmond 2004). Thus the UK and the USA are still characterized by a low incidence of temporary employment, despite the recent dramatic growth of some types of temporary work. It has been suggested that 'it is precisely because the regulation of standard forms of employment in the UK and the US is relatively modest that we observe a low incidence of temporary employment', in contrast to France and Spain (Robinson 1999: 96). The recent though short-lived growth of temporary work in the UK and the USA has been attributed to organizational restructuring as part of a concern to improve flexibility and reduce labour costs in both the private and public sectors (Carré 1992; Conley 2002). This suggests that the expansion of the temporary workforce was driven by the demands of employers rather than the preferences of employees, around 40 per cent of whom in the UK would prefer a permanent job (Atkinson et al. 1996; Robinson 1999), and that it was increasingly used by employers as a cost-effective way of dealing with variable demand.

Table 8.2   Percentage distribution of bad job characteristics by employment status

	% of all employees	% with low wages	% with no sick pay	% with no pension	% with no career ladder
Full-time	77.2	22.3	31.1	31.1	46.3
Permanent	71.2	21.4	29.4	29.0	44.9
Temporary	6.0	32.0	53.7	57.4	64.4
Part-Time	22.8	52.4	53.1	55.8	67.1
Permanent	20.1	52.7	50.3	54.3	68.2
Temporary	2.7	32.0	53.7	57.4	64.4
All	100	28.9	36.1	36.7	51.1

Source: Abridged from McGovern et al. (2004: 236)

The main debate regarding temporary work was inspired by Beck's destandardization of work thesis and concerns the quality of it *vis-à-vis* standard work, especially in terms of security of employment, but also other intrinsic and extrinsic features such as skill, pay, benefits and prospects. In other words, does the growth of temporary work, and non-standard work in general, mean that non-standard work is inferior to standard work?

The security of temporary work has been well researched in the UK. A major survey of this issue found that 'the temporary workforce clearly did experience relatively high levels of job insecurity' in comparison with permanent workers (Gallie et al. 1998: 185). The same study also revealed that as far as other aspects of work are concerned, there was a contrast between temporary workers on contracts of less than a year who were trapped in low-skill, minimal repsonsibility, dead-end jobs and those on longer contracts, up to a maximum of three years, who were more like permanent workers with respect to the same features, although still more insecure. As Table 8.2 shows, this pattern has been confirmed by another UK study which showed that non-standard types of workers, especially temporary and part-time workers, are more likely than permanent workers to experience low pay, no sick pay, no pension, and no career ladder (McGovern et al. 2004). Other research in the UK has also shown that employment insecurity is highly gendered, with women more concentrated in the short-term, low-paid and low-skilled temporary work (Purcell 2000). Research in the USA found that different forms of temporary work, such as help agency and on-call workers, were more likely than other non-standard and standard workers 'to have low pay, and to lack insurance and pension benefits' and confirmed the gender dimension (Kalleberg et al. 2000: 273; see also Rosenberg and Lapidus 1999). Elsewhere, for example continental Europe and Japan, recent research has shown that temporary agency work tends to be dominated by women and the young, who receive little training and low wages, and that this is also potentially detrimental to employers (Burgess and Connell 2004). Beck's temporal destandardization of work thesis has been largely confirmed in terms of both insecurity and inferior quality. However, there is little evidence that workers in general are feeling more insecure now that in the 1980s (Robinson 2000).

In view of the marked expansion of agency temporary work in the UK and the USA in the recent past, the implications of this trend for security and wages warrants further comment. A study of two such agencies in the UK concluded that the interventions of agencies have 'facilitated, reinforced and regulated the employment of temporary workers' which 'exacerbated the contingent and insecure nature of temporary working for agency temps' (Forde 2001: 642). Unlike a number of other European societies, the absence of regulations seems to have encouraged the growth and enhanced role of agencies in the labour market. Similarly, research into the operation of temporary employment agencies in Chicago found that their focus on the bottom end of the labour market was adding to the labour market insecurity and exploitation of the lowest paid temporary workers (Peck and Theodore 1998). These studies suggest that the continued growth of employment agencies will have a deleterious effect on the pay and conditions of temporary workers to the clear advantage of employers in terms of increased flexibility and reduced costs. Temporary workers may be a small proportion of the labour force in the UK and the USA, but temporary work is arguably one of the most precarious and least desirable forms of non-standard work, and for the rapidly expanded number of agency temps, it personifies just-in-time labour.

Total destandardization: paid informal work

Informal work, also known as hidden, irregular, invisible, underground, off-the-books, and so on, embodies the destandardization of work in all respects – contractural, spatial and temporal – and as such is totally unprotected. The term 'informal' is thought to be the most commonly used adjective and arguably the most apt because it implies a contrast between this kind of work and formal work (Williams and Windebank 1998). Prior to the development of industrial capitalism, informality characterized most paid work (discussed in Chapter 1 with reference to the irregularity of pre-modern work). From this historical perspective, the transformation of work wrought by industrial capitalism represents the increasing formalization of work that culminated in full employment and a welfare state, known as 'the formalization thesis' (Williams and Windebank 1998: 27), and of course Fordism (Leonard 1998).

However, informal work, both paid and unpaid, persisted, and when Fordism started to decline in industrial capitalist societies in the late 1970s, paid informal economic activity was not only rediscovered but, along with other types of non-standard work, thought to be increasing at the expense of formal or standard work (Mattera 1985). As noted at the beginning of this chapter, the expansion of non-standard work was theorized as an expression of the growing destandardization of work in Beck's increasing job insecurity thesis and in Castells' emergent network enterprise society theory, notwithstanding the difficulties of defining and measuring the incidence of informal work.

Informal work covers a great variety of income-generating economic activities, which range from work that is legal but unreported, and therefore in violation of tax and other state regulations, such as those concerning minimum wages and health and safety, to work which is illegal and, of necessity therefore, hidden as far as possible from public view. This distinction between legitimate but unregulated informal work and criminal activity is commonly made in analyses of informal work, although they often overlap where criminals employ workers informally (Leonard 1998; Mattera 1985). As befits a book on the sociology of work, the focus will be on legitimate informal work since criminal activities are not only even more difficult to measure, but what constitutes criminal activity varies over time and between societies (Thomas 1992). For example, gambling and prostitution are legal in some parts of America, such as Nevada, but not in others.

There are essentially two approaches to measuring of the incidence of informal work: directly, via surveys, and indirectly, by examining discrepancies between national income and expenditure data (Mattera 1985). Both methods are inherently unreliable since they depend upon the accuracy of the information reported to either survey researchers or to those who collect data for the state, something which is highly problematic in the case of work that is undertaken with a view to avoiding tax, insurance, and other regulations (Thomas 1992). Even when similar indirect measures are used, the estimates of the scale of informal work in any one country vary considerably, ranging from just over 4 per cent to one-third of GNP (Portes and Sassen-Koob 1987). Given the difficulty of 'measuring the unmeasurable', Mattera has suggested the '10 per cent solution' as a realistic and reasonable compromise guestimate of the extent of the informal work for the UK and the USA (1985: 53). However, this solution does not address the issue of changes over time or differences between societies. Thus claims on the basis of statistical data that the magnitude of informal work has increased or declined over the past couple of decades should be regarded with extreme caution.

Although reliable evidence of changes in the scale of informal work is not available, there are several grounds for suggesting that this type of non-standard work has increased since the decline of Fordism in the 1970s. First, it is thought that the growth of subcontracting, self-employment and other small-scale enterprises 'provide the most appropriate setting for casual hiring, nonreporting of income, and other informal practices' (Portes and Sassen-Koob 1987: 42). According to this view, informalization is easier to achieve in small firms in part due to the absence of trade unions and in part due to the numbers involved and the type of worker recruited, namely immigrants and women. In their search for greater flexibility and reduced costs following the decline of Fordism, companies transferred their work to agencies and small-scale enterprises, which is not only conducive to informal work but, as noted earlier in this chapter, to all forms of non-standard work. In support of this explanation for the alleged growth of informal work, Portes and Sassen-Koob (1987) cite research into informal work in the garment and construction industries in New York and Miami, although they acknowledge that case study evidence of this kind illustrates the plausibility of the theory but that it is not generalizable. Williams and Windebank (1998) have expressed the reservation that neither small businesses nor subcontracting are inevitably related to informalization since it also occurs in areas not characterized by these ways of organizing production.

A second factor that arguably encourages informal work concerns the role of the state, either in terms of increasing the costs of formal sector work to both employers and employees in the form of national insurance contributions, VAT and income tax, and/or by the weak enforcement of costly statutory regulations such as the 'lax enforcement of minimum wage and labour standards in areas of Europe and the United States in which informal activities proliferate' (Portes and Sassen-Koob 1987: 56; see also Leonard 1998). The positive impact of the state on informal work is thought to have been especially influential in the period after the 1970s when taxes and other contributions increased (Mattera 1985). The main limitation of this explanation of the apparent rise in informal work over the past three decades in advanced societies is that it assumes that the sole motive for engaging in informal work is economic. Yet there is considerable empirical evidence which shows that social and cultural factors influence participation in the informal sector, hence it is more about a 'way of life' than profit maximization (Williams and Windebank 1998: 40). For example, informal work is often valued for the autonomy and satisfaction it provides, thereby enhancing personal freedom and social bonds (Pahl 1984). This applies particularly to those already employed in the formal sector, whose regular income provides security, whereas any irregular income from informal work is regarded as a bonus, to be spent on less essential items (Edgell and Hart 1988). By the same token, financial considerations are more important for the 'working unemployed', as Henry (1982) calls them, but even among the unemployed, working informally is not without its social significance for a person's sense of well-being and confidence (Ferman and Berndt 1981). Thus, for some informal workers and their employers, tax and regulatory evasion may be important, but for others, less so since participation in informal work is undertaken as much for social and cultural reasons as for economic ones.

Third, undocumented immigration from less developed to the more developed industrial capitalist societies is also thought to lead to the growth of informal work (Mattera 1985). Following the 1970s global recession, many advanced societies attempted to restrict immigration, which resulted in a decline in legal immigrant workers and an expansion of undocumented ones (Thomas 1992). Without a work permit, immigrant workers tend to gain employment in low-wage and highly insecure off-the-books work since regular legitimate employment is not an option. The high-risk character of such work is exemplified by the fate of the undocumented Chinese cockle pickers who perished in Morecambe Bay in the summer of 2004. Undocumented immigrants are clearly a major source of informal workers, although the exact scale of the supply of such workers is impossible to estimate accurately.

Finally, there is evidence that dense social networks facilitate informal work by providing information about work opportunities and enhancing the trust essential to avoiding detection by the authorities (Williams and Windebank 1998). Close-knit social networks can develop on the basis of one or more of the following: shared family, shared space, and shared ethnicity (Leonard 1998), and shared occupational culture, for instance firefighters (Edgell and Hart 1988). However, it has been argued that close ties are unlikely to favour informal work 'if all their members are unable to pay for such goods and services', as in the case of communities dominated by long-term unemployment (Williams and Windebank 1998: 41). Therefore it is not just a matter of social network density, but the usefulness of one's network, with family and friends in work more likely to have information about job opportunities.

In addition to the grounds for thinking that informal work has increased in the recent past, there are also reasons for suggesting that it has declined. First, initially it was thought that the rise in unemployment in the most developed industrial capitalist societies in the 1980s would lead to an increase in informal work as redundant workers sought 'to escape chronic unemployment and to supplement paltry official relief', thereby expanding the 'supply of labour available for informal activities' (Portes and Sassen-Koob 1987: 55). When empirical research caught up with theoretical speculation, it was shown that the unemployed were less involved in informal work than other social groups because they not only lacked the resources needed to engage in informal work, such as finance, skills and useful social contacts, but were also more 'likely to be reported by their neighbours' whilst working off-the-books (Pahl 1988: 248). Consequently, the unemployed may be available and in need of extra income, but they are at a marked disadvantage compared with the employed in their chances of obtaining informal work. Therefore a rise in unemployment is likely to depress the scale of informal work, not inflate it.

Studies of the unemployed have found that involvement in informal work is considered to be a poor substitute for employment in the formal sector of the economy. An American study showed that this is because informal work typically provides only a small and irregular income, hence it tends to be regarded by the unemployed as a temporary supplement to state benefits, although it can enhance social contact and boost confidence (Ferman and Berndt 1981). Empirical research in Britain has confirmed these findings and has also shown that informal jobs often involve 'hard work, long hours, dangerous and unhealthy conditions, poor pay and few of the conditions of employment normally afforded workers', and 'were irregular, infrequent and demanded greater flexibility' (MacDonald 1994: 527). For all these reasons, it is widely agreed that the unemployed are far less likely to engage in informal work than the employed.

The second factor that discourages informal work concerns the efficacy of the local and national state in enforcing the relevant regulations applicable to employment. For example, during the 1980s the governments of the UK and the USA both successfully increased their efforts to investigate and retrieve unpaid taxes by people working informally (Mattera 1985). However, there are practical problems with this approach to discouraging informal work, including the issue of civil liberties in the USA (Mattera 1985), and cost effectiveness in the UK (Pahl 1984). The main limitation of this factor is that governments, and therefore policies, change, hence a consistently tough approach to the control of informal work is unlikely over the long term. In fact it may well be that, as noted above, informal work may be tolerated to a greater or lesser extent since to do otherwise may threaten the viability of those parts of the economy that rely heavily on informal labour, such as agriculture and construction.

A third reason for the decline of informal work since the demise of Fordism is the growth of self-provisioning or home production for use rather than exchange (Leonard 1998). Self-provisioning, such as growing food, making clothes and baking bread, was widespread before the advent of industrial capitalism, but these skills were lost by most people when mass production provided goods more cheaply. When Fordism was at its peak during the 1950s and 1960s, self-provisioning in Britain had declined to the point where it was widely assumed that households were almost completely dependent on employment in the formal sector for wages/salaries in order to be able to purchase goods and services in the market, although empirical data showing the exact extent of this process of commodification tends to be lacking (Williams 2002). However, from about the mid-1970s, at more or less the end of Fordism, on the basis of trade figures, Pahl claims that self-provisioning expanded in the form of increased home, garden and car maintenance, due to the rise in home-ownership, 'the combination of lower disposable incomes and higher labour costs', and the decline in standard working hours (1984: 101). Also, 'new tools and cheap, readily available materials encouraged experimentation in providing domestic comforts and improvements' (Pahl 1984: 102). Thus, instead of employing others to repair or maintain the house, garden and car, there was a tendency in Britain during the 1980s to adopt the less expensive strategy of doing the work oneself. In other words, the decline of formal work does not lead automatically to the rise in informal work; it can also lead to a switch of productive work from the paid formal sector to the unpaid domestic sector.

This trend for self-provisioning to increase since the decline of Fordism in industrial capitalist societies is not unique to Britain. Mingione claims that self-help building 'expanded greatly in the 1970s' in Italy (1988: 560), and Glatzer and Berger (1988) found that self-provisioning was extensive in West Germany in 1980, with around two-thirds of households repairing their houses and maintaining their cars. These and other studies also show that self-provisioning is highly gendered, with males specializing in car maintenance and females in dressmaking (Leonard 1998). There is also a class pattern, with more self-provisioning in resource-rich households than in resource-poor households (Williams and Windebank 2002). Thus, although precise data on the extent of self-provisioning during the development of Fordism are not available, there is evidence to show that it was extensive and expanding during the 1970s and 1980s, and is probably still increasing in Britain, perhaps stimulated by the plethora of house and garden makeover programmes on television.

Fourth, whilst the restructuring of employment may encourage informal work, the restructuring of urban spaces tends not to as community ties are disrupted and with them the close relationships upon which trust is built (Morris 1994; Roberts 1994). This factor is related to unemployment since such neighbourhoods are likely to have a high proportion of residents on benefits, which, as noted above, reduces their ability to finance and conceal informal economic activity. There are exceptions to this tendency, notably in Northern Ireland, where informal work is condoned and the political situation makes it more difficult to police informal work (Leonard 1998). However, even in this distinctive locality, the scale of informal work is limited due to the depressed state of the local economy. In general, therefore, when formal work moves away from a locality, informal work opportunities tend to go with them. Deindustrialized, derelict communities are not fertile environments for informal work.

The variability of the presence or absence of the factors that encourage or discourage informal work prompted Williams and Windebank to conclude that 'there is neither universal formalization nor universal informalization across the advanced economies' (1998: 177). Having rejected the search for 'over-simplistic and universal tendencies', they proposed a 'geographically-refined approach to informal employment' in order to comprehend 'both its heterogeneity and the commonalities between areas' (1998: 178). Pivotal to their 'tentative typology' of high and low levels of informal work localities is the distinction between good-quality autonomous and poor-quality exploitative informal work in terms of skill and pay. They outline four types of localities:

1   Areas of high levels of mostly exploitative informal work, for example, poorer areas of southern Europe characterized by small-scale businesses concerned with reducing production costs, relatively deprived populations, and authorities who tend to 'passively tolerate the existence of informal employment' (1998: 105).
2   Areas of high levels of mostly autonomous informal work, for example, affluent areas of northern Europe dominated by small firms concerned with 'high value-added production through technological innovation', relatively affluent locals, and authorities who are relaxed about regulation.
3   Areas of low levels of mostly exploitative informal work, for example, inner-city areas of northern Europe characterized by a high level of unemployment, an economically deprived community, and authorities that are strict about off-the-books work.
4   Areas of low levels of mostly autonomous informal work, for example, wealthy suburbs of affluent cities where unemployment is almost non-existent, the inhabitants are relatively affluent, and the authorities enforce thoroughly the relevant rules and regulations regarding employment.

The first three areas outlined by Williams and Windebank have been widely researched but the type-four area has not, which makes this type the most speculative theorization. They conclude that the kind and scale of informal work in any one area depends on a complex range of economic, social and political factors which results in a tendency for localities to be characterized by predominantly high or low levels of either autonomous or exploitative work.

This contribution is a valiant effort to make sense of the complexity of the patterning of informal work in modern societies. It also underlines the importance of the national and local states and government policies in terms of encouraging and discouraging informal work, a point that has been emphasized by Leonard (1998) and Thomas (1992). Unlike Mattera (1985), Williams and Windebank do not use the language of class, but the thrust of their analysis is the same, namely that the patterning of informal work is similar to that of work in the formal sector. This is particularly clear from their suggestion that informal work 'usually reinforces rather than mitigates the plight of marginal groups' since it implies that the uneven distribution of different kinds of informal work reflects the class structure of the formal employment system (1998: 176). The main weakness of their typology is that the key distinctions between high and low levels of informal work and mostly exploitative or mostly autonomous informal work, lack quantification, without which it is impossible to know other than impressionistically whether or not the four different areas categorized under these types are comparable. Williams and Windebank are fully aware of this difficulty, hence their warning that 'the concepts of "higher" and "lower" levels of informal employment have to be used with great care' (1998: 110).

Summary and conclusions

The idea of the destandardization of work is predicated on the idea that standard work is associated with the rise of Fordism and is usually conceptualized in terms of three key dimensions: the labour contract, the work site, and working hours. From their different perspectives, according to Beck's risk society thesis (1992, 2000) and Castells' network enterprise theory (2000, 2001), non-standard work is increasing at the expense of standard work and is characterized by flexibility, individualization and insecurity, but with potential social benefits for workers in terms of their work–life balance.

The destandardization of the work contract can refer to any aspect of an employment contract, but here self-employment was considered as its opposite since it lacks a contract of any kind. Homeworking was discussed as the embodiment of spatial destandardization, temporary work to exemplify temporal destandarization, and informal work to represent total destandardization. Problems of definition, and therefore measurement, afflict all forms of non-standard work, but are especially acute in the case of informal work because it does not appear in official employment statistics directly. Consequently, of all the forms of non-standard work, historical and cross-national data on informal work are not available and this means that it is virtually impossible to generalize about the incidence of this type of work. Williams and Windebank's tentative typology of the predominance of exploitative and autonomous informal work in different areas is an interesting middle-range compromise that reveals the variety of factors that encourage or discourage these two types of informal work.

The overlap between different types of non-standard work are extensive. Consequently, simply adding up each type is likely to overstate the scale of the destandardization of work process. Historically, contractural, spatial and temporal forms of non-standard work had not disappeared completely with the rise of Fordist standard work, yet evidence of their growth since the 1970s, particularly self-employment and homeworking, was unexpected. Notwithstanding the difficulties of measuring accurately the incidence of non-standard types of work, it has been estimated that in most industrial capitalist societies approximately one-third of the workforce was engaged in non-standard work by the 1990s. Overall, the trend has been one of uneven growth in terms of time and place. For example, self-employment and homeworking increased quite dramatically in the UK in the 1980s but have hardly changed more recently, and temporary work grew from a low base in the UK and USA but it has tailed off since 1998. Yet even in the UK and USA some forms of temporary work have expanded markedly, notably agency temps. There is also evidence that standard work itself has become less standard, especially in relation to working hours and security of employment, thereby blurring the distinction between standard and non-standard work. These changes in the nature of standard work and the uneven growth of non-standard forms of work provide only limited support for Beck's and Castells' claim that non-standard work is expanding. Moreover, the revival of standard work and the decline in volume of non-standard work in the leading national economy, the USA, also suggests that their destandardization of work thesis is exaggerated and that the trend is more complex than they allow. The growth of different types of non-standard work in most advanced societies undermines the idea that it is a myth (Bradley et al. 2000), but the cessation of the growth of non-standard work, with notable exceptions such as the continued expansion of temporary agency jobs, albeit from a very low base, in Silicon Valley, does not amount to a total transformation of work arrangements, just yet.

A mixture of employee- and employer-based reasons have been advanced for the growth of non-standard work, although the exact mix is not the same for every type of non-standard work. From the standpoint of employers, one factor seems to be present in every case, namely changes to the organization of production. Changes to the organization of production date from the crisis of Fordism in the late 1970s and are linked to the globalization of competition which constrained companies to introduce just-in-time labour to complement just-in-time production. The consequent managerial concern for increased numerical flexibility and lower costs of production has resulted in both the tendency for standard work to become less standard and for the three measurable types of non-standard work discussed in the chapter – self-employment, homeworking and temporary work – to expand, albeit unevenly. In view of the overlap between the different types of non-standard work, it is unsurprising that the expansion of every type has been attributed largely to changes to the organization of production.

The role of the state has also been influential in the growth of non-standard work: first, by its policies to encourage directly and indirectly certain types of non-standard work, as in the case of self-employment in the UK; second, by the absence of regulation, such as the operation of temporary employment agencies in the USA; and third, by its limited enforcement of regulations which favours the expansion of non-standard work, notably informal work. Government policies were an integral component of Fordism and they continue to play an important part ideologically via their advocacy of the flexibility of non-standard (and standard work) and, practically, by the presence or absence of regulations that affect the incidence and quality of non-standard work. Indeed, the unevenness of the expansion of different types of non-standard work may be due in large part to national variations in state legislation covering work conditions and rewards, which has influenced both individual and company decisions to embrace non-standard types of work.

An interesting variation of the 'role of the state' theme is the suggestion that the increased sense of insecurity perceived by workers in the UK during the 1990s was not related to the destandardization of labour, since long-term employment has increased, but to the 'critical role of government intervention' which has 'manufactured uncertainty' by policies such as 'the marketization of public services, the withdrawal or weakening of the social protection system, and the opening of national economies to international competition' (Doogan 2001: 439). Doogan is not denying that there is a growing sense of job insecurity, but arguing that Beck is mistaken about the cause. Unfortunately, Doogan only considers full-time and part-time employment patterns. As a result he does not address fully the issue of the growth of other types of potentially precarious non-standard work.

A range of other factors were found to be linked to the growth of certain types of non-standard work that apply to both employees and employers, including technological innovations and homeworking, and social networks and informal work. Technological innovations, especially information technologies, are regarded by Beck and Castells as central to the transformation of work from standard to non-standard. Research on self-employment and homeworking has confirmed that technological changes have reduced the cost of the former and encouraged the latter, although the diffusion, and therefore influence, of advanced information technologies on the expansion of non-standard work is possibly less than that envisaged by Beck and Castells. Technology is arguably not a direct cause of change, but tends to facilitate certain types of non-standard work in conjunction with the re-organization of production. The significance of social networks, or social capital as it is sometimes termed, implies that who you know is more important than what you know, and has long been seen as an important factor that influences who gets what kind of job in the labour market for standard work (Fevre 1992). In the case of the acquisition of non-standard work, social networks seem to be particularly crucial to those seeking informal work, and for those with a social network of limited usefulness, temporary employment agencies can make good this handicap.

From the distinct perspective of the worker, the growth of non-standard work can be in part attributed to the increasing demand for flexibility, such as being able to combine paid work with unpaid work without leaving the home, or more generally improving one's work–life balance, both of which are advanced by Beck and Castells as reasons for the increasing popularity of non-standard work. The evidence from this review of different types of non-standard work suggests that those who are pushed or converted into self-employment by governments keen to reduce unemployment, or employers who are interested in reducing costs, or those who take a temporary job having failed to obtain a permanent one, are not doing so for the potential benefits of flexibility. The exact proportion of reluctant non-standard workers is difficult to estimate but in the case of temporary workers it is around 40 per cent and rising in the UK. Among homeworkers in the UK a majority report a preference for not working outside the home. More generally, what little research exists currently on the demand for more flexible work shows that it is small and that there is concern about the implications of increased flexibility for job security and benefits (McRae 1989). These findings provide only limited support for the view that non-standard work is growing at the behest of the workers and suggest that workers are aware of the economic and social risks of opting for such work in preference to standard work.

A major issue regarding the decline of standard work and the expansion of non-standard types of work is that it involves a deterioration in the quality of jobs, particularly in terms of security, but also in pay, prospects and fringe benefits. In short, fewer standard jobs and more non-standard jobs means fewer good jobs and more bad jobs. Surveys in the UK and USA have broadly confirmed that this is the case, although there are some exceptions, such as self-employed males who often earn more than equivalent standard employees but were still less likely to receive fringe benefits. The tendency for non-standard jobs to be inferior to standard jobs suggests that flexibility comes at a high price for employees and a low price for employers. However, variations in the degree of security, relatively good for part-timers (discussed in Chapter 7) but far less so temporary agency workers, indicates a need to distinguish carefully between types of such work rather than bracket them together (Robinson 2000). Thus, the insecurity dimension of Beck's destandardization thesis is at best unevenly supported by the data for the UK and USA.

Finally, it has been argued that the opportunity to achieve a 'better harmonization of familial and wage labour' (Beck 1992: 146) and 'improved family relationships' (Castells 2001: 290) fuels the demand for all types of non-standard work. The patterning of different types of non-standard work suggests that this may apply to somewhere between one-third and two-thirds of non-standard workers, depending upon the type of non-standard work undertaken. There is also some data to show that men and women view flexibility somewhat differently, with the former being more focused on their leisure activities and the latter on their unpaid domestic work (McRae 1989). Thus it is too early to say whether or not the optimism expressed by Beck and Castells regarding the impact of greater work flexibility on the work–life balance is justified. The extent to which, if any, changes in the partial re-organization of both standard and non-standard work since the demise of Fordism has influenced the organization of unpaid domestic and voluntary work is the subject of the next chapter.

Further reading

The main proponents of the destandardization thesis are Beck's (1992) *Risk Society: Towards a New Modernity* and (2000) *The Brave New World of Work*, and Castells' (2001) *The Rise of the Network Society* (2nd edn). There are two good overviews of the debate: one that focuses on job security by Heery and Salmon (eds) (2000) *The Insecure Workforce*, and another on the different types of non-standard work by Felstead and Jewson (eds) (1999) *Global Trends in Flexible Labour*. With the exception of temporary work, there are good sociological studies of each type of non-standard work, including Curran and Blackburn (eds) (1991a) *Paths of Enterprise: The Future of the Small Business*, Feldstead and Jewson (2000) *In Work, At Home: Towards an Understanding of Homeworking*, and Leonard

(1998) *Invisible Work, Invisible Workers: The Informal Economy in Europe and the US.* The most sceptical view of the destandardization thesis can be found in Bradley et al. (2000) *Myths at Work.*

Questions for discussion and assessment

1. Evaluate the evidence that non-standard work is growing in the UK and the USA.
2. To what extent is non-standard work inferior to standard work?
3. Why has self-employment expanded in the UK since the 1980s?
4. Consider the view that homeworking mainly benefits employers.
5. Examine the advantages and disadvantages of temporary work.
6. Account for the heterogeneous development of informal work.

CHAPTER NINE

Unpaid Work Domestic Work and Voluntary Work

In the first chapter it was argued that during the rise of industrial capitalism in Britain, in the absence of any restrictions on who could be employed and for how long, the opportunities for women to work outside the home were quite good, although they tended to undertake the relatively less skilled and less well paid types of work. However, the employment of large numbers of women outside the home, especially mothers, created problems for men whose authority was threatened, and employers whose supply of able-bodied workers was threatened. The solution was to limit the employment of women and children via a variety of practical and ideological forces that reduced a woman's role to domestic matters. The emergent division of labour involved men specializing in working for pay outside the home, enabling them to reassert their authority, and women to working in an unpaid capacity inside the home, ensuring the maintenance and future supply of healthy workers. The male breadwinner and female homemaker model that evolved in Britain, and elsewhere to a greater or lesser extent but not universally, tended to be adopted far more by middle-class families than working-class ones who could less well afford a financially dependent wife, although support for this ideal was widespread. Ironically, the middle-class wife did not so much do the domestic work as employ and organize single working-class women to do it (Oakley 1976). This arrangement left them free to undertake other unpaid work, namely voluntary work, and did not threaten the ideal of feminine domesticity nor that of male economic provider, and had the added advantage of demonstrating the prosperity of the household, thereby enhancing the status of the male head.

The emergence of a dominant conception of work, with its emphasis on paid employment outside the home in the late nineteenth century, was reflected and affirmed in the Census categories in Britain which from 1881 onwards excluded unpaid domestic work (Hakim 1980). Hakim noted that although the Census Report acknowledged the importance of such work, it was excluded for 'spurious methodological reasons' (1980: 558). Paid domestic workers continued to be counted as economically active, which shows that by this time only the production of goods and services exchanged in the market were deemed to be worthy of being included as work (Beneria 1988). The long-term effect of not counting full-time unpaid domestic work from national statistics on work was to discount and hence undervalue women's economic contribution.

By the beginning of the twentieth century, largely as a consequence of the physical separation of the home from work, and in due course the relative exclusion of men from unpaid domestic work inside the home and women from paid work outside the home, the tradition of women being primarily responsible for the housework and children, referred to here as domestic work, was established, albeit in the form of an aspiration rather than a reality in working-class families. Taking his cue from Veblen's theory of women's subordination (1970 [1899]), Galbraith has suggested that '[t]he conversion of women into a crypto-servant class was an accomplishment of the first importance', and that thanks to the development of industrial capitalism, 'the servant-wife is available, democratically, to almost the entire present male population' (1979: 49). Thus, instead of the gender-neutral term 'houseworker', the widely held assumption in modern societies is that wives are primarily responsible for domestic work, hence the term 'housewife' (Martin and Roberts 1984).

During the first half of the last century, aside from the exceptions of the two world wars when women entered the labour market in Britain temporarily as a matter of expediency and therefore did not challenge the dominant conception of work, the economic activity rate of adult women remained more or less static at around 33 per cent between 1901 and 1951, compared to a male rate that ranged from 84 per cent to 91 per cent (Hakim 1996). In fact, in the UK, the gender dimension of the dominant conception of work was reinforced by the Beveridge-inspired post-war welfare state, which assumed that the wife's place was at home performing 'vital but unpaid labour' and that the husband's was at work full-time (Williams and Williams 1987: 51). This gender division of labour was part of the Fordist compromise which privileged men in relation to standard work outside the home, thereby freeing them from major domestic responsibility, and 'constructed women's work in relationship to motherhood' (Gottfried 2000: 239). It has been argued that the male breadwinner and female houseworker ideal characterizes nearly all welfare regimes to a greater or lesser extent, with some countries, such as Britain and Germany, considered to be examples of a strong version of the model (Lewis 1992), although there are exceptions (Janssens 1997; Pfau-Effinger 2004). Thus, in the mid-to-late twentieth century, it was still clear who was expected to, and actually did, undertake most of the unpaid work inside the home.

The other main type of unpaid work to be considered in this chapter is voluntary work for non-profit organizations that are generally regarded as part of the social economy or third sector, separate from, and an alternative to, not only profit-oriented private organizations but also to non-profit public organizations (Borzaga and Defourney 2001). The boundaries of the non-profit and voluntary sector are increasingly blurred due to changes in the funding and responsibilities of this sector *vis-à-vis* business and government (Frumkin 2002). For example, 98 per cent of the funding of the British social care charity Turning Point comes from contracts with local authorities and National Health Service commissioners (Benjamin 2004). The non-profit sector includes co-operative enterprises, mutual societies, plus a great variety of voluntary organizations that are often concerned with the amelioration of needs unmet by the market system, in spite of the (uneven) growth of welfare states (Kendall and Knapp 1995). In addition to this unpaid formal voluntary work, there is informal unpaid voluntary work, often referred to as community work and usually excluded from surveys of voluntary work on the grounds that potentially it contains elements of reciprocity and obligation (Finch 1989; Finch and Groves 1983; Gregory and Windebank 2000).

The non-profit sector in general and formal voluntary work in particular predates industrialization, for example friendly societies animated by mutual aid and self-help, but expanded in the nineteenth century, often inspired by religious and secular ideologies concerned with the plight and lack of providence of the working classes in the context of the economic and social costs of the transformations wrought by the rise of industrial capitalism before a state system of welfare was established (Birchall 1997; Kendall and Knapp 1996). Notwithstanding extensive middle-class philanthropy and working-class self-help and informal neighbourhood work (Taylor 2004), the class and gender image of formal voluntary work that dates from this period is of the rich ministering to the needs of the poor, epitomized by the charitable activities of 'ladies of leisure'. According to Veblen, the cultural imperative to avoid paid work in order to perform vicarious leisure that affirms a husband's pecuniary status 'applies more rigorously to upper-class women than to any other class' (1970 [1899]: 228). The class dimension of this stereotype was still apparent in the UK in the 1990s when a survey showed that the higher socio-economic group the greater the likelihood of formal volunteering (www.ivr.org.uk/nationalsurvey.htm). The gender dimension of this stereotype has been sustained by the public visibility of women volunteers with collection tins on the street and behind the counters of charity shops. Yet in contrast to unpaid domestic work and informal voluntary work, both of which are female-dominated (Finch and Groves 1983; Gregory and Windebank 2000), men and women participate in formal voluntary work about equally (www.ivr.org.uk/nationalsurvey.htm).

Neither domestic nor formal and informal voluntary work are included in national statistics on work, which reflects the continued pre-eminence of the dominant conception of work that undervalues unpaid work. However, whereas domestic work has been the focus of research over the past forty years, due in large measure to a feminist critique of the devaluation of women's work, voluntary work, especially the formal kind, remains notoriously under-researched except by social and political policy analysts (Taylor 2004). Taylor has suggested that one possible explanation for the neglect of (formal) voluntary work by sociologists is that it falls between the two stalls of public sphere paid work, theorized within mainstream economics, and the private sphere unpaid work, not theorized within mainstream economics. Arguably, unpaid private sphere work tends to be theorized with reference to gender. In the case of informal voluntary work, it is similarly neglected by mainsteam economists since it is unpaid, but it is nearer to unpaid domestic work in that it is embedded in kinship and neighbourhood relationships. Figure 9.1 shows that formal voluntary work occurs in the public sphere but it is like private sphere work in that it is unpaid, and informal voluntary work is undertaken partly in the public sphere (i.e., neighbourhood work) and partly in the private sphere (i.e., kinship work). Presenting these

Public sphere work
Paid formal work – Male-dominated
Formal voluntary work
Unpaid voluntary organization work – neither male- nor female-dominated
Informal voluntary work
Unpaid kinship and neighbourhood work – Female-dominated
Private sphere work
Unpaid domestic work – Female-dominated

Figure 9.1   Spheres and types of work

Source: Adapted from Taylor (2004: 32)

distinctions between different types of paid and unpaid work in this way suggests that as one moves nearer to the private sphere and away from the public sphere, women tend to dominate and vice versa.

The paucity of sociological research on voluntary work contrasts with the importance of this sector, estimated in the 1990s to be of major and growing economic significance in terms of paid employment, accounting for over 3 per cent of all jobs in the UK and 7 per cent in the USA (www.jrf.org.uk/knowledge/findings/socialpolicy/SP82.asp). Far from shrinking after the development of state welfare, the voluntary sector has expanded over the past half century, especially since the 1980s restructuring of state welfare. The recent growth of the voluntary sector is supported by left- and right-wing politicians, with the former tending to emphasize the democratic and community service aspects and the latter with limiting the role of the state and personal responsibility as part of the attempt to revive self-help and enterprise (Deakin 1995). Governments in the UK and USA over the past two decades have turned to this sector to compensate for the reduction in services following cuts in public welfare provision (Borzaga and Defourney 2001; Castells 1997; Frumkin 2002).

The relative neglect of voluntary work by sociologists and the increasing attention devoted to domestic work is aptly reflected in the contributions of Beck (1992, 2000) and Castells (1997, 2001), who focus on the politics of the former and egalitarian aspects of the latter. Briefly, since more detail will be forthcoming below and in the next chapter, Beck's distinction between early and later modern society informs one current theorization of voluntary work and both Beck and Castells discuss the decline of the patriarchal family. These are among the issues that will be addressed in this chapter on the character and changing patterns of domestic and voluntary work.

Unpaid domestic work

The gender-neutral term 'domestic work', like that of 'houseworker', is misleading since it has been so thoroughly feminized and is synonymous with the role of a wife that the idea of a househusband is greeted invariably with sniggers. Yet the historical association in theory and practice between married women and unpaid domestic work, encapsulated by the term 'housewife', dates from the mid-to-late nineteenth century (Oakley 1976). It was not until 100 years later that sociologists started to research it as a type of work, although general sociology textbooks still tend to discuss it under the heading 'gender' (e.g., Macionis 2001), rather than in the context of work, as in the notable exception of Giddens (1997). The first study of housework as an 'occupation' was undertaken by Lopata (1972) in the USA and based on data collected in the 1950s and 1960s from a sample of 568 Chicago housewives aged between 19 and 84, of whom 468 were full-time housewives. This was followed in the UK by Oakley (1974), who studied housework as 'work' and interviewed 40 full-time London housewives in 1971, all of whom were mothers aged between 20 and 30. The findings of these two pioneering studies were broadly similar regarding full-time housewives who were mothers, despite differences in the size and representativeness of their samples.

Both Lopata (1972) and Oakley (1974) note the low social status of the 'job' of housewife and suggest that this is mainly due to the lack of payment, but also because preparation and recruitment to it are informal, entry is via marriage or cohabitation, and that it is ascribed on the basis of gender rather than achieved via formal training and testing. Employment outside the home does not negate the status of, and hence a wife's primary responsibility for, domestic work, although it may diminish the work load with other family and/or non-family members undertaking more work. The low status of the housewife is indicated by commonly used words and phrases to refer to this unpaid work role, such as 'cabbage' or 'just a housewife' (Oakley 1974: 47, 48), and is reflected in the 'dislike of the title "housewife" expressed by many of the women' interviewed by Lopata (1972: 78). The widespread denigration of the housewife role derives from the conventional representation of domestic work as a boring activity, and this epithet attaches to those who do it. In order to assess whether or not this image of housework is justified, the perspective advanced by Oakley (1974, 1976), and to a lesser extent Lopata (1972), will be adopted. This involves analysing unpaid domestic work in the same way as any paid work role, rather than as something that is intrinsic to femininity in modern societies. Thus unpaid domestic work will be analysed as far as possible in terms of the interrelated characteristics of work featured in the earlier chapters on paid work, including alienation, satisfaction, skill, hours and conditions. Moreover, as will become apparent below, the impact of technological change is also relevant to any account of the sociology of domestic work as work.

In Chapter 2 it was noted that Blauner operationalized alienation with reference to four dimensions: powerlessness, meaninglessness, social isolation and self-estrangement. Empirical research on domestic work shows that the power to exercise control over the scheduling of work tasks and how to accomplish them without direct supervision was extensive and valued highly by full-time housewives (Lopata 1972; Oakley 1974). This freedom from interference in the work environment compared favourably with most paid work situations outside the home. However, the autonomy enjoyed by housewives was more 'theoretical than real' due to the 'obligation to see that housework gets done' (Oakley 1974: 43), and the presence of children creates demands than cannot be ignored and leads to a sense of 'being tied down' (Lopata 1972: 194). Other research has shown that housewives are constrained by the need to accommodate the demands of the husband's work since this is vital to the economic success of the family (Edgell 1980), and that when husband's work at home, 'household routines get organized around the male breadwinner's work' (Finch 1983: 55). These limitations on the freedom experienced by a housewife suggest that an unpaid domestic worker shares with the self-employed a sense of being one's own boss but in practice it is contradicted on a daily basis.

The evidence on meaninglessness and domestic work is also mixed in that some aspects are a major source of purposefulness, notably child-rearing, and others, such as the more regular domestic tasks of washing-up and cleaning, are regarded as far less rewarding and endlessly repetitive. The housewives interviewed by Lopata and Oakley both reported considerable satisfaction with motherhood, although Lopata noted that '[t]he combination of being tied down and having a heavy workload leads many women in their twenties to wish for a maid or cleaning help' (1972: 196), and a majority of Oakley's sample expressed dissatisfaction with the monotony of housework. This pattern has been confirmed by subsequent research, notably in a study of 50 working-class and middle-class mothers which found that children 'gave them a purpose and in pursuing this purpose, they experienced their lives as meaningful', but also that they found it 'very demanding and frustrating' (Boulton 1983: 104, 128). The parallels between rewarding child-care work and unrewarding housework and different types of paid work is instructive in that Blauner argued that '[w]orking on a unique and individuated product is almost inherently meaningful', whereas it is 'more difficult to develop and maintain a sense of purpose in contributing toward a standardized product since this inevitably involves repetitive work cycles' (1964: 23). Unsurprisingly, though arguably unconvincingly, Oakley concluded that with respect to housework and dissatisfaction, 'housewives have more in common with assembly line workers than with factory workers engaged in more skilled and less repetitive work' (1974: 182).

At the child-rearing stage of the family cycle social isolation has been found to be extensive, especially among housewives at the beginning of this stage in urban neighbourhoods. Lopata noted that, among other things, child-care involves 'isolation from interaction and intellectual stimulation' (1972: 193), and according to Oakley, 'loneliness is an occupational hazard for the modern housewife, who is often cut off not only from community life but often from family life' (1974: 88). The main reason for the lack of social interaction is the housebound nature of having a young child whose needs are paramount, and the tendency for domestic work to be undertaken alone rather than as part of a work group. The problem of social isolation can be mitigated to some extent by living in a neighbourhood with lots of other young families (Lopata 1972), and/or the same neighbourhood as one's kinship group (Oakley 1974). Moreover, once the young child joins a pre-school play group or starts school, opportunities for social interaction are enhanced considerably as the housewife has an increased chance of meeting people and more free time to enjoy adult company. Other strategies that can reduce the social isolation of housewives include working part-time for pay or in a voluntary organization such as a Parent Teacher Association (Gavron 1968; Lopata 1972). Thus, although social isolation is potentially an acute problem for mothers with young children and a major source of discontent, the housebound dimension for most is short-lived, but the inherently isolated nature of the domestic workplace endures.

Finally, as far as Blauner's four dimensions of alienation are concerned, self-estrangement or self-expression, characterized by a lack of involvement in work, is also applicable to domestic work. Lopata found that, on the one hand, the housewife who becomes a mother experiences an identity crisis due to the 'limitation of occasions to display a wide range of personality behaviours in a variety of social contexts which show the uniqueness of self', on the other hand, it 'is experienced as an increase in maturity, in capacities and abilities' (1972: 193). The tension between the potentially challenging, involving, and rewarding character of child-rearing, and the perceived boring nature of much of the housework associated with it was apparent from Boulton's study of motherhood (1983). The positive and negative possibilities of domestic work were also outlined by Oakley, who contrasted the assembly-line character of ironing to the 'creative potential' of cooking, although the latter may be limited by the preferences and demands of husbands and children (1974: 58).

This review of the degree to which domestic work for mothers is alienating in Blauner's sense of the term suggests that there are some features of housework that are quite alienating, such as the more arduous and repetitive tasks, and that there are others which are far less so, notably child-rearing. In view of the mixed experience of domestic work, overall it could be argued that domestic work at the child-rearing stage of the family cycle is alienating to a medium rather than high or low degree. However, if certain routine features of domestic work are separated from the mother role, the degree of alienation is higher. This has been confirmed by Oakley's likening of the experience of monotony, fragmentation and pace of work for housewives to that of factory and assembly-line work, notwithstanding the greater autonomy and task variation characteristic of housework and valued by housewives. Domestic work is clearly a dissatisfying activity for the most part, and although child-care is a major source of meaning and purpose, it also contributes to a housewife's workload and restricts her freedom and social interaction.

As far as the other characteristics of work featured in the early chapters are concerned, domestic work encompasses a wide range of work roles and skill levels, including relatively unskilled manual work (e.g., cleaning), relatively skilled manual work (e.g., cooking), emotional work (e.g., child-care), service work (e.g., shopping and driving children to school), and a variety of non-manual work activities that put a premium on administrative and social skills (e.g., organizing work tasks and managing people). Clearly, domestic work involves a great variety of labour-intensive jobs, characterized by multiple tasks and skills, which can be rotated by choice within the constraints generated by the needs and demands of other family members. The 'heterogeneity' and import of the work activities undertaken by contemporary housewives is unmistakable and noted by both Lopata (1972: 364) and Oakley (1974: 183), though less impressive than in the pre-modern era when a knowledge of horticulture, animal husbandry, and making clothes were also an essential part of the job. Arguably, the managerial dimension of domestic work has increased in significance over time, and technology has caused 'a deskilling of housework' as well as reducing the physical drudgery (Offe, cited in Beck 1992: 110).

Domestic work: conditions and technology

Studies of the working hours of full-time housewives date back to the 1920s in the USA and show there was little change between the 1920s and 1960s, averaging about 52 hours in the mid-1920s and 55 hours a week in the mid-1960s, which 'is longer than the average person in the labour force' (Vanek 1980 [1974]: 83). Oakley compared the surveys of housework hours in the USA, France, and Britain over a similar period and also found that, aside from small fluctuations, between 1929 and 1971 the average weekly hours spent on domestic work was reasonably stable with a slight increase over time (Oakley 1974). In other words, whilst the average number of hours worked by factory workers each week decreased during this period by around 10 hours to 40 hours, those worked by the full-time housewives in her sample was 77 hours, which is nearly twice the hours worked in industry.

One explanation advanced by both Vanek and Oakley for the conundrum that despite the introduction of electrically powered technology in the form of labour-saving appliances into the home, such as washing and cleaning machines, the long working week of housewives has remained remarkably stable, and if anything has increased, focuses in large part on increased productivity and the related rise in standards of cleanliness and cooking. A good example of higher productivity and expectations concerns doing the laundry with the aid of a washing machine and tumble drier which enables this activity to be undertaken once or more a day rather than once or twice a week. Thus, in the more affluent contemporary society, 'people have more clothes now than they did in the past and they wash them more often' (Vanek 1980 [1974]: 84–5). In addition to agreeing with the Vanek and Oakley thesis that domestic technology has increased the productivity and time spent on housework and their explanation, Cowan claims that, due to the introduction of complex industrial goods into households, 'houseworkers are as alienated from the tools with which they labour as assembly-line people' (1983: 7). More recent Australian time–use data has confirmed the tendency that 'owning domestic technology rarely reduces unpaid housework' and that in some circumstances it 'marginally increases the time spent on the relevant task' (Bittman et al. 2004: 412). These researchers also attributed this trend to the wish to improve the quantity and quality of domestic work outputs. Thus, technological change has not reduced the housewife's working week, although it has undoubtedly reduced the physical demands of domestic work.

A second possible explanation of the myth of time-saving electrical appliances suggested by Vanek concerns the under-valuation of domestic work in modern societies, which prompts those responsible for it to increase the quality and quantity of their output and hence expand the time spent on it in order to demonstrate the importance of their contribution. Vanek argues that the homemaker's contribution to the family economy is less clear 'compared to the more easily measurable and transparent significance of wages and that long working hours help to indicate the value of domestic work' (1980 [1974]: 88). A slightly different line of argument is offered by Oakley, who contends that the tendency for full-time housewives to set continuously exacting standards and routines is a form of 'job enlargement' that increases work satisfaction and working hours (1974: 111). Considered together, these explanations of the expansion of domestic work time could be construed as an attempt to legitimize what is conventionally regarded as an essentially mundane and unsatisfying job.

Another reason proposed by Vanek (1980 [1974]) for the constancy of the time spent on domestic work between the 1920s and 1960s by full-time housewives is that there has been a redistribution of time expended on various activities. For example, whilst less time is spent on food preparation, more time is devoted to shopping and child-care. The increase in shopping, including travelling, not only reflects the decline in producing one's own food and clothes (Cowan 1983), but also the desire to escape the confines of the house and meet people, thereby alleviating the social isolation of domestic work (Oakley 1974). The expansion of time spent on child-care activities, despite the historical decline in family size, is indicative of the increasingly child-centred character of modern societies (Oakley 1976), and the tendency in western culture to allocate primary responsibility for child-care to mothers rather than other relatives or non-family organizations (Boulton 1983).

An alternative view on the issue of domestic work time in general, and the impact of technology in particular, has been put forward by Gershuny, who first of all qualifies Vanek's domestic work time thesis by arguing that in the UK the 'apparent constancy in the total' number of hours spent on unpaid domestic work is 'an artefact produced by the downwards effect of the new domestic technologies on working-class women, and the substantial increase in work caused by the loss of paid domestic service in middle-class households' (Gershuny 2000: 67). Second, and following from the previous point, Gershuny shows that there was a 'strong middle-class bias' in the survey data used by Vanek which underpins the apparent growth in the time spent on domestic work (2000: 67). Third, although he agrees that the initial impact of domestic appliances is to increase productivity and hence the time spent on a particular activity, he also claims that as more efficient machines are made available, the time spent on 'the core housework tasks of cooking and cleaning' declines (Gershuny 2000: 67; see also Gershuny 2004). Gershuny concluded that domestic appliances increased productivity but is very sceptical of the view that it results unambiguously in increased domestic work time.

There are several difficulties with the attempt to measure the amount of time spent on domestic work following the introduction and diffusion of electrical appliances into the home. First, there is the methodological problem of dividing the day up into specified time slots, such as half-hour periods, and asking respondents to record the main activity undertaken within each. This approach tends to overlook 'very short activities and secondary or concurrent activities' and therefore underestimates the total amount of domestic work and the fragmentation of such work (Thomas and Zmroczek 1988: 107; see also Wajcman 1995: 222). A similar point has been expressed by Hakim, who has noted that '[t]he number of hours of work can be misleading, given flexibility in the housewife's use of time' (1996: 47). This criticism raises serious doubts about the accuracy of this way of measuring domestic work participation. It is clear from Gershuny's 'Reflections on Time-Diary Methodology' that he is not unaware of this issue (2000: 249).

Second, it is difficult to isolate the time impact of one specific technological change, for example the introduction of washing machines, from other related technological changes, such as the use of fabrics made from synthetic fibres and soaps made from synthetic detergents (Thomas and Zmroczek 1988). It may be that the availability of clothes made from materials that are cheaper to buy and easier to wash and dry, for instance drip-dry shirts, encouraged people to buy more clothes and wear them shorter periods and this could account, in part, for the increase in time spent on laundry work. Once again, Gershuny is fully cognisant of this problem since he notes: 'It is very hard to disentangle the various strands of change' (2000: 181).

Third, technological developments do not occur in a social vacuum; 'fundamental social factors' are involved, notably the number of other people in a household and the amount of domestic work they create and undertake (Wajcman 1995: 222). In the Australian study cited above it was found that electrical kitchen appliances 'do not save women any time', whereas they do result in a reduction in the time men spend on domestic work (Bittman et al. 2004: 409). Cowan has suggested that this is 'partly because they believe that the work simply cannot be onerous, but also because some of the "extra" appliances actually relieve them of sex-related, or sex-acceptable chores' (1983: 200). Thus if men conventionally help with the washing up, as is often the case, the impact of the purchase of a dishwashing machine would be to reduce their domestic work time contribution. Hence one of the major ironies of domestic appliances is that it saves men time and is implicated in the creation of more work for women. This is not meant to suggest that women have missed out completely on the time-saving potential of domestic technologies since, as Cowan also argues, the diffusion of washing machines, dishwashers, microwave ovens, frozen food and so on were 'catalysts' of the increased participation of women in paid work (1983: 209). However, this development was a mixed blessing for women in terms of the total amount of time expended on paid and unpaid work by men and women, as the following section makes clear.

Gender and the division of domestic work: the symmetrical family thesis

One theory that links the development of industrial capitalism to the changing pattern of domestic work is Young and Willmott's symmetrical family thesis. They proposed a four-stage historical sequence starting with: (1) the eighteenth-century pre-industrial family in which men and women worked together as a unit of production; (2) the nineteenth-century early industrial family characterized by the physical and social segregation and inequality between men and women; (3) the less segregated, more equal and hence symmetrical twentieth-century (later) industrial family; and (4) the twenty-first-century multiple family types ranging from the asymmetrical to the symmetrical 'two demanding jobs for the wife and two for the husband' (Young and Willmott 1973: 278).

From the standpoint of who is responsible for and undertakes domestic work the key stages are 2 and 3, since the first is no longer relevant to the vast majority of families and the fourth refers to a number of speculative possibilities that will be discussed later. The stage 2 family corresponds to the male breadwinner and female houseworker model discussed earlier and is characterized by a clear differentiation of roles within and outside the home. The husband's job was to earn money which he controlled and it was the wife's job to do virtually all the domestic work, even if she worked out of necessity having overcome the practical and ideological barriers designed to prevent married women from obtaining paid work employment, and to spend the housekeeping money on the family: 'There was a man's sphere and a woman's sphere, in spending as in other functions' (Young and Willmott 1973: 82). In the highly segregated and gendered division of labour, '[i]f the husbands did any "work" at all at home the tasks that they, and their wives, thought proper to them were those to which male strength and male manual skill lent themselves' (Young and Willmott 1973: 94). In industries with multiple shift systems, such as coal mining, the gendered character of domestic work was especially crucial to the organization of industrial work (Beynon and Austrin 1994).

This changed during the twentieth century with the rise of the stage 3 symmetrical family, which, via the 'Principle of Stratified Diffusion', spread from the middle classes to the working classes so that by 1970 it was the predominant pattern among Young and Willmott's large London area research sample (1973: 19). The three defining features of this new type of family are that it is home-centred, focused on the nuclear family and, most importantly from the perspective of the sociology of work, a less segregated and more equal relationship. In practical terms this translates into a husband doing more unpaid domestic work although primary responsibility is retained by the wife, and a wife doing more paid work with the husband retaining the major responsibility for economic support, and this 'egalitarian tendency works with a time lag' (Young and Willmott 1973: 20). Young and Willmott qualify their thesis, such as when they use the phrase 'more symmetrical' and note that '[w]e are only talking of trends' (1973: 32, 265). Yet there is no escaping the main thrust of their argument, namely that in modern Britain there is now a more equal division of paid and unpaid work which started at the top and worked its way down the class structure to the point where the 'great majority of married people in our sample were members of the dominant type of new family' (1973: 94).

Young and Willmott suggest that a variety of factors caused the change from the male-dominated and highly segregated nineteenth-century family to the more equal and less segregated twentieth-century family, including affluence, migration, establishment of the welfare state, the reduced paid working hours of men, and the employment of married women outside the home, but seem to place particular weight on technology and feminism. The rise of feminism was successful to the extent that it improved the status of women, legally, economically, politically and socially, and the role of technology was similarly multifaceted in that it helped to improve the quality of home life via smaller families (i.e., contraceptive technology), better housing (i.e., access to clean water plus new sources of energy), and the availability of consumer goods (i.e., washing machines). The idea that technology transforms work and family largely for the better, to the extent that it upskills paid jobs and improves the quality of home life, corresponds to Bell's post-industrial society thesis (discussed in Chapter 4) and is acknowledged as a 'major influence on their thinking' (Young and Willmott 1973: 19).

The main weakness of the symmetrical family thesis is a lack of convincing empirical evidence, even from Young and Willmott's own London-centric data. First, although they present qualitative and quantitative data that purports to show increasing symmetry, their analysis does not provide unequivocal support for their thesis. For example, Oakley has noted that there was only one question on the domestic division of labour out of an interview schedule of over 100 and the table (No. 8) that summarizes the answers to this 'poorly worded question' reveals a limited degree of male domesticity (1974: 164). The same key table also demonstrates the weakness of the class diffusion dimension of their symmetrical family thesis since it shows that husbands in clerical jobs 'help in the home' more than any other occupational class, including the more unambiguously middle-class professional and managerial categories (Young and Willmott 1973: 95). Young and Willmott concede that among their respondents, 'it was in virtually all not expected that men should do more than *help* their wives' and that wives 'retain primary responsibility for domestic work' (1973: 96, italics in the original). However, rather than revise their theory about increasing symmetry, they maintain that 'the extent of sharing is probably still increasing' (Young and Willmott 1973: 94).

The results of empirical research in Britain, the USA, and other modern societies since Young and Willmott's study was first published in 1973 were no more encouraging for the symmetrical family thesis in that study after study revealed little evidence of behavioural symmetry, even among the strategic case of middle-class couples (e.g., Berk 1985; Berk and Berk 1979; Bond and Sales 2001; Edgell 1980; Gregory and Windebank 2000; Martin and Roberts 1984; Morris 1990; Newell 1993; Picchio 2003; Wajcman 1996). Although these and other studies found some evidence of less traditional attitudes towards the division of domestic work, they also found that the majority of husbands did not share it equally.

This is not surprising in households where the wife does not work outside the home for pay and the husband does, but the symmetrical family thesis places great weight on the rise in married women's employment and the tendency for husbands to do more domestic work: 'In the interests of symmetry it was only fair, as husbands and wives saw it, for the men to do more so that their wives could do less' (Young and Willmott 1973: 114). The crucial question is how much more? As can be seen

Table 9.1 Average weekly hours spent in paid work and unpaid domestic work

	Men	Women working full-time	Women working part-time	Women not in paid work
Paid work and travel to work	49.5	40.2	26.3	–
Domestic work	9.9	23.1	35.3	45.5
Total	59.4	63.3	61.6	45.5

Source: Adapted from Young and Willmott (1973: 113)

from Table 9.1, according to Young and Willmott when a wife works part-time her domestic working hours each week are reduced by about ten hours, and when she works full-time they are reduced by just over another ten hours. In terms of total working hours, that is paid and unpaid work, women who are employed full-time outside the home work on average four hours each week longer than their husbands, and those who are employed part-time work two hours a week longer. In a year this adds up to married women working over 200 or 100 hours more than their husbands if they are employed full-time or part-time respectively. If an average working week for men, including travel to work time, is approximately 50 hours a week, as was the case in Young and Willmott's sample, then married women work at about a month or two weeks longer than married men. Clearly, married men are doing more, as Young and Willmott put it, but if their wives have a paid job they still work longer hours in total each week/year.

A similar calculation has been made by Hochschild on the basis of 1960s and 1970s time–use studies which showed that 'women worked roughly fifteen hours longer each week than men', or 'an extra month of twenty-four-hour days a year' and concluded that 'most women work one shift at the office or factory and a "second shift" at home' (1990: 3–4). The marked difference between the two estimates may be due to sampling in that Young and Willmott's figures refer to 'married men and women aged 30 to 49' whereas the Hochschild ones only include two-earner families with children. Both calculations are well below the 77-hour average working week of Oakley's sample of housewives, all of whom were mothers of young children (1974), yet still provide evidence of an extra domestic work burden for married women who undertake paid work, and that this ranges from four to 15 hours each week depending on circumstances such as the number and age of children in the family, and of course, 'upon how much of it the husband will share' (Young and Willmott 1973: 277).

What is vital to an evaluation of the symmetrical family thesis is the extent to which husbands increase their participation in domestic work when their wives go out to work on a part- or full-time basis. In other words, if, according to Young and Willmott, wives reduce their domestic work time by approximately 25 per cent when they work part-time and by 50 per cent when they work full-time, do husbands increase their domestic work time by similar proportions? Young and Willmott answered this question indirectly and imprecisely when they reported, on the basis of a flawed question, highlighted by Oakley and noted above, that more husbands 'help in the home' when their wives go out to work part-time, and slightly more when they work full-time (1973: 115). Using a different but similarly indirect and imprecise measure, Hochschild's data on the participation of husbands in domestic work found that '[o]f the men who earned more than their wives, 21 per cent shared housework. Of the men who earned about the same, 30 per cent shared. But among the men who earned *less* than their wives, *none* shared' (1990: 221, italics in the original). Hochschild concluded that since only a small minority of husbands share equally the domestic work when their wives go out to work, this represents a 'stalled revolution', one that 'is in danger of staying stalled' (1990: 12, 267). Thus, neither of these studies, nor the others cited earlier, provide very much support for the symmetrical family thesis, although they do show that husbands undertake more domestic work when their wives go out to work. The optimism of the symmetrical family thesis is punctured by these more pessimistic findings which found that symmetry did not even characterize the middle-class vanguard.

It is not all bad news for Young and Willmott's symmetrical family thesis, however. There is some evidence of a change in attitudes and behaviour with middle-class husbands expressing the view that they should and did do more child-care domestic work, which they preferred to cleaning or ironing, at certain stages of the work and family career cycles (Edgell 1980). However, this was a temporary modification to an otherwise segregated and unequal division of domestic work participation by husbands and wives, and consequently did not threaten the primacy of their respective breadwinner and houseworker roles.

Less traditional attitudes were also found in a large-scale representative survey of adults living in Britain in the mid-1980s (Witherspoon 1985). This study found a marked inequality of participation in various household tasks, but less inegalitarian attitudes regarding who should do them. For example, the married and the never married consistently favoured a more equal division of domestic labour, with 62 per cent of the former and 68 per cent of the latter expressing the view that shopping should be shared equally compared to 39 per cent that actually did, and 45 per cent of the married and 56 per cent of the never married reporting that household cleaning should be shared compared to 23 per cent that actually did. The slightly less inegalitarian attitudes revealed by this survey, especially among the younger never married and married women who worked full-time outside the home, is a small crumb of comfort for those who are looking for evidence of symmetry.

More encouragement for the symmetrical family thesis is provided by the higher percentages of married and cohabiting couples who actually shared various domestic tasks and thought that they should be shared in Britain in 1991 (Whitmarsh 1995) and elsewhere (Crompton and Harris 1999). In terms of the core domestic tasks referred to above, the 'actually shared' percentage was up to 47 per cent for shopping and 27 per cent for household cleaning, and the 'should be shared' percentages were up to 76 per cent and 62 per cent respectively for the same tasks, although some domestic tasks were still markedly gendered, notably the female-dominated activity of ironing and the male-dominated one of repairing equipment (Whitmarsh 1995).

There was also a decline in the percentage of adults who agreed with the idea of male breadwinning and female houseworkers between 1987 and 1994 in Britain. Thus between the mid-1980s and the early 1990s there was a clear trend of increasing egalitarianism in terms of both behaviour and attitudes, though there were still no domestic tasks that were actually shared equally by a majority of the married and cohabiting couples included in the sample.

Further support for the symmetrical family thesis has been provided by UK time–budget data which shows that husbands were doing more domestic work in 1987 than in 1975, although the husbands of wives who worked full-time for pay outside the home were still doing a 'substantially smaller proportion of the total work of the household' (Gershuny et al. 1994: 179; see also Horrell 1994). This pattern was not unique to the UK but was apparent in all modern societies for which time–use survey data is available for this period. Gershuny et al. concluded that 'married men's proportion of the total of domestic work time has a regular and substantial growth over the past three decades', and that 'the women's proportion of the total of paid and unpaid work increases in most countries over this period' (1994: 185–6). This is interpreted as a case of 'lagged adaptation' which implies that it is only a matter of time before men compensate fully for the entry of women into paid work. Gershuny et al. commented that 'even if lagged adaptation does lead to a "symmetry" in the Young and Willmott sense that the total of work may in the longer term tend towards equality between husband and wife, still the differential pattern of responsibilities for paid and unpaid work provides substantial advantages to the husband in terms of earnings and status' (1994: 188). This is an important qualification since it suggests that meaningful symmetry in the sense of gender equality in paid and unpaid work is a long way off. It should also be borne in mind that time–budget data underestimates women's unpaid work time and overestimates men's paid work time because short rest-breaks tend to be recorded for unpaid domestic work but not for paid work away from home (Gershuny et al. 1994). The contention of Gershuny et al. that as more women are employed outside the home, men will eventually increase their participation in domestic work has been criticized, on the basis of empirical research on dual-earner couples in Britain and France, for being 'somewhat optimistic, if not totally unfounded' (Windebank 2001: 286). More promisingly for the Gershuny theory of lagged adaptation is the finding that women in particular occupations have the relational resources, notably interpersonal skills, that enable them to challenge successfully the traditional domestic division of labour (Benjamin and Sullivan 1999). Meanwhile, notwithstanding the evidence of a trend towards more widely held egalitarian attitudes, desegregation, and an increased sharing of domestic work, the division of domestic work remains quite unequal with women still undertaking the bulk of the domestic work.

Leaving aside that in the future the division of domestic work may be more equal than it is at the moment, the key issue concerns the relative lack of change regarding the persistence of female-dominated participation in unpaid work. Morris (1990) has suggested three interconnected explanations: (1) institutional constraints, (2) normative constraints, and (3) power inequalities within the household. The first includes a labour market in which women still tend to be secondary earners and this makes it difficult for them to challenge, let alone alter in a radical way, a traditional division of labour that assigns primary responsibility for domestic work to women. Institutional constrains also refers to welfare regimes that operate to a greater or lesser extent on the assumption that husbands are breadwinners and wives are houseworkers and therefore reinforce rather than undermine a gendered and unequal division of domestic work, although welfare regimes are in the process of changing (Pascall and Lewis 2004). Whilst this essentially economic explanation of the persistence of a female-dominated pattern of domestic work and male domination of major financial decisions may well apply to most couples, even middle-class ones, the tendency for unemployed husbands to shun domestic work indicates that ideas about masculinity and femininity are also relevant (Morris 1990).

Although there is evidence that gender norms are changing to the extent that fewer people support the idea that men should be the primary breadwinners and women the primary houseworkers, there is also evidence which shows that more women than men express non-traditional attitudes and that women continue to undertake most domestic work (Griffin et al. 1998; Morris 1990). One possible interpretation of the tendency for women to do less domestic work when they enter the labour market and for men to resist undertaking proportionally more domestic work is that women operate with reference to the economics of the household, which results in a reduction of their unpaid domestic work burden, whereas men operate with reference to a gender framework, which constrains them to resist doing more domestic work for fear of losing their masculinity. This theory has been advanced by Brines, who has summed it up by noting that 'she gets to do less housework as she provides, while he gets to do gender while she provides' (1994: 684). In the aforementioned study by Hochschild, the findings were not interpreted explicitly in terms of the operation of economic forces and gender norms, although the limitations of the 'logic of the pocketbook' was noted and it was contended that it was a matter of 'balancing' the loss of one form of power by relying on another form of power (1990: 221). This study concluded that men and women engage in power balancing and that 'the political struggle behind a cultural shift and not the timeless logic of the pocketbook seems to determine how much men help in the home' (Hochschild 1990: 225).

Following from the previous point, the third possible explanation for the lack of fundamental change in the division of domestic work concerns the distribution of power with a family. Power can be conceptualized in terms of the three analytically different ways of controlling people – physically, economically, and normatively (Etzioni 1964). The power of the hand may have declined, although in contemporary Britain one in four women will experience domestic violence during their lifetime and one in five men admit using violence against their partner or ex-partner at least once, which suggests that it has not disappeared (www.domesticviolencedata.org/4_faqs/faq01.htm). However, the power of the purse is still apparent from the persistence of income inequalities between men and women outside and inside the home (Allen 1999; Arber and Ginn 1995; Hurst 2004), even in highly egalitarian societies such as Sweden (Nyman 1999). Similarly, the power of cultural norms regarding gender roles and identities, and specifically that women's place is in the home and men's is in the workplace, also show little sign of disappearing completely, with large minorities of women (just under a quarter) and men (just over a quarter) expressing support for this division of labour (Griffin et al. 1998). The enduring influence of traditional ideas about gender roles is clear from studies of two-job families in which women continue to do most of the domestic work (Brannen and Moss 1991; Hochschild 1990). In view of the labour-intensive, monotonous, and dissatisfying character of most domestic work, it is not difficult to imagine why men draw upon whatever source(s) of power they can to resist increasing their participation significantly in domestic work and tend to cherry pick the more creative tasks and avoid the less appealing ones, like cleaning the toilet.

The symmetrical family thesis is concerned with trends in the twentieth century whereas Young and Willmott's stage 4 families model is essentially about changes at the beginning of the twenty-first century. In keeping with their 'Principle of Stratified Diffusion', or what the higher classes do today, the lower classes will do tomorrow, Young and Willmott begin their speculations about stage 4 families by considering 'the impact of the top strata of the two chief forces', namely technology and feminism (1973: 271). First, they argue that the introduction of technology into the paid workplace will reduce the number of physically demanding and monotonous jobs, there will be an expansion of more interesting jobs and 'the greater attachment to work of middle-class people will extend downwards' (Young and Willmott 1973: 271). This will mean more intrinsically rewarding and therefore satisfying jobs for men and women, with possibly longer working hours outside the home. Second, feminism would reinforce this trend, encouraging women to expect and achieve work satisfaction outside as well as inside the home. Young and Willmott summarize the implications of the combined impact of technology and feminism on the paid and unpaid work roles of men and women by noting: 'By the next century – with the pioneers of 1970 already at the front of the column – society will have moved ... to two demanding jobs for the wife and two for the husband. The symmetry will be complete' (1973: 278). Young and Willmott suggest that this is a prospect fraught with problems, notably a high rate of marital breakdown, which risks the well-being of children, and 'if people by their own hyper-activity threatened their own inner stability, they would slowly turn the line of the march in another direction' (1973: 282). They speculate that this could involve less emphasis on paid work, such as shorter and/or more flexible working hours, and the transfer of paid work to the home, all of which would enable people to reconcile the competing demands of work and home. According to this analysis, unless people cut back their focus on earning and spending money, the social costs of a more complete symmetry could outweigh the social benefits.

Another possibility is that there will be an increase in shiftwork and weekend work due to the growth of technology and 24-hour production, and the growth of the service sector and 24-hour consumption. Young and Willmott suggest that this will constrain husbands and wives to work at different times and, consequently, '[t]he life of the family can hardly be enhanced', specifically, 'the family's joint life is challenged' (Young and Willmott 1973: 273). At the time of this research, this development mostly affected manual workers, but was expected to spread to non-manual workers; in other words, 'in a manner directly contrary to the Principle [of Stratified Diffusion]' (Young and Willmott 1973: 273). This possibility potentially undermines symmetry in the sense that a shared social life is difficult if couples work different shifts and, according to Young and Willmott's analysis of unsocial working hours, it disrupts family life and creates extra work, such a cooking meals for family members at different times.

Recent research in Britain on flexible paid work and household arrangements found that working nights was very unpopular with both men and women, and that women particularly disliked working weekends and that men disliked working evenings (Horrell et al. 1994). The main reasons for these preferences were that it created difficulties for child-care, especially for women, and both men and women were concerned about the impact of working nights and weekends on their social life. Men and women were open to flexible working so long as it was 'under their control not the employer's' (Horrell et al. 1994: 129). Although this research did not address the issue of symmetry, it did show that resistance to flexibility was founded on a concern to minimize the disruption to prevailing household arrangements, especially in terms of the women's responsibility for child-care.

A final possibility covered by Young and Willmott was based on their material on managing directors whose demanding paid work and high economic rewards were found to be more conducive to asymmetry than symmetry. They describe the family life of extremely work-centred managing directors as 'husband-dominated', where the wife is mobilized to support the husband's career as a 'hostess', although there was the compensation of staff to mitigate her extra domestic burden (Young and Willmott 1973: 276). Young and Willmott suggest that this highly segregated and unequal type of family was, and was likely to remain, a minority pattern, but this does little to minimize the damage of this finding to the increasing symmetry or the stratified diffusion dimensions of their theory.

The idea that wives experience a triple burden, which is implicit in Young and Willmott's analysis of the work-centred rather than home-centred family life of managing directors, has been advanced by Finch's theory of wives' incorporation in men's work. She argues that employed wives often 'end up doing *three jobs*' in that in addition to their paid work and unpaid domestic work, they contribute in various ways to the husband's paid work career (Finch 1983: 149, italics in the original). For example, if a husband works at home and/or is self-employed, his wife is likely to be recruited as an unpaid receptionist, and if his work involves entertaining colleagues, she will be expected to act as a hostess. In these and other ways, Finch suggests that the hierarchy of priorities that assigns primacy to the male breadwinner's work career ensures the wife's incorporation into her husband's work. Thus the asymmetry of many middle-class couples is traced to the enduring asymmetry of the work–family nexus, noted by, among others, Edgell (1980). Not to be outdone, as it were, Castells has noted that due to the increased involvement of women in paid work, the burden carried by women in their everyday lives correspondingly increased to a 'quadruple shift (paid work, homemaking, child rearing, and night shift for the husband)' (1997: 125). However the roles of working mothers are conceptualized and counted, the general point is that such women tend to shoulder a greater paid and unpaid work burden than their husbands.

Outsourcing domestic work

One potential solution to the problem of a woman's heavier domestic work load is to pay someone else to do it, known as domestic outsourcing or contracting out housework. This includes direct substitution in the form of paid labour (e.g., a cleaner or child-carer), and indirect substitution in the form of manufactured goods (e.g., ready-made meals), or appliances that aid productivity (e.g., vacuum cleaners) (Bittman et al. 1999). The focus here will be almost exclusively on the first type since the second has been covered to some extent above with reference to technology and domestic work.

As noted earlier in this chapter, it has been argued that the decline of paid domestic servants between the 1930s and 1960s in Britain increased considerably the domestic work time of middle-class housewives (Gershuny 2000). For many middle-class families in 1980s Britain this problem was solved to some extent by paying someone else to undertake the particularly labour-intensive domestic work. The resurgence in demand for paid domestic workers, mostly for cleaning and child-care work, but also gardening, has been attributed primarily to the increase in paid work among middle-class women, plus a concern with '"leisure time" and "quality time"' (Gregson and Lowe 1994: 95). In the case of the decision to employ a cleaner, it was the demanding nature of such work that created a time difficulty in dual-career households, plus a reluctance among middle-class husbands to increase their already minimal contribution to domestic work, and for some couples it helped to avoid conflict over a husband's relative lack of participation in this domestic work task. In the case of the employment of someone to undertake child-care work, Gregson and Lowe argue that this was 'essential' if a dual-career couple with pre-school aged children wanted to 'maintain this employment pattern' (1995: 157).

Whilst the employment of cleaners and child-carers conform to the social relations of waged labour, Gregson and Lowe argue that cleaners enjoy a degree of autonomy and that the relationship between child-carers and their employers is distinctive in that it is 'shaped by both wage and false-kinship relations', with the latter dominating everyday interaction (1995: 159). In both forms of substitution, though, the typically female employee relates primarily to the wife in middle-class dual-career households since domestic work is regarded by both parties as women's work. Hence, the employment of paid domestic workers amplifies the managerial dimension of the middle-class wife who also undertakes paid work outside the home. Gregson and Lowe concluded that from the standpoint of the dual-career family it solves the problem of getting essential domestic work done, but at the cost of a higher work load for wives than husbands.

A study of the domestic work arrangements of male and female managers found that in contrast to male managers, who tend to be 'serviced by their wives' even when the wife works part-time, 'women managers are serviced by housewife substitutes in the form of other women's labour' (Wajcman 1996: 626). Thus, this research confirmed that in addition to undertaking a disproportionate volume of domestic work, working wives organize and supervise paid domestic workers. The lack of symmetry among this middle-class sample studied a generation later than Young and Willmott's sample shows that husbands have yet to adapt to the domestic work implications of the employment of their wives, other than to agreeing to the hiring of substitute labour.

The generalization that paid domestic work invariably involves hard work, long hours, and relatively low pay and status has been widely confirmed, as Gregson and Lowe note, but a number of criticisms have been directed at their study. First, their claim that the outsourcing of house cleaning and child-care domestic work has expanded markedly in Britain since the 1980s has been shown to be an exaggeration based on a flawed method of estimating the demand for these services, namely advertisements in a journal (Bittman et al. 1999). Second, Australian household expenditure data for the mid-1990s found that the outsourcing of food preparation at nearly 90 per cent of households exceeded that of all other types of outsourcing added together, including laundry (10 per cent) and child-care (10 per cent), and that the outsourcing of male-dominated tasks such as gardening at 9 per cent occurred over twice as often as the outsourcing of the female-dominated task of cleaning at 4 per cent (Bittman et al. 1999). Third, Gregson and Lowe have been criticized by Anderson (1996) for neglecting black and migrant domestic workers on the grounds that 'in contemporary Britain, no such close association exists between ethnicity, female migration and waged domestic work' (Gregson and Lowe 1994: 123). Anderson claims that Home Office figures show that this is not the case and argues that Gregson and Lowe's crucial cleaner/nanny analytical distinction 'does not hold for migrant women' (Anderson 1996: 581). Following from this point, it could also be argued that Gregson and Lowe neglected the informal dimension of paid domestic work, yet it has been shown that off-the-books workers often undertake domestic work, including child-care, and the employment of such vulnerable workers increases the power of the employer and reduces that of the employee, especially if the workers lack documentation (Leonard 1998: 130). This dimension has implications for the work conditions in general, and the autonomy of cleaners in particular, since in contrast to Gregson and Lowe's account, such workers tend to experience greater exploitation and, specifically, may find it more difficult to control for whom, when and what they clean.

At best, outsourcing domestic work is a partial solution to the problem of a lack of time among some dual-earner couples at a particular stage of the family cycle; at worst, it increases the work load of wives and is an expensive option that is available only to the relatively affluent.

Unpaid voluntary work

In a national survey of trends in the UK, voluntary work was defined as 'any activity which involves spending time, unpaid, doing something which aims to benefit someone (individuals or groups) other than or in addition to, close relatives, or to benefit the environment' (www.ivr.org.uk/nationalsurvey.htm). The essence of formal voluntary work is that it is unpaid and involves a 'gift' in the sense that it reflects a sense of community (Titmuss 1973). Since it is undertaken freely, one can effectively choose what, when and how often to do it, and it is therefore the opposite of virtually every kind of other work, especially the more alienating types of paid work. Informal voluntary work is similarly unpaid but it potentially involves reciprocity between friends or neighbours and kinship obligation, although reciprocity may also characterize kin exchange and obligation friendship and neighbourhood relations. Consequently, it is sometimes excluded from studies of voluntary work.

The UK survey found that the proportion of adults engaged in formal and informal voluntary work declined slightly from a peak of 51 per cent and 76 per cent respectively in 1991 to 48 per cent and 74 per cent in 1997. Although fewer people were undertaking formal voluntary work (down from 23 to 22 million), they were working longer hours (2.7 hours per week in 1991, 4.05 hours in 1997), hence there was a marked increase in the total number of hours volunteered, up from just over 60 million hours in 1991 to nearly 90 in 1997. Estimates of volunteering in the USA vary from 45 per cent to 52 per cent of the adult population engaged in either formal or informal voluntary work in the late 1980s (Pearce 1993; Wuthnow 1991). These surveys suggest that currently around half of all adults in the UK and the USA are involved in unpaid voluntary work, a not inconsiderable amount of what has been called non-monetized exchange (Williams 2002).

The UK national survey also found that the higher the social class, the greater the participation in formal voluntary work and that this pattern was less clear-cut for informal voluntary work. Moreover, those in paid employment were more likely to undertake voluntary work than the unemployed (there was no difference between the participation rates of women and men) and that since 1991 fewer young and more older people were participating in unpaid volunteering (www.ivr.org.uk/ nationalsurvey.htm). Public debate about the economic cost of an ageing population seems to overlook the increasing contribution of retired people to unpaid voluntary work and hence to the quality of community life. The main focus of voluntary work were sports, education, religion, and health and social welfare, with men particularly active in the sports, and women in education and social welfare. The main type of voluntary activities were fundraising, organizing events, committee work, and transporation, with the young and women especially active in fundraising and men and older adults more prominent on committees. This suggests that the over-representation of men at the top and women at the bottom of paid work organizational hierarchies are mirrored in voluntary work organizations.

The gendered character of unpaid voluntary work is also apparent from the tendency for women to be over-represented in unpaid informal care work, largely as a result of 'the cultural designation of women as carers', for whom it is considered natural and which in practical terms means that 'wives care for husbands, mothers for handicapped children and daughters for their elderly parents or disabled siblings. Care is also provided by female neighbours and volunteers' (Finch and Groves 1980: 499).

Notwithstanding the increasing commodification of care work (Ungerson 1985, 1997), and the decline of the male breadwinner and female houseworker model of the family upon which the idea of women as primary carers was founded (Crompton 1999; Finch and Groves 1980), the provision of unpaid care in the community, or what has been called the 'care economy', remains female-dominated in the UK and other similar societies, such as France (Gregory and Windebank 2000; Himmelweit 1999). The persistence of the tendency for women to be over-represented in unpaid voluntary caring work not only increases their burden of unpaid domestic work but also has important implications for their paid work careers, particularly in terms of its continuity, which in turn can have a deleterious effect on their pension benefits since these are often based on an individual's employment record (Finch and Groves 1983). It also has a wider social impact in the sense that the extensive unpaid caring work undertaken informally by women reduces their availability for paid work and creates a need for them to be financially supported by the state and/or husbands (Finch and Groves 1983; Himmelweit 1999). Thus the contribution of women to informal voluntary work, whilst of enormous though under-valued benefit to the social welfare of people and the social fabric of communities, is largely at the cost of women's paid work careers, yet is often excluded from definitions and hence surveys of voluntary work on the grounds that it may not be entirely freely given, in the sense that there could be an element of reciprocity, and may not be freely chosen since it could be a matter of kinship obligation (Sheard 1995). The disqualification of female-dominated caring work in the community from conventional conceptualizations of voluntary work merely reinforces the perception that it is an extension of women's traditional domestic work role as wives and mothers.

However, unpaid informal caring for others, especially if they are disabled or elderly, is clearly work. In fact, it is often quite hard physical and emotional work, and undertaking it can be an isolating experience that generally exacerbates the relentless repetitiveness of domestic work (Baldwin and Glendinning 1983; Finch and Groves 1983). Interestingly, the sex of single carers affected the amount of support provided by a local authority in that sons received 'far more' than daughters, thereby reinforcing the traditional gender division of labour (Wright 1983: 96). The same study also showed that if a women combines unpaid care work with paid work outside the home, there is likely to be considerable and constant tension between the two, for example, deciding whether to work part-time, give up paid work entirely, and/or take time off in an emergency. It is a measure of the continued pervasiveness of the male breadwinner and female houseworker model that women are still designated as the main source of unpaid carers in what is considered a modern society. Moreover, even where this model is considered weak, the theory and practice of female caregiving remains strong (Millar 1999).

There have been very few focused studies on unpaid informal work among friends and neighbours, aside from the evidence created as a 'by-product of investigations into either other forms of work or the way in which care is provided for specific social groups' (Gregory and Windebank 2000: 92). Gregory and Windebank's comparative study found that what little data that has been garnered in this way shows that in

Britain and France it is less widespread than kinship-based unpaid informal work, but that the gender inequalities that pervade both unpaid domestic work and unpaid informal work among kin also characterizes unpaid informal work among friends and neighbours. Moreover, the kind of work undertaken on this basis was also highly gendered, with women providing social and emotional support and men goods and services.

In addition to the aforementioned decline in younger volunteers and growth of older volunteers, the age dimension of volunteering was particularly marked with reference to the motives for undertaking this type of unpaid work in that young volunteers stressed the opportunity to learn new skills and were more critical of this type of work than older volunteers, who were more concerned about using their free time to meet community needs. This suggests that younger voluntary workers tend to be more reflective and instrumentally motivated and that older ones tend to be more committed and altruistic (www.ivr.org.uk/nationalsurvey.htm). Instrumentalism is also apparent from a small-scale study of the unemployed and voluntary work which found that 'the experience of taking part in voluntary activities was considered to enhance job prospects' and helped to relieve boredom and maintain motivation during the search for paid work (Elam and Thomas 1997). For certain types of paid work career, such as youth work, voluntary work was considered vital experience and therefore crucial to their future employment prospects. This is not to suggest that voluntary work by the unemployed was totally lacking in any sense of giving, especially among older unemployed people. The positive benefits of volunteering in terms of self-esteem and satisfaction applies to everyone who undertakes it for whatever reason (Wilson 2000).

The difference between the formal voluntary work orientations of the young and old has been conceptualized in ideal-typical terms as corresponding to traditional or collective and new or reflexive styles of voluntary work and are associated respectively with early modern and late modern types of society (Hustinx and Lammertyn 2003). The distinction between early and late modern society has been theorized by Beck, for whom the transition from the first to the second stage of modern society represents a more complete or advanced version of modern society that he characterizes as 'reflexive modernization' (1992: 21). In the first type of modern society the key anchorage points for individuals include class and family, which dissolve under pressure from the process of increasing individualization. Having been 'set free from the social formations of industrial society', individuals become reflexive and individual trajectories become a matter of choice and decisions rather than constrained by established institutional structures (Beck 1992: 87). The process of individualization applies to unpaid voluntary work as well as paid work in that traditional voluntary work, organized bureaucratically, is declining, and 'more short-term, more specific, more deliberate but also more cooperative' voluntary work is increasing (Beck 2000: 139).

Hustinx and Lammertyn develop this argument by noting that the culture of the collective volunteer is rooted in their class, gender, religious and/or community identities, and is typical of the early stage of the modernization of society. At the later stage these cultural links are undermined by the processes of individualization and globalization, and a new style of reflexive volunteering develops in which 'feelings of belonging are increasingly self-selected on the basis of shared interests' (Hustinx and Lammertyn 2003: 178). Whereas collective volunteerism also tends to be altruistic, organized hierarchically and involve unconditional long-term commitment, reflexive volunteerism tends to be pragmatic, organized democratically and involve conditional short-term commitment. They further suggest, in line with Beck, that old-style volunteering is in decline and that new-style volunteering is growing and that contemporary voluntary workers will exhibit a mixture of the two, but note that empirical research has yet to clarify the 'consequences for the nature of volunteering', (Hustinx and Lammertyn 2003: 183). By drawing upon Beck's model of early and late modern society, this theory of the reflexive volunteer confirms that there are clear parallels between the flexible paid worker and the flexible unpaid voluntary worker and that this development creates potential problems for both volunteers and voluntary organizations.

As yet empirical support for this theory is limited in that among the few studies that cover the issue of voluntary work as work, the indications are that the character of volunteering is currently changing in ways that Hustinx and Lammertyn hypothesize. For example, the aforementioned national survey of volunteering in the UK noted that the trend for younger volunteers to be more instrumental and critical than older volunteers fits their theory. Similarly, Wuthnow's American research found that '[i]nstead of cultivating lifelong ties with their neighbours, or joining organizations that reward faithful long-term service, people are coming together around specific needs and to work on projects that have definite objectives' (1998: 8). These organizations enhance the power and involvement of their members, who are linked by looser connections, such as via the internet, in marked contrast to the old-style hierarchic organizations based on closer connections. An in-depth study of 20 young voluntary workers by Hustinx (2001) contributed to, and confirmed, the more pragmatic and individualized character of the new style of volunteering. Finally, the case studies described by Taylor include, among others, a young graduate who has 'worked as a volunteer for several charities for over a year' as part of a conscious strategy to obtain relevant experience for paid work in the voluntary sector, and a middle-aged voluntary worker who has been a politically committed voluntary worker in his ethnic community for a number of years. The first case matches clearly the pragmatically oriented reflexive volunteering style and the second the traditional style of volunteering. However, until large-scale and more representative empirical research specifically designed to test Hustinx and Lammertyn's theory of reflexive volunteering has been undertaken, it remains just a theory, albeit a most promising one.

The beginning of a theoretically informed empirical analysis of the changing motivation and commitment of voluntary workers is to be applauded, but it masks the dearth of equivalent research on the experience of volunteering as unpaid work. One notable exception is Pearce's (1993) US study of 14 matched volunteer-staffed and employee-staffed organizations. The main findings were that most volunteers worked part-time, had autonomy, expressed positive attitudes to their work, and worked in egalitarian organizations, whilst most of the paid employees worked full-time, had little autonomy, expressed few positive attitudes to their work, and worked in more hierarchical organizations. Yet voluntary work was also found to be intrinsically problematic due to the uncertainty about whether it was work or leisure and was often undertaken in understaffed circumstances. Thus, voluntary work may be less alienating in Blauner's sense of the term, but it was not without it sources of stress.

Summary and conclusions

The gender-neutral terms, unpaid domestic work and housework conceal the ascriptive tendency for women to undertake the bulk of this type of work. Yet the rise of the full-time housewife is a relatively recent development that was associated with the rise of the male breadwinner as an idea and practice in the late nineteenth century in Britain and other industrial capitalist societies. This model prevailed to a greater or lesser extent in virtually all modern societies during the twentieth century and involved relative exclusion from paid work and economic dependency for wives and relative exclusion from unpaid domestic work and economic independence for husbands. Although the male breadwinner and female houseworker model is on the wane, it has yet to be eclipsed totally by alternative arrangements, even among most dual-career couples.

Domestic work is not only unpaid, but essentially a form of deskilled manual work involving a multitude of tasks, although the managerial dimension has arguably increased in the recent past, especially if domestic work is outsourced. The combination of no pay and hence financial dependency, and repetitious and hence monotonous physical work, ensures that domestic work is perceived widely, including by those who undertake most of it, as a low-status and dissatisfying job. The studies of domestic work as an occupational role by Lopata and as work by Oakley revealed that is was comparable to factory work in terms of Blauner's operationalization of alienation. First, control was highly valued, especially the lack of close supervision, but elusive due mainly to the demands of others, especially husbands, upon whose agenda-setting primary paid work the household depends for it economic survival. Second, domestic work involves some meaningful activities, notably child-rearing, but mostly many routine ones that tend to be repeated, often several times a day or week. Third, social isolation was inherent in the sense that domestic work was typically undertaken alone, and in some circumstances it was acute, for instance during the early years of the child-rearing stage, although it could be mitigated by developing a network of family, friends and neighbours. Fourth, opportunities for self-expression are somewhat limited given that the majority of domestic tasks tend to be repeated in a routine way on a relentless basis. Even the creative potential of some domestic work tasks, such as cooking, was more apparent than real, as the data on technological short-cuts in food preparation testify. Overall, whilst domestic work may not be as highly alienating as assembly-line work, it seems to be moderately alienating at the very least.

The impact of technological change on domestic work, including the introduction of electrical appliances and other technological innovations, such as non-iron materials and ready-made meals, has lessened the physical demands of domestic work but does not seem to have led to a marked reduction in the amount of time spent on domestic work, especially by full-time housewives. This has been explained with reference to the higher productivity and standards facilitated by the diffusion of domestic technologies, and to the increased time spent on buying, operating, cleaning and maintaining the new technologies. Ironically, some domestic technologies may have reduced the time men spend on domestic work, dishwashing machines being the favoured example. The alternative view, advanced by Gershuny among others, is that the decline of domestic servants increased the domestic work load for middle-class housewives and technology reduced the time spent on core domestic tasks, namely cleaning and cooking, although he does concede that domestic technology increased productivity and in the short term this may have led to an increase in domestic work time. Critics of this account of the impact of technology on time spent on domestic work have pointed out that it is based on time–budget data, which is unreliable and tends to underestimate domestic work time. Although it is difficult to separate out the impact of technology from other influences on domestic work, there are some circumstances in which the use of technology does result in less time being spent on domestic work, for example in dual-earner households, and there are others when it does not, for example when it stimulates an increase in certain domestic activities, such as laundry work. Whether directly or indirectly, domestic technology tends not to be the time-saving panacea of marketing rhetoric.

The symmetrical family thesis also highlighted the impact of technological change on domestic work, along with the role of feminism and the growth of women's work outside the home, as factors that contributed to the change from segregated and unequal marital relationships to more desegregated and equal ones during the last century. The problematic data that Young and Willmott provided, ostensibly in support of their thesis, has been found to be flawed, and subsequent empirical research in Britain and similar societies has tended to show that whilst attitudes have become less traditional, domestic work behaviour remains less than symmetrical. Other evidence, particularly when derived from time–budget dairies, show that there has been an increase in the sharing of domestic work between couples and that this trend can be expected to continue in the future in accordance with the theory of lagged adaptation. The inconsistency of findings on this issue may be due to variations in the measurement and interpretation of domestic work patterns, although when this possibility was taken into account, little change was found, thereby confirming that the revolution had stalled (Warde and Hetherington 1993). One way to reconcile the conflicting evidence regarding the symmetrical family thesis is to conclude that there is weak support for a strong version of the symmetrical family thesis and strong support for a weak version.

Various explanations have been advanced for the lack of any radical change in the tendency for women to continue to be primarily responsible for domestic work and men for the economic prosperity of the household. These include the persistence of the economic, cultural and political (in the sense of power) advantages of men over women outside and inside the household. Thus, no one factor alone can account for the continued inequitable distribution of unpaid domestic work between men and women in the same household, and whilst women have taken more responsibility for breadwinning, men have yet to match this change by taking a commensurate degree of responsibility for domestic work.

Young and Willmott discussed three possible future developments with reference to the fate of the symmetrical family in the twenty-first century. The first is predicated on the general upskilling of paid work, which is thought to lead to increasing involvement in such work. The second assumes that temporal flexibility will characterize more and more jobs as the economy continues to deindustrialize and become dominated by service work. The third is a variation of the first in that it focuses on the exceedingly work-centred lives of managing directors. All three eventualities are problematic for the prospects of symmetry since they imply that paid work is likely to be more of a priority in the future than in the past for both men and women in general and especially for those with demanding paid work careers. This suggests that paid work trends seem to favour the growth of asymmetry rather than symmetry in the domestic division of labour in the longer term.

One possible solution to the discordant issue of who does the unpaid domestic work is to outsource some or all of it, especially the more labour-intensive and routine tasks like cleaning and the laundry. For a wife or female partner in a dual-career household this strategy is often vital to the success of her paid work career and can reduce conflict over who does certain domestic tasks. In effect, for a women, the employment of someone else, usually another women, to undertake the more time-consuming domestic activities is a damage limitation exercise in terms of her work and family careers. However, this option is only available to relatively affluent couples and even then the female partner tends to be responsible for organizing and supervising the employee(s).

Throughout the analysis of unpaid domestic work, the nub of the issue of who does it is male resistance to sharing this type of work equally. According to Beck, whilst women have raised their expectations of increased equality outside and inside the family, 'men have practiced a *rhetoric of equality*, without matching their words with deeds' (1992: 104, italics in the original). For Beck, the current antagonism between men and women is rooted in the development of industrial society which created the separate spheres of public paid work for men and private domestic work for women. As a consequence of this arrangement, gender roles and statuses were ascribed, but whereas men were assigned primary responsibility for paid work and can obtain a sense of economic independence, women were assigned primary responsibility for domestic work and were consigned to dependence upon others. The increasing feminization of paid work has helped to free men 'from the yoke of being *sole* supporter of the family', and various social factors have freed women to some extent, but not entirely, from their 'gender fate', including longer life expectancy, family planning, the technological restructuring of domestic work, and the trend towards the equalization of educational and occupational opportunities

(Beck 1992: 110, 112). The ensuing gap 'between women's expectations of equality and the reality of inequality in occupations and the family', prompted Beck to predict that conflict between men and women in their private relationships will increase and 'fill the corridors of the divorce courts or waiting rooms of marriage counsellors and psychotherapists' (1992: 120, 121). To paraphrase Beck, women are still struggling to lessen the yoke of being mainly responsible for domestic work, but in the meantime they continue to carry a dual, triple, quadruple burden!

Unpaid voluntary work can be either formal, for organizations in which men and women participate about equally, or informal, for family, friends and neighbours which is female-dominated. Informal voluntary work is often excluded from definitions and hence surveys of voluntary work because it involves elements of obligation, especially in the case of kinship, and reciprocity, particularly in the case of non-kin, and is therefore neither a gift nor an entirely free choice. Rather than exclude informal voluntary work on the grounds that it is not entirely freely chosen or freely given, perhaps it could be included as quasi-voluntary work, thereby recognizing that it is different from formal voluntary work but a widespread form of voluntary activity. Unpaid informal work among kin is often very hard work, and tends to be dominated by women, which has deleterious consequences for their economic independence and well-being throughout their adult lives. The limited and mostly indirect research on unpaid informal work among non-kin shows that it too is female-dominated and therefore tends to add to a women's burden of unpaid work. Reviews of non-kinship exchange also show that in times of economic restructuring, support among friends and neighbours tends to be widespread and crucial to surviving change (Morris 1995).

Unpaid formal voluntary work is arguably the least well researched type of work by sociologists, although there are signs that this situation is beginning to be addressed. Pearce's small-scale study found that it was typically undertaken on a part-time basis and was far less alienating than similar paid work, though it could also be quite stressful. A promising line of enquiry has been advanced by Hustinx and Lammertyn, who have built upon Beck's theorization of the increasing individualization that accompanies the transition from early to late modern society, to hypothesize that collective volunteerism is in decline and reflexive volunteering is increasing. The little empirical research that has been undertaken on the changing character of formal voluntary work tends to support this thesis. However, more research needs to be done, not only to confirm Pearce's tentative conclusions and the theory of reflexive volunteering, but also to clarify the consequences of the growth of reflexive volunteering for volunteers and voluntary organizations.

Further reading

The classic studies of domestic work by Oakley have yet to be surpassed and cover both the history of housework with reference to the rise of industrial capitalism, *Housewife*

(1976), and domestic work as work, *The Sociology of Housework* (1974). Similarly, the pre-eminent study of technology and domestic work, not least because it is very readable, remains Cowan's (1983) *More Work for Mother: The Ironies of Household Technology from the Open Hearth to the Microwave*. For a critique of, and an alternative to, the view that technology does not reduce the time spent on domestic work, the many publications of Gershuny (and his associates) should be consulted, notably *Changing Times: Work and Leisure in Postindustrial Society* (2000). Young and Willmott's (1973) *The Symmetrical Family: A Study of Work and Leisure in the London Region* should be read carefully and critically as the point of departure for the ongoing debate about to what extent and why the domestic division of labour changed during the twentieth century, and may change again in this century. A summary of the relevant theories and data can be found in Morris (1990) *The Workings of the Household: A US–UK Comparison*. A useful collection of theoretically informed empirical research on various aspects of the changing pattern of domestic work is M. Anderson et al. (eds) (1994) *The Social and Political Economy of the Household*. Unpaid informal voluntary work is well documented, notably the edited collection by Finch and Groves (1983) *A Labour of Love: Women, Work and Caring*, and the study by Gregory and Windebank (2000) *Women's Work in Britain and France: Practice, Theory and Policy*. The best sources on formal voluntary work are the articles by Hustinx and Lammertyn (2003) and Taylor (2004), and Pearce's (1993) *Volunteers: The Organizational Behaviour of Unpaid Workers*.

Questions for discussion and assessment

1. Consider the view that domestic work is as alienating as factory work.
2. Does technology reduce the time spent on domestic work?
3. Evaluate critically the symmetrical family thesis.
4. Explain the apparent reluctance of husbands to share domestic work equally.
5. Discuss the sociological significance of women's unpaid informal voluntary work among kin, friends and neighbours.
6. How and to what extent has formal voluntary work changed in the recent past?

CHAPTER TEN

Globalization and the Transformation of Paid and Unpaid Work

In the journey from what is often regarded as non-alienating work in hunting and gathering societies, to the most alienating factory work in industrial capitalist societies, and finally to arguably the least alienating form of contemporary work, namely voluntary work, the concept of globalization has been an intermittent presence, explicitly or implicitly. As recently as the late 1980s some dictionaries of sociology (e.g., Abercrombie et al. 1988) did not include an entry for globalization, and even in the early 1990s some textbooks on the sociology of work (e.g., Hall 1994) treated the issue of globalization in a cursory manner. However, it would be remiss not to discuss it in reasonable depth now, such is the prominence of these concepts in public discourse and sociological analysis (e.g., Cohen and Kennedy 2000).

At various points in the earlier analysis, the issue of globalization was particularly pertinent, such as in the discussions of the post-Fordism and network enterprise (Chapter 6) and non-standard work (Chapter 8). Likewise in the contributions of Beck (1992, 2000), broached at many junctures in the earlier chapters, the idea of globalization was referred to but not discussed in detail. In view of the current estimation of the importance of globalization, it is now time to consider the meaning, causes and implications of this process and those of one other process that is thought to be inextricably related to it, namely changes in women's work and consciousness, for both paid and unpaid work. Thus the purpose of this chapter is to consider globalization and the parallel transformation of women's position with reference to their impact on different types of paid and unpaid work, plus the implications of these processes for the dominant conception of work outlined, and the alleged growth of non-standard work discussed in the previous chapters.

────────────────────────── **Globalization** ──────────────────────────

Marx and Engels were among the first social theorists to refer to the global character of industrial capitalism: 'The need of a constantly expanding market for its products chases the bourgeoisie over the whole surface of the globe. It must nestle everywhere, settle everywhere, establish connexions everywhere' (n.d. [1848]: 54). Thus capitalism was the spur to the globalization of production and exchange, and in the process capital sought to 'tear down every spatial barrier to intercourse' and 'annihilate this space with time' (Marx 1973 [1857–58]: 539). Among other things, Marx (and Engels) was suggesting that globalization was an economic process with many major political and social ramifications and that it was not a natural force but a capitalist imperative rooted in the need to accumulate capital, aided and abetted by political policies that favoured capitalist expansion or risk decline in the face of increasingly international competition. These themes are still apparent in contemporary discussions of globalization which typically refer to the 'widening, deepening and speeding up of worldwide interconnectedness in all aspects of social life' (Held et al. 1999: 2).

Three approaches to contemporary globalization have been identified: hyperglobalists, such as Albrow (1996), for whom it represents something totally new; sceptics, such as Hirst and Thompson (1996), for whom it is not new but merely a continuation of past developments; and transformationalists, such as Scholte (2000) and Castells (2001), for whom it is 'historically unprecedented such that states and societies across the globe are experiencing a process of profound change as they try to adapt to a more interconnected but highly uncertain world' (Held et al. 1999: 2). Scholte has summarized the first two approaches as 'an "all change" thesis' and 'an "all continuity" thesis' respectively, and considers them both 'flawed' on the grounds that the former 'suffers from historical myopia' and the latter 'from insensitivity to proportion' (2000: 62). The alternative transformationalist perspective effectively adopts a middle position in that it recognizes that both continuities and distinctive features characterize contemporary globalization (Held et al. 1999; Scholte 2000).

The main continuity with past phases of globalization is the movement of people, goods and ideas across the world, whereas the distinctiveness of contemporary globalization includes what Scholte refers to as 'supraterritoral relations' rather than mere 'interterritorial relations' in that it 'entails a reconfiguration of geography, so that social space is no longer wholly mapped in terms of territorial spaces' (2000: 16). This focus on the 'spatial-temporal' dimension of globalization is in keeping with the approaches of Held et al. (1999: 430) and Castells (2001). A precise definition of globalization that takes into account 'spatial-temporal processes of change' defines it as 'a process (or set of processes) which embodies a transformation in the spatial organization of social relations and transactions – assessed in terms of their extensity, intensity, velocity and impact – generating transcontinental or interregional flows and networks of activity, interactions, and the exercise of power' (Held et al. 1999: 16).

In the light of this approach to globalization, Scholte (2000) has distinguished between three distinct phases of globalization:

1   Global imagination: to the eighteenth century,
2   Incipient globalization: 1850s to 1950s,
3   Full-scale globalization: 1960s to the present

In terms of the historical periodization outlined in Chapter 1 (see Figure 1.1), these three phases correspond to pre-modern, early modern, and late modern globalization. This chronology is also comparable to Beck's analysis in that he distinguishes between the simple globalization of the first modernity, based on territorial principles, and globalization of the second, or reflexive modernity, based on the 'deterritorialization of space' (2000: 26). In addition, Scholte's model implies that globalization is a complex historical process in the sense that initially it was essentially a matter of consciousness and international connections among a minority, also referred to as 'proto-globalization' (Cohen and Kennedy 2000: 42). Second, it developed 'beyond the imagination into more substantive social relations' which were manifested in the cross-border character of communications, markets, organizations and production, as well as consciousness (Scholte 2000: 65) Third, contemporary globalization is considered to be quantitatively and qualitatively different since transworld relations have expanded in terms of their 'number, variety, intensity, institutionalization, awareness and impact' (Scholte 2000: 74).

The conceptual framework advanced by Held et al. 'provides the basis for both a quantitative and qualitative assessment of the historical patterns of globalization' (1999: 17). Thus, contemporary globalization is characterized by extensive networks, intensive flows within networks, speedy, frequent instantaneous global interactions, all of which impact on all areas of economic, social and political life, and affect everyone in the world to a greater or lesser extent. Somewhat more prosaically, there is a tendency to refer to the marked expansion of the global scale of interconnections in terms of global communications (e.g., electronic mass media), global markets (e.g., global products), global production (e.g., global production chains), global money (e.g., global credit cards), global finance (e.g., global banking), global organizations (e.g., global companies and agencies), and global consciousness (e.g., global events). The acceleration of global relations is indicated similarly by data that shows a marked and sometimes spectacular increase over the past thirty to forty years of transborder relations, such as the growth of transnational corporations (e.g., IBM), international governmental organizations (e.g., the United Nations), international non-governmental organizations (e.g., Greenpeace), the consumption of global products (e.g., Coca-Cola), and the use of global communications devices (e.g., computers) (Castells 2001; Cohen and Kennedy 2000; Scholte 2000).

The revealing thing about such lists, and the statistics that accompany them, is that many of the indicators pre-date full-scale or contemporary globalization dating from the second half of the twentieth century, including those which transcend geographical space such as the telegraph, the fax and the computer. Moreover, even the most fervent advocates of the idea that the global economy is here already, and differs from previous forms of globalization, admit that 'not everything is global in the economy: in fact most production, employment, and firms are, and will remain, local and regional' (Castells 2001: 101). Although such data tends to confirm the view that contemporary globalization has roots in the past, involves distinctive ways of organizing activities in terms of space and time, and is ongoing, some words of caution are appropriate. First, there is the possibility of confusing 'economic global-ization with internationalization of the economy' (Beck 2001: 120). Second, eco-nomic trends still have to be interpreted carefully – such data is not unambiguous evidence of globalization (Held et al. 1999). Third, quantitative evidence cannot, by itself, 'confirm or deny the "reality" of globalization' since qualitative changes are also essential, for example, the 'exercise of power', and such 'shifts' are 'rarely cap-tured by statistical data' (Held et al. 1999: 11).

There are two other concepts, which are related to the process of globalization, that are relevant to the analysis and therefore worthy of comment: globality and global-ism. Robertson (1992) is credited by Beck with being the first to distinguish between globalization as an external process and globality as the 'extent to which people are conscious of living in the world as one place' (Beck 2001: 88). In effect, globalization refers to objective reality and globality to the subjective awareness of that reality (Cohen and Kennedy 2000). Buying products over the internet illustrates perfectly the external or objective reality of globalization, and events as diverse as interna-tional sporting competitions and humanitarian disasters that prompt a global response raise consciousness of the world as a single place. Globalism is usually taken to mean the 'neo-liberal ideology of world market domination' and as such is the political-economic dimension of the contemporary phase of globalization (Beck 2001: 118). Beck has criticized contemporary globalism on the grounds that it is based on 'an antiquated economism projected on a gigantic scale', not least because the idea of free world trade is a myth, yet policies based on this premise often lead to increased inequality (2001: 117; see also Gray 1998). In the following analysis, the primary focus is the economic aspects of globalization since these are the most per-tinent to the sociology of work.

Causes of globalization

Four main and interrelated factors are thought to have caused the expansion of global-ization: rationalism, capitalism, technology, and regulation (Scholte 2000). No one fac-tor is considered causally paramount in the following account, though this is not always the case. For example, those writing within the Marxian tradition highlight the decisive role of capitalism, whereas neo-Weberians emphasize the influence of rationalism.

Rationalism refers to a type of knowledge that is thought to have assisted the growth of global thinking and hence globalization. Rationalism has four key distinguishing aspects: it is secularist, anthropocentric, scientist and instrumental, which together give it primacy over other types of knowledge, such as religious ideas (Scholte 2000). Thus, rationalist knowledge does not recognize boundaries based on nationhood, religion, ethnicity, and so on, and in this sense is thought to have encouraged globalization.

Capitalism refers to a distinctive way of organizing economic activity oriented to making a profit and this aspect of capitalism is regarded as a key force behind globalization. The unceasing concern to accumulate a surplus or fail constrains capital to seek out cheaper production sites and new markets for their products, which in practical terms means the world. Thus, in a fully globalized system of production and consumption, global companies operate in a global market in production sites, for labour, and their products (Fröbel et al. 1980).

Technology refers the application of knowledge, typically scientific knowledge, to solve practical problems, which, from the standpoint of the sociology of work, means problems to do with the production and consumption of goods and services. Technological innovations in production and transportation were prominent during the early modern phase of globalization, for example, electrical power, while technological innovations in information and communication are often singled out as particularly important during late modern phase of globalization. In both cases technological change is thought to have enabled individuals and companies to develop global connections.

Regulation refers to the politico-legal framework that provides the rules and procedures which govern global relationships without which globalization could not develop, let alone prosper. In the early modern phase of globalization the relevant rules and procedures emanated from individual nation states which were especially prominent in promoting globalization, such as Britain in the second half of the nineteenth century and the USA in the first half of the twentieth century. In the late modern phase of globalization, international government organizations (e.g., the United Nations), and international non-governmental organizations, such as the International Organization for Standardization and the World Intellectual Property Organization, have tended to become more influential in setting the rules and procedures of globalization. Thus international agreements regarding cross-border socio-economic relations have created the regulatory framework within which globalization has flourished.

Castells' theory of the network society (discussed in Chapter 6 with reference to the transformation of paid work) illustrates the interrelated character of the driving forces behind globalization. Castells seems to give pride of place to the revolution in information technology because it 'provided the indispensable, material basis' for the creation of the new global economy (2001: 77). Yet he emphasizes that firms do not invest in 'technology for the sake of technological innovation', they do so in the hope that they will be rewarded in terms of improved competitiveness and greater profitability (Castells 2001: 94). Moreover, Castells argues that globalization emerged towards the end of the twentieth century, originally in America, as part of the neo-liberal-inspired restructuring of companies and financial markets following the economic crisis of the 1970s, which in turn prompted the diffusion of the then new information and communication technologies, and that the 'decisive agents in setting up a new, global economy were governments', especially those of the richest nations, led by the USA, and 'their ancillary international institutions, the International Monetary Fund, the World Bank, and the World Trade Organization' (2001: 137). There were three interrelated parts to the neo-liberal project that laid the foundations for the contemporary phase of capitalist globalization: deregulation, the liberalization of trade and privatization. Thus, for Castells, globalization is essentially a complex technological and capitalist phenomenon that was promoted actively by the governments of the most advanced nation states acting in a rational self-interested manner in accordance with a revived neo-liberal ideology, although there is an undoubted tension between the technological and the capitalist dimensions in terms of which was paramount. The evidence from the most detailed account of the development of globalization is that multicausal explanations are superior to monocausal ones, hence it concluded that the contemporary process of globalization is a 'product of a unique conjuncture of social, political, economic and technological forces' (Held et al. 1999: 429).

The parallel transformation of women's condition

Whilst the majority of analyses of contemporary social change consider globalization to be the dominant force affecting the world in general and different types of work in particular, it is not the only influential factor. Castells suggests that there are other transformations that 'develop in parallel' with globalization and which are in part connected to globalization and in part autonomous (2000: 21). Prominent among the parallel changes discussed by Castells are 'proactive movements, aiming at transforming human relationships at their most fundamental level, such as feminism and environmentalism' (1997: 2). From the standpoint of the sociology of work, the most relevant is feminism since it is concerned with dismantling patriarchy inside and outside the home. First-wave feminism predates contemporary globalization by over a century, was predominantly an upper- and middle-class movement, and was successful in achieving a degree of political (e.g., the vote) and legal (e.g., access to divorce and education) equality for women (Walby 1990). In other words, first-wave feminism coincided with early modern globalization and was focused primarily on women as equal citizens.

Second-wave feminism dates from the 1960s and therefore coincided with the latest phase of globalization, is more of a mass movement, and is correspondingly far more diverse and radical in its concerns, though united in its 'historical effort, individual as well as collective, formal and informal, to redefine womanhood in direct opposition to patriarchalism' (Castells 1997: 176). Consequently, second-wave feminism parallels the development of late modern globalization and is focused on the reconstruction of woman's identity. Specifically, Castells' argument is that patriarchalism 'is being challenged in this end of the millennium by the inseparably related processes of the transformation of women's work and the transformation of women's consciousness' (1997: 135). Among the 'driving forces behind these processes' are the emergence of the informational, global economy, which Castells claims improves women's paid work opportunities, technological innovations that have increased women's control over child-bearing and reproduction, and the 'rapid diffusion of ideas in a globalized culture' (1997: 137). In Castells' estimation, the ongoing revolution in gender relations is of the utmost importance 'because it goes to the roots of society and to the heart of who we are' (1997: 135). As a result of these ongoing changes in women's condition and consciousness, Castells concluded that the patriarchal family is in crisis. Thus, according to Castells, the feminization of the labour force and feminism are the most important of several overlapping and mutually reinforcing transformations operating at the end of the twentieth century, with globalization not just implicated heavily in all of them, but arguably the pivotal factor given its part in creating flexible employment for women and in the dissemination of feminist ideas.

Beck's analysis of the current transformation of women's condition resembles Castells' account in several ways, notwithstanding their different conceptual furniture and theoretical focus. First, Beck too considers the issue of gender relations to be of fundamental importance and the ongoing conflict between women and men to have reached an 'explosive' stage and the 'opposition of the sexes will determine the coming years' (1992: 103, 104; see also Beck and Beck-Gernsheim 2002). Second, Beck argues that among the factors that contribute to the as yet incomplete transformation of women's situation and consciousness are technological control over contraception, women's improved educational opportunities, women's increased participation in paid labour, and globalization in the sense of facilitating 'transnational women's networks' (2000: 166). Of these, as with Castells, most weight seems to be placed on the increased significance of paid work in women's lives because 'money allows and educates for greater autonomy than women could achieve while financially dependent on parents or a husband' (Beck and Beck-Gernsheim 2002: 62). Third, Beck concurs with Castells that the patriarchal family has reached a crisis point, although he frames this conclusion, and indeed his whole analysis with reference to the 'contradiction between modernity and counter modernity within industrial society', namely the modernization of paid work and the traditionalism of the nuclear family with its male breadwinner and female houseworker, which is in the process of detraditionalization. In contrast to Castells, Beck also argues that the technological 'deskilling of housework' is a factor that is conducive to women seeking fulfilment outside the home (1992: 110). Thus, for Beck, as in the case of Castells, the aspirations of women, and their ability to achieve them, are a product of a multiplicity of factors, prominent among which are changes in education and work opportunities, plus globalization, notwithstanding their contrasting terminologies and theoretical concerns.

The respective accounts of the acute state of contemporary gender relations by Beck and Castells are similarly wide-ranging and as such there are weaknesses in their arguments. In the case of Castells, he tends to exaggerate the transforming power of the feminization of the paid labour force since women's over-representation in part-time and other types of non-standard work is of limited value as a 'catalyst for wider social and political change' (Hakim 1996: 79). Although Beck recognizes the precarious character of many of the jobs women are employed in and that women still have less continuous paid work histories than men, he tends to be over-confident about the labour-saving qualities of domestic technology and does not attend to the possibility that some women, according to Hakim (1996), prefer a homemaking career to a paid work one.

The transformation paid work?

The earlier analysis of paid work in the most advanced societies showed that there was evidence during the recent past, albeit of a contested nature, of a growing polarization between upskilled, functionally flexible work, and deskilled, numerically flexible work, plus a related but uneven tendency for an increasing division between a shrinking proportion of secure, permanent, full-time, well-paid workers and an expanding proportion of temporary, part-time, low-paid, though not necessarily insecure, workers. Thus, over the past thirty years or so, standard jobs were improving in quality but arguably declining in number, whereas non-standard jobs were declining in quality but possibly increasing in number. These trends were part of an attempt to overcome the limitations of Fordism, notably its inflexible, low-skilled workforce, by reforming it, namely neo-Fordism characterized by greater flexibility and multi-task jobs, or by revolutionizing it, namely post-Fordism characterized by considerable flexibility and multi-skilled jobs. In sum, the decline of Fordism was attributed to its inflexibility, and the development of alternatives to Fordism were informed by the promise of flexibility.

The earlier discussion of these changes in the nature of paid work and the changing pattern of employment sometimes alluded to, and sometimes referred to, the role of globalization. However, there is a strand of recent theorizing which seeks to understand these changes through the prism of globalization. This globalization perspective of the restructuring of industrial capitalism has been well summarized by Debrah and Smith: 'Faced with the imperative of gloablization, management constantly seek greater wage flexibility, functional and numerical flexibility. Thus, the competitive pressures associated with economic globalization induce shifts in workforce composition, labour demand, and the inter-temporal deployment of workers' (2002: 9). For example, it will be recalled that in the discussion of Castells' network enterprise thesis (Chapter 6), he argued that the three key interrelated features of the new type of economy are that it is informational, global and networked, as well as capitalist, and that the network enterprise was its characteristic organizational form, in which 'internal adaptability and external flexibility' are paramount (2001: 258). Similarly, in the earlier discussion of non-standard paid work (Chapters 7 and 8), the contributions of Castells (2001) and Beck (1992, 2000) suggested that globalization was heavily implicated in the (uneven) growth of different types of non-standard paid work. Specifically, Castells argued: 'Induced by globalization, and the network enterprise, and facilitated by information/communication technologies, the most important transformation in employment patterns concerns the development of flexible work, as the predominant form of working arrangements', namely all types of non-standard paid work (2000: 11). In short, globalization puts additional competitive pressure on capitalist enterprises to be functionally and numerically flexible.

One of Beck's more provocative and speculative conclusions is that if the free-market version of contemporary globalization continues to develop in an unconstrained way, it could result in the most advanced industrial capitalist societies resembling semi-industrialized countries like Brazil, where only a minority work full-time and 'the majority earn their living in more precarious conditions' (2000: 1). Beck refers to this as the 'Brazilianization of the West', as a short-hand for the extreme deregulation, informalization, criminalization, and flexibilization of work (2000: 93). This is a dystopian vision since it involves masses of low-quality jobs in terms of pay, productivity, security, and so on, without the safety net of a public welfare system. Beck considers that the USA is already well down the road of Brazilianization since it too does not have a well developed welfare state and that the increase in inequality and insecurity is a major threat to social cohesion and hence democracy.

Empirical research on transnational vehicle production in Brazil also concluded that it was a model for the future, but for a totally different reason from that advanced by Beck. Abreu et al. (2000) have argued that the VW truck plant in Resende represents a new way of organizing production in a global economy. It is located on a greenfield site in an area famed for its conservative unionism, well away from those known for a tradition of strong trade unions, and created, with the usual benefit of tax breaks and other fiscal support, a skilled and competitive 'dream factory'. The distinctiveness of this plant, aside from the lack of automation compared to auto plants in Europe, the USA and Japan, is that VW limited its risk and role to strategic issues, plus quality, product, marketing and sales, whilst subcontracting to firms focused on production, and deal with the problem of labour discipline, and only get paid when the vehicles are sold. Abreu et al. liken this radical change in the relationship between the assembler and component suppliers to the 'department stores [which] routinely allocate their floor space to other companies' (2000: 271). The study concluded tentatively that in this version of Brazilianization, 'labour compliance and involvement is being achieved through the wage contract (with the hours bank) and a strong emphasis on training provision than through teamworking and other advanced forms of human resource management' (Abreu et al. 2000: 280). Whilst this is a low-wage plant, even by Brazilian standards, it is relatively skilled and secure work and, given the size and expansion of auto transplants in Brazil by Chrysler, Ford and Fiat, among others, it is indicative of a possible alternative to Beck's apocalyptic vision. Perhaps also it is an echo of Fordism and the male breadwinner and female houseworker model.

Globalization is not the only process involved in the transformation of paid work, the feminization of the labour force is also an integral factor. Castells argues that although women are less well paid than men for similar work, are over-represented in social and personal services work, and in part-time employment, they are increasingly employed at the higher levels of multi-skilled informational work, the fastest-growing area of employment. Therefore, they 'are not being relegated to the lowest skilled service jobs' (1997: 165). However, Beck's reference to 'precarious feminization' indicates that he is more aware that the feminization of work is not all good news for women (2000: 64).

Arguably the most profound transformation of work concerns the relationship between capital and labour in a globalizing economy since it affects all aspects of work. On this point Beck and Castells are in complete agreement, and even use similar language to articulate the strengthening of capital and the weakening of labour as a result of the free market character of contemporary capitalist globalization. Thus, Beck has noted that: '[c]apital is global, work is local' (2000: 27), whilst Castells has written that '[a]t its core, capital is global. As a rule, labour is local' (2001: 506). Castells elaborates the argument by summarizing the impact of the current phase of globalization on the main protagonists in a capitalist system, however developed or underdeveloped: 'Labour is disaggregated in its performance, fragmented in its organization, diversified in its existence, divided in its collective action', (2001: 506). But as far as capital is concerned. 'Networks converge toward a meta-network of capital that integrates capitalist interests at the global level and across sectors and realms of activity' (Castells 2001: 506). In short, capital is well organized and labour is disorganized.

In the case of labour, Beck argues that, as a result of globalization and related social processes, class will fade in significance 'beside an individualized society of employees' (1992: 100). Whereas for Castells, the combination of organizational restructuring facilitated by information technology, 'and stimulated by global competition, is ushering in a fundamental transformation of work: *the individualization of labour in the labour process*' (2001: 282, italics in the original). By this Castells means that each employee's role is defined individually and that s/he has to negotiate the terms and conditions of his/her employment individually. Hence, under the 'new management rules of the global economy ... labour lost institutional protection and became increasingly dependent on individual bargaining conditions in a constantly changing labour market' (Castells 2001: 301–2). Thus, confronted by the growing wealth and mobility of capital in the form of global firms and global networks of firms, supported by national governments and international non-governmental organizations, labour became more vulnerable to the vicissitudes of the global capitalist market.

The increased power of capital and the reduced power of labour can be demonstrated with reference not only to the trend noted by Beck and Castells for capital to be organized on a global scale and labour to be organized on a national scale, which considerably reduces the effectiveness of collective action, but also to several other related tendencies. First, most governments support transnational corporations by offering financial incentives in the form of grants and tax concessions to transnational corporations, and/or by modifying or even suspending labour legislation, in the hope that these policies will persuade transnational corporations to set up in business and create more jobs (Sklair 2002). Second, transnational corporations have the ability to relocate their business(es) to countries where labour is available most cheaply, and/or is least regulated (Gray 1998). Third, the historic tendency for capital to be concentrated among fewer and fewer companies has increased markedly due to globalization, and this has enhanced the power of capital in relation to both individual employees and individual governments (Scholte 2000). As a result of the increased power of capital in the 'new international division of labour' (Fröbel et al. 1980), it is argued that flexibility is invariably on the employer's terms and that these tend to be to the disadvantage of employees with respect to pay and conditions, such as work loads, hours and security.

An extreme example of the global power of capital and the local powerlessness of labour is afforded by free-trade areas known as Export Processing Zones (hereafter EPZ), located mainly in the less developed part of the world. EPZs are notorious due to the tendency for transnational corporations to re-locate production in such areas to take advantage of tax breaks, cheap, non-unionized, flexible and mostly female labour, and minimal health, safety and environmental regulations (Fröbel et al. 1980; Sklair 2002). The highly exploitative, sweatshop conditions of factories in EPZs have been described in detail by Klein (2000), who, along with other politically concerned individuals and groups, has used naming and shaming plus consumer boycotts in an attempt to persuade global manufactures, such as Nike, to improve their employment practices. Defenders of EPZs claim, not without some justification, that they provide jobs in less developed societies and cheaper consumer goods in developed societies.

This picture of seriously empowered capital and disempowered labour has been contested on the grounds that governments also place restrictions on transnational corporations (Dicken 1992), that unions are beginning to organize transnationally and transform themselves into 'global social movement uinionism' (Bezuidenhout 2002: 111), and that the empirical evidence on the deleterious effect of globalization on pay and conditions is mixed (Blyton et al. 2002). The strength of these three lines of argument are weakened by the pervasiveness of the neo-liberal ideology among political and business leaders that informs contemporary globalization and which considers trade unions and welfare benefits as impediments to enterprise and the efficient operation of the market. There is also the evidence of the extreme exploitation and oppression that characterize the flexibilization of work at the end of the subcontracting supply chain in EPZs (Klein 2000; Raworth 2004). Despite these qualifications, it is clearly premature to announce the total eclipse of collective labour and workers rights in the face of the co-ordinated globalization of capital, and therefore that the complete reversal of the work conditions and relations achieved during the Fordist era has been accomplished.

The transformation of unpaid work?

Arguably, the patterning of unpaid domestic and voluntary work has changed far less than that of paid work, though they have not been entirely immune to external pressures

Table 10.1   Hours spent on housework by managers

[Housework is defined as cooking, cleaning, laundry, shopping and child-care.]

Family form	Men	Men's partners	Women	Women's partners
Dual-career family (i.e., both employed full-time)	9*	19*	20*	11
Manager with partner employed part-time	9	34	–	–
Manager with partner not employed (i.e., full-time housewife)	11	51	–	–
Single/divorced manager	9	–	15	–

*Respondents with children reported more hours of housework – the women 34 hours and the men 14 hours.

Source: Wajcman (1996: 619)

for change. As indicated in the previous chapter, and above, the theories that deal with the potentially transforming influences on unpaid work in an historically informed way are Castells' account of the rise of the informational global economy, and Beck's account of the detraditionalization of the nuclear family.

To recap, Beck (1992), along with others, notably Castells (1997), claims that the patriarchal nuclear family is in crisis. According to Beck, the acrimonious state of contemporary gender relations can be traced back to the partial modernization of industrial capitalism in that men were freed from traditional constraints rooted in the family, class and community, which enabled them to participate fully and equally in the public sphere of paid work, but women were not. In fact, it was women's lack of freedom from unpaid domestic work that allowed men to achieve independence, and research on the domestic basis of the managerial career indicates that this still applies, as Table 10.1 shows dramatically (Wajcman 1996). However, this male breadwinner and female houseworker model, though never universally accepted or practised, particularly by those who could not afford to conform to it, is in decline (Crompton 1999). Beck's explanation of the loosening of women's 'feudal' ties includes, among other things, the equalization of educational and employment opportunities, which have changed women's economic condition, and the revival of feminism, which has raised their consciousness of the persistence of gender inequalities. These changes are part of a more general process of individualization that is associated with globalization, especially in relation to the individualization of work. With more and more women entering the public sphere of paid work, they too are becoming part of the 'individualized society of employee' (Beck 1992: 99). Although it is still the case that whilst women participate in paid work in increasing numbers, men have not increased their participation in unpaid domestic work to the same extent. Hence, for Beck, the crux of the issue of the highly gendered pattern of unpaid domestic work is how to resolve the conflicting demands of paid work outside the home and unpaid work inside the home, and the persistence of gender inequalities associated with them?

According to Beck, there are three, 'by no means mutually exclusive', possible outcomes to this contradiction: 'return to the family in its traditional from; equalization according to the male model; and experimentation with new forms of living beyond male and female roles' (1992: 119). Beck considers the first two options to be 'pseudo-alternatives' which either reaffirm the traditional family or acknowledge the dominance of the needs of the market (1992: 124). Specifically, the first would undermine the modernization of the public sphere of employment by reconsigning women to the private sphere of the family, and the second would undermine the private sphere of family relationships by prioritizing the public sphere of paid work, the logical conclusion of which is 'not harmony with equal rights, but isolation in courses and situations that run counter and apart from each other' (Beck 1992: 123). It is only the third option that offers the possibility of reconciling the demands of the two (currently) diametrically opposed institutions. This will only be achieved 'if arrangements are made enabling both functions to be combined throughout the couple's life together' (Beck and Beck-Gernsheim 1995: 163). Thus, the organization of paid work and family life will have to be modified so that the social and economic needs of individuals can be met satisfactorily, such as more family-friendly paid work arrangements and more unpaid work friendly-family arrangements. Beck suggests that couple mobility could replace, where appropriate, individual mobility and that several families could share child-rearing instead of arranging it on an individual family basis. In these and other ways, paid work and family life could be reunified without destroying either institution.

A more empirically grounded version of the range of possibilities between a 'traditional' male breadwinner and female carer work and family system and 'less-traditional' dual earner and dual carer one has been advanced by Crompton on the basis of data from many European countries (1999: 205). As shown in Figure 10.1, in between these ends of the continuum, there are three possible paid work and unpaid domestic work or 'earning (that is breadwinning) and caring alternatives', which include dual earner/female part-time carer, dual earner/state carer, and dual earner/marketized carer arrangements (Crompton 1999: 205). Crompton's review of the cross-national comparative research into contemporary changes in gender systems leads her to four main conclusions. First, that the male breadwinner/female carer model is in terminal decline to varying degrees in all industrial capitalist societies, due mainly to a combination of the feminization of paid work and feminism, which in turn have resulted in alterations to welfare regimes and gender norms. Second, the dual earner/female part-time carer model, adopted most noticeably in Britain, has only modified the traditional gender arrangement since women tend to retain primary responsibility for unpaid domestic work. Third, in situations where women work full-time and resort to either private or public substitute care, various outcomes are possible in terms of gender equality depending on how woman-friendly the welfare state is, the prevailing gender culture, and the quality of the paid work undertaken by women. For example, Scandinavia has adopted a more woman-friendly welfare state, has been influenced

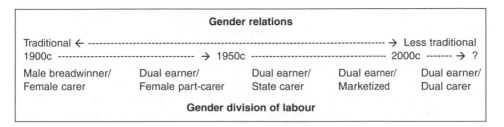

Figure 10.1   Options beyond the male breadwinner/female carer model

Source. Adapted from Crompton (1999: 205)

more by feminism, and has provided more high-quality jobs than other parts of Europe. Consequently, it is nearer to the dual earner/dual carer model than ex-communist countries. Fourth, the dual earner/dual carer model remains an aspiration at best in all the countries studied, with Norway coming nearest to this less traditional ideal.

The range of possible work and family options outlined by Beck and Crompton are comparable in the sense that they both start with the assumption that the male breadwinner/female houseworker model prevailed to a greater or lesser extent in all industrial capitalist societies at the beginning of the twentieth century. Also, they both contend that this ideal is being eroded by the feminization of work and feminism, and that the dual earner/dual carer model represents the most radical departure from the traditional family. The Crompton framework spells out the intermediate positions in greater detail with reference to many European countries and acknowledges the important part that welfare state regimes play in reinforcing or modifying gender relations. This suggests that in Europe at least, the unrestrained market solution is not a realistic option given the deep historical roots of welfare statism. Crompton's dual earner/state carer or marketized carer possibilities are the equivalent to Beck's gender equality via the male model, although these options depend upon the availability of public child-care provision and the relative affluence of the dual earner couples respectively. Finally, Crompton and Beck note that for meaningful and widespread gender equality to be achieved, dramatic changes in the ways that paid work and unpaid domestic work are organized is imperative, which implies an increased role for the state in terms of the regulation of paid work and the provision of child-care, and a reduction in men's paid working hours and an expansion of their domestic work contribution.

In the case of Castells' analysis of the transformation of unpaid work, it was noted earlier in this chapter that it is framed by his account of the rise of the informational global economy, featuring all the usual suspects, namely the feminization of work, feminism, and technological advances in contraception and family planning. Castells is in no doubt that in virtually all societies, but especially the most advanced ones, the patriarchal family is in crisis, by which he means that the traditional male breadwinner and female houseworker model has been seriously weakened by the above forces and that this is reflected in the statistical trends in such things as divorce, separation, marriage rates, non-marital births, and single-parent households.

Of all the forces affecting the decline of the male breadwinner and female houseworker model, Castells places great weight on globalization and the 'expansion of women's employment in the 1990s' at all levels and skills, which he attributes in large part to 'their flexibility as workers' plus their relative cheapness and social skills (1997: 173). Castells claims that the congruence between the need of the new economy for flexible labour also 'fits the survival interests of women who, under the conditions of patriarchalism, seek to make compatible work and family, with little help from their husbands' (1997: 173). This has two major consequences for the family: 'female bargaining power in the household increases significantly' and patriarchal ideology is 'decisively undermined' (1997: 173). In the absence of supportive welfare services, women's consciousness of their difficulty in juggling paid and unpaid work is raised further by the growth of feminist movements and their ideas.

The almost universal crisis of the patriarchal family 'manifests itself in the increasing diversity of partnership arrangements among people to share life and raise children', illustrated by Castells with reference to American data (1997: 221). Hence, in many cases, the patriarchal family is history already, notably in the 'growing proportions of female-headed households, and seriously challenged in most other families' (Castells 1997: 228). Moreover, in the growing proportion of non-family households, estimated by Castells to be approaching 40 per cent, the issue of patriarchalism is avoided altogether. Thus, for Castells, the crisis of the patriarchal family seems to have been resolved in many households in the sense that the taken-for-granted role structure of the traditional family no longer applies, although the possibility of a conservative backlash cannot be ruled out. In the current complex diversity of family relationships, no one standard family form predominates as in the past, hence the patterning of gender relations in the future is uncertain.

The impact of globalization on unpaid voluntary work is readily apparent at an individual level by the increase in the popularity of taking a 'gap year' from education or employment among young people in the UK, since this often includes a voluntary work component (Jones 2004), and theoretically by the claim that the growth of a new style of reflexive volunteering among young people is in large part a consequence of globalization (Hustinx 2001). More generally, it has been argued that contemporary globalization is associated with the weakening and restructuring of the state, class and communities, and the increasing influence of the market in everyday life (Scholte 2000). It is further argued that these changes have created a crisis for the voluntary sector in the sense that the traditional forms of volunteering are in decline and that voluntary organizations are finding it difficult to recruit and manage volunteers, who seek more flexibility and expect to have more say in the running of voluntary organizations (Hustinx and Lammertyn 2000).

As far as female-dominated informal unpaid voluntary work is concerned, the feminization of the labour force has reduced the supply of unpaid carers at a time when the demand for them has increased, not least because of the reduction in welfare state services and the expansion of groups in need of care, notably the elderly. It is in this context that the call by politicians for a renewal of community volunteerism has been interpreted as 'an ideological screen not to face the cynical abandonment of collective responsibility under the pretext of exercising individual responsibility' (Castells 1997: 294). Meanwhile, in many European countries, cash payment is being introduced for what was previously unpaid informal care work undertaken on a voluntary basis (Millar 1999). The increasing commodification of caring can take three forms: payments to care-givers (e.g., Italy and Norway), payments to care-receivers (e.g., Germany and Spain), or a combination of both (e.g., France and UK). The debate at the end of 2004 between the main UK political parties about how to fund child-care for all, with the Labour Party promising more public provision and the Conservative Party promising payment for informal care by relatives and friends, indicates the growing importance of this issue and neatly reflects the two main policy options: more/less commodification and/or more/less collectivization.

Beck's solution to the crisis in formal voluntary work is that it should be transformed into 'civil labour', which is defined as 'voluntary, self-organized labour where what should be done, and how it should be done, are in the hands of those who actually do it' (2000: 129). Civil labour would be 'rewarded with civic money and thereby socially recognized and valued' at a rate that 'at least matches the level of income support' (Beck 2000: 126). Beck suggests that this would provide a basic income for voluntary workers, temper the emphasis on economic growth, and afford 'an alternative source of activity and identity which not only gives people satisfaction, but also creates cohesion in individualized society by breathing life into everyday democracy' (2000: 127). Beck's vision of civil labour is that it is global in its orientation and organized by a 'public welfare entrepreneur, a kind of cross between Mother Teresa and Bill Gates' (2000: 129). In the UK, where there is a well developed tradition of using entrepreneurial skills for the common good, such people are referred to as social entrepreneurs and the organizations as social enterprises (Leadbeater 1997).

Beck concedes that for his vision of democratic voluntary work of this type to become a reality, paid work in the market economy and unpaid work in the household would need to be reduced and more evenly distributed between men and women, otherwise not everybody would have the time get involved in voluntary work. This is a tall order given the increasing polarization of paid work in the global economy and the persistence of an unequal gender division of unpaid work despite the decline of the male breadwinner and female houseworker tradition.

Summary and conclusions

Globalization is a highly contested concept although there seems to be an emerging consensus that the essence of contemporary capitalist globalization concerns the compression of time and space. The focus of the analysis has been on economic globalization more than on the political or socio-cultural aspects of this complex historical process since this dimension is the most relevant to the impact of globalization on different types of paid and unpaid work.

Historically, three main phases of globalization have been identified: pre-modern, modern, and late modern or contemporary globalization corresponding to the progressive deterritorialization of space. The key indicators of the current globalization phase include the global interconnections between societies, institutions, especially economic and political ones, and people.

The major causes of globalization include ideas (e.g., rationalism), economic forces (e.g., capitalism), technological factors (e.g., information and communication technologies), and regulatory frameworks (e.g., liberalization of the international movement of capital). In view of the complexity of the globalization process, and hence the difficulty of separating out one cause from another, it is widely thought that multi-causal explanations are the most appropriate. There is also general agreement that the growth of contemporary globalization was not inevitable but was promoted actively by the governments of the most advanced industrial capitalist societies, notably the USA, and the leading international corporations, hence its neo-liberal character. However, once the process of globalization has advanced to the stage where transworld interconnections are so extensive that virtually everyone is affected by them directly or indirectly, it has effectively become an irreversible process.

The growth of the global economy during the second half of the twentieth century coincided with parallel developments on a world-wide scale, such as social movements, including feminism, and global trends, such as the feminization of work. These and other factors, such as biological technologies, contributed to the ability of networks of women to challenge patriarchalism, and influence the nature and direction of globalization.

Paid work has been transformed by globalization and associated factors, notably new information and communication technologies, feminism, and the feminization of work, in that standard work has not only changed in terms of flexibility in every sense, but it has also declined relative to non-standard work. Women tend to be over-represented in most types of non-standard work, including part-time, temporary and home-based work, which also happen to be less well paid with less desirable conditions of employment in terms of such things as health and holiday entitlements. Castells is adamant that the feminization of work does not involve them being channelled into the less skilled jobs, although he does note that they are paid less than men for similar work. Conversely, Beck has noted that the feminization of work mainly affects non-standard work and has expressed the view that the growth of this type of low-paid and insecure work relative to well-paid and secure, standard work is inextricably associated with unrestrained capitalist globalization. Moreover, this trend raises the worrying possibility that the future of advanced industrial capitalist societies can be seen in the less advanced societies, such as Brazil, which is characterized by flexible labour markets and the informalization of work. However, recent research on vehicle production by global corporations in Brazil shows that they provide work contracts, albeit at low pay.

A major debate surrounding contemporary globalization concerns the enhanced power of capital organized transnationally relative to the power of labour which tends to be organized locally. Whilst acknowledging the economic advantages of globalization, in terms of increased employment and the diffusion of inexpensive quality goods and services, the social costs, in the form of dramatic levels of work oppression and exploitation, represent the unacceptable face of capitalist globalization. The increased power of global capital, largely beyond the control of any one nation state, and the decreased power of local labour, largely within the control of individual national states, is illustrated clearly with reference to EPZs where female-dominated jobs have often reduced the scale of unemployment at the cost of repressive labour practices. However, there is some evidence that labour and other political movements are beginning to organize on a transnational scale in order to try to limit the worst excesses of unbridled global capitalism. The weakness of labour during the rise of neo-liberal global capitalism is comparable to the situation confronted by workers during the rise of industrial capitalism, or the early modern phase of globalization, in that this was also an era of free trade and unconstrained competition. In both cases independent trade unions and state intervention designed to regulate excessive exploitation and provide an economic safety net were/are regarded as a obstacles free enterprise.

The transformation of unpaid domestic work has progressed more slowly than that of paid work, notwithstanding the decline during the twentieth century of the male breadwinner and female houseworker model, due to a variety of factors including the usual suspects of feminism and the feminization of work. Consequently, women still tend to do the bulk of the domestic work, including child-care, if they work outside the home for pay on a part-time basis, and still retain primary responsibility for it when they work full-time, in which case private or public substitute domestic workers are often used. Thus, the detraditionalization of family and work roles has yet to be transformed totally and most couple households fall somewhere between the extremes noted by Crompton and Beck in their gender systems framework of options.

The patriarchal crisis discussed at length by Beck and Castells may not apply to an increasing proportion of households, but where it does, most couples operate a compromise rather than a radical solution. Castells' argument that the 'process of full incorporation into the labour market, and into paid work, has important consequences for the family', namely the increased bargaining power of women and the delegitimation of male domination, is overly optimistic (1997: 173). This is because although Castells acknowledges that women are paid less than men and documents the over-representation of women in part-time work in all the 17 countries for which he presents trend data, ranging from just under 60 per cent in Greece to nearly 90 per cent in Belgium, he fails to take into account Hakim's (1996) point that part-time women workers are nearer to full-time housewives than full-time women workers in their financial dependence and primary responsibility for unpaid domestic work. Since women have been partially, not fully, incorporated into the labour market, this tends to augment rather than undermine the male breadwinner and female houseworker model.

Unpaid informal voluntary work is in the process of being transformed following the feminization of work, the restructuring of welfare services, and the expansion of groups in need of care work, such as the elderly. There is evidence in Europe of a tendency for female-dominated informal care work to be commodified, although there is also pressure on the state not only to pick up the bill directly, but also to provide more care services on a collective basis.

Unpaid formal voluntary work is similarly experiencing change at the turn of the century, notably with reference to the expansion of new and more flexible forms of volunteering which threaten to undermine the old style of volunteering. This was founded on long-term commitment and was rooted in class and other types of traditional communities. Beck's somewhat utopian vision of civil labour rewarded with civic money, a sort of semi-commodified work, and organized by social entrepreneurs, with everyone animated by transnational concerns, promises more voluntary worker satisfaction, more social cohesion, and a more vibrant democracy. The problem is that for this to become a practical reality for most people given their other work time commitments and schedules, a less unequal division of paid work and unpaid domestic work is deemed essential.

Concluding remarks on continuity and change and 'work'

Beck's thoughts on civil labour are an integral part of his vision of an alternative to the current work society dominated by the priorities of the capitalist global economy, a society based 'upon political freedom' that he calls 'a multi-activity society in which housework, family work, club work and voluntary work are prized alongside paid work and returned to the centre of public and academic attention' (2000: 125). This is another way of saying that what was referred to in the first chapter as the dominant conception of work needs to be transcended. This fusion of capitalist, industrial, modern and patriarchal aspects of work was established by the beginning of the twentieth century, relegating other forms of work, such as unpaid domestic and voluntary work, to a degree of marginality verging on invisibility.

As far as the dominant conception of work is concerned, there is little evidence that the capitalist dimension has been eroded, yet the combined forces of globalization, technological innovations, feminism, and the feminization of paid work have modified to some degree the industrial, modern and patriarchal dimensions. First, the diffusion of technological innovations in information and communication in the global economy has encouraged the expansion of working at and from the home in a more flexible way than was possible when all work was undertaken at a site away from the home, thereby diminishing the idea instigated by industrialism that paid work is something that happens in a separate place, away from the household. Second, the unexpected and marked expansion of self-employment, spurious or otherwise, formal or informal, is not unconnected to the flexibilization of work in the global economy, and involves the recrudescence of ascription on the basis of family membership, or other types of high trust groups, which contrasts with the modern principle of universalistic achievement. Third, feminism and the feminization of paid work in the global economy have not only reduced patriarchalism in the public sphere of paid employment, but have also challenged patriarchalism in the private sphere of unpaid domestic work. Furthermore, along with the reduced availability of family child-care, they have prompted a domestic work problem that has been resolved in part by an increase in domestic outsourcing, and in part by a small increase in men's participation in this domestic work. However, it is apparent from the material presented in the earlier chapters that paid work and unpaid domestic work remain highly gendered and unequal, and that women continue to take the strain, albeit less so than when the male breadwinner and female houseworker model was more pervasive.

Meanwhile, the primacy of capitalist institutions and values have been entrenched further by the development of the most recent phase of economic globalization in several ways. This includes the revival of neo-liberalism, the attempt to create an enterprise culture, and the privatization, marketization and general intrusion of entrepreneurialism into the provision of public services, including the related commodification of previously collectivized public goods and services. By the same token, the removal of institutional supports that legitimize capitalism, particularly legislation regarding labour and welfare, are an indication of the hegemony of the profit motive. The reinvigoration of capitalism is also reflected in the shift in the balance of power in favour of capital relative to labour. Yet, global corporations tend to deny that a conflict of class interests is built into modern capitalism and resort to fostering an egalitarian culture via 'specialized symbols, ideology, language and rituals', for example the tendency of Japanese multinationals to refer to their employees euphemistically as 'associates' (Graham 1994: 138) or 'partners', as in the case Starbucks (2002). Thus the dominant conception of work is still largely intact to the extent that the key capitalist dimension has been strengthened by the ubiquity of the twin principles of limitless production and limitless consumption and hence profit, and by its contamination of the public sector, whilst the other dimensions, the industrial, modern and patriarchal, have only been nibbled away at the edges. Consequently, the dominant conception of work remains highly influential to the extent that real work is still equated with being paid for a job obtained on the basis of universalistic criteria, and working away from home in capitalist organizations dominated by men at the top of the hierarchy.

Within the parameters of paid work, it will be recalled that during the first half of the twentieth century the Fordist model of work, characterized by the standardization of the contractural, spatial and temporal dimensions, became the standard form of employment. In theory, the idea of standard work is gender neutral, but in practice it was based on the male breadwinner and female houseworker gender arrangement which favoured men since they were effectively exempted from primary responsibility for domestic work whereas women were not. Fordism was also predicated on the nation state in the sense that it was actively complicit in the relationship between capital and labour, not least in terms of providing an appropriately gendered and standardized benefits system. The crisis of Fordism in the mid-1970s and its subsequent decline (discussed in Chapter 5) has been attributed to changes in demand and supply, both of which are associated with the rise of globalization. In fact, for one sociologist: 'The most important factor that that has led to the downfall of Fordism, and something which is often thought of as a defining characteristic of the post-Fordist era, is globalization' (Webster 2002: 68). Whatever the causes, Fordism certainly fragmented into neo-Fordist and post-Fordist production systems, which imply continuity and change respectively, and flexibility became the key issue for employers and employees.

Arguably, the most profound change in the patterning of work over the past thirty years or so concerns the destandardization of the Fordist-inspired model of standard work, not least because it is associated with the polarization of work. In terms of Beck's three dimensions of standard work, contractural standardization has been undermined by the growth of paid work lacking an employment contract, spatial standardization by the expansion of working at or from home, and temporal standardization by the increase in various types of part-time and temporary work, on and/or off the books, as a flexible employee or self-employed worker. In addition, the implicit patriarchal element of standard work, namely the male breadwinner and female houseworker model, has also been weakened by the feminization of work. In sum, there has been a decline of inflexible and secure standard work and a growth of many overlapping forms of flexible and insecure non-standard work, a trend that is thought to be increasing. However, the destandardization of paid work thesis needs to be qualified by the recognition that standard work was not as universal or secure as the model implies, and that some forms of non-standard work are not as insecure as the stereotype suggests. Thus, the standard work model is less pervasive in industrial capitalist societies, though far from being extinct, and may even be enjoying a renaissance. Moreover, the distinction between standard and non-standard work has blurred in that they have both been subject to the process of flexibilization. Those who adopt a strong view on the transformation of paid work tend to overlook the persistence of neo-Fordist mass production, especially in developing societies, the resilience of collective labour, and the continuing political support for the state regulation of employment.

Overall, continuity more than change seems to characterize the recent history of the dominant conception of work that developed with the rise of industrial capitalism, and whilst there have been some changes to the more recent and less universal Fordist model of standard paid work, notably the uneven expansion of non-standard work and the limited decline of the male breadwinner and female homemaker model, it is premature to conclude that Fordism has been completely transformed.

Finally, this sociological analysis of paid and unpaid work has shown that variations in the patterning of paid and unpaid work need to be historically and geopolitically located. Second, that all forms of work also need to be understood with reference to the increasing globalization of economic life. Third, that each type of work impacts on every other type of work and therefore no one type of paid or unpaid work can be understood in isolation. Furthermore, and following from this point, the hope of a more symmetrical or 'egalitarian' family pattern, expressed in their different ways by, among others, Castells (1997: 242), Beck (2000), and of course Young and Willmott (1973), depends in large part upon changes in the nature and distribution of paid work. Whilst it is good to have a vision of a more democratic and balanced pattern of paid and unpaid work, it is more likely to become a reality if all dreamers participate in trying to bring about the desired changes.

Further reading

A good introduction to globalization is Scholte (2000) *Globalization: A Critical Introduction.* A more detailed account of the economic and political aspects of contemporary globalization can be found in Held et al. (1999) *Global Transformations: Politics, Economics and Culture.* An excellent text on sociology from a global perspective, which includes material on the development of globalization and paid work, is Cohen and Kennedy (2000) *Global Sociology.* The most comprehensive, theoretically informed empirical analysis of globalization and related transformations in relation to work is Castells (2001) *The Rise of the Network Society* (2nd edn) and (1997) *The Power of Identity.* Two books by Beck, *Risk Society: Towards a New Modernity* (1992) and *The Brave New World of Work* (2000), also discuss globalization, plus the destandardization of paid work, the detraditionalization of the family, and changes in unpaid voluntary work in interesting and provocative ways. The monograph edited by Crompton (1999) *Restructuring Gender Relations and Employment: The Decline of the Male Breadwinner* covers national variations in Europe in the patterning of women's employment.

Questions for discussion and assessment

1. What is globalization and how has it changed historically?
2. Account for the rise and distinctiveness of contemporary globalization.
3. Consider the impact of globalization on paid work.
4. How has unpaid domestic work changed since the advent of the global economy?
5. In what ways and to what extent is the dominant conception of work still dominant?
6. Examine critically the destandardization of labour thesis.

.... Glossary

Cautionary note: Definitions of social science terms are invariably contested. It is therefore imperative to consult the relevant section(s) of the text, making a note of any variations. In other words, do not be deceived by the apparent simplicity of the definitions and read carefully the sources cited.

Agrarian society: An advanced (third) type of pre-industrial human society character-ized by the use of animal power for farming and transport, such as horses for plough-ing and riding.

Alienation: A concept used by Marx to describe the exploited and oppressed condition of labour under an industrial capitalist mode of production, and operationalized by Blauner in order to examine empirically the impact of different types of technology. The latter's conceptualization emphasized a worker's powerlessness, the meaningless-ness of work, social isolation and self-estrangement.

Capitalism: A type of economic organization oriented to the accumulation of profit involving the private ownership of the means of production and the employment of free wage labour.

Commodification: A process by which goods and services are produced by profit-ori-ented organizations and exchanged for money under a market system.

Conspicuous consumption: A concept developed by Veblen that refers to a zero sum game involving the competitive, conspicuous consumption of leisure (time), goods and services (money), and resources (waste) in order to demonstrate one's economic prowess and high social status.

Cultural lag: When two previously harmonious features of society become dissociated due to one changing more radically than the other.

Domestic work: A form of unpaid work involving tasks undertaken in and around the home, including child-care, also referred to as housework and domestic labour.

Enterprise culture: Ideas and practices concerned with initiative and self-reliance oriented to making a profit.

Family wage: A male wage sufficient to support a family without financial contributions from other family members that was based on the model that the ideal family comprised a male breadwinner and dependent full-time housewife.

Feminism: A social movement/set of ideas concerned with challenging male domination, thereby improving the condition of women and achieving equality.

Flexibility: The ability to change production easily by altering the size of the workforce (numerical flexibility), the roles of the workforce (functional flexibility), and/or the output of the workforce (product flexibility).

Flexible specialization: A model of work organization associated primarily with Piore and Sabel that involves the combination of craft skills and advanced technology which enables companies to supply high-quality customized products to diversified markets.

Fordism: A system of mass production and consumption pioneered by Henry Ford in America at the beginning of the twentieth century. The main features include the fragmentation and simplification of tasks, the moving assembly line, and the standardization of parts and low-quality products.

Globalization: A complex historical process characterized by increasing economic, political and socio-cultural interconnections that compress time/space.

Homeworking: Income-generating economic activity derived from working at and/or from home.

Horticultural society: A (second) type of human society which evolved from semi-nomadic hunting and gathering societies to become a settled horticultural one based on the use of metal tools for the production of food.

Hunting and gathering society: The earliest known (first) type of human society dominated by the use of stone weapons and tools for hunting animals and the gathering of food, such as berries, and hence nomadic.

Individualization: A concept developed by Beck that refers to the tendency for individuals in late modern society to be set free from traditional sources of collective identity rooted in early modern society, such as class, family and community.

Industrial capitalism: A type of society in which economic organizations are privately owned and use large-scale machinery powered by inanimate sources of energy.

Industrialization: The transformation of an essentially agrarian economy into a manufacturing one characterized by the use of inanimate sources of energy such as steam to power large-scale machinery, epitomized by factory production.

Informal work: Work that is legal or illegal but undeclared to the tax and other regulatory authorities.

Japanization: Ways of organizing work that are associated with Japanese companies which have been adopted by western companies, such as Just-in-Time (the supply of parts and material etc. when they are needed) and Total Quality Control (the emphasis on zero defects), also known as lean production.

Leisure class: A parasitic class which abstains from useful work because it regards it as demeaning and instead engages in the conspicuous consumption of time (leisure), money (expensive goods and services) and resources (waste). The leisure class is analysed in detail by Veblen.

McDonaldism: A neo-Fordist form of service production system characterized by qualified Taylorized social and manual work tasks, a modified assembly line, and limited destandardization of parts and medium-quality products.

Male breadwinner/female houseworker model: The idea that men should be the primary economic providers in a family and that women should be the primary unpaid domestic workers.

Marriage bar: A prohibition on the hiring of women workers, often operated in conjunction with a retain bar, which prohibited the retention of women when they married.

Modernization: The social and cultural dimensions of (western) industrialization involving the decline of traditionalism and characterized by literacy, rationality and urbanization.

Neo-Fordism: A reformed version of Fordism involving qualified Taylorized work tasks, a modified assembly line, a limited destandardization of parts and a wider range of higher-quality products.

Neo-liberalism: An economic (and political and social) set of ideas that dates from the rise of capitalism which stresses the importance of a free market and unrestrained competition. When this doctrine was revived in the 1990s it was sometimes referred to as New Right ideology.

Network enterprise: A business model made up of companies or sections of companies thought by Castells to have superseded individual and collective capitalist units.

Network society: A concept developed by Castells to refer to a new type of society that is informational, global and networked.

Non-standard work: Forms of paid work, such as part-time and temporary work, which deviate from what had become standard by the mid-to-late twentieth century in western industrial capitalist societies, namely regular, full-time employment based on a contract specifying wages, hours and benefits. Also known as contingent work and flexible work.

Patriarchy: Ideas and practices by which males dominate females.

Post-Fordism: A radical alternative to Fordism involving flexible multi-skilled work, flexible computer technology, and flexible parts and high-quality customized products.

Post-industrial society: A type of society in which services and service work (white-collar) rather than manufacturing and factory work (blue-collar) dominate the economy.

Pre-industrial society: Any type of society dominated by non-manufacturing economic activities, including hunting and gathering, horticulture and farming.

(Protestant) work ethic: The idea that work is a virtuous activity (a sign of election among Calvinists) and that one should work conscientiously, consume ascetically, and eschew idleness. The Prostestant source of this idea was examined by Weber.

Self-employment: Workers who own and operate the means of production either alone or in combination with others.

Skill: One or more competences required by a specific job, possessed by an individual, or associated with particular types of work or occupation. A decline in skill is usually termed deskilling and an increase in skill is usually termed upskilling, whereas a tendency for both to occur is termed polarization.

Standard work: Work in the form of full-time employment involving a contract that typically includes regular pay for a specified number of hours and a range of benefits, notably sick pay and a pension. This form of work is thought to have become the norm by the mid-to-late twentieth century in western industrial capitalist societies as a result of what some have called the Fordist compromise to match mass production and mass consumption.

Taylorism (or scientific management): Principles of work organization advocated by Taylor, notably the transfer of all discretion from workers to management and the fragmentation and simplification of tasks.

Teamworking: Working as part of a group instead of individually and adopted by Volvo and Japanese car makers during the late twentieth century. It is associated with increased functional flexibility and the ideology of egalitarianism.

Technology: The application of scientific knowledge to solve practical problems.

Technological determinism: The assumption that technology – productive technique including both the material objects and their social organization – determines social relationships.

Temporary work: Employment that is regarded by employers and employees to be of a limited duration that can range from casual work lasting a few hours to contract work lasting a few years.

Traditionalism: Ideas and practices handed down form one generation to another.

Underemployment: An inadequate employment situation in terms of time, education/skill, or income/pay. Time-related underemployment is the most commonly researched, notably involuntary part-time work.

Unemployment: A situation of being without paid employment. A concept that is inextricably associated with the development of industrial capitalism which involved the demise of alternative sources of income.

Voluntary work: Unpaid work undertaken as a gift and freely chosen for non-profit organizations, often referred to as formal voluntary work. Informal voluntary work is also unpaid but can involve elements of reciprocity, for instance in friendship or neighbourhood exchange, and obligation, typically among members of the same family.

References

●●●●●●●●

Abercrombie, N., Hill, S. and Turner, B.S. (1988) *Dictionary of Sociology* (2nd edn). London: Penguin.

Abreu, A., Beynon, H. and Ramalho, J.R. (2000) 'The dream factory: VW's modular production system in Resende, Brazil', *Work, Employment and Society*, 14 (2): 265–82.

Aglietta, M. (1987 [1976]) *A Theory of Capitalist Regulation: The US Experience*. London: Verso.

Aguren, S., Hansson, R. and Karlsson, K.G. (1976) *The Volvo Kalmar Plant: The Impact of New Design on Work Organization*. Stockholm: The Rationalization Council SAF–LO.

Albrow, M. (1996) *The Global Age*. Cambridge: Polity.

Allan, E.A. and Steffensmeier, D.J. (1989) 'Youth, unemployment and property crime: differential effects on job availability and job quality on juvenile and young adult arrest rates', *American Sociological Review*, 54 (1): 107–23.

Allatt, P. and Yeandle, S. (1992) *Youth Unemployment and the Family*. London: Routledge.

Allen, J. and du Gay, P. (1994) 'Industry and the rest: the economic identity of services', *Work, Employment and Society*, 8 (2): 255–71.

Allen, J., Braham, P. and Lewis, P. (1992) *Political and Economic Forms of Modernity*. Cambridge: Polity.

Allen, S. (1999) 'Gender inequality and divisions of labour', in H. Beynon and P. Glavanis (eds), *Patterns of Social Inequality*. London: Longman. pp. 20–55.

Allen, S. and Wolkowitz, C. (1987) *Homeworking: Myths and Realities*. London: Macmillan.

Amin, A. (ed.) (1994a) *Post-Fordism: A Reader*. Oxford: Blackwell.

Amin, A. (1994b) 'Post-Fordism: models, fantasies and phantoms of transition', in A. Amin (ed.), *Post-Fordism: A Reader*. Oxford: Blackwell. pp. 1–39.

Anderson, B. (1996) 'Review of *Servicing the Middle Classes*, by N. Gregson and M. Lowe', *Work, Employment and Society*, 10 (3): 581–3.

Anderson, M. (1971) *Family Structure in Nineteenth-Century Lancashire*. Cambridge: Cambridge University Press.

Anderson, M., Bechhofer, F. and Gershuny, J. (eds) (1994) *The Social and Political Economy of the Household*. Oxford: Oxford University Press.

Anthony, P.D. (1977) *The Ideology of Work*. London: Tavistock.

Applebaum, H. (1992) *The Concept of Work: Ancient, Medieval and Modern*. New York: State University of New York Press.

Arber, S. and Ginn, J. (1995) 'The mirage of gender equality: occupational success in the labour market and within marriage', *British Journal of Sociology*, 46 (1): 21–43.

Aronowitz, S. and DiFazio, W. (1994) *The Jobless Future: Sci-Tech and the Dogma of Work*. Minneapolis: University of Minnesota Press.

Ashton, D.M. (1986) *Unemployment under Capitalism: The Sociology of British and American Labour Markets*. Brighton: Wheatsheaf.

Atkinson, J., Morris, R.J. and Williams, M. (1996) *Temporary Work and the Labour Market*. Brighton: University of Sussex, Institute of Employment Studies.

Attewell, P. (1989) 'The clerk deskilled: a study of false nostalgia', *Journal of Historical Sociology*, 2 (4): 357–88.

Auer, P. and Cazes, S. (2000) 'The resilience of the long-term employment relationship: evidence from the industrialized countries', *International Labour Review*, 139 (4): 379–408.

Bailyn, L. (1988) 'Freeing work from the constraints of location and time', *New Technology, Work and Employment*, 3 (2): 143–52.

Baldwin, S. and Glendinning, C. (1983) 'Employment, women and their disabled children', in J. Finch and D. Groves (eds), *A Labour of Love: Women, Work and Caring*. London: Routledge and Kegan Paul. pp. 53–71.

Baran, B. (1988) 'Office automation and women's work: the technological transformation of the insurance industry', in R. Pahl (ed.), *On Work: Historical, Comparative and Theoretical Approaches*. Oxford: Blackwell. pp. 684–706.

Bechhofer, F. and Elliot, B. (1968) 'Small shopkeepers and the class structure', *European Journal of Sociology*, 9: 180–202.

Bechhofer, F., Elliot, B., Rushforth, M. and Bland, R. (1974) 'The *petits bourgeois* in the class structure: the case of the small shopkeepers', in F. Parkin (ed.), *The Social Analysis of Class Structure*. London: Tavistock. pp. 103–28.

Beck, U. (1992) *Risk Society: Towards a New Modernity*. London: Sage.

Beck, U. (2000) *The Brave New World of Work*. Cambridge: Polity.

Beck, U. (2001) *What is Globalization?* Cambridge: Polity.

Beck, U. and Beck-Gernsheim, E. (1995) *The Normal Chaos of Love*. Cambridge: Polity.

Beck, U. and Beck-Gernsheim, E. (2002) *Individualization: Institutionalized Individualism and its Social and Political Consequences*. London: Sage.

Beder, S. (2000) *Selling the Work Ethic: From Puritan Pulpit to Corporate PR*. London: Zen Books.

Beechey, V. and Perkins, T. (1987) *A Matter of Hours: Part-time Work and the Labour Market*. Cambridge: Polity.

Bell, D. (1976 [1973]) *The Coming of Post-industrial Society: A Venture in Social Forcasting*. London: Penguin.

Bell, D. (1980) 'The information society: the social framework of the information society', in T. Forester (ed.), *The Microelectronics Revolution: The Complete Guide to the New Technology and Its Impact on Society*. Oxford: Blackwell. pp. 500–49.

Beneria, L. (1988) 'Conceptualizing the labour force: the underestimation of women's economic activities', in R. Pahl (ed.), *On Work: Historical, Comparative and Theoretical Approaches*. Oxford: Blackwell. pp. 372–91.

Benjamin, A. (2004) 'Lord of the Manor', *The Guardian*, 29 September.

Benjamin, O. and Sullivan, O. (1999) 'Relational resources, gender consciousness and possibilities of change in marital relationships', *Sociological Review*, 47 (4): 794–820.

Benner, C. (2002) *Work in the New Economy: Flexible Labour Markets in Silicon Valley*. Oxford: Blackwell.

Berg, M. (1988) 'Women's work, mechanization and early industrialization', in R. Pahl (ed.), *On Work: Historical, Comparative and Theoretical Approaches*. Oxford: Blackwell. pp. 61–94.

Berg, M. (1994) *The Age of Manufactures 1700–1820: Industry, Innovation and Work in Britain* (2nd edn). London: Routledge.

Berggren, C. (1992) 'New production concepts in final assembly – the Swedish experience', in S. Wood (ed.), *The Transformation of Work: Skill, Flexibility and the Labour Process*. London: Routledge. pp. 172–203.

Berggren, C. (1993a) *The Volvo Experience: Alternatives to Lean Production in the Swedish Auto Industry*. London: Macmillan.

Berggren, C. (1993b) 'Lean production – the end of history?', *Work, Employment and Society*, 7 (2): 163–88.

Berk, R.A. and Berk, S.F. (1979) *Labour and Leisure at Home: Content and Organization of the Household Day*. London: Sage.

Berk, S.F. (1985) *The Gender Factory: The Apportionment of Work in American Households*. New York: Plenum.

Beynon, H. (1975) *Working for Ford*. Wakefield: E.P. Publishing.

Beynon, H. and Austrin, T. (1994) *Masters and Servants: Class and Patronage in the Making of a Labour Organization*. London: Rivers Oram Press.

Bezuidenhout, A. (2002) '"What we do" or "What we are"? Trade union responses to globalization and regionalization in South Africa', in Y.A. Debrah and I.G. Smith (eds), *Globalization, Employment and the Workplace: Diverse Impacts*. London: Routledge. pp. 85–114.

Birchall, J. (1997) *The International Co-operative Movement*. Manchester: Manchester University Press.

Bittman, M., Matheson, G. and Meagher, G. (1999) 'The changing boundary between home and market: Australian trends in outsourcing domestic labour', *Work, Employment and Society*, 13 (2): 249–73.

Bittman, M., Rice, J. and Wajcman, J. (2004) 'Appliances and their impact: the ownership of domestic technology and time spent on household work', *British Journal of Sociology*, 55 (3): 401–23.

Blackburn, R.M. and Mann, M. (1979) *The Working Class in the Labour Market*. London: Macmillan.

Blanchflower, D.G. and Freeman, R. (eds) (2000) *Youth Unemployment and Joblessness in Advanced Societies*. Chicago: University of Chicago Press.

Blauner, R. (1964) *Alienation and Freedom: The Factory Worker and His Industry*. Chicago: University of Chicago Press.

Blom, R. and Melin, H. (2003) 'Information society and the transformation of organizations in Finland', *Work and Occupations*, 30 (2): 176–93.

Blyton, P., Lucio, M.M., McGurk, J. and Turnbull, P. (2002) 'Globalization, restructuring and occupational labour power: evidence from the international airline industry', in Y.A. Debrah and I.G. Smith (eds), *Globalization, Employment and the Workplace: Diverse Impacts*. London: Routledge. pp. 24–40.

Bogenhold, D. and Staber, U. (1991) 'The decline and rise of self-employment', *Work, Employment and Society*, 5 (2): 223–39.

Bond, S. and Sales, J. (2001) 'Household work in the UK: an analysis of the British Household Panel Survey', *Work, Employment and Society*, 15 (2): 223–50.

Boris, E. and Prugl, E. (eds) (1996) *Homeworkers in Global Perspective: Invisible No More*. London: Routledge.

Borzaga, C. and Defourney, J. (eds) (2001) *The Emergence of Social Enterprise*. London: Routledge.

Boserup, E. (1970) *Women's Role in Economic Development*. London: Allen and Unwin.

Boulton, M.G. (1983) *On Being a Mother: A Study of Women with Pre-school Children*. London: Tavistock.

Bowles, S. and Gintis, H. (1976) *Schooling in Capitalist America*. London: Routledge and Kegan Paul.

Box, S. (1987) *Recession, Crime and Punishment*. London: Macmillan.

Boyle, E. (1994) 'The rise of the reluctant entrepreneurs', *International Small Business Journal*, 12 (2): 63–9.

Bradley, H. (1989) *Men's Work, Women's Work: A Sociological History of the Sexual Division of Labour in Employment*. Cambridge: Polity.

Bradley, H., Erickson, M., Stephenson, C. and Williams, S. (2000) *Myths at Work*. Cambridge: Polity.

Brannen, J. and Moss, P. (1991) *Managing Mothers: Dual Earner Households after Maternity Leave*. London: Unwin Hyman.

Brannen, J. and Nilsen, A. (2002) 'Young people's time perspective: from youth to adulthood', *Sociology*, 36 (3): 513–37.

Braverman, H. (1974) *Labour and Monopoly Capital: The Degradation of Work in the Twentieth Century*. New York: Monthly Review Press.

Bresnen, M.J., Wray, K., Bryman, A., Beardsworth, A.D., Ford, J.R. and Keil, E.T. (1985) 'The flexibility of recruitment in the construction industry; formalization or re-casualization?', *Sociology*, 19 (1): 108–24.

Bright, J.R. (1958) 'Does automation raise skill requirements?', *Harvard Business Review*, 36 (4): 85–98.

Brines, J. (1994) 'Economic dependency, gender and the division of labour at home', *American Journal of Sociology*, 100 (3): 652–88.

Brown, R.K. (1992) *Understanding Industrial Organizations*. London: Routledge.

Brynin, M. (2002) 'Overqualification in employment', *Work, Employment and Society*, 16 (4): 637–54.

Burawoy, M. (1979) *Manufacturing Consent: Changes in the Labour Process under Monopoly Capitalism*. Chicago: University of Chicago Press.

Burawoy, M. (1996) 'A classic of its time: review of *Labour and Monopoly Capital* by H. Braverman', *Contemporary Sociology*, 25 (3): 296–9.

Burchell, J., Day, D., Hudson, M., Ladipo, D., Mankelow, R., Nolan, J.P., Reed, H., Wichert, I.C. and Wilkinson, R. (1999) *Job Insecurity and Work Intensification*. York: Joseph Rowntree Foundation.

Burgess, J. and Connell, J. (2004) *International Perspectives on Temporary Agency Work*. London: Routledge.

Burnett, J. (1994) *Idle Hands: The Experience of Unemployment, 1790–1990*. London: Routledge.

Burrows, R. (ed.) (1991) *Deciphering the Enterprise Culture: Entrepreneurship, Petty Capitalism and the Restructuring of Britain*. London: Routledge.

Burrows, R. and Curran, J. (1991) 'Not such a small business: reflections on the rhetoric, the reality and the future of the enterprise culture', in M. Cross and G. Payne (eds), *Work and the Enterprise Culture*. London: Falmer. pp. 9–29.

Callender, C. (1985) 'Unemployment: the case for women', in C. Jones and M. Benton (eds), *Yearbook of Social Policy in Britain 1984/5*. London: Routledge. pp. 47–73.

Campbell, I. and Burgess, J. (2001) 'Casual employment and temporary employment in Europe: developing a cross-national comparison', *Work, Employment and Society*, 15 (1): 171–84.

Carr, D. (1996) 'Two paths to self-employment: women and men's self-employment in the United States, 1980', *Work and Occupations*, 23 (1): 26–53.

Carré, F.J. (1992) 'Temporary employment in the eighties', in V.L. duRivage (ed.), *New Policies for the Part-time and Contingent Workforce*. New York: M.E. Sharpe. pp. 45–87.

Carré, F.J., Ferber, M.A., Golden, L. and Herzenberg, S.A. (eds) (2000) *Nonstandard Work: The Nature and Challenges of Changing Employment Arrangements*. Champaign, IL: Industrial Relations Research Association, University of Illinois at Urbana-Champaign.

Casey, B. (1991) 'Survey evidence on trends in "non-standard" employment', in A. Pollert (ed.), *Farewell to Flexibility*? Oxford: Blackwell. pp. 179–99.

Casey, B. and Laczko, F. (1989) 'Early retired or long-term unemployed: the situation of non-working men aged 55–64 from 1979–1986', *Work, Employment and Society*, 3 (4): 509–26.

Castells, M. (1997) *The Power of Identity*. Oxford: Blackwell.

Castells, M. (2000) 'Materials for an exploratory theory of the network society', *British Journal of Sociology*, 51 (1): 5–24.

Castells, M. (2001) *The Rise of the Network Society* (2nd edn). Oxford: Blackwell.

Cato, M.S. (2004) *The Pit and the Pendulum: A Co-operative Future for Work in the Welsh Valleys*. Cardiff: University of Wales Press.

Charles, N. and James, E. (2003) 'The gender dimensions of job insecurity in a local market', *Work, Employment and Society*, 17 (3): 531–52.

Clarke, S. (1992) 'What in the F——-'s name is Fordism', in N. Gilbert, R. Burrows and A. Pollert (eds), *Fordism and Flexibility: Divisions and Change*. London: Macmillan. pp. 13–30.

Cockburn, C. (1983) *Brothers: Male Dominance and Technological Change*. London: Pluto.

Coffield, F., Borrill, C. and Marshall, S. (1986) *Growing up at the Margins: Young Adults in the North East*. Milton Keynes: Open University Press.

Cohen, R. and Kennedy, P. (2000) *Global Sociology*. London: Macmillan.

Collins, R. (1979) *The Credential Society: An Historical Sociology of Education and Stratification*. New York: Academic Press.

Collinson, D. and Knights, D. (1986) '"Men only": theories and practices of job segregation in insurance', in D. Knights and H. Willmott (eds), *Gender and the Labour Process*. Aldershot: Gower. pp. 140–78.

Collinson, M. and Collinson, D. (1996) '"It's only Dick": the sexual harassment of women managers in insurance sales', *Work, Employment and Society*, 10 (1): 29–56.

Conley, H. (2002) 'A state of insecurity: temporary work in the public services', *Work, Employment and Society*, 16 (4): 725–37.

Cooley, M. (1987 [1980]) *Architect or Bee? The Human Price of Technology*. London: Hogarth Press.

Copps, A. (2000) 'Comment', *The Times*, 7 February.

Coriat, B. (1980) 'The restructuring of the assembly line: a new economy of time and control', *Capital and Class*, 11: 34–43.

Corrigan, P. (1977) 'Feudal relics or capitalist monuments?', *Sociology*, 11 (3): 411–63.

Cotgrove, S. (1972) 'Alienation and automation', *British Journal of Sociology*, 23 (4): 437–51.

Cowan, R.S. (1983) *More Work for Mother: The Ironies of Household Technology from the Open Hearth to the Microwave*. New York: Basic Books.

Coyle, A. (1984) *Redundant Women*. London. Women's Press.

Cragg, A. and Dawson, T. (1984) *Unemployed Women: A Study of Attitudes and Experiences*, Research Paper No. 47. London: Department of Employment.

Creighton, C. (1996) 'The rise and fall of the male breadwinner family: a reappraisal', *Comparative Studies in Society and History*, 38: 310–37.

Crompton, R. (1990) 'Professions in the current context', *Work, Employment and Society*, Special Issue, May. pp. 147–66.

Crompton, R. (1997) *Women and Work in Modern Britain*. Oxford: Oxford University Press.

Crompton, R. (ed.) (1999) *Restructuring Gender Relations and Employment: The Decline of the Male Breadwinner*. Oxford: Oxford University Press.

Crompton, R. (2002) 'Employment, flexible working and the family', *British Journal of Sociology*, 53 (4): 537–58.

Crompton, R. and Harris, F. (1998) 'Explaining women's employment patterns: "orientations to work" revisited', *British Journal of Sociology*, 49 (1): 118–36.

Crompton, R. and Harris, F. (1999) 'Attitudes, women's employment, and the changing domestic division of labour: a cross-national analysis', in R. Crompton (ed.), *Restructuring Gender Relations and Employment: The Decline of the Male Breadwinner*. Oxford: Oxford University Press. pp. 105–27.

Crompton, R. and Jones, G. (1984) *White Collar Proletariat: Deskilling and Gender in Clerical Work*. London: Macmillan.

Crompton, R. and Reid, S. (1982) 'The deskilling of clerical work', in S. Wood (ed.), *The Degradation of Work?: Skill, Deskilling and the Labour Process*. London: Hutchinson. pp. 163–78.

Crompton, R., Gallie, D. and Purcell, K. (eds) (1996) *Changing Forms of Employment: Organizations, Skills and Gender*. London: Routledge.

Crouch, C. (1999) *Social Change in Western Europe*. Oxford: Oxford University Press.

Curran, J. and Blackburn, R.A. (eds) (1991a) *Paths of Enterprise: The Future of the Small Business*. London: Routledge.

Curran, J. and Blackburn, R.A. (1991b) 'Changes in the context of enterprise: some socio-economic and environmental factors facing small firms in the 1990s', in J. Curran and R.A. Blackburn (eds), *Paths of Enterprise: The Future of Small Business*. London: Routledge. pp. 163–92.

Cusumano, M.A. (1985) *The Japanese Automobile Industry: Technology and Management at Nissan and Toyota*. Cambridge, MA: Harvard University Press.

Cutler, T. (1978) 'The romance of "labour"', *Economy and Society*, 7 (1): 74–95.

Dale, A. (1986) 'Social class and the self-employed', *Sociology*, 20 (3): 430–4.

Dale, A. (1991) 'Self-employment and entrepreneurship: notes on two problematic concepts', in R. Burrows (ed.), *Deciphering the Enterprise Culture: Entrepreneurship, Petty Capitalism and the Restructuring of Britain*. London: Routledge. pp. 35–52.

Daniel, W.W. (1990) *The Unemployed Flow*. London: Policy Studies Institute.

d'A.Jones, P. (1965) *The Consumer Society: A History of American Capitalism*. London: Penguin.

Davies, C. (1980) 'Making sense of the Census in Britain and the USA: the changing occupational classification and the position of nurses', *Sociological Review*, 28 (3): 581–609.

Davies, C. and Rosser, J. (1986) 'Gendered jobs in the health service: a problem for labour process analysis', in D. Knights and H. Willmott (eds), *Gender and the Labour Process*. Aldershot: Gower. pp. 94–116.

Deakin, N. (1995) 'The perils of partnership: the voluntary sector and the state, 1945–1992', in J.D. Smith, C. Rochester and R. Headley, (eds), *An Introduction to the Voluntary Sector*. London: Routledge. pp. 40–65.

Debrah, Y.A. and Smith, I.G. (eds) (2002) *Globalization, Employment and the Workplace: Diverse Impacts*. London: Routledge.

Delsen, L. (1998) 'Where and why is part-time work growing in Europe?', in J. O'Reilly and C. Fagan (eds), *Part-time Prospects: An International Comparison of Part-time Work in Europe, North America and the Pacific Rim*. London: Routledge. pp. 57–76.

deWitte, M. and Steijn, B. (2000) 'Automation, job content and underemployment', *Work, Employment and Society*, 14 (2): 245–64.

Dex, S. (1985) *The Sexual Division of Work: Conceptual Revolutions in the Social Sciences*. Brighton: Harvester.

Dex, S. and McCullock, A. (1997) *Flexible Employment: The Future of Britain's Jobs*. London: Macmillan.

Dex, S., Willis, J., Peterson, R. and Sheppard, E. (2000) 'Freelance workers and contract uncertainty: the effects of contractual changes in the television industry', *Work, Employment and Society*, 14 (2): 283–305.

Dicken, P. (1992) *Global Shift: The Internationalization of Economic Activity* (2nd edn). London: Paul Chapman Publishing.

Dimitrova, D. (2003) 'Controlling teleworkers: supervision and flexibility revisited', *New Technology, Work and Employment*, 18 (3): 181–95.

Dohse, K., Jürgens, U. and Malsch, T. (1985) 'From "Fordism" to "Toyotism"?: the social organization of the labour process in Japanese automobile industry', *Politics and Society*, 14 (2): 115–46.

Doogan, K. (2001) 'Insecurity and long-term employment', *Work, Employment and Society*, 15 (3): 419–41.

Dooley, D. and Prause, J. (2004) *The Social Costs of Underemployment: Inadequate Employment as Disguised Unemployment*. Cambridge: Cambridge University Press.

Doray, B. (1988) *From Taylorism to Fordism: A Rational Madness*. London: Free Association Books.

duRivage, V.L. (ed.) (1992) *New Policies for the Part-time and Contingent Workforce*. New York: M.E. Sharpe.

Eardley, T. and Corden, A. (1994) 'Dependency or enterprise?: social security or self-employment', in S. Baldwin and J. Falkingham (eds), *Social Security and Social Change: New Challenges to the Beveridge Model*. Hemel Hempstead: Harvester Wheatsheaf. pp. 116–31.

Edgell, S. (1980) *Middle Class Couples: A Study of Segregation, Domination and Inequality in Marriage*. London: Allen and Unwin.

Edgell, S. (1993) *Class*. London: Routledge.

Edgell, S. (2001) *Veblen in Perspective: His Life and Thought*. New York: M.E. Sharpe.

Edgell, S. and Duke, V. (1991) *A Measure of Thatcherism: A Sociology of Britain*. London: HarperCollins.

Edgell, S. and Hart, G. (1988) 'Informal work: a case study of moonlighting firemen', *Salford Papers in Sociology*, No. 6. Salford: University of Salford.

Edwards, R. (1979) *Contested Terrain: The Transformation of the Workplace in the Twentieth Century*. London: Heinemann.

Eichengreen, B. (1989) 'Unemployment and underemployment in historical perspective: introduction', *Institute of Industrial Relations*, Working Paper Series. Berkeley CA: University of California (http://respositories.cdlib.org/iirwps-018-89).

Elam, G. and Thomas, A. (1997) *Stepping Stones to Employment: Part-time Work and Voluntary Activities whilst Claiming Out-of-work Security Benefits*. Department of Social Security, Research Report No. 71. London: HMSO.

Elam, M. (1994) 'Puzzling out the post-Fordist debate: technology, markets and institutions', in A. Amin (ed.), *Post-Fordism: A Reader*. Oxford: Blackwell. pp. 43–70.

Eldridge, J.E.T. (1971) *Sociology and Industrial Life*. London: M. Joseph.

Elger, T. (1991) 'Task flexibility and the intensification of labour in UK manufacturing in the 1980s', in A. Pollert (ed.), *Farewell to Flexibility?* Oxford: Blackwell. pp. 46–66.

Elger, T. and Smith, C. (eds) (1994) *Global Japanization? The Transnational Transformation of the Labour Process*. London: Routledge.

Epstein, C.F., Seron, C., Oglensky, B. and Saute, R. (1999) *The Part-time Paradox: Time Norms, Professional Life, Family and Gender*. New York: Routledge.

Erickson, R.J. and Wharton, A.S. (1997) 'Inauthenticity and depression: assessing the consequences of interactive service work', *Work and Occupations*, 24 (2): 188–213.

Etzioni, A. (1964) *Modern Organizations*. Englewood Cliffs, NJ: Prentice-Hall.

Ewen, S. (1977) *Captains of Consciousness: Advertising and the Social Roots of Consumer Culture*. New York: McGraw-Hill.

Fagan, C. and O'Reilly, J. (1998) 'Conceptualising part-time work: the value of an integrated comparative perspective', in J. O'Reilly and C. Fagan (eds), *Part-time Prospects: An International Comparison of Part-time Work in Europe, North America and the Pacific Rim*. London: Routledge. pp. 1–31.

Feldberg, R.L. and Glenn, E.N. (1979) 'Male and female: job versus gender models in the sociology of work', *Social Problems*, 26 (5): 524–38.

Felstead, A. (1991) 'Franchising: a testimony to the "enterprise economy" and economic restructuring in the 1980s', in A. Pollert (ed.), *Farewell to Flexibility?* Oxford: Blackwell. pp. 215–38.

Felstead, A. and Jewson, N. (1996) *Homeworkers in Britain*. London: HMSO.

Felstead, A. and Jewson, N. (eds) (1999) *Global Trends in Flexible Labour*. London: Macmillan.

Felstead, A. and Jewson, N. (2000) *In Work, At Home: Towards an Understanding of Homeworking*. London: Routledge.

Felstead, A., Gallie, D. and Green, F. (2002) *Work Skills in Britain: 1986–2001*. Department of Education and Skills. London: HMSO.

Felstead, A., Jewson, N., Phizacklea, A. and Walters, S. (2001) 'Working at home: statistical evidence for seven key hypotheses', *Work, Employment and Society*, 15 (2): 215–31.

Ferman, L.A. and Berndt, L.E. (1981) 'The irregular economy', in S. Henry (ed.), *Can I Have it in Cash? A Study of Informal Institutions and Unorthodox Ways of Doing Things*. London: Astragal Books. pp. 26–42.

Fevre, R. (1987) 'Subcontracting in steel', *Work, Employment and Society*, 1 (4): 509–27.

Fevre, R. (1992) *The Sociology of Labour Markets*. London: Harvester Wheatsheaf.

Finch, J. (1983) *Married to the Job: Wives' Incorporation in Men's Work*. London: Allen and Unwin.

Finch, J. (1989) *Family Obligations and Social Change*. Cambridge: Polity.

Finch, J. and Groves, D. (1980) 'Community care and the family: a case of equal opportunities', *Journal of Social Policy*, 9 (4): 487–511.

Finch, J. and Groves, D. (eds) (1983) *A Labour of Love: Women, Work and Caring*. London: Routledge and Kegan Paul.

Fine, B. (1995) 'From political economy to consumption', in D. Miller (ed.), *Acknowledging Consumption: A Review of New Studies*. London: Routledge. pp. 127–63.

Fineman, S. (1983) *White Collar Unemployment: Impact and Stress*. Chichester: Wiley.

Finifter, A.W. (ed.) (1972) *Alienation and the Social System*. New York: Wiley.

Forde, C. (2001) 'Temporary arrangements: the activities of employment agencies in the UK', *Work, Employment and Society*, 15 (3): 631–44.

French, H. (2000) 'Pretending 9–5', *The Guardian*, 20 December.

Friedman, A.L. (1977) *Industry and Labour: Class Struggle at Work and Monopoly Capitalism*. London: Macmillan.

Friedmann, G. (1955) *Industrial Society: The Emergence of the Human Problems of Automation*. Glencoe, Ill.: Free Press.

Fröbel, F., Heinrichs, J. and Kreye, O. (1980) *The New International Division of Labour: Structural Unemployment in Industrialized Countries and Industrialization in Developing Countries*. Cambridge: Cambridge University Press.

Frumkin, P. (2002) *On Being Nonprofit: A Conceptual and Policy Primer*. Cambridge, MA: Harvard University Press.

Gabe, J., Calnan, M. and Bury, M. (eds) (1990) *The Sociology of the Health Service*. London: Routledge.

Galbraith, J.K. (1979) *Economics and the Public Purpose*. London: Penguin.

Gallie, D. (1978) *In Search of the New Working Class: Automation and Social Integration within the Capitalist Enterprise*. Cambridge: Cambridge University Press.

Gallie, D. (1991) 'Patterns of skill change: upskilling, deskilling or the polarization of skills?', *Work, Employment and Society*, 5 (3): 319–51.

Gallie, D., Marsh, C. and Vogler, C. (eds) (1994) *Social Change and the Experience of Unemployment*. Oxford: Oxford University Press.

Gallie, D. and Paugam, S. (eds) (2000) *Welfare Regimes and the Experience of Unemployment*. Oxford: Oxford University Press.

Gallie, D. and Vogler, C. (1994) 'Unemployment and attitudes to work', in D. Gallie, C. Marsh and C. Vogler (eds), *Social Change and the Experience of Unemployment*. Oxford: Oxford University Press. pp. 115–53.

Gallie, D., White, M., Cheng, Y. and Tomlinson, M. (1998) *Restructuring the Employment Relationship*. Oxford: Oxford University Press.

Garrahan, P. and Stewart, P. (1992) *The Nissan Enigma: Flexibility at Work in a Local Economy*. London: Routledge.

Gavron, H. (1968) *The Captive Wife: Conflicts of Housebound Mothers*. London: Penguin.

Gershuny, J. (1994) 'The psychological consequences of unemployment: an assessment of the Jahoda thesis', in D. Gallie, C. Marsh and C. Vogler (eds), *Social Change and the Experience of Unemployment*. Oxford: Oxford University Press. pp. 213–30.

Gershuny, J. (2000) *Changing Times: Work and Leisure in Postindustrial Society*. Oxford: Oxford University Press.

Gershuny, J. (2004) 'Domestic equipment does not increase work: a response to Bittman, Rice and Wajcman', *British Journal of Sociology*, 55 (3): 425–31.

Gershuny, J., Goodwin, M. and Jones, S. (1994) 'The domestic labour revolution: a process of lagged adaptation', in M. Anderson, F. Bechhofer and J. Gershuny (eds), *The Social and Political Economy of the Household*. Oxford: Oxford University Press. pp. 151–97.

Giddens, A. (1971) *Capitalism and Modern Social Theory: An Analysis of the Writings of Marx, Durkheim and Max Weber*. Cambridge: Cambridge University Press.

Giddens, A. (1973) *The Class Structure of Advanced Societies*. London: Hutchinson.

Giddens, A. (1997) *Sociology* (3rd edn). Cambridge: Polity.

Glatzer, W. and Burger, R. (1988) 'Household composition, social networks and household production', in R. Pahl (ed.), *On Work: Historical, Comparative and Theoretical Approaches*. Oxford: Blackwell. pp. 513–26.

Glucksmann, M. (1990) *Women Assemble: Women Workers and the New Industries in Inter-War Britain*. London: Routledge.

Goldthorpe, J.H. (1966) 'Attitudes and behaviour of car assembly workers: a deviant case and a theoretical critique', *British Journal of Sociology*, 17 (3): 227–44.

Goldthorpe, J.H., Lockwood, D., Bechhofer, R. and Platt, J. (1969) *The Affluent Worker and the Class Structure*. Cambridge: Cambridge University Press.

Goode, W.J. (1970) *World Revolution and Family Patterns*. New York: Free Press.

Gorz, A. (1999) *Reclaiming Work: Beyond the Wage-based Society*. Cambridge: Polity.

Gottfried, H. (2000) 'Compromising positions: emergent neo-Fordisms and embedded gender contracts', *British Journal of Sociology*, 51 (2): 235–59.

Gottfried, H. and Graham, L. (1993) 'Constructing difference: the making of gendered subcultures in a Japanese automobile assembly plant', *Sociology*, 27 (4): 611–28.

Graham, L. (1994) 'How does the Japanese model transfer to the United States? A view from the line', in T. Elger and C. Smith (eds), *Global Japanization? The Transnational Transformation of the Labour Process*. London: Routledge. pp. 123–51.

Graham, L. (1995) *On the Line at Subaru-Isuzu: The Japanese Model and the American Worker*. Ithaca, NY: Cornell University Press.

Gramsci, A. (1971) *Selections from the Prison Notebooks of Antonio Gramsci*. Edited and translated by Q. Hoare and G. Nowell Smith. London: Lawrence and Wishart.

Granger, B., Stanworth, J. and Stanworth, C. (1995) 'Self-employment career dynamics: the case of "unemployment push" in UK book publishing', *Work, Employment and Society*, 9 (3): 499–516.

Granovetter, M. (1985) 'Economic action and social structure: the problem of embeddedness', *American Journal of Sociology*, 91 (3): 481–510.

Gray, J. (1998) *False Dawn: The Dimensions of Global Capitalism*. London: Granta.

Greenwood, J. (1977) *Worker Sit-ins and Job Protection*. Farnborough: Gower.

Gregory, A. and Windebank, J. (2000) *Women's Work in Britain and France: Practice, Theory and Policy*. London: Macmillan.

Gregson, N. and Lowe, M. (1994) *Servicing the Middle Classes: Class, Gender and Waged Domestic Labour in Contemporary Britain*. London: Routledge.

Gregson, N. and Lowe, M. (1995) '"Too much work?": Class, gender and the reconstruction of middle-class domestic labour', in T. Butler and M. Savage (eds), *Social Change and the Middle Class*. London: UCL Press. pp. 148–65.

Griffin, R., Hill, C., Perfect, D., Smith, A., Speed, L. and Symmonds, T. (1998) *Social Focus on Women and Men*. London: HMSO.

Grint, K. and Woolgar, S. (1997) *The Machine at Work: Technology, Work, and Organization*. Cambridge: Polity.

Gruneberg, M.M. (1979) *Understanding Job Satisfaction*. London: Macmillan.

Guardian (2001) 'Job fears after Ford shake-up', *The Guardian*, 30 October.

Guardian (2002) 'Deadline set for cutting working hours', *The Guardian*, 6 February.

Hakim, C. (1980) 'Census reports as documentary evidence: the Census commentaries 1801–1951', *Sociological Review*, 28 (3): 551–80.

Hakim, C. (1982) 'The social consequences of high unemployment', *Journal of Social Policy*, 11 (4): 433–67.

Hakim, C. (1988) 'Self-employment in Britain: a review of recent trends and current issues', *Work, Employment and Society*, 2 (4): 421–50.

Hakim, C. (1995) 'Five feminist myths about women's employment', *British Journal of Sociology*, 46 (3): 429–55.

Hakim, C. (1996) *Key Issues in Women's Work: Female Heterogeneity and the Polarization of Women's Employment*. London: Athlone.

Hakim, C. (1998) *Social Change and Innovation in the Labour Market*. Oxford: Oxford University Press.

Hakim, C. (2000) *Work–Lifestyle Choices in the 21st Century: Preference Theory*. Oxford: Oxford University Press.

Hakim, C. (2003) 'Public morality versus personal choice: the failure of social attitude surveys', *British Journal of Sociology*, 53 (3): 339–45.

Hall, R.H. (1994) *Sociology of Work: Perspectives, Analyses and Issues*. Thousand Oaks, CA: Pine Forge Press.

Hammersley, B. (2000) 'World's workers united', *The Times*, 7 February.

Harrison, B. (1997) *Lean and Mean: The Changing Landscape of Corporate Power in the Age of Flexibility*. New York: Guilford Press.

Harrison, R. and Zeitlin, J. (eds) (1985) *Divisions of Labour: Skilled Workers and Technological Change in Nineteenth Century Britain*. Brighton: Harvester.

Hartmann, H. (1979) 'The unhappy marriage of Marxism and Feminism: towards a more progressive union', *Capital and Class*, 8: 1–33.

Harvey, M. (1999) 'Economics of time: a framework for analysing the restructuring of employment relations', in A. Felstead and N. Jewson (eds), *Global Trends in Flexible Labour*. London: Macmillan. pp. 21–41.

Heery, E. and Salmon, J. (eds) (2000) *The Insecure Workforce*. London: Routledge.

Held, D., McGrew, A., Goldblatt, D. and Perration, J. (1999) *Global Transformations: Politics, Economics and Culture*. Cambridge: Polity.

Henry, S. (1982) 'The working unemployed: perspectives on the informal economy and unemployment', *Sociological Review*, 30 (3): 460–77.

Hill, C.P. (1971) *British Economic and Social History 1700–1964* (3rd edn). London: Edward Arnold.

Hill, S. (1981) *Competition and Control at Work*. London: Heinemann.

Hilton, G.W. (1960) *The Truck System, Including a History of the British Truck Acts, 1465–1960*. Westport, CT: Greenwood Press.

Himmelweit, S. (1999) 'Accounting for care', *Radstats Journal*, 70: 1–6. (www.radstats.org.uk/no070/article1.htm)

Hirst, P. and Thompson, G. (1996) *Globalization in Question: The International Economy and Possibilities of Governance*. Cambridge: Polity.

Hobbs, D. (1991) 'Business as a master metaphor: working-class entrepreneurship and business-like policing', in R. Burrows (ed.), *Deciphering the Enterprise Culture: Entrepreneurship, Petty Capitalism and the Restructuring of Britain*. London: Routledge. pp. 107–25.

Hobsbawm, E.J. (1969) *Industry and Empire*. London: Penguin.

Hochschild, A. (1990) *The Second Shift: Working Parents and the Revolution in the Home*. London: Piatkus.

Horrell, S. (1994) 'Household time allocation and women's labour force participation', in M. Anderson, F. Bechhofer and J. Gershuny (eds), *The Social and Political Economy of the Household*. Oxford: Oxford University Press. pp. 198–224.

Horrell, S., Rubery, J. and Burchell, B. (1994) 'Working-time patterns, constraints and preferences', in M. Anderson, F. Bechhofer and J. Gershuny (eds), *The Social and Political Economy of the Household*. Oxford: Oxford University Press. pp. 100–32.

Hounshell, D. (1984) *The American System of Mass Production 1800–1932: The Development of Manufacturing Technology in the United States*, Baltimore, MD: Johns Hopkins University Press.

Houseman, S. and Osawa, M. (1998) 'What is the nature of part-time work in the United States and Japan?', in J. O'Reilly and C. Fagan (eds), *Part-time Prospects: An International Comparison of Part-time Work in Europe, North America and the Pacific Rim*. London: Routledge. pp. 232–51.

Hudson, P. and Lee, W.R. (1990) *Women's Work and the Family Economy in Historical Perspective*. Manchester: Manchester University Press.

Hughes, E.C. (1958) *Men and their Work*. Glencoe, IL: Free Press.

Hull, F., Friedman, N.S. and Rogers, T.F. (1982) 'The effect of technology on alienation from work: testing Blauner's inverted U-curve hypothesis for 110 industrial organizations and 245 retrained printers', *Work and Occupations*, 9 (1): 31–57.

Hurst, C.E. (2004) *Social Inequality: Forms, Causes and Consequence*. Boston, MA: Pearson.

Hustinx, L. (2001) 'Individualization and new styles of youth volunteering: an empirical exploration', *Voluntary Action*, 3 (2): 57–76.

Hustinx, L. and Lammertyn, F. (2000) 'Solidarity and volunteering under a reflexive-modern sign: towards a new conceptual framework'. Paper presented at the *International Society for Third Sector Research*. Dublin, Ireland, 5–8 July.

Hustinx, L. and Lammertyn, F. (2003) 'Collective and reflexive styles of volunteering: a sociological modernization perspective', *Voluntas*, 14 (2): 167–87.

Hutson, S. and Jenkins, R. (1989) *Taking the Strain: Families, Unemployment and the Transition to Adulthood*. Milton Keynes: Open University Press.

Irwin, S. (1995) 'Social reproduction and change in the transition from youth to adulthood', *Sociology*, 29 (2): 293–315.

Jahoda, M. (1982) *Employment and Unemployment: A Social-Psychological Analysis*. Cambridge: Cambridge University Press.

Jahoda, M., Lazarsfeld, P.F. and Zeisel, H. (1974 [1933]) *Marienthal: The Sociography of an Unemployed Community*. London: Tavistock.

Janssens, A. (1997) 'The rise and decline of the male breadwinner family? An overview of the debate', *International Review of Social History*, Supplement 5, 41: 1–23.

Jenson, J. (1992) 'The talents of women, the skills of men: flexible specialization and women', in S. Wood (ed.), *The Transformation of Work? Skill, Flexibility and the Labour Process*. London: Routledge. pp. 141–55.

Jessop, B. (1994) 'Post-Fordism and the state', in A. Amin (ed.), *Post-Fordism: A Reader*. Oxford: Blackwell. pp. 251–79.

John, A.V. (ed.) (1988) *Unequal Opportunities: Women's Employment in England 1800–1918*. Oxford: Blackwell.

Jones, A.M. (2004) *Review of Gap Year Provision*. Department of Education and Skills, Research Report 555. London: HMSO.

Jordan, B. (1982) *Mass Unemployment and the Future of Britain*. Oxford: Blackwell.

Joyce, P. (1982) *Work, Society and Politics*. London: Methuen.

Jürgens, U. (1992) 'The transfer of Japanese management concepts in the international automobile industry', in S. Wood (ed.), *The Transformation of Work? Skill, Flexibility and the Labour Process*. London: Routledge. pp. 204–18.

Kamata, S. (1984) Japan in the Passing Lane: An insider's account of Life in a Japanese auto factory. London: Unwin.

Kalleberg, A.L., Reskin, B.F. and Hudson, K. (2000) 'Bad jobs in America: standard and non-standard employment relations and job quality in the United States', *American Sociological Review*, 65 (2): 256–78.

Keat, R. and Abercrombie, N. (eds) (1991) *Enterprise Culture*. London: Routledge.

Kelly, A. (1991) 'The enterprise culture and the welfare state: restructuring the management of the health and personal services', in R. Burrows (ed.), *Deciphering the Enterprise: Entrepreneurship, Petty Capitalism and the Restructuring of Britain*. London: Routledge. pp. 126–51.

Kelvin, P. and Jarrett, J.E. (1985) *Unemployment: Its Social and Psychological Effects*. Cambridge: Cambridge University Press.

Kendall, J. and Knapp, M. (1995) 'A loose and baggy monster: boundaries, definitions and typologies', in J.D. Smith, C. Rochester and R. Headley (eds), *An Introduction to the Voluntary Sector*. London: Routledge. pp. 66–95.

Kendall, J. and Knapp, M. (1996) *The Voluntary Sector in the United Kingdom*. Manchester: Manchester University Press.

Kenney, M. and Florida, R. (1988) 'Beyond mass production: production and the labour process in Japan', *Politics and Society*, 16 (1): 121–58.

Kilpern, K. (2001) 'A call for change', *The Guardian*, 19 February.

Kivisto, P. (1998) *Key Ideas in Sociology*. Thousand Oaks, CA: Pine Forge Press.

Klein, N. (2000) *No Logo*. London: Flamingo.

Kumar, K. (1978) *Prophecy and Progress: The Sociology of Industrial and Post-Industrial Society*. London: Penguin.

Kumar, K. (1988a) *The Rise of Modern Society: Aspects of the Social and Political Development of the West*. Oxford: Blackwell.

Kumar, K. (1988b) 'From work to employment and unemployment', in R. Pahl (ed.), *On Work: Historical, Comparative and Theoretical Perspectives*. Oxford: Blackwell. pp. 138–64.

Kumar, K. (1995) *From Post-Industrial to Post-Modern Society: New Theories of the Contemporary World*. Oxford: Blackwell.

Land, H. (1980) 'The family wage', *Feminist Review*, 6: 55–77.

Lash, S. and Urry, J. (1994) *Economies of Signs and Space*. London: Sage.

Layte, R., Levin, H., Hendrickx, J. and Bisou, I. (2000) 'Unemployment and cumulative disadvantage in the labour market', in D. Gallie and S. Paugam (eds), *Welfare Regimes and the Experience of Unemployment in Europe*. Oxford: Oxford University Press. pp. 153–74.

Layton, E.T. (1971) *The Revolt of the Engineers*. Cleveland, OH: The Press of Case Western Reserve University.

Leadbeater, C. (1997) *The Rise of Social Entrepreneurialism*. London: Demos.

Lee, D. (1981) 'Skill, craft and class: a theoretical critique and critical case', *Sociology*, 15 (1): 56–78.

Lee, D. and Newby, H. (1983) *The Problem of Sociology: An Introduction to the Discipline*. London: Hutchinson.

Leidner, R. (1996) 'Rethinking questions of control: lessons from McDonald's', in C.L. MacDonald and C. Sirianni (eds), *Working in the Service Society*. Philadelphia: Temple University Press. pp. 29–49.

Leidner, R. (2002) 'Fast-food work in the United States', in T. Royle and B. Towers (eds), *Labour Relations in the Global Fast-Food Industry*. London: Routledge. pp. 8–29.

Leiter, J. (1985) 'Work alienation in the textile industry: reassessing Blauner', *Work and Occupations*, 12 (4): 479–99.

Leonard, M. (1998) *Invisible Work, Invisible Workers: The Informal Economy in Europe and the US*. London: Macmillan.

Letkemann, P. (2002) 'Unemployed professionals, stigma management and derived stigmata', *Work, Employment and Society*, 16 (3): 511–22.

Lewchuk, W. (1995) 'Men and mass production: the role of gender in managerial strategies in the British and American automobile industries', in H. Shiomi and K. Wada (eds), *Fordism Transformed: The Development of Production Methods in the Automobile Industry*. Oxford: Oxford University Press. pp. 219–42.

Lewchuk, W. and Robertson, D. (1997) 'Production without empowerment: work reorganization from the perspective of motor vehicle workers', *Capital and Class*, 63: 37–64.

Lewenhak, S. (1980) *Women and Work*. Glasgow: Fontana.

Lewis, J. (1992) 'Gender and the development of welfare regimes', *Journal of European Social Policy*, 2 (3): 159–73.

Lipietz, A. (1992) *Towards a New Economic Order: Postfordism, Ecology, and Democracy*. Cambridge: Polity.

Lipietz, A. (1994) 'Post-Fordism and democracy', in A. Amin (ed.), *Post-Fordism: A Reader*. Oxford: Blackwell. pp. 338–57.

Littler, C.R. (1982) *The Development of the Labour Process in Capitalist Societies*. Aldershot: Gower.

Littler, C.R. and Salaman, G. (1984) *Class at Work: The Design, Allocation and Control of Jobs*. London: Batsford.

Lomba, C. (2005) 'Beyond the debate over "Post"- vs "Neo"-Taylorism: the contrasting evolution of industrial work practices', *International Sociology*, 20 (1): 71–91.

Lopata, H.Z. (1972) *Occupation: Housewife*. Oxford: Oxford University Press.

Love, J.F. (1995) *McDonald's: Behind the Arches* (revised edn). New York: Bantam.

Lown, J. (1990) *Women and Industrialization: Gender and Work in Nineteenth-century England*. Cambridge: Polity.

Lowenthal, M. (1981) 'Non-market transactions in an urban community', in S. Henry (ed.), *Can I Have it in Cash? A Study of Informal Institutions and Unorthodox Ways of Doing Things*. London: Astragal Books. pp. 90–104.

Macauley, C. (2003) 'Changes to self-employment in the UK: 2002 to 2003', *Labour Market Trends*, 111 (12): 623–8.

MacDonald, C. and Sirianni, C. (eds) (1996) *Working in the Service Society*. Philadelphia: Temple University Press.

MacDonald, K.M. (1995) *The Sociology of the Professions*. London: Sage.

MacDonald, R. (1994) 'Fiddly jobs, undeclared working and the something for nothing society', *Work, Employment and Society*, 8 (4): 507–30.

MacDonald, R. (1996) 'Welfare dependency, the enterprise culture and self-employed survival', *Work, Employment and Society*, 10 (3): 431–47.

McGovern, P., Smeaton, D. and Hill, S. (2004) 'Bad jobs in Britain: nonstandard employment and job quality', *Work and Occupations*, 31 (2): 225–49.

McIntosh, I. (1995) '"It was worse than Alcatraz": Working for Ford in Trafford Park', *Manchester Regional History Review*, 9: 66–76.

McIvor, A.J. (2001) *A History of Work in Britain, 1880–1950*. Basingstoke: Palgrave.

Mackenzie, G. (1977) 'The political economy of the American working class', *British Journal of Sociology*, 28 (2): 244–52.

McKenzie, J. (2001) *Changing Education: A Sociology of Education since 1944*. London: Prentice Hall.

McOrmond, T. (2004) 'Changes in working conditions over the past decade', *Labour Market Trends*, 112 (1): 25–36.

McRae, S. (1989) *Flexible Working Time and Family Life: A Review of Changes*. London: Policy Studies Institute.

McRae, S. (2003a) 'Constraints and choices in mothers' employment careers: a consideration of Hakim's preference theory', *British Journal of Sociology*, 54 (3): 317–38.

McRae, S. (2003b) 'Choice and constraints in mothers' employment careers: McRae replies to Hakim', *British Journal of Sociology*, 54 (4): 585–92.

Macionis, J.J. (2001) *Sociology* (8th edn). Upper Saddle River, NJ: Prentice-Hall.

Maguire, K. (2003) 'Nissan factory staff ballot strike?', *The Guardian*, 18 November.

Mair, A. (1994) *Honda's Global Local Corporation*. London: Macmillan.

Malcomson, R.W. (1988) 'Ways of getting a living in eighteenth-century England', in R. Pahl (ed.), *On Work: Historical, Comparative and Theoretical Approaches*. Oxford: Blackwell. pp. 48–60.

Mann, M. (1986) 'Work and the work ethic', in R. Jowell, S. Witherspoon and L. Brook (eds), *British Social Attitudes: The 1986 Report*. Aldershot: Gower. pp. 17–38.

Marglin, S. (1980) 'The origins and functions of hierarchy in capitalist production', in T. Nichols (ed.), *Capital and Labour: A Marxist Primer*. Glasgow: Fontana. pp. 237–54.

Marsden, D. (1982) *Workless: An Exploration of the Social Contract between Society and the Worker* (revised and enlarged edn). London: Croom Helm.

Marshall, G. (1984) 'On the significance of women's unemployment: its neglect and significance', *Sociological Review*, 32 (2): 234–59.

Martin, J. and Roberts, C. (1984) *Women and Employment: A Lifetime Perspective*. London: HMSO.

Marx, K. (1970 [1887]) *Capital*, Vol. 1. London: Lawrence and Wishart.

Marx, K. (1970 [1959]) *Economic and Philosophical Manuscripts of 1844*. London: Lawrence and Wishart.

Marx, K. (1973 [1857–58]) *Grundrisse: Foundations of the Critique of Political Economy*. London: Penguin.

Marx, K. and Engels, F. (1962 [1845]) *On Britain* (2nd edn). Moscow: Foreign Languages Publishing House.

Marx, K. and Engels, F. (n.d. [1848]) *Manifesto of the Communist Party*. Moscow: Foreign languages Publishing House.

Mattera, P. (1985) *Off the Books: The Rise of the Underground Economy*. London: Pluto.

Mellor, M., Hannah, J. and Stirling, J. (1988) *Worker Co-operatives in Theory and Practice*. Milton Keynes: Open University Press.

Merton, R.K. (1957) *Social Theory and Social Structure*. New York: Free Press.

Meszaros, I. (1970) *Marx's Theory of Alienation*. London: Merlin.

Milkman, R. and Pullman, C. (1991) 'Technological change in an auto assembly plant: the impact on workers' tasks and skills', *Work and Occupations*, 18 (2): 123–47.

Millar, J. (1999) 'Obligations and autonomy in social welfare', in R. Crompton (ed.), *Restructuring Gender Relations and Employment: The Decline of the Male Breadwinner*. Oxford: Oxford University Press. pp. 26–39.

Mills, C.W. (1968 [1951]) *White Collar: The American Middle Classes*. Oxford: Oxford University Press.

Mingione, E. (1988) 'Work and informal activities in urban southern Italy', in R. Pahl (ed.), *On Work: Historical, Comparative and Theoretical Approaches*. Oxford: Blackwell. pp. 548–78.

Montgomery, D. (1979) *Workers' Control in America: Studies in the History of Work, Technology and Labour Struggles*. Cambridge: Cambridge University Press.

Morris, J. (1988) 'The characteristics of sweating: the late nineteenth-century London and Leeds tailoring trade', in A.V. John (ed.), *Unequal Opportunities: Women's Employment in England 1800–1918*. Oxford: Blackwell. pp. 95–121.

Morris, L. (1990) *The Workings of the Household: A US–UK Comparison*. Cambridge: Polity.

Morris, L. (1994) 'Informal aspects of social divisions', *International Journal of Urban and Regional Research*, 18 (1): 112–26.

Morris, L. (1995) *Social Divisions: Economic Decline and Social Stratification*. London: UCL Press.

Mumford, L. (1934) *Technics and Civilization*. New York: Harcourt, Brace & World.

Murakami, T. (1997) 'The anatomy of teams in the car industry: a cross national comparison', *Work, Employment and Society*, 11 (4): 749–58.

Murray, F. (1987) 'Flexible specialization in the "Third Italy"', *Capital and Class*, 33: 84–94.

Mythen, G. (2004) *Ulrich Beck: A Critical Introduction to the Risk Society*. London: Pluto.

Newall, S. (1993) 'The superwoman syndrome: gender differences in attitudes towards equal opportunities at work and towards domestic responsibilities', *Work, Employment and Society*, 7 (2): 275–89.

Nichols, T. and Beynon, H. (1971) *Living with Capitalism: Class Relations and the Modern Factory*. London: Routledge and Kegan Paul.

Nisbet, P. (1997) 'Dualism, flexibility and self-employment in the UK construction industry', *Work, Employment and Society*, 11 (3): 459–79.

Nisbet, R.A. (1970) *The Sociological Tradition*. London: Heinemann.

Nolan, P. and Lenski, G. (1999) *Human Societies: An Introduction to Macrosociology* (8th edn). New York: McGraw-Hill.

Nyman, C. (1999) 'Gender equality in "the most equal country in the world"? Money and marriage in Sweden', *Sociological Review*, 47 (4): 766–93.

Oakley, A. (1974) *The Sociology of Housework*. Oxford: Martin Robertson.

Oakley, A. (1976) *Housewife*. London: Penguin.

Ohno, T. (1988) *Toyota Production System: Beyond Large-scale Production*. Cambridge, MA: Productivity Press.

Oliver, N. and Wilkinson, B. (1997) *The Japanization of British Industry: New Developments in the 1990s*. Oxford: Blackwell.

Ollman, B. (1971) *Alienation: Marx's Conception of Man in Capitalist Society*. Cambridge: Cambridge University Press.

O'Reilly, J. and Fagan, C. (eds) (1998) *Part-time Prospects: An International Comparison of Part-time Work in Europe, North America and the Pacific Rim*. London: Routledge.

Osborne, D. and Gaebler, T. (1992) *Reinventing Government: How the Entrepreneurial Spirit is Transforming the Public Sector*. Reading, MA: Addison-Wesley.

Pahl, R.E. (1984) *Divisions of Labour*. Oxford: Blackwell.

Pahl, R.E. (1988) 'Some remarks on informal work, social polarization and the social structure', *International Journal of Urban and Regional Research*, 12 (2): 247–67.

Palloix, C. (1976) 'The labour process: from Fordism to neo-Fordism', The Labour Process and Class Strategies, Conference of Socialist Economists, pamphlet No.1: 46–76.

Parker, M. and Slaughter, J. (1990) 'Management by stress: the team concept in the US auto industry', *Science as Culture*, 8: 27–58.

Pascall, G. and Lewis, J. (2004) 'Emerging gender regimes and policies for gender equality in a wider Europe', *Journal of Social Policy*, 33 (3): 373–94.

Payne, J. and Payne, C. (1993) 'Unemployment and peripheral work', *Work, Employment and Society*, 7 (4): 513–34.

Pearce, J.L. (1993) *Volunteers: The Organizational Behaviour of Unpaid Workers*. London: Routledge.

Peck, J. and Theodore, N. (1998) 'The business of contingent work: growth and restructuring in Chicago's temporary employment industry', *Work, Employment and Society*, 12 (4): 655–74.

Peck, J. and Tickell, A. (1994) 'Searching for a new institutional fix: the after-Fordist crisis and the global–local disorder', in A. Amin (ed.), *Post-Fordism: A Reader*. Oxford: Blackwell. pp. 280–315.

Penn, R.D. (1990) *Class, Power and Technology: Skilled Workers in Britain and America*. Cambridge: Polity.

Pennington, S. and Westover, B. (1989) *A Hidden Workforce: Homeworkers in England, 1850–1985*. London: Macmillan.

Pfau-Effinger, B. (1993) 'Modernization, culture and part-time employment: the example of Finland and West Germany', *Work, Employment and Society*, 7 (3): 383–410.

Pfau-Effinger, B. (2004) 'Socio-historical paths to the male breadwinner model – an explanation of cross-national differences', *British Journal of Sociology*, 55 (3): 377–99.

Phillips, A. and Taylor, B. (1980) 'Sex and skill: notes towards a feminist economics', *Feminist Review*, 6: 79–88.

Phizacklea, A. and Ram, M. (1996) 'Being your own boss: ethnic entrepreneurs in comparative perspective', *Work, Employment and Society*, 10 (2): 319–39.

Picchio, A. (ed.) (2003) *Unpaid Work and the Economy: A Gender Analysis of the Standard of Living*. London: Routledge.

Pinchbeck, I. (1969 [1930]) *Women and the Industrial Revolution, 1750–1880*. London: Frank Cass.

Pine, B.J. (1993) *Mass Customization: The New Frontier in Business Competition*. Boston, MA: Harvard Business School Press.

Piore, M. and Sabel, C.F. (1984) *The Second Industrial Divide*. New York: Basic Books.

Piven, F.F. and Cloward, R.A. (1974) *Regulating the Poor: The Functions of Public Welfare*. London: Tavistock.

Platt, S. (1986) 'Recent trends in parasuicide ("attempted suicide") and unemployment among men in Edinburgh', in S. Allen, A. Waton, K. Purcell and S. Wood (eds), *The Experience of Unemployment*. London: Macmillan. pp. 150–67.

Polivka, A.E., Cohany, S.R. and Hipple, S. (2000) 'Definition, composition and economic consequences of the nonstandard workforce', in F. Carre, M.A. Ferber, L. Golden and S.A. Herzenberg (eds) *Non-Standard Work: The Nature and Challenges of Changing Employment Arrangements*. Champaign, IL: Industrial Relations Research Association, University of Illinois Urbana-Champaign. pp. 41–94.

Pollert, A. (1988) 'The "flexible firm": fiction or fact?', *Work, Employment and Society*, 2 (3): 281–316.

Portes, A. and Sassen-Koob, S. (1987) 'Making it underground: comparative material on the informal sector in western market societies', *American Journal of Sociology*, 93 (1): 30–61.

Purcell, K. (2000) 'Gendered employment insecurity?', in E. Heery and J. Salmon (eds), *The Insecure Workforce*. London: Routledge. pp. 112–39.

Pyoria, P. (2003) 'Knowledge work in distributed environments: issues and illusions', *New Technology, Work and Employment*, 18 (3): 166–80.

Rainbird, H. (1991) 'Small entrepreneurs or disguised wage labourers?', in A. Pollert (ed.), *Farewell to Flexibility?* Oxford: Blackwell. pp. 200–14.

Ransome, P. (1996) *The Work Paradigm: A Theoretical Investigation of Concepts of Work*. Aldershot: Avebury.

Raworth, K. (2004) *Trading Away Our Rights: Women Working in Global Supply Chains*. Oxford: Oxfam.

Reich, R. (1991) *The Work of Nations: Preparing Ourselves for the 21st Century*. New York: Knopf.

Rendall, J. (1990) *Women in an Industrializing Society: England 1750–1880*. Oxford: Blackwell.

Rhode, S. (2002/03) *The History of Credit and Debt*. Myvesta, A Nonprofit Consumer Education Organization (www.dca.org/history_installment.htm).

Richards, E. (1974) 'Women in the British economy since about 1770: an interpretation', *History*, 59: 337–57.

Richardson, P. and Hartshorn, P. (1993) 'Business start-up training: the gender dimension', in S. Allen and C. Trueman (eds), *Women in Business: Perspectives on Women Entrepreneurs*. London: Routledge. pp. 86–100.

Richie, J. (1991) 'Enterprise cultures: a frame analysis', in R. Burrows (ed.), *Enterprise Culture: Entrepreneurship, Petty Capitalism and the Restructuring of Britain*. London: Routledge. pp. 17–34.

Ridyard, D., Jones, I. and Foster, R. (1989) 'Economic evaluation of the loan guarantee scheme', *Employment Gazette*, August: 417–21.

Rinehart, J. (2001) *The Tyranny of Work: Alienation and the Labour Process* (4th edn). Toronto: Harcourt.

Rinehart, J., Huxley, C. and Robertson, D. (1997) *Just Another Factory? Lean Production and Its Discontents*. Ithaca, NY: Cornell University Press.

Rinehart, J., Robertson, D., Huxley, C. and Wareham, J. (1994) 'Reunifying conception and execution of work under Japanese production management? A Canadian case study', in T. Elger and C. Smith (eds), *Global Japanization? The Transformation of the Labour Process*. London: Routledge. pp. 152–74.

Ritzer, G. (1996) *The McDonaldization of Society: An Investigation into the Changing Character of Contemporary Social Life* (revised edn). Thousand Oaks, CA: Pine Forge Press.

Ritzer, G. (1998) *The McDonaldization Thesis: Explorations and Extensions*. London: Sage.

Roberts, B. (1994) 'Informal economy and family strategies', *International Journal of Urban and Regional Research*, 18 (1): 6–23.

Roberts, E. (1995) *Women's Work, 1840–1940*. Cambridge: Cambridge University Press.

Roberts, K. (1984) *School Leavers and their Prospects: Youth and the Labour Market in the 1980s*. Milton Keynes: Open University Press.

Roberts, K., Clark, S.C. and Wallace, C. (1994) 'Flexibility and individualization: a comparison of transitions into employment in England and Germany', *Sociology*, 28 (1): 31–54.

Roberts, K. and Parsell, G. (1988) *Opportunity Structures and Career Trajectories from Age 16–19. ESRC 16–19 Initiative*, Occasional Paper No. 1. London: City University.

Roberts, K. and Parsell, G. (1992) 'Entering the labour market in Britain: the survival of traditional opportunity structures', *Sociological Review*, 46 (4): 726–53.

Robertson, R. (1992) *Globalization: Social Theory and Global Culture*. London: Sage.

Robins, K. and Webster, F. (1989) *The Technical Fix: Education, Computers and Industry*. London: Macmillan.

Robinson, P. (1999) 'Explaining the relationship between flexible employment and labour market participation', in A. Felstead and N. Jewson (eds), *Global Trends in Flexible Labour*. London: Macmillan. pp. 84–99.

Robinson, R. (2000) 'Insecurity and the flexible workforce: measuring the ill-defined', in E. Heery and J. Salmon (eds), *The Insecure Workforce*. London: Routledge. pp. 25–38.

Rose, M. (1988) *Industrial Behaviour: Research and Control*. London: Penguin.

Rose, M. (1989) 'Attachment to work and social values', in D. Gallie (ed.), *Employment in Britain*. Oxford: Blackwell. pp. 128–56.

Rosenberg, S. and Lapidus, J. (1999) 'Contingent and non-standard work in the United States: towards a more poorly compensated, insecure workforce', in A. Felstead and N. Jewson (eds), *Global Trends in Flexible Labour*. London: Macmillan. pp. 62–83.

Rothman, R.A. (1998) *Working: Sociological Perspectives* (2nd edn). Upper Saddle River, NJ: Prentice-Hall.

Royle, T. and Towers, B. (eds) (2002) *Labour Relations in the Fast-Food Industry*. London: Routledge.

Rubery, J. (1980) 'Structured labour markets, worker organization and low pay', in A.H. Amsden (ed.), *The Economics of Women and Work*. London: Penguin. pp. 242–70.

Rubery, J. (1998) 'Part-time work: a threat to labour standards?', in J. O'Reilly and C. Fagan (eds), *Part-time Prospects: An International Comparison of Part-time Workers in Europe, North America and the Pacific Rim*. London: Routledge. pp. 137–55.

Rubery, J. and Grimshaw, D. (2003) *The Organization of Employment: An International Perspective*. Basingstoke: Palgrave Macmillan.

Sabel, C.F. (1984) *Work and Politics: The Division of Labour in Industry*. Cambridge: Cambridge University Press.

Salaman, G. (1974) *Community and Occupation: An Exploration of Work/Leisure Relationships*. Cambridge: Cambridge University Press.

Salaman, G. (1986) *Working*. London: Tavistock.

Samuel, R. (1977) 'Workshop of the world: steam power and hand technology in mid-Victorian Britain', *History Workshop Journal*, 3 (1): 6–72.

Sayer, A. (1989) 'Postfordism in question?', *International Journal of Urban and Regional Research*, 13 (4): 666–95.

Sayer, A. and Walker, R. (1992) *The New Social Economy: Reworking the Division of Labour*. Oxford: Blackwell.

Scase, R. and Goffee, R. (1980) *The Real World of the Small Business Owner*. London: Croom Helm.

Scase, R. and Goffee, R. (1982) *The Entrepreneurial Middle Class*. London: Croom Helm.

Schiller, H. (1996) *Information Inequality: The Deepening Social Crisis in America*. London: Routledge.

Scholte, J.A. (2000) *Globalization: A Critical Introduction*. London: Macmillan.

Schonberger, R.J. (1982) *Japanese Manufacturing Technologies: Nine Hidden Lessons in Simplicity*. London: Collier-Macmillan.

Scott, J. (1985) *Corporations, Classes and Capitalism* (2nd edn). London: Hutchinson.

Scott, J. (1991) *Who Rules Britain?* Cambridge: Polity.

Scott, J.W. and Tilly, L.A. (1975) 'Women's work and family in nineteenth-century Europe', *Comparative Studies in Society and History*, 17 (1): 36–64.

Seeman, M. (1959) 'On the meaning of alienation', *American Sociological Review*, 24 (6): 783–91.

Sennett, R. (1998) *The Corrosion of Character: Personal Consequences of Work in the New Capitalism*. New York: W.W. Norton.

Sheard, J. (1995) 'From Lady Bountiful to active citizen: volunteering and the voluntary sector', in J.D. Smith, C. Rochester and R. Hadley (eds), *An Introduction to the Voluntary Sector*. London: Routledge. pp. 114–27.

Shepard, J.M. (1971) *Automation and Alienation: A Study of Office and Factory Workers*. Boston, MA: Colonial Press.

Shiomi, H. (1995) 'Introduction', in H. Shiomi and K. Wada (eds), *Fordism Transformed: The Development of Production Methods in the Automobile Industry*. Oxford: Oxford University Press. pp. 1–7.

Shorter, E. (1976) 'Women's work: what difference did capitalism make?', *Theory and Society*, 3 (4): 513–29.

Silverman, D. (1970) *The Theory of Organizations: A Sociological Framework*. London: Heinemann.

Simic, M. (2002a) 'Underemployment and overemployment in the UK', *Labour Market Trends*, 110 (8): 339–414.

Simic, M. (2002b) 'Volume of underemployment and overemplyment in the UK', *Labour Market Trends*, 110 (10): 511–22.

Sinfield, A. (1981) *What Unemployment Means*. Oxford: Martin Robertson.

Sklair, L. (2002) *Globalization: Capitalism and Its Alternatives*. Oxford: Oxford University Press.

Smart, B. (1992) *Modern Conditions, Postmodern Controversies*. London: Routledge.

Smeaton, D. (2003) 'Self-employed workers: calling the shots or hesitant independents?', *Work, Employment and Society*, 17 (2): 379–91.

Smelser, N.J. (1972 [1959]) *Social Change in the Industrial Revolution: An Application of Theory to the Lancashire Cotton Industry, 1770–1840*. London: Routledge and Kegan Paul.

Smith, M., Fagan, C. and Rubery, J. (1998) 'Where and why part-time work is growing in Europe', in J. O'Reilly and C. Fagan (eds), *Part-time Prospects: An International Comparison of Part-time Work in Europe, North America and the Pacific Rim*. London: Routledge. pp. 35–56.

Social Trends (2001) *Social Trends*, No. 31. London: HMSO.

Stabile, D. (1984) *Prophets of Order: The Rise of the New Class, Technocracy and Socialism in America*. Boston, MA: South End Press.

Standing, G. (1997) 'Globalization, labour flexibility and insecurity: the era of market regulation', *European Journal of Industrial Relations*, 3 (1): 7–37.

Stanworth, J. and Stanworth, C. (1991) 'Enterprise 2000: workbase the electronic cottage?', in J. Curran and R.A. Blackburn (eds), *Paths of Enterprise: The Future of Small Businesses*. London: Routledge. pp. 34–50.

Starbucks (2002) 'How are we doing?', *Customer Service Questionnaire*. London: Starbucks Coffee Company.

Stark, D. (1980) 'Class struggle and the transformation of the labour process: a relational approach', *Theory and Society*, 9 (1): 89–130.

Stedman Jones, G. (1984) *Outcast London: A Study in the Relationships between Classes in Victorian Society*. London: Penguin.

Sussman, W.I. (1974) 'Comment 1', in J.H.M. Laslett and S.M. Lipset (eds), *Failure of a Dream? Essays in the History of American Socialism*. Garden City, NY: Anchor/Doubleday. pp. 443–55.

Swingewoord, A. (1975) *Marx and Modern Social Theory*. London: Macmillan.

Taylor, P. and Bain, P. (1999) '"An assembly line in the head": work and employee relations in the call centre', *Industrial Relations Journal*, 30 (2): 111–17.

Taylor, P., Mulvey, G., Hyman, J. and Bain, P. (2002) 'Work organization, control and the experience of work in call centres', *Work, Employment and Society*, 16 (1): 133–50.

Taylor, R. (2003) 'Managing workplace change'. *ESRC Future of Work Programme* (www.esrc. ac.uk).

Taylor, R. (2004) 'Extending conceptual boundaries: work, voluntary work and employment', *Work, Employment and Society*, 18 (1): 29–49.

Taylor, S., Smith, S. and Lyon, P. (1998) 'McDonalization and consumer choice in the future: an illusion or the next marketing revolution?', in M. Alfino, J.S. Caputo and R. Wynyard (eds), *McDonaldization Revisited: Critical Essays on Consumer Culture*. Westport, CT: Praeger. pp. 105–19.

Thomas, G. and Zmroczek, C. (1988) 'Household technology: the "liberation" of women from the home', in P. Close and R. Collins (eds), *Family and Economy in Modern Society*. London: Macmillan. pp. 101–28.

Thomas, J. (1988) 'Women and capitalism: oppression or emancipatiom? A review article', *Comparative Studies in Society and History*, 30 (3): 534–49.

Thomas, J.J. (1992) *Informal Economic Activity*. Hemel Hempstead: Harvester Wheatsheaf.

Thompson, E.P. (1967) 'Time, work-discipline, and industrial capitalism', *Past and Present*, 38: 56–97.

Thompson, E.P. (1970) *The Making of the English Working Class*. London: Penguin.

Thompson, E.P. (1983) *The Nature of Work: An Introduction to Debates on the Labour Process*. London: Macmillan.

Thornley, C. (1996) 'Segmentation and inequality in the nursing workforce: re-evaluating the evaluation of skills', in R. Crompton, D. Gallie and K. Purcell (eds), *Changing Forms of Employment: Organizations, Skills and Gender*. London: Macmillan. pp. 160–81.

Tilgher, A. (1977 [1930]) *Work: What It Has Meant to Men through the Ages*. New York: Arno Press.

Tilly, C. (1992) 'Short hours, short shrift: the causes and consequences of part-time employment', in V.L. duRivage (ed.), *New Policies for the Part-time and Contingent Workforce*. New York: M.E. Sharpe. pp. 15–44.

Titmuss, R.M. (1973) *The Gift Relationship*. London: Penguin.

Tomaney, J. (1994) 'A new paradigm of work organization', in A. Amin (ed.), *Post-Fordism: A Reader*. Oxford: Blackwell. pp. 157–94.

Ungerson, C. (1985) 'Paid work and unpaid caring: a problem for women or the state', in P. Close and R. Collins (eds), *Family and Economy in Modern Society*. London: Macmillan. pp. 146–61.

Ungerson, C. (1997) 'Social politics and the commodification of care', *Social Politics*, 4 (3): 362–81.

Urry, J. (1990) 'Work, production and social relations', *Work, Employment and Society*, 4 (2): 271–80.

Vallas, S. (1988) 'New technology, job content, and worker alienation: a test of two rival perspectives', *Work and Occupations*, 15 (2): 148–78.

Vallas, S. (1999) 'Rethinking post-Fordism: the meaning of workplace flexibility', *Sociological Theory*, 17 (1): 68–101.

Vallas, S. and Yarrow, M. (1987) 'Advanced technology and worker alienation: comments on the Blauner/Marxian debate', *Work and Occupations*, 14 (1): 126–42.

Vanek, J. (1980 [1974]) 'Time spent on housework', in A.H. Amsden (ed.), *The Economics of Women and Work*. London: Penguin. pp. 82–90.

Veblen, T. (1964 [1914]) *The Instinct of Workmanship and the State of the Industrial Arts*. Clifton, NJ: Kelley.

Veblen, T. (1966 [1915]) *Imperial Germany and the Industrial Revolution*. Ann Arbor, MI: University of Michigan Press.

Veblen, T. (1970 [1899]) *The Theory of the Leisure Class: An Economic Study of Institutions*. London: Unwin Books.

Veblen, T. (1975 [1904]) *The Theory of the Business Enterprise*. Clifton, NJ: Kelley.

Vickerstaff, S.A. (2003) 'Apprenticeship in the "golden age": were youth transitions really smooth and unproblematic back then?', *Work, Employment and Society*, 17 (2): 269–87.

Wajcman, J. (1991) 'Patriarchy, technology and conceptions of skill', *Work and Occupations*, 18 (1): 29–45.

Wajcman, J. (1995) 'Domestic technology: labour-saving or enslaving?', in S. Jackson and S. Moores (eds), *The Politics of Domestic Consumption*. London: Prentice Hall. pp. 217–30.

Wajcman, J. (1996) 'The domestic basis for the managerial career', *Sociological Review*, 44 (4): 609–29.

Walby, S. (1986) *Patriarchy at Work*. Cambridge: Polity.

Walby, S. (1990) *Theorizing Patriarchy*. Oxford: Blackwell.

Warde, A. and Hetherington, K. (1993) 'A changing division of labour? Issues of measurement and interpretation', *Work, Employment and Society*, 7 (1): 23–45.

Weber, M. (1961 [1948]) *From Max Weber: Essays in Sociology*. Translated by H.H. Gerth and C. Wright Mills. London: Routledge and Kegan Paul.

Weber, M. (1964 [1947]) *The Theory of Social and Economic Organization*. Translated by A.M. Henderson and T. Parsons. New York: Free Press.

Weber, M. (1976 [1930]) *The Protestant Ethic and the Spirit of Capitalism*. London: Allen and Unwin.

Webster, F. (2002) *Theories of the Information Society* (2nd edn). London: Routledge.

Webster, J. (1996) *Shaping Women's Work: Gender, Employment and Information Technology*. London: Longman.

Wedderburn, D. and Crompton, R. (1972) *Workers' Attitudes and Technology*. Cambridge: Cambridge University Press.

Weir, G. (2003) 'Self-employment in the UK', *Labour Market Trends*, 111 (9): 441–51.

Westergaard, J., Noble, I. and Walker, A. (1989) *After Redundancy*. Cambridge: Polity.

Whipp, R. (1987) '"A time to every purpose": an essay on time and work', in P. Joyce (ed.), *The Historical Meanings of Work*. Cambridge: Cambridge University Press. pp. 210–36.

Wigley, J. and Lipman, C. (1992) *The Enterprise Economy*. London: Macmillan.

Whitmarsh, A. (1995) *Social Focus on Women*. London: HMSO.

Williams, C.C. (2002) 'A critical evaluation of the commodification thesis', *Sociological Review*, 50 (4): 525–42.

Williams, C.C. and Windebank, J. (1998) *Informal Employment in the Advanced Societies: Implications for Work and Welfare*. London: Routledge.

Williams, C.C. and Windebank, J. (2002) 'The uneven geographies of informal economic activities: a case study of two British cities', *War, Employment and Society*, 16 (2): 231–50.

Williams, K., Cutler, T., Williams, J. and Haslam, C. (1987) 'The end of mass production', *Economy and Society*, 16 (3): 405–39.

Williams, K., Haslam, C. and Williams, J. (1992) 'Ford versus "Fordism": the beginning of mass production?', *Work, Employment and Society*, 6 (4): 517–55.

Williams, K., Mitsui, H. and Haslam, C. (1994) 'How far from Japan? A case study of Japanese press shop practice and management calculation', in T. Elger and C. Smith (eds), *Global Japanization? The Transformation of the Labour Process*. London: Routledge. pp. 60–90.

Williams, K. and Williams, J. (eds) (1987) *A Beveridge Reader*. London: Allen and Unwin.

Wilson, J. (2000) 'Volunteering', *American Review of Sociology*, 26: 215–40.

Windebank, J. (2001) 'Dual-earner couples in Britain and France: gender divisions of domestic labour and parenting work in different welfare states', *Work, Employment and Society*, 15 (2): 269–90.

Witherspoon, S. (1985) 'Sex roles and gender issues', in R. Jowell and S. Witherspoon (eds), *British Social Attitudes: The 1985 Report*. Aldershot: Gower. pp. 55–94.

Womack, J.P., Jones, D.T. and Roos, D. (1990) *The Machine that Changed the World*. New York: Rawson Associates.

Wood, S. (ed.) (1982) *The Degradation of Work? Skill, Deskilling and the Labour Process*. London: Hutchinson.

Wood, S. (ed.) (1992) *The Transformation of Work? Skill, Flexibility and the Labour Process*. London: Routledge.

Woodfield, R. (2000) *Women, Work and Computing*. Cambridge: Cambridge University Press.

Wright, E.O. (1997) *Class Counts: Comparative Studies in Class Analysis*. Cambridge: Cambridge University Press.

Wright, F. (1983) 'Single carers: employment, housework and caring', in J. Finch and D. Groves (eds), *A Labour of Love: Women, Work and Caring*. London: Routledge and Kegan Paul. pp. 89–105.

Wuthnow, R. (1991) *Acts of Compassion: Caring for Others and Helping Ourselves*. Princeton, NJ: Princeton University Press.

Wuthnow, R. (1998) *Loose Connections: Joining Together America's Fragmented Communities*. Cambridge, MA: Harvard University Press.

www.domesticviolencedata.org/4_faq/faq01.htm

www.hm-treasury.gov.uk/newsroom_and_speeches/press/2004

www.ivr.org.uk/economic.htm

www.ivr.org.uk/nationalsurvey.htm

www.jrf.org.uk/knowledge/findings/socialpolicy/SP82.asp
www.oecd/dataoecd January 2004
www.oldsmobile.com/enthusiasts/defaultd69c.html
www.statistics.gov.uk 2004
Yeandle, S. (1999) 'Women, men and non-standard employment', in R. Crompton (ed.), *Restructuring Gender Relations and Employment: The Decline of the Male Breadwinner*. Oxford: Oxford University Press. pp. 80–104.
Young, M. and Willmott, P. (1973) *The Symmetrical Family: A Study of Work and Leisure in the London Region*. London: Routledge and Kegan Paul.
Zeitlin, J. (1985) 'Engineers and compositors: a comparison', in R. Harrison and J. Zeitlin (eds), *Divisions of Labour: Skilled Workers and Technical Change in Nineteenth Century England*. Brighton: Harvester. pp. 185–250.

Name Index

●●●●●●●●

Abercrombie, N. 134, 182
Abreu, A. 190
Aglietta, M. 81, 89
Aguren, S. 85–6
Albrow, M. 183
Allan, E.A. 119
Allatt, P. 110
Allen, J. 75, 94
Allen, S. 19, 138, 168
Amin, A. 80, 84–5
Anderson, B. 172
Anderson, M. 6, 10, 13, 19, 22
Anthony, P.D. 6
Applebaum, H. 4–5
Arber, S. 168
Aronowitz, S. 60, 71, 103
Ashton, D.M. 103–5, 108–10, 112–15
Atkinson, J. 140
Attewell, P. 54
Auer, P. 127
Austrin, T. 163

Bailyn, L. 138
Bain, P. 64
Baldwin, S. 174
Baran, B. 66
Bechhofer, F. 130
Beck, U. 25, 78–9, 102, 104, 116, 119–21,
    123–4, 126–9, 132, 141, 148–51, 156,
    160, 175–6, 179–80, 182, 184–5,
    188–91, 193–5, 197–200, 202–3
Beck-Gernsheim, E. 188, 194
Beder, S. 15, 105
Beechey, V. 123
Bell, D. 61–71, 92, 120, 164
Beneria, L. 153
Benjamin, A. 154
Benjamin, O. 167
Benner, C. 126–7, 140
Berg, M. 9, 21, 67

Berger, R. 146
Berggren, C. 85–6, 89, 92, 98–9
Berk, R.A. and S.F. 164
Berndt, L.E. 144–5
Beynon, H. 42–5, 74–5, 77–8, 163
Bezuidenhout, A. 192
Birchall, J. 155
Bittman, M. 160, 162, 171–2
Blackburn, R.A. 133, 135
Blackburn, R.M. 56–7
Blanchflower, D.G. 111–12
Blauner, R. 28, 30–47, 51, 68, 73, 157–9, 177
Blom, R. 98
Blyton, P. 192
Bogenhold, D. 133
Bond, S. 164
Booth, Charles 102
Boris, E. 137
Borzaga, C. 154, 156
Boserup, E. 5
Boulton, M.G. 158–9, 161
Bowles, S. 13
Box, S. 112
Boyle, E. 135
Bradley, H. 21, 23, 127, 149
Brannen, J. 112, 169
Braverman, H. 40, 48–53, 61, 65, 67–8, 70–1
Bright, James R. 51–3, 68
Brines, J. 168
Brown, R.K. 55, 73
Brynin, M. 67
Burawoy, M. 53, 59–60
Burchell, J. 127
Burgess, J. 140–1
Burnett, J. 17, 25, 102–3, 108, 114–15
Burrows, R. 133, 136

Callender, C. 24
Campbell, I. 140
Carr, D. 135

Carré, F.J. 104, 116, 126, 140
Casey, B. 110, 128, 131–2, 140
Castells, M. 25, 70, 84, 97–8, 103, 116,
    120–1, 126, 128–9, 132, 138, 140,
    142, 148–51, 156, 170, 183–91,
    193, 195–9, 203
Cato, M.S. 115
Cazes, S. 127
Charles, N. 120
Clarke, S. 85
Cloward, R.A. 103
Cockburn, C. 57
Coffield, F. 110
Cohen, R. 182, 184–5
Collins, R. 13
Collinson, D. 57
Collinson, M. 57
Conley, H. 140
Connell, J. 140–1
Cooley, M. 59, 66, 71
Copps, A. 78
Corden, A. 129
Coriat, B. 86
Corrigan, P. 5, 8
Cotgrove, S. 42
Cowan, R.S. 160–2
Coyle, A. 114
Cragg, A. 112–14
Creighton, C. 23
Crompton, R. 42–5, 58, 65–6, 80, 117,
    123–4, 166, 174, 193–5, 199
Crouch, C. 120
Curran, J. 133, 135
Cusumano, M.A. 87–9, 92
Cutler, T. 54

d'A.Jones, P. 75
Dale, A. 130
Daniel, W.W. 109–10
Davies, C. 21–2, 57
Dawson, T. 112–14
de Witte, M. 69
Deakin, N. 156
Debrah, Y.A. 189
Defourney, J. 154, 156
Delsen, L. 123
Dex, S. 25, 117, 132
Dicken, P. 192
DiFazio, W. 60, 71, 103
Dimitrova, D. 138–9
Dohse, K. 87, 90, 92
Doogan, K. 150
Dooley, D. 118, 123
Doray, B. 12–13, 77
du Gay, P. 94

Duke, V. 66, 103–4
duRivage, V.L. 64, 116
Durkheim, Emile 7, 20, 30

Eardley, T. 129
Edgell, S. 7–8, 16, 20, 25, 61, 66,
    103–4, 136, 144, 158, 166
Edwards, R. 55, 74
Eichengreen, B. 104
Elam, G. 175
Elam, M. 91
Eldridge, J.E.T. 34, 36–8, 41
Elger, T. 87, 96
Elliot, B. 130
Engels, F. 14, 19, 102, 183
Epstein, C.F. 119
Erickson, R.J. 94
Etzioni, A. 168
Ewen, S. 75

Fagan, C. 60, 64, 71, 118
Feldberg, R.L. 39, 46, 68
Felstead, A. 135, 137–9
Ferman, L.A. 144–5
Fevre, R. 6, 150
Filene, Edward 75
Finch, J. 19, 155, 158, 170, 173–4
Fine, B. 133
Fineman, S. 109
Finifter, A.W. 28
Florida, R. 92
Ford, Henry 74, 76, 78
Forde, C. 140, 142
Freeman, R. 111–12
French, H. 109
Friedman, A.L. 55–6
Friedmann, G. 53
Fröbel, F. 186, 192
Frumkin, P. 154, 156

Gabe, J. 66
Gaebler, T. 66
Galbraith, J.K. 154
Gallie, D. 36–8, 40, 43–4, 55, 57–8, 64,
    69, 105, 108, 110, 114, 120, 127, 141
Garrahan, P. 90, 92
Gavron, H. 159
Gershuny, J. 107, 113, 161–2, 167, 171, 178
Giddens, A. 7–8, 20, 157
Ginn, J. 168
Gintis, H. 13
Glatzer, W. 146
Glendinning, C. 174
Glenn, E.N. 39, 46, 68
Glucksmann, M. 79

Goffee, R. 130–1, 136
Goldthorpe, J.H. 16, 41–2
Goode, W.J. 20
Gorz, A. 105
Gottfried, H. 80, 89, 154
Graham, L. 89, 92, 201
Gramsci, A. 79
Granger, B. 133
Granovetter, M. 18
Gray, J. 185, 192
Greenwood, J. 115
Gregory, A. 155, 164, 174–5
Gregson, N. 171–2
Griffin, R. 168–9
Grimshaw, D. 99
Grint, K. 10
Groves, D. 155, 173–4
Gruneberg, M.M. 36

Hakim, C. 21–2, 24, 80, 107, 110, 112, 114, 116–17, 123–4, 130–3, 135–6, 153–4, 162, 189, 199
Hall, R.H. 182
Hammersley, B. 78
Harris, F. 80, 117, 166
Harrison, B. 96, 117–18
Harrison, R. 42
Hart, G. 144
Hartmann, H. 23
Hartshorn, P. 135
Harvey, M. 139
Heery, E. 120
Held, D. 183–5, 187
Henry, S. 144
Hetherington, K. 178
Hill, C.P. 13
Hill, S. 38, 41
Hilton, G.W. 17
Himmelweit, S. 174
Hirst, P. 183
Hobbs, D. 134
Hobsbawm, E.J. 12, 21
Hochschild, A. 165–6, 168–9
Horrell, S. 167, 170
Hounshell, D. 74, 76
Houseman, S. 120
Hudson, P. 21, 23
Hughes, E.C. 6
Hull, F. 42
Hurst, C.E. 168
Hustinx, L. 175–6, 180, 196
Hutson, S. 111

Jahoda, M. 106–8, 114–15, 122
James, E. 120

Janssens, A. 23, 154
Jarrett, J.E. 105
Jenkins, R. 111
Jenson, J. 96
Jessop, B. 73, 78
Jewson, N. 137–9
John, A.V. 22
Jones, A.M. 196
Jones, G. 58
Jordan, B. 112
Joyce, P. 14
Jürgens, U. 87

Kalleberg, A.L. 129, 141
Kamata, S. 90
Keat, R. 134
Kelly, A. 134
Kelvin, P. 105
Kendall, J. 155
Kennedy, P. 182, 184–5
Kenney, M. 92
Kilpern, K. 64
Kivisto, P. 7
Klein, N. 192
Knapp, M. 155
Knights, D. 57
Kumar, K. 10, 12, 61, 64–7, 104

Laczko, F. 110
Lammertyn, F. 175–6, 180, 196
Land, H. 23
Lapidus, J. 128, 141
Lash, S. 133
Layte, R. 110
Layton, E.T. 55
Leadbeater, C. 197
Lee, D. 7, 70
Lee, W.R. 21, 23
Leidner, R. 93–4
Leiter, J. 42
Lenski, G. 2–3, 5, 11
Leonard, M. 142–4, 146–7, 172
Letkemann, P. 109
Lewchuck, W. 77, 90–1
Lewenhak, S. 20–1, 23
Lewis, J. 154, 168
Lipietz, A. 78, 81
Lipman, C. 130, 134–5
Littler, C.R. 54, 56, 77
Lomba, C. 73
Lopata, H.Z. 157–60, 177
Love, J.F. 93, 95
Lowe, M. 171–2
Lown, J. 21–2

Macauley, C. 131–2
McCullock, A. 117
MacDonald, C. 65
McDonald, Dick 93
MacDonald, K.M. 16
MacDonald, R. 133–5, 145
McGovern, P. 141
McIntosh, I. 77
Macionis, J.J. 157
McIvor, A.J. 77, 103
Mackenzie, G. 56
McKenzie, J. 13
McOrmond, T. 140
McRae, S. 117, 123, 151
Maguire, K. 92
Mair, A. 87, 91
Malcolmson, R.W. 6, 17
Mann, M. 56–7, 105
Marglin, S. 10
Marsden, D. 25
Marshall, G. 112
Martin, J. 111, 154, 164
Marx, Karl 7–9, 11–12, 14–16, 19–20, 28–30, 32,
    36–8, 45–6, 48–9, 53, 61, 70–1, 102, 131, 183
Mattera, P. 142–5
Mayhew, A. 102
Mayo, E. 49
Melin, H. 98
Mellor, M. 25, 115
Merton, R.K. 112
Meszaros, I. 28
Milkman, R. 58, 69
Millar, J. 174, 197
Mills, C.W. 30, 38, 53
Mingione, E. 146
Montgomery, D. 55
Morris, J. 22
Morris, L. 6, 146, 164, 167–8, 180
Moss, P. 169
Mumford, L. 12
Murray, F. 96
Mythen, G. 121

Newby, H. 7
Newell, S. 164
Nichols, T. 42–5
Nilsen, A. 112
Nisbet, P. 130
Nisbet, R.A. 7, 30
Nolan, P. 2–3, 5, 11
Nyman, C. 168

Oakley, A. 4, 20–1, 23, 25, 153,
    157–61, 164–6, 177
Offe, C. 160

Ohno, T. 87–8, 90–1
Oliver, N. 87–8
Ollman, B. 29
O'Reilly, J. 60, 64, 71, 118
Osawa, M. 120
Osborne, D. 66

Pahl, R.E. 17, 144–6
Palloix, C. 89
Parker, M. 90
Parsell, G. 111
Pascall, G. 168
Paugum, S. 114
Payne, G. 115
Payne, J. 115
Pearce, J.L. 173, 176–7, 180
Peck, J. 77, 79, 84, 142
Penn, R.D. 58, 64
Pennington, S. 137
Perkins, T. 123
Pfau-Effinger, B. 23–4, 80, 154
Phillips, A. 57
Phizacklea, A. 133
Picchio, A. 164
Pinchbeck, I. 20–1
Pine, B.J. 94
Piore, M. 81, 95–7
Piven, F.F. 103
Platt, S. 109
Polivka, A.E. 126–7
Pollert, A. 127
Portes, A. 143–5
Prause, J. 118, 123
Prugl, E. 137
Pullman, C. 58, 69
Purcell, K. 120, 140–1
Pyoria, P. 139

Rainbird, H. 135
Ram, M. 133
Ransome, P. 24
Raworth, K. 192
Reich, R. 69
Reid, S. 58, 65
Rendall, J. 21–3
Rhode, S. 75
Richards, E. 20–1, 23
Richardson, P. 135
Richie, J. 134
Ridyard, D. 135
Rinehart, J. 89–92
Ritzer, G. 93, 95
Roberts, B. 146
Roberts, C. 111, 154, 164
Roberts, E. 23

Roberts, K. 111–12
Robertson, D. 90–1
Robertson, R. 185
Robins, K. 66
Robinson, P. 126–7, 140
Robinson, R. 120, 141, 151
Roper, M. 32
Rose, M. 46, 54, 59, 105
Rosenberg, S. 128, 141
Rosser, J. 57
Rothman, R.A. 6
Royle, T. 95
Rubery, J. 56, 99, 118

Sabel, C.F. 81, 95–7
Salaman, G. 53, 77, 109
Sales, J. 164
Salmon, J. 120
Samuel, R. 73
Sassen-Koob, S. 143–5
Sayer, A. 81, 84–5, 87
Scase, R. 130–1, 136
Schiller, H. 66
Scholte, J.A. 183–6, 192, 196
Schonberger, R.J. 88–90
Scott, J. 8, 18
Scott, J.W. 20–1, 23
Seeman, M. 30
Sheard, J. 174
Shepard, J.M. 44–6
Shiomi, H. 77
Shorter, E. 20
Silverman, D. 41
Simic, M. 115–17
Sinfield, A. 112
Sirianni, G. 65
Sklair, L. 192
Slaughter, J. 90
Smart, B. 66
Smeaton, D. 132
Smelser, N.J. 9, 18
Smith, C. 87
Smith, I.G. 189
Smith, M. 117–18, 120
Stabile, D. 55
Stabler, U. 133
Standing, G. 126–7
Stanworth, C. and J. 132, 135, 138–9
Starbucks Coffee Company 201
Stark, D. 54–5
Stedman Jones, G. 17, 102
Steffensmeier, D.J. 119
Steijn, B. 69
Stewart, P. 90, 92
Sullivan, O. 167

Sussman, W.I. 76
Swingewood, A. 29

Taylor, B. 57
Taylor, Frederick Winslow 49–50, 56
Taylor, P. 64–5
Taylor, R. 127, 155–6, 176
Taylor, S. 94
Theodore, N. 142
Thomas, A. 175
Thomas, G. 162
Thomas, J. 20
Thomas, J.J. 143–4, 147
Thompson, E.P. 9–12, 21, 102
Thompson, G. 183
Thompson, P. 41, 55, 59
Thornley, C. 57
Tickell, A. 77, 79, 84
Tilgher, A. 5
Tilly, C. 117–18
Tilly, L.A. 20–1, 23
Titmuss, R.M. 173
Tomaney, J. 92
Tonnies, Ferdinand 7
Towers, B. 95

Ungerson, C. 174
Urry, J. 94, 133

Vallas, S. 42, 46–7, 97, 99
Vanek, J. 160–1
Veblen, T. 3–7, 16–17, 19–20, 23,
    30, 76, 154–5
Vickerstaff, S.A. 110
Vogler, C. 105, 110, 114

Wajcman, J. 57, 162, 164, 172, 193
Walby, S. 5, 20, 23, 56, 187
Walker, R. 81, 84, 87
Warde, A. 178
Weber, Max 7–8, 13–16, 19–20, 30,
    61, 71, 131
Webster, F. 64, 66, 68, 98, 202
Webster, J. 54, 60
Wedderburn, D. 42–5
Weir, G. 131
Westergaard, J. 105
Westover, B. 137
Wharton, A.S. 94
Whipp, R. 12
Whitmarsh, A. 166
Wigley, J. 130, 134–5
Wilkinson, B. 87–8
Williams, C.C. 25, 142–8, 173
Williams, J. 154

Williams, K. 74–6, 81, 84, 88, 96, 154
Willmott, P. 162–72, 178–9, 203
Wilson, J. 175
Windebank, J. 142–8, 155, 164, 167, 174–5
Witherspoon, S. 166
Wolkowitz, C. 19, 138
Womack, J.P. 74, 87, 92
Wood, S. 68, 71, 84–5, 96
Woodfield, R. 55
Woolgar, S. 10

Wright, E.O. 70–1, 130–3, 135
Wright, F. 174
Wuthnow, R. 173, 176

Yarrow, M. 42, 46
Yeandle, S. 110, 133
Young, M. 162–72, 178–9, 203

Zeitlin, J. 42, 55–6
Zmroczek, C. 162

Subject Index

• • • • • • • •

absolute poverty 114–15
activity alienation 29
Acts of Parliament 13, 22
adaptable marketing system (AMS) 94
age factors
  underemployment 117–18
  unemployment consequences 108, 110–12
  voluntary work 173, 175–6
ageism 110
agencies, temporary work 140–2
agrarian societies 2, 3–4
alienation
  Blauner's thesis 30–45
  domestic work 157–9
  empirical research 30–6, 41–5
  Fordism 80–1
  machinery 9
  Marx's theory 28–30
  paid work 28–47
  production systems 73
  questions 47
  summary and conclusions 45–7
  technology 30–47
America
  deskilling 49
  homeworking 137–8
  informal work 145
  Japanese neo-Fordism 87
  New Deal 103
  non-standard work 126–8, 131,
      137–8, 140, 142, 145
  self-employment 131
  Taylorism 56
  temporary work 140, 142
  unemployment/underemployment
      105, 115–18, 121–2
  upskilling 61, 63–4, 70
  voluntary work 173
AMS see adaptable marketing system

anomie theory 112
assembly-line technology
  alienation thesis 31–3, 34–5
  empirical research 41–2
  Fordism 74
  McDonaldism 93
  neo-Fordism 85–6, 90
Austrian unemployment study 106–8
automation 35, 51–2, 68–9
  see also continuous-process technology;
      machinery
automobile industry
  alienation 31–2, 34–5
  Brazilianization 190
  Fordism 73–101
autonomy
  domestic work 157–8
  homeworking 138
  informal work 147–8
  self-employment 130

blue-collar workers 69
  see also individual types
Brazilianization 190
Britain
  homeworking 137–8
  informal work 145–7
  non-standard work 127, 131–8,
      140–2, 145–7
  self-employment 131–6
  temporary work 140–2
  unemployment/underemployment
      102–3, 105, 114–16, 121–2
  voluntary work 173, 176
bureaucracy 19

CAD see computer-aided design
call centres 64–5
Calvinism 15

capitalism
   definition 1, 7
   globalization 183, 186–7, 191–2, 201
   mode of production 49
   threats to hegemony 24
   unstable character 20
   see also industrial capitalism
car industry see automobile industry
care work 173–4, 194–5, 196–7
carrier systems, assembly-lines 85–6
causality model, alienation 32–3
change see continuity and change;
      transformation of work
chemical industry 31–2, 35, 40, 42–4
child-rearing 158–9, 161, 170–2
child workers 13
civil labour model 197, 200
class
   deskilling thesis 50, 55–6
   domestic work 153–4, 161,
      164, 166, 171–2
   industrial capitalism 14, 23
   informal work 147–8
   pre-industrial societies 4, 5–6
   Principle of Stratified Diffusion
      163, 169–70
   self-provisioning 146
   skill changes 70
   underemployment 117–18
   unemployment consequences 108–10
   voluntary work 155, 173
   women and work 23
   youth unemployment 111–12
cleaning work 171–2
clerical work 52, 54
   see also office work
collective volunteering 175–6, 197
commodification of caring 197
commodification of knowledge 66
computer-aided design (CAD) 59
computerization 54–5, 58, 65
   see also information technology;
      technology
conceptual critique, alienation thesis 37–8
conflict 19–20
consent, game playing 59
Conservative governments 103, 104, 133–5
conspicuous consumption 4
consumption 4, 133
   see also mass consumption
contingent work 116
   see also underemployment
continuity and change 200–3
continuous-process technology 31–2,
      35, 40, 42–4

continuous work patterns 112–13
contractural destandardization 128, 129–36, 202
co-operative enterprises 115
correspondence theory 13
craft technology
   alienation 31–2, 33, 35
   deskilling 53–6
   empirical research 41–2
   flexible specialization 96
   Taylorism 50
crime 112, 119, 143
cultural lag 6
customer expectations 93–4

de-alienation 28, 30
degree of alienation/type of technology
      thesis (Blauner) 34–5
deindustrialization see post-industrial society
demand-side approach to Fordism 81–2
de-marginalization of self-employment 136
demise theory, self-employment 136
dependency culture 134
dependent variable, alienation 32–4
deskilling 48–60
   Braverman's thesis 48–59
   domestic work 160
   Fordism 71, 76, 80–1
   polarization of skills 68–70
   upskilling theses 61, 65–6, 68
destandardized work 104, 126–52
   contractual 128, 129–36, 202
   information technology 119
   Japanese vehicle manufacturers 90–1
   questions 152
   spatial 128, 136–9, 202
   summary and conclusions 148–51
   temporal 128, 140–2, 202
   total destandardization 142–8
   see also non-standard work;
      underemployment
determinism see technological determinism
discontinuous work patterns 112–13
division of labour
   alienation thesis 32–3
   gender 153–4, 162–71, 194–5
   industrial capitalism 10–11, 13
   pre-industrial societies 5
domestic violence 168
domestic work 153–60
   care work burden 174
   conditions 160–2
   continuity and change 201
   industrial capitalism 22–5
   measurement 161–2
   outsourcing 171–2

domestic work *cont.*
  questions 181
  status 157
  summary and conclusions 177–80
  symmetrical family thesis 162–71
  technology 160–2, 164, 169, 188–9
  transformation 192–6, 197
  unemployment 113, 114
  see also self-provisioning
dominant concept of work 23–5,
      127, 153–4, 200–2
dual earner/dual carer model 194–5

early modern society 175–6
economic activity, work as 1–27
economic factors
  globalization 183, 185–7
  self-employment 131–3
  unemployment 102–3, 110, 113–14
economic structure of industry 32–3
economic system, industrial
      capitalism 14–15
education
  deskilling thesis 53
  enterprise culture 134
  industrial capitalism 13
  underemployment 115–16, 119
  unemployment 111–12
  upskilling thesis 63, 67
embeddedness of work 17–19
empirical research, alienation
      30–6, 41–5
employer alienation 29
employer preferences 127–8
employment, work as 1–27
engineering work 58
Enterprise Allowance Scheme 134, 135
enterprise culture 134–6
Enterprise Insight Campaign 134
EPZs *see* Export Processing Zones
equality, gender 163–71
estrangement 29
  see also alienation; self-estrangement
ethnicity 108, 137, 172
European Fordism 76–7
exploitative informal work 147–8, 172
Export Processing Zones (EPZs) 192

factory system
  deskilling thesis 51–2
  education 13
  Fordism 73–4
  industrial production 9, 10–11
  spatial destandardization 136–7
  time 12–13

family unit
  embeddedness of work 18–19
  industrial capitalism 10, 15
  pre-industrial societies 6
  symmetrical family thesis 162–71, 202–3
  transformation 188, 193–6
  unemployment effects 113
family wage 23
fast-food industry 93–5
feminism
  domestic work 164, 169
  dominant concept of work 200–1
  flexible specialization 96–7
  globalization 187–8
  threat to dominant concept 24
  unpaid work 196
feminization of labour 98, 188–9, 191,
      196, 200–1
  see also women
first-wave feminism 187
  see also feminism
flexible manufacturing system (FMA) 94
flexible mass production 91–2
flexible specialization (FS) 80–2, 84, 95–7
flexible work 119–20
  definition 116
  gender dimension 151
  globalization 189–92
  homeworking 138–9
  Just in Time system 88
  network enterprise thesis 97–8
  symmetrical family thesis 170
  voluntary 176
  women 196
  see also non-standard work; underemployment
fluidity of unemployment 110–11
FMA *see* flexible manufacturing system
food production industry 93–5
Fordism 73–83
  demise 80–2
  deskilling 71
  development 77–80
  formal/informal work 142
  globalization 189, 201–2
  production system 74–5, 76, 80
  questions 83, 101
  rise of 73–7
  self-provisioning 146
  solutions to crisis 84–101
  standard work 127
  summary and conclusions 82, 98–100
  unemployment/underemployment
      103, 105, 111, 116–17
  welfare 115
  see also neo-Fordism; post-Fordism

Fordist compromise 78–9, 81, 103, 105
formal voluntary work 155–6, 173,
    175–6, 197
formalization thesis 142
franchising 135
fraternalism 77–80
free market economy 14
freelance workers 132
French alienation study 43–4
FS *see* flexible specialization
The Full Monty (film) 109
full-time work
  hours of work 122
  job characteristics 141
  symmetrical family 165–6
functional flexibility 88, 91–2

game playing 59
gender
  alienation thesis 39–40
  deskilling thesis 56–8
  division of labour 153–4, 162–71, 194–5
  flexibility 151
  flexible specialization 96–7
  Fordism 79–80
  homeworking 137, 139
  industrial capitalism 20–5
  network enterprise thesis 98
  non-standard/standard work
    models 128
  polarization of skills 69
  pre-industrial societies 5
  self-provisioning 146
  standard work 128, 201–2
  temporary work 141
  transformation 187–9
  underemployment 117–19, 123–4
  unemployment consequences
    106–8, 112–15
  unpaid domestic work 153–60, 193–6
  upskilling thesis 67–8
  voluntary work 155, 173–5
  youth unemployment 111–12
  see also women
General Motors Corporation 75–6, 91
globalism/globality 185
globalization 183–5
  causes 185–7
  continuity and change 200–3
  deskilled jobs 70
  industrial capitalism 3, 8, 24
  phases 184
  questions 203
  summary and conclusions 197–200
  transformation of work 182–203

government policies
  care work 197
  globalization 186, 187
  informal work 144, 145, 147
  self-employment 133–6
  unemployment/underemployment
    102–3, 104
  voluntary work 156
  welfare 78

hegemony 24
heterogeneity of domestic work 159–60
historical alienation trends 35
home/work separation 8, 18–19
homemaker career women 112, 113
homeworking 22, 136–9
horizontal organization, network
    enterprises 97
horticultural societies 2, 3
hours of work *see* time; working hours
household economy *see* family unit
housework *see* domestic work
Hoxie Report 55
hunting and gathering societies 2–3
hyperglobalism 183

idealization 64–5
  see also romanticism
ideological function, self-employment 130
IE *see* industrial engineering
ILO *see* International Labour Organization
immigration 144, 172
income... *see* pay...
independent variable, alienation 32–4
individualization
  globalization 193
  industrial production 10
  risk model 78–9
  self-employment 133
  unemployment/underemployment 103
  voluntary work 175
industrial capitalism
  alienation 28–30
  choice of term 2
  definition 1, 7
  deskilling 48–60
  division of labour 10–11, 13
  dominant concept of work 23–5,
    127, 153–4, 200–2
  economic system 14–15
  education and recruitment 13
  embeddedness of work 17–19
  features of work 8–20
  formal/informal work 142
  globalization 3, 8, 24, 183

industrial capitalism *cont.*
  initial phase 1800-40s 21–2
  mature phase 1850-90s 22–3
  meaning of work 15–16
  non-standard work 126–7
  patriarchy 23–5
  payment 16–17
  production system 8–10, 49–50
  purpose of work 16
  self-employment 131
  spatial destandardization 136–7
  symmetrical family thesis 162–3
  time 11–13
  transition to 6
  unemployment/underemployment
    102–3, 105
  unit of production 10
  unstable character 19–20
  upskilling 61–72
  women and development 20–3
  work in society 7–8
  see also capitalism
industrial engineering (IE) 90
industrial society (IS) 62–3
  see also industrial capitalism
industrialization 7
informal work 126, 128–9, 142–8
  domestic outsourcing 172
  measurement 143
  voluntary 155–6, 173–5, 196–7
'information society' 64
  see also post-industrial society
information technology 119, 186–7
  see also technology
institutional division of domestic
  work 167
instrumentalism, voluntary work 175
International Labour Organization
  (ILO) 104–5, 116
interpretative critique, alienation
  thesis 38–41
intervening variables, alienation
  32–3, 38
IS *see* industrial society
Italy, flexible specialization 96

Japanese vehicle manufacturers 87–92, 99
JIT system *see* Just-in-Time system
job model 39–40, 68
job satisfaction surveys 36, 38
job security 120
Just-in-Time (JIT) system 87–90, 126

kaizen 88
Kalmar car plant 85–6

Keynesianism 78, 103
kinship links 18–19, 173, 175
knowledge
  commodification 66
  upskilling thesis 61, 66–7

labour-capital relations 191–2
  see also trade unions
Labour governments 134–5
labour-saving appliances 160–2
lagged adaptation theory 167
late modern society 175–6
laundry work 160, 162
lean production 87–92, 99
leisure class 4
Loan Guarantee Scheme 133, 135
local distinctions, informal work 146–7
Luddism 9–10

McDonaldism 73, 84–5, 92–5, 99–100
  see also neo-Fordism
machine-tending technology 31–2, 33–5, 42
machinery
  alienation 9
  deskilling thesis 50–2, 54
  division of labour 11
  see also automation
maintenance work 58
male breadwinner/female carer model
  194–6, 201–2
  see also dominant concept of
    work; gender
management
  deskilling thesis 55–6
  domestic work 159–60
  homeworkers 138
  Japanese vehicle manufacturers 88–9, 92
  neo-Fordism 86
  Taylorism 49–50
managerial work 170–2, 193
manual workers 69
  see also individual types
marginalization of self-employment 136
Marienthal unemployment study 106–8, 113
market economy 14
market saturation 81
marriage bar 23
marriage problems 106–7, 169
Marxism 70
  see also name index
masculinity 57, 168
  see also gender
mass consumption 80–2
mass customization 94
mass markets 81

mass production 71, 80–2, 91–2, 95–6
   see also Fordism
meaning of work
   industrial capitalism 15–16, 23–5
   pre-industrial societies 5–6
   women 23
meaninglessness 30–2, 34–5, 43–4, 158
measurement
   domestic work 161–2
   informal work 143
   underemployment 115–18
   unemployment 104–6
men, domestic work 164–6, 169
   see also gender
mental health 107, 109, 118
methodological critique, alienation
   thesis 36–7
middle classes
   domestic work 153, 161, 164, 166, 171–2
   outsourcing 171–2
   unemployment consequences 109–10
   voluntary work 155
   see also class
migrant workers 144, 172
mode of production, capitalism 49
modern society
   definition 1
   reflexive volunteering 175–6
   threats to hegemony 24
Morecambe Bay cockle pickers 144
multi-tasking skills 95

national Fordisms 79
neo-Fordism 73, 84–95, 98–100
   globalization 189, 202
   Japanese production 87–92
   key features 100
   service work 92–5
   Swedish production 85–6
   underemployment 116–17
   see also McDonaldism
neo-liberalism 103, 192
network enterprise thesis (NET)
   84, 97–8, 189
network societies 97, 184, 186–7
   see also social networks
New Deal 103
NGOs (non-governmental organizations) 186
night work 170
Nissan 88–90
nomadic societies 3
non-capitalist societies 24
non-governmental organizations
   (NGOs) 186
non-profit organizations 154–5

non-standard work 104, 126–52
   definition 116
   globalization 182, 189–90
   key dimensions 128
   questions 152
   standard work distinction 202
   summary and conclusions 148–51
   see also destandardized work;
      underemployment
normative division of domestic work 168
Northern Ireland 146–7
nuclear families 193
   see also family unit
numerical flexibility 88, 91–2, 138–9

occupational structure
   industrial capitalism 11
   polarization of skills 69–70
office work 50–2, 54–5, 58, 65
   see also clerical work
older people 110, 173, 175–6
Oldsmobile 75–6
optimistic perspective
   skill change 48, 61–72
   women in industrial capitalism 20–1
organizational restructuring 132, 135, 140
   see also re-organization of production
outsourcing domestic work 171–2
overemployment 122

paid work
   alienation 28–47
   care work burden 174
   deskilling 48–60
   domestic outsourcing 171–2
   informal work 142–8
   non-standard 126–52
   symmetrical family thesis 162–71
   transformation of work 189–92, 193–4
   unemployment/underemployment
      102–25
   unpaid work distinctions 153–6
   upskilling 61–72
   voluntary work comparison 176–7
   volunteering in preparation 175
   women's transformation 188
   working hours 164–6
part-time work 115–20, 128, 141, 165–6
particularism 18
paternalism 14, 77–80
patriarchy
   deskilling thesis 56–8
   feminist challenge 188, 201
   industrial capitalism 23–5
   unpaid work 193–6

pay-related underemployment
 115–16, 118–19
payment, industrial capitalism 16–17
peripheral Fordism 79, 84
permanent work 141
 see also standard work
pessimistic perspective
 skill change 48–60
 women in industrial capitalism 20–1
PIS *see* post-industrial society
polarization of skills 48, 50, 68–70,
 97–8, 189
political factors
 self-employment 133–4
 skill 57
post-Fordism 73, 84–5, 95–8
 flexible specialization 95–7
 globalization 189
 key features 100
 network enterprise thesis 97–8
 self-employment 133
 underemployment 116–17
 upskilling 71
post-industrial society (PIS)
 industrial contrasts 62–3
 self-employment 131–2
 underemployment 120
 upskilling 61–72
poverty 114–15
powerlessness 30–2, 34–5, 37–8, 43,
 157–8, 168–9
pre-industrial societies 4–6
 domestic work 160
 gender division of labour 163
 industrial capitalism contrasts 8–9
 informal work 142
 payment 16–17
 romanticization 54
 self-employment 130–1
 time 11–12
 work in 1–6
preference theory 117, 127–8
primary sector work 11
Principle of Stratified Diffusion 163, 169–70
printing industry 31–2, 33, 35
private sector voluntary work 154–6
product alienation 29
product flexibility 88
production systems
 concepts 73
 Fordism 74–5, 76, 80, 84–101
 industrial capitalism 8–10, 49–50
 neo-Fordism 100
 post-Fordism 100
 pre-Fordism 75

production systems *cont.*
 re-organization 84–101
 see also mass production; organizational
 restructuring
professional work 16, 62, 65–7, 108–9
profit motive 14, 16
proletarianization 50, 52
Protestant work ethic 15, 105–6
psychological consequences
 underemployment 118
 unemployment 107, 109
public sector
 professionals 66
 voluntary work 154–6
purpose of work 16

quality control 88–90

race 108
 see also ethnicity
racism 110
rationalism 185–6
rationalization of education 13
reciprocity 173
recruitment 13, 18–19
redundancies 115
reflexive volunteering 175–6, 196
reformism 36
regulation
 Fordism 80–2
 globalization 186
relative poverty 114–15
relief workers 91
re-location of production 84
re-organization of production 84–101
 see also organizational
 restructuring
responsibility 51, 69
risk model, individualization 78–9
robots 84
romanticism 54
 see also idealization
routine white-collar work 65–6

sceptical position, globalization 183
scientific management *see* Taylorism
second-wave feminism 187–8
 see also feminism
secondary sector work 11
self-employment 128, 129–36
 definition 130
 dominant concept of work 200–1
 economic factors 131–3
 homeworking overlaps 137–8
 informal work 143

self-employment *cont.*
  political factors 133–4
  socio-cultural factors 134
self-estrangement 30–2, 34–5, 37, 43–4, 159
self-provisioning 146
  see also domestic work
semi-skilled workers 108–9
service work
  deskilling thesis 51, 57
  gender dimension 67–8
  idealization 64–5
  neo-Fordism 92–5
  self-employment 132
  upskilling thesis 62–5, 67–8
sexism 110
  see also gender
shiftwork 169–70
shopping 161
Silicon Valley, California 126, 140
silk industry 21–2
skill
  Bell's thesis 63
  Braverman's definition 53–5, 56–7
  changes
    class and sex 69
    occupational structure 70
    optimistic perspective 48, 61–72
    pessimistic perspective 48–60
    production systems 73
  definitions 48, 53–5, 56–7
  deskilling 48–60
  domestic work 159–60
  indicators 69
  polarization 48, 50, 68–70, 97–8, 189
  underemployment 119
  upskilling 61–72
small businesses 143
  see also self-employment
social alienation 29
social consequences
  underemployment 118–19
  unemployment 106–15
social exclusion 114
social isolation 30–2, 34–5, 43, 158–9, 161
social networks 144–5
  see also network societies
social organization, alienation 32–3, 38
social provisions of Fordism 77
social security 129–30
  see also welfare regimes
social skills 70, 94–5
socio-cultural factors, self-employment 134
spatial destandardization 128, 136–9, 202
spatial separation *see* home/work separation
spatial-temporal globalization 183–4

specialization 5
species alienation 29
standard work
  Beck's key aspects 129
  gender 201–2
  key aspects 128–9
  non-standard comparison 126–7
  see also paid work; permanent work
standardization
  flexible specialization alternative 95–6
  Fordism 77, 78–80
  Japanese vehicle manufacturers 89
  McDonaldism 93–4
  see also destandardized work
state policies *see* government policies;
    welfare regimes
status
  domestic work 157
  pre-industrial societies 5–6
steam engines 9
stigma
  part-time work 118–19
  unemployment 109
Stratified Diffusion Principle 163, 169–70
subcontractors 132, 143
subsistence system 17
supply-side approach to Fordism 81–2
sweated trades 22
Swedish vehicle manufacturers 85–6, 99
symmetrical family thesis 162–71, 202–3

taxation 129–30, 142–4, 145
Taylorism
  deskilling 49–50, 51–2, 54, 55–6
  division of labour 11
  Fordism's overlaps 73
  Ford's adoption 74, 76
  Japanese vehicle manufacturers 89–90
  McDonaldism 93
  neo-Fordism 86
  upskilling critique 65–6
teamwork 88–9, 94–5, 98
technicist approach, skill 56
technological determinism 41
technology
  alienation 30–47
  Blauner's four types 31, 36–7
  domestic work 160–2, 164, 169, 188–9
  dominant concept of work 200
  globalization 186–7
  homeworking 138
  self-employment 132
  see also computerization; information
    technology
teleworkers 132, 135, 139

temporal destandardization 128, 140–2, 202
   see also part-time work
temporal dimension of globalization 183–4
temporary work 128, 140–2
tertiary sector work 11
textile industry 21–2, 31–5, 39–40, 42
theoretical critique, alienation thesis 37–8
'Third Italy' 96
time
   domestic work 160–2, 164–7, 169, 193
   homeworking 139
   industrial capitalism 11–13
   unemployment 106–8
   see also temporal...
time and motion studies 86
time-related underemployment
   115–19, 123–4
total destandardization 142–8
Total Quality Control 88
Toyota 87–9
trade unions 38–9, 67, 78, 92, 115
traditionalism 24
transborder relations 184
transformation of work 1–27
   globalization 182–203
   industrial capitalism 7–25
   paid work 189–92, 193–4
   pre-industrial societies 1–6
   questions 27
   summary and conclusions 25–6
   unpaid work 192–7
   women and work 20–5, 187–9
transformationalism 183
transition to adulthood thesis 110–11
transnational corporations 191–2
truck system 17
type of technology/degree of alienation
   thesis (Blauner) 34–5

Uddevalla car plant 85–6
UK *see* Britain
underemployment 102–25
   Beck's thesis 119–21, 123–4
   meaning and measurement 115–18
   questions 125
   social consequences 118–19
   summary and conclusions 121–4
   working hours 122
undocumented immigration 144
unemployment 102–25
   gender patterns 25
   industrial capitalism 17, 25
   informal work 145, 146
   meaning and measurement 104–6
   questions 125

unemployment *cont.*
   self-employment opportunities
      133, 134, 135
   social consequences 106–8
      age 108, 110–12
      class 108–10
      gender 108, 112–15
      summary and conclusions 121–4
   voluntary work 175
   working hours 122
unions *see* trade unions
unit of production, industrial
   capitalism 10, 21
universalism 18
unpaid work 153–81
   domestic 153–72, 177–81,
      188–9, 192–7, 201
   dominant concept of work 127
   homeworking 139
   questions 181
   summary and conclusions 177–80
   transformation of work 192–7
   voluntary 154–6, 172–7, 180–1,
      192–3, 196–7
   working hours 164–6
unskilled workers 108–9
unstable industrial capitalism 19–20
upskilling 61–72
   alienation thesis 46–7
   Bell's thesis 61–70
   Braverman's critique 52–3, 57–8
   network enterprise thesis 97–8
   polarization of skills 68–70
   questions 72
   summary and conclusions 71
USA *see* America

vehicle manufacturers *see* automobile
   industry
verificational research, alienation 36
voluntary work 154–6, 172–7
   definition 172–3
   questions 181
   summary and conclusions 180
   transformation 192–3, 196–7
   women 23
Volvo 85–6

wage increases, Fordism 74–5
wage labour 6, 14
weekend work 169–70
welfare regimes
   division of domestic work 168, 194–5
   Fordism 78
   underemployment 118

welfare regimes *cont.*
  unemployment 104, 114–15
  see also social security
white-collar workers 44–5, 62–3, 65–6, 69
'wife's incorporation' theory 170
women
  alienation thesis 39–40
  deskilling thesis 56–8
  dominant concept of work 153–4
  Fordism 79–80
  globalization 182, 187–9, 191
  homeworking 137, 139
  industrial capitalism 20–5
  polarization of skills 69
  self-employment 132, 135
  symmetrical family thesis 163–71
  temporary work 141
  underemployment 117–19, 123–4
  unemployment 106–8, 112–15

women *cont.*
  unpaid domestic work 153–60, 193–6
  upskilling thesis 67–8
  voluntary work 173–5
  'wife's incorporation' theory 170
  youth unemployment 111
  see also gender
work ethic 15, 105–6
working classes
  domestic work 153, 154
  unemployment consequences 109–10
  voluntary work 155
  see also class
working hours
  domestic work 160–2, 164–7, 169, 193
  employment situations 122
  see also time

young people 110–12, 141, 173, 175–6, 196